BLUE BLOOD

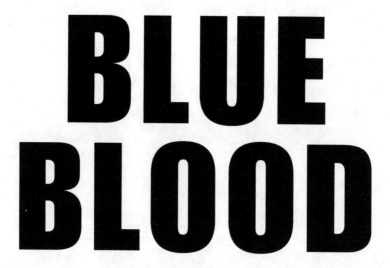

BLUE BLOOD

Duke-Carolina: Inside the
Most Storied Rivalry in College Hoops

Art Chansky

With a Foreword by Dick Vitale

THOMAS DUNNE BOOKS ST. MARTIN'S PRESS 🕮 NEW YORK

THOMAS DUNNE BOOKS.
An imprint of St. Martin's Press.

www.stmartins.com

Library of Congress Cataloging-in-Publication Data

Chansky, Art.
    Blue blood : Duke-Carolina, inside the most storied rivalry in college hoops / Art Chansky ; with a foreword by Dick Vitale.—1st ed.
        p. cm.
    ISBN 0-312-32787-0
    EAN 978-0-312-32787-3
    1. Duke Blue Devils (Basketball team)—History.   2. North Carolina Tar Heels (Basketball team)—History.   3. Duke University—Basketball—History.   4. University of North Carolina at Chapel Hill—Basketball—History.   5. Sports rivalries—North Carolina—History.   6. College sports—North Carolina—History.   I. Title.

GV885.43.D85C43 2005
796.323'63'097565—dc22   2005048469

10   9   8   7   6   5   4

To my father-in-law, Harold Bolick,

a Duke engineer who taught me about building bridges

CONTENTS

ACKNOWLEDGMENTS

This book took twice as long to write as I expected for two reasons.

First, I couldn't decide how to tell the story of Duke-Carolina basketball the way it deserves to be told. By simple chronology? By the great players and coaches at each program? By the classic games they have played? By the recruits they sought simultaneously? By the fans who help make it the most famous rivalry in American college sports?

Second, the rivalry didn't reignite as we all expected during the 2004 season, the first year of Roy Williams versus Mike Krzyzewski. There were two close, hard-fought games, both going down to the last possession and both won by Duke. The Blue Devils and Tar Heels did not meet in the ACC Tournament, or the NCAA East Regional, when they could have. Duke's season ended in heartbreak, Carolina's in disappointment. Who wanted to read a story that stopped there?

So we combined all the formats, using a chronology but incorporating the games and personalities and recruiting battles that have helped define the rivalry. We also waited one more year when Williams's program was back on par with Krzyzewski's. *Blue Blood* is a bit longer, but it has to be that way. Doing Duke-Carolina basketball justice takes time, thousands of words, and, most important, the work of a lot of people.

As a UNC graduate, and longtime Tar Heel fan, I made "accuracy and balance" my personal mantra for this book. That's what I told every Dukie who raised an eyebrow and every Heel who snickered about a certain coach's profanity.

The biggest break occurred when Al Featherston was laid off from the Durham *Herald-Sun* because new ownership wanted to cut the payroll. "Feather" had worked there more than thirty years and was one of the highest-paid employees—deservedly so. He agreed to help insure that *Blue Blood* was indeed "accurate and balanced," and the newspaper's loss is this book's clear gain.

Lending his perspective, reason, and wealth of factual information to the

ACKNOWLEDGMENTS

manuscript, Featherston contributed far more than his thoughtful, historical introduction. He conducted a long interview with former Duke All-American Art Heyman and contributed his file on the famous fight between Heyman and UNC's Larry Brown in 1961 that changed Duke-Carolina basketball forever. Featherston is a history buff and always the voice of accuracy and balance. He made sure there was a Tommy Amaker for a Kenny Smith and a Stuart Scott for a Jay Bilas and, as this rivalry goes, a reaction for every action. Thank you, Al. This book is as much yours as mine.

Thanks also to Eddy Landreth, the veteran sportswriter who conducted interviews with former players and coaches and lent early direction to the project. His contemporary commentary and insistence that "K has become just like Dean" helped weave the various eras together. I couldn't have gotten started without Eddy.

Like Landreth, Fred Kiger was in on the earliest meetings and proofread initial drafts to help give the book focus. Kiger is an acclaimed high school history teacher and spends much of his professional time wearing an engineer's headset for the various networks that telecast ACC sports. He has written moving openings for Duke-Carolina TV games, and his industry contacts were invaluable.

Others to thank are Jon Drew, a young AP writer in Columbus, Ohio, who got the first interview Pete Gaudet gave about his Duke days since he was booted out of Krzyzewski's program after the disastrous 1995 season. Drew is a Vanderbilt graduate and one of the new breed I refer to as "Young Theos"—after Boston Red Sox General Manager Theo Epstein, who personifies the brilliant twenty-somethings with wisdom and knowledge beyond their years and a mastery of modern technology beyond most of us over forty.

Another Young Theo who assisted on *Blue Blood* was Dan Satter, who read and edited manuscripts pretending he was a person of his generation with no knowledge of the past. His job was to make sure someone who dropped in from Mars would understand who Dick Groat and Lennie Rosenbluth were. Jim Wilson, not quite a Young Theo, also lent his editing expertise.

At the other end of the age scale, Bill Brill may be known as the ultimate Dukie, but there is not a fairer or finer follower of the Blue Devils anywhere. The seventy-five-year-old Brill, who supposedly retired when he left the *Roanoke Times* in 1991, has worked harder than ever since moving to Durham and covering Duke and the ACC for *Blue Devil Weekly* and several national publications. He authored *A Season Is a Lifetime* with Mike and Mickie Krzyzewski after Duke's back-to-back national championships in 1991–92. He first wrote *Duke Basketball: An Illustrated History* in 1987 and last year finished the sequel following Duke's one hundredth anniversary. Brill was available for conversations, long and short, about the rivalry and his six-decade point of view.

ACKNOWLEDGMENTS

Author and columnist Barry Jacobs, perhaps the most knowledgeable person on this planet about ACC basketball, led the long list of sportswriters who offered their time, opinions and recollections to *Blue Blood*. Another famous writer once said, "Borrowing from one source is plagiarism, borrowing from many sources is research." A complete list of writers, and their various books and articles on Duke and/or Carolina, would fill up two more pages. Suffice it to say that if anyone has ever written anything of note on the rivalry, a piece of your work is probably somewhere in this book.

Thanks to Matt Bowers, Rick Brewer, and Steve Kirschner in the UNC Sports Information Office and to their counterpart Jon Jackson at Duke for providing anecdotes, stats, and access to their overflowing files. These guys handle the throng of media covering both programs with aplomb and friendship; Kirschner has even baby-sat Jackson's daughter. Thanks also to Tom Drew, Johnny Moore, and Mike Sobb, who are my great friends and Duke insiders who drop a tidbit here and there without ever giving away the ranch. And to Mike Cragg, Krzyzewski's right hand man whose insight into the empire his boss has built was invaluable.

Dean Smith retained his policy of giving no extensive interviews on this or any subject, a position he took before and since penning his own autobiography in 1999. Smith did answer specific questions when asked, and often said more when he had the time, hand-writing replies on e-mails that his secretaries, Linda Woods and Ruth Kirkendall, printed out, gave to him and then returned by mail. When asked what year he was offered the Knicks head-coaching job by Sonny Werblin, Smith could only remember that he was in New York and Ron "Guidry pitched the first World Series game in Yankee Stadium." That turned out to be 1978.

Krzyzewski was not asked for a personal interview ("books are not a priority," said publicist Jackson) but candidly answered my "historical" questions at the end of every pertinent press conference over the last two years. Roy Williams was insistent that the facts be right about his controversial, misunderstood decisions to turn down and then accept the UNC head-coaching job. He agreed to read files compiled on his years at Kansas and provided valuable new information.

On literally his last day in Chapel Hill, Matt Doherty sat for a two-hour interview on his turbulent tenure as the Tar Heels' coach. Amidst half-packed boxes and furniture being moved out of his large home in Chapel Hill, Doherty talked about what went right and what went wrong, elaborating on his two wins over Duke—the infamous "ugly cheerleader" game in Durham in 2001 and the near-fight between him and Duke assistant Chris Collins in March of 2003. "Good luck with the book," Doherty said just before he and his family drove out of town to their new home outside of Charlotte.

ACKNOWLEDGMENTS

"Good luck with your new job at Florida Atlantic University," I say now.

Vic Bubas and Bucky Waters told (almost) all about their cumulative thirteen years at Duke in either recent or older files from both former coaches. Retired Athletics Director Tom Butters was enthused and entertaining when he phoned back from Florida and talked for ninety minutes, "on my nickel," he pointed out. On the UNC side, thanks to Larry Brown and the late Frank McGuire for their fascinating interviews over the years.

Thanks also to Tate Armstrong, Fred Barakat, Kevin Best, Jay Bilas, Mike Brey, John Clougherty, Mike Cooke, Johnny Dawkins, Jim Delany, Left Driesell, John Dubis, Eli Evans, Eddie Fogler, Pete Gaudet, Dave Gavitt, Bob Gersten, Rich Gersten, Mike Gminski, Lou Goetz, Dick Groat, Tracey Groat Goetz, Jim Heavner, Art Heyman, Tommy Hunt, Bobby Hurley, Donna Keane, Mitch Kupchak, Will Lane, Matthew Laurance, David Lawrence, Clyde Lear, Ashley McGeachy, Mick Mixon, Eric Mlyn, Eric Montross, Ron Morris, Vic Sapp, Lee Shaffer, Gary Sobba, Barbara Semonche, David Thompson, Steve Vacendak, Bucky Waters, Johh Wildhack, Scott Williams, and Mike Wood.

As a bushy-haired child of the '60s, I went south from Boston with only the Red Sox and Celtics in my heart (the Patriots have since replaced the Celts). Among the first Duke-Carolina games I saw were a triple overtime (won by Duke), an ACC championship comeback for the ages (authored by Charlie Scott), and a bad team rising up to upset a very good one (thanks, Robby West). Add to that the inebriating atmospheres at the Indoor Stadium and Carmichael Auditorium, the legendary stories about Glamack and Groat, Heyman and Brown, Mullins, Marin, and Miller—and the games they played against each other—and I was hooked. Big time.

When covering the Blue Devils for the *Durham Morning Herald* from 1973–80, I always considered Duke athletes, coaches and administrators among the most intelligent and candid of their peer group. I felt almost the same about Carolina players, although they were a bit more muzzled by Smith's inside-the-family philosophy.

Since then, millions more have gotten hooked on the rivalry that, at first, was the special secret of two schools only eight miles apart. Now, with nearly every game that they both play on television, there are Duke and Carolina cults all over the country that come together in a tribal war of sorts the two or three times their teams meet each season. When their own warriors aren't in action, they play close watch to the opposing tribe.

This has gone on now, in earnest, for more than fifty years. Fads don't last a half century. When this rivalry loses its balance, it only seems to matter who is coaching or playing for short periods. Bubas outlasted McGuire, Smith survived Bubas and stayed thirty-six seasons. Now Krzyzewski has coached twenty-five of the one hundred years Duke has been playing the game. Williams won't coach at Carolina that long, but he could last longer than Coach K. If and when that happens, don't expect Duke to fall very far behind.

Thanks to St. Martin's Senior Editor Peter Wolverton for helping me find the right formula to tell this story. His assistant, Katie Gilligan, did much of the hands-on work as we headed for press. Greg Dinkin and Frank Scatoni were beyond literary agents; they were friends and critics when either was called for. My wife, Jan, and son, Ryan, allowed me to consume one full room in our home for about twice as long as I told them I needed it. Thanks for your love and support.

The project got more massive with every bit of research and recollection; it was simply amazing to see how much the two programs have been entwined— far beyond the actual games they play against each other. Because alumni and fans from each school are so proud and prejudiced, they have added to the history by loving one team and loving to hate the other. Since McGuire and Smith and Bubas and Krzyzewski built programs that mirrored each other so, it became habit to judge Duke by Carolina and vice versa.

Of course, those diehard followers of the Blue Devils and Tar Heels can recite chapter and verse on the rivalry and tell many more stories than are within these pages—where they were when Heyman dropped 40 on Carolina; when Walter capped the greatest comeback of all-time; when the developing Devils stunned the Jordan Heels; when Laettner and Montross literally butted heads; and when Battier blocked Forte from behind. Such a rivalry could only be reared between the baselines and sidelines by players who wanted to be the best and, year in and year out, came pretty darn close. Thanks to all of them.

Finally, thanks to the Atlantic Coast Conference which, in its infinite wisdom, made the Duke-Carolina rivalry even bigger. By expanding to twelve schools and then trying to *create* balance with a confusing basketball schedule that few fans like and fewer comprehend, the ACC did just the opposite. The only rivalry that persevered was the one that needed no preservation. Because Duke and Carolina will always play twice each season while everyone rotates primary partners, home-and-home series, and one-year stands, ACC basketball is now, more than ever, the Big Two and all the rest.

As other traditional rivalries try to hang on, and new ones attempt to sprout, Duke-Carolina remains the constant against which all others are measured. The era of Roy and K is really just beginning, and the beat of these two basketball bluebloods goes on.

FOREWORD
By Dick Vitale

I have the greatest job in the world. I get paid money to talk about something I love, college basketball. Don't tell ESPN, but I would do it for free, baby!

Complete strangers approach me all the time to talk college hoops. How can I possibly say no? I could be eating at a restaurant, walking through an airport, or preparing for a broadcast. It doesn't matter where I am or what I'm doing—I'll always talk roundball. My beautiful wife, Lorraine, will tell you I'll talk about it in my sleep! People want to discuss the odds of their favorite school winning it all. They want to argue about the greatest games and the best rivalries. And more often than not, they want to talk about two schools in particular: Duke and Carolina.

There's absolutely no doubt in my mind, baby—Duke-Carolina is the best rivalry in college basketball, and probably in all of athletics. Even a one-eyed broadcaster can see that!

Every time these two titans clash, the hair on the back of my neck stands up. If I had any on the top of my head, it would also be at attention, saluting the Dukies and the Tar Heels. There is no keener competition anywhere than between these two roundball giants. When one of them wins the ACC championship, it means they're automatically a favorite for the national championship. Nothing else as great exists as in the eight mile radius covering Chapel Hill and Durham.

There are other great rivalries—Kentucky-Louisville, Kansas-Missouri, Xavier-Cincinnati—but, let me tell you, there's nothing better than Duke-Carolina because it's the only one that has all of what I call the three P's: Power, Passion, and Proximity.

Power stands for the success these two juggernauts have achieved, winning a total of seven NCAA championships and being the cream of the college-hoops crop. Kentucky is the only Division I program that has won more games than UNC, and Duke is fourth all-time. Since 1977, Duke and Carolina have advanced to a combined twenty-one Final Fours—twenty-one times in twenty-eight years! Are you kidding me, America?

Passion is for the feelings these two stir in not just their students and alumni, but in all college basketball fans. At least twice a year, when they meet, everybody in the country watches. The best game I broadcast every year is the first regular-season Duke-Carolina matchup of the season we call on ESPN2. In those special years when these two power programs meet for a third time in the ACC Tournament, it's icing on the cake, an ESPN Instant Classic, baby. I can't even imagine what it would be like if they ever met in the NCAA Tournament, or with the national championship on the line. It almost happened last season—two games away from the Final Four!

Proximity represents the short distance between the two schools. Just ten miles, baby! I'd walk on my head from one school to the other if that's what it took to get a ticket inside Cameron Indoor Stadium or the Dean Dome. Being located so close to each other means they're constantly trying to top what the other is doing. They're completely intertwined—you can't possibly discuss one without bringing up the other. I mean, the players sometimes play pickup games together in the summer. They even go to the same barbershop!

I absolutely love this rivalry. It's everything that's pure and right about college athletics. You never hear a trace of an NCAA infraction with either program. The student-athletes donning both shades of blue not only play the game with class, they go to class. Superstars such as Michael Jordan and Vince Carter went back to Chapel Hill to get their degrees, while Christian Laettner and Grant Hill stayed all four years at Duke. All of them walked down the aisle during graduation.

It all starts at the top, baby. How about all of the amazing coaches who have patrolled the sidelines in Chapel Hill and Durham. Frank McGuire, Vic Bubas, Dean Smith, Bill Foster, Mike Krzyzewski, and, now, Roy Williams.

Coach K is the best in the business. How can you not respect the job Michael Krzyzewski has done since Tom Butters took a chance on him in 1980? Three national championships, ten Final Fours, the premiere program in the country. Duke has developed into what the Yankees were under Casey Stengel or the Packers under Vince Lombardi. This Blue Devil era is the closest we've come to a college basketball dynasty since the days when John Wooden, the Wizard of Westwood, held a rolled-up program on the UCLA bench.

Surprisingly, for the longest time K wasn't even considered the best coach in his own *state*. Back then, it was all Michelangelo, baby. Dean Edwards Smith was the king, and has been since taking Carolina to three straight Final Fours from '67 to '69. And to think, in his fourth season students hung him in effigy after a loss at Wake Forest.

Fortunately, Dean survived and held his throne for thirty-six years. I called him Michelangelo because the basketball court was his canvas. He innovated and inspired. Four Corners offense, pointing to the passer, huddling at the free-throw line—no wonder Dean is the all-time winningest coach!

If people think I'm a Duke-lover now, they must have never heard me in Dean's day. One time I went to my mailbox and there was a letter from his top lieutenant, Bill Guthridge, who led the Heels to two Final Fours in three years as a head coach. He said how flattered they were by all the attention I gave them, thanked me for what I've done for them and then politely asked if I wouldn't toot their horns as much!

Hey, who am I to argue with two guys who have only about nine hundred more career wins than me? So instead, I'll brag about their protégé, Roy Williams, who has returned to his alma mater and taken the Tar Heels back to the top in only two years!

Roy is the real deal. You don't win four hundred games in fifteen years at Kansas unless you're big time. What a job he did with his alma mater last season—he made me look brilliant as the Heels were my No. 1 pick back in October! When Roy cut the nets down in St. Louis, he sent a loud, clear message that Carolina basketball was back among the elite programs.

Now the Dukies are my No. 1 pick for *this* season.

Duke vs. Carolina. Coach K, the Hall of Famer, versus the future Hall of Famer, Roy Williams, just adds electricity to the hottest rivalry in all of college sports. Sorry, pigskin lovers who sing the praises of Michigan-Ohio State, there is nothing else quite like the Dukies and the Tar Heels!

A book chronicling the classic players, coaches, and contests that Carolina and Duke have produced is long overdue, and there's no one in America more qualified to write it than Art Chansky, who's lived and breathed this rivalry for the last thirty-five years. This book is awesome, baby, it tells the whole story!

I'm proud to write this foreword for Art, but since Coach K wrote one for *my* latest book I'm going to call upon Roy Williams to do it for my next book. No question, having Coach K and Roy will be Awesome, with a capital A! But, Roy, you're going to have to toot my horn a little bit, too!

RIVALRY FACTS

- **Years Playing Basketball:** Duke 100; Carolina 95
- **First Coaches:** Duke, W. W. "Cap" Card; Carolina, Nat Cartmell
- **First Duke-Carolina Game (January 24, 1920)**
  UNC 36, Duke 25
- **Rivary Record Through 1954**
  Carolina won 45; Duke won 37
  UNC won 16 straight between 1921 and 1928
- **Football Rivalry Through 1954**
  Duke won 20; Carolina won 17 (3 ties)
  The schools did not play each other in football from 1895–1921
- **All-Time Basketball Records**
  Carolina 1,861–681 (.732); Duke 1,764–807 (.691)

INTRODUCTION

THE LEGEND OF TOBACCO ROAD

There was not much attention paid outside of Tobacco Road when North Carolina visited Duke Indoor Stadium for the final basketball game of the 1955 regular season.

Why should anybody outside the brand new ACC have cared about the game? There was nothing of national significance at stake that February night in Durham. The 17–7 Blue Devils needed a win to clinch second place in the ACC standings, while the 10–9 Tar Heels were trying to finish above .500 in the second season of ACC play. UNC boasted high-scoring sophomore Lennie Rosenbluth, but the slender forward from New York couldn't overcome coach Harold Bradley's potent inside-outside combo of Joe Belmont and Ronnie Mayer.

It's only in retrospect that Duke's 96–74 victory stands out as a landmark game. It's only by looking back across a half century that has seen the Duke-North Carolina series develop into the best rivalry in college basketball—maybe the best rivalry in all of sports—that the Feb. 25, 1955 meeting in Durham assumes its true significance: That was the last time that Duke and North Carolina met on the basketball court and neither was ranked.

The two Tobacco Road rivals have faced each other 134 times since and one or the other has been ranked in every single one of those games. North Carolina has been ranked in 110 of them, Duke in 82 of them. *Both* teams have been ranked in 58 of the 134 match-ups, including 38 times when both were ranked in the top 10.

Their parallel climb to prominence has turned the rivalry from a neighborhood brawl into a national phenomenon. In the half-century since that obscure 1955 match-up, North Carolina and Duke have combined to win seven national titles (four by UNC; three by Duke), play in 29 Final Fours (15 by UNC; 14 by Duke) and win a combined 169 NCAA Tournament games (86 by UNC; 83 by Duke).

Their dual dominance has become even more apparent in recent years. Since the adoption of the modern sixty-four/sixty-five-team NCAA Tournament field in 1985, Duke and North Carolina have been the two most successful programs in college basketball—and no one is even close. Between them, the two schools have won more titles (5), played in more title games (9), and made more Final Four appearances (17) than any entire *conference*.

Is it any wonder that the first annual Duke-Carolina game, coming as it does in early February, is normally the sports' highest-rated regular-season TV property?

Start outside Cameron Indoor Stadium, since, after all, Duke's arena was there first.

Turn right out of the circle that fronts the stadium's faux-Gothic façade and take Whitford Drive for just over a tenth of a mile, past Duke's baseball stadium, to Science Drive. A left turn and a drive of about three hundred yards takes you to Cameron Boulevard, like the basketball gym named for Duke's long-time basketball coach and athletics director Eddie Cameron. Take a right and go down the hill to the Highway 15–501 overpass. Turn left into the southbound lanes and follow the four-lane road into Chapel Hill.

The name changes to Fordham Boulevard at the Eastgate Shopping Center. You still have another two miles to go before turning right onto Manning Drive. Go just a couple of hundred yards and make a final left turn onto Skipper Bowles Drive, named for the former North Carolina politician who chaired the fundraising efforts that built the Dean E. Smith Center—which suddenly pops into view on your left.

The entire trip covers exactly 10.5 miles and takes—depending on your luck with the traffic lights along the way—between fifteen and twenty minutes. It may be a little quicker to cut across to Highway 54 by taking Garrett Road or cutting across on Interstate 40, but both are more miles. As the crow flies, however, it is actually—the distance that is most often cited—only eight miles.

Outsiders are often shocked to discover how close together the two great universities are. Even Mike Krzyzewski said that when he first came to Duke, he knew that both schools were in North Carolina, but not that they were almost within a J. J. Redick three-pointer of each other. Now he lives on an isolated estate in the Duke Forest and his back property line is also the Chapel Hill town limits, although he has never visited Franklin Street that abuts the UNC campus.

Proximity helps explain a lot about the rivalry. Students from the two schools party in the same bars, eat in the same restaurants and visit the same movie the-

INTRODUCTION

aters. For years, Duke and North Carolina players have had their hair cut at the same South Durham barber shop. Krzyzewski and former UNC coach Dean Smith each sent their daughters to the same piano teacher.

It's an incestuous rivalry. Families are divided. Former high school class-mates find themselves on opposite sides of the blue divide. Workplaces are war zones—the Duke-Carolina tensions only leavened by the presence of partisans from the other two Big Four powers—N.C. State and Wake Forest.

While proximity alone could account for a passionate local rivalry, Duke-Carolina has burst out of its geographical boundaries. It's become a national rivalry—not just because the two schools are close together, but because two of the nation's premier basketball programs are so close together.

How did these two Southern Universities evolve into the twin giants of the college basketball world?

The University of North Carolina, the nation's first state-supported university to open its doors, welcomed its first students in the winter of 1795. The Chapel Hill institution was the South's largest university in the days before the Civil War, when Normal College in Randolph County changed its name to Trinity College and first affiliated with the Methodist Church.

The small private school moved to Durham—barely those ten miles away from UNC's burgeoning campus—in 1892, thanks to a generous grant from tobacco baron Washington Duke. His son James B. Duke made a far larger gift in 1924 and the university changed its name to Duke University.

By that time, the neighboring colleges had become rivals on a number of athletic terrains. Baseball was probably the first "money" sport at the two schools, although the new sport of football rapidly gained a rabid following. Even before Trinity's move to Durham, the small private school defeated the state university in Chapel Hill 16–0 in the first football game played below the Mason-Dixon Line. The next spring, Trinity again defeated UNC, but when the two teams tried to meet again in the fall of 1889 a dispute over the site of the game led both teams to claim a forfeit—a one-game discrepancy in the records that exists to this day.

The UNC-Trinity football rivalry didn't make it to the twentieth century. In 1895, the Trinity faculty—reportedly disturbed by signs of growing profession-alism in Chapel Hill—banned the violent sport and for the next quarter century, the schools would have to find other venues for their rivalry.

It's still not clear whether the South's first basketball game was a game be-tween Wake Forest College and Guilford College or was, as most historians be-lieve, a game between Wake Forest and Trinity that was played on March 2,

1906, in a white-frame gymnasium that still stands on the East Campus of Duke University. The early father of the sport was Wilbur Wade "Cap" Card, a 1900 Trinity graduate who learned "basket ball" (as it was called) from its inventor, Dr. James Naismith, while he was a graduate student at Harvard.

North Carolina was a latecomer to the sport, not fielding a team until the winter of 1911. It would be another nine years before UNC and Trinity College met on the basketball court—and far longer than that before their collisions on the court would mean anything beyond the insular world of Big Four sports.

The Tar Heels did field some strong basketball teams in the early 1920s, winning Southern Conference Tournament titles in 1922, 1924, 1925, and 1926. The undefeated 1924 team, coached by Norman Shepard and starring the likes of Jack Cobb and Cartwright Carmichael, was especially impressive, compiling a 26–0 record against the best teams in the South. Two decades later, that record would convince a committee appointed by the Helms Foundation to award the 1924 team a retroactive national championship.

UNC's first "national title" would—like the 1889 double forfeit—become one of the cornerstones of contention in the Duke-Carolina rivalry. Every time the Tar Heels held up their Helms championship, critics pointed out that the '24 White Phantoms (as the UNC teams were then known) played nobody north of the Mason-Dixon Line (at a time when the best basketball was played in the East and Midwest) and failed to participate in the AAU's national tournament won by Butler University, which also claims the 1924 title.

Whatever the true value of that 1924 title, basketball remained an off-season sport at North Carolina and at the new Duke University, which resumed football with a passion in 1920. The school's mammoth new football stadium was an integral part of the new building program that became Duke's West Campus and to fill it to its fifty thousand-plus capacity, the school hired celebrated coach Wallace Wade from Alabama.

Wade—to this day the only Duke or North Carolina coach ever to grace the cover of *Time* magazine—delivered on his promise, building a football giant that challenged Tennessee and Georgia Tech for Southern football supremacy. North Carolina, which just missed a Rose Bowl bid when trounced by Duke in the 1935 finale, struggled to keep up with Wade's juggernaut in the years just before and during World War II. It wasn't until UNC coach George Barclay landed a swivel-hipped halfback from Asheville, North Carolina, that the Tar Heels could finally gain the upper hand in the rivalry.

Charlie "Choo Choo" Justice captured the imagination of the state's sports fans in a way that no athlete before or since has ever quite managed. He brought North Carolina football to national prominence—three top 10 finishes and three major bowl games between 1947 and 1949. More importantly, Justice was 4–0 against Duke. In his last college game, played in Duke Stadium in front of the largest crowd ever to see a football game in the state of North Carolina, Justice led the Tar Heels to a heart-stopping 21–20 victory that was only secured when All-America end Art Weiner blocked a potential game-winning field goal by Duke's Mike Souchak, a future golf pro of some note.

At that moment, football was still king in North Carolina, just as it was almost everywhere else in the South. Could anyone who watched that thrilling 1949 Duke-Carolina football game have foreseen that in a few short years football would be a secondary sport and King Basketball would begin its rule on Tobacco Road?

The first exhibition of Naismith's new sport was played at the Springfield, Massachusetts YMCA. In the early days of the sport, the amateur teams fielded by the various YMCAs gave the top college teams a run for their money.

In the years before North Carolina began its rivalry with Trinity/Duke, the university engaged in a hotly contested series of games with the Durham YMCA. The first UNC team in 1911 beat the Durham Y twice, but the YMCA team edged North Carolina on its home court to open the next two seasons.

Even when North Carolina first emerged as a power in the Southern Conference, the state university continued to dot its schedule with YMCA opponents. That led to what may have been the first basketball game in the state of North Carolina to capture the public's imagination.

UNC entered the 1921–22 season with a powerful team, headed by Monk McDonald and the Carmichael brothers—Billy and Cartwright. It was a team that would earn North Carolina its first conference title, but in the opener in Durham against the Durham YMCA, an overflow crowd of almost three thousand fans watched big man Myril "Footsie" Knight dominate the university boys inside. The 6' 3" giant led the YMCA team to a decisive 41–18 victory—and just to prove it was no fluke, Knight did it again a month later, leading the Durham Y to a 46–25 victory in Chapel Hill.

The YMCA teams soon faded to insignificance, but Knight remained in Durham to plant the seed of Tobacco Road's basketball mania. He became director of the Durham YMCA and began training generations of basketball players. Rufus and Bunn Hackney, brothers who captained the UNC basketball team in the late 1920s, were products of Knight's program. So was their baby brother Elmore Hackney, who crossed the blue divide and starred in football at Duke.

The members of the legendary Durham High basketball team that won 71 straight games between 1939 and 1941 were all graduates of Knight's YMCA program. Duke's coach Cameron, who was using his new arena to build a powerhouse in Durham, landed all of the Durham High stars except one and rode them to Southern Conference titles in 1942 and 1944.

The one who got away from Cameron was the best of all—6' 6" forward Horace "Bones" McKinney. The loquacious forward—who was sort of a cross between fellow North Carolinians Andy Griffith and Meadowlark Lemon—first enrolled at N.C. State, where he led the Wolfpack to the Southern Conference title game in 1942, but after his military service in World War II, he resurfaced in Chapel Hill, where he teamed with All-Americans Jim Jordan and John "Hook" Dillon to lead UNC to the 1946 national title game.

By that time, there was a new face on Tobacco Road, one who would take the basketball seed planted by Knight and nurture the sport until it overran the region.

The irony is that N.C. State hired Indiana high school legend Everett Case because Wolfpack officials decided that they couldn't compete with Duke and North Carolina on the football field. They made the conscious decision to dominate their rivals in basketball—and by doing so, ignited the greatest rivalry in college sports.

Only they wouldn't be a part of it.

Case didn't take long to make his mark on Tobacco Road. His first ten Wolfpack teams won nine conference titles—six in the old Southern Conference and the first three awarded by the new ACC. Not only did Case win, he sold basketball to the Southerners who had previously treated the sport as an interesting winter diversion. He traveled the state, talking to civic groups, passing out basketballs and erecting hoops on old barns. He added color to the games with pep bands, net-cutting ceremonies, and a fast-breaking style of up-tempo basketball.

In the end, Case was so successful that his rivals in Chapel Hill and Durham were unbearably envious and forced to respond. North Carolina went out and hired the best college coach the school could find—luring a dapper Irishman from St. John's University after his Final Four appearance with the Johnnies. Duke, which thought it had Red Auerbach lined up to take over the Blue Devil program, finally settled on Case's right-hand man, an eager young coach who would revolutionize recruiting in the ACC.

The new North Carolina and Duke coaches would not only compete with N.C. State's "Gray Fox"—both would surpass him on their way to respective greatness. Their battle for ACC supremacy would ignite the Duke-Carolina rivalry and take the sport to places even Case never could have imagined.

—Alwyn Featherston, Duke, Class of 1974

BLUE BLOOD

OVERALL RIVALRY RECORD
- Carolina has won 124; Duke has won 95

IN CHAPEL HILL
- Carolina has won 57; Duke has won 29

IN DURHAM
- Duke has won 47; Carolina has won 42

NEUTRAL COURTS
- Carolina has won 25; Duke has won 19

COACH K VERSUS CAROLINA
- In Durham: 14–10 (missed 1995 game)
- In Chapel Hill: 9–15 (missed 1995 game)
- Neutral Courts: 7–4

ALL-TIME ACC RECORDS
- Carolina 525–212 (.712); Duke 474–260 (.646)

FIRST IN ACC REGULAR SEASON
- Carolina 24 times (9 shared); Duke 17 times (2 shared)

ACC TOURNAMENT RECORDS
- Carolina 76–36 (.678); Duke 77–37 (.675)

ACC TOURNAMENT CHAMPIONSHIPS
- Duke 15; Carolina 15

1

TIDES OF MARCH

The Dean Smith Center was empty, except for the cleanup crew. The words "ACC Champions" were still illuminated on the new electronic boards on the fascia of the upper deck. Carolina had just beaten Florida State, surviving a 60 percent shooting half by the Seminoles, to clinch at least a tie for first place in the 2005 Atlantic Coast Conference standings.

One regular-season game remained, the biggest. It was more than sixth-ranked Duke coming in on Sunday afternoon. More than national TV with broadcasters Jim Nantz and Billy Packer sitting courtside. More than the latest renewal of the greatest rivalry in college basketball or perhaps any sport on any level.

The Tar Heels *had* to win this game for the preservation of their own collective sanity. Duke had won 15 of the last 17 meetings dating back to 1999, its most dominant stretch in the ninety-year history of the series. That statistic more than anything else had made the rivalry a moot point with many Blue Devil fans.

Duke coach Mike Krzyzewski was the new king of college basketball, a twenty-first century sideline CEO with power and prestige that pushed the legend of UNC coach Dean Smith further into the past. Roy Williams's arrival from Kansas as Carolina's new coach was supposed to erase the memory of a disastrous transition from the Smith era and begin evening the score with Duke.

Yet Williams had lost two heartbreakers during his first year in Chapel Hill when the Blue Devils returned to another Final Four. This season, 2005, Carolina finally had the better team in terms of depth and talent. However, the Tar Heels had failed to prove it the previous February 9 at Duke, where they had lost again.

Thus, Carolina owned an ironic form of pressure. Looking *up* from the top.

A win would give the Tar Heels the ACC regular-season title outright for the first time since 1993 and only three years after three seniors on the team and their fans had suffered through an 8–20 debacle. A loss to Duke would still leave them in first place but with a hollow title after having been swept by the Blue Devils a second straight season.

If Williams didn't beat Krzyzewski soon, the comparison he had tried so hard to avoid would stick like Velcro. His second Tar Heel team was ranked higher than Duke with fewer losses in both the ACC and overall. The Blue Devils were down to six healthy dependable players; despite not having ill Rashad McCants for the fourth consecutive game, Carolina was still deeper.

There was also the emotion of playing at home in front of a sold-out crowd of nearly twenty-two thousand fans on Senior Day for Jackie Manuel, Melvin Scott, and Jawad Williams, the trio that had somehow survived two years and 36 defeats under coach Matt Doherty. UNC had everything in its favor. The Tar Heels *had* to win.

Roy Williams knew that. On Sunday morning, he told Smith Center Director Angie Bitting to have two tall ladders in the tunnel after the game.

Two hours before the 4:00 P.M. tip-off, thousands of fans had descended upon the Dean Dome, hanging around in sunny, 60-degree weather. Thirsting to beat the Blue Devils, they had the hottest and most valuable tickets of any Duke-Carolina game in memory. A seller's market if there were any sellers.

A Chapel Hill man was there with his two grade-school daughters. He was offered $5,000 for his three tickets. "I have a choice for you," he said to his girls, "I can sell these tickets and we can all go to Disney World next week. Or we can go to the game." They tugged at his hand and kept walking.

Duke's team bus pulled into the tunnel beneath the arena at 2:30 P.M. Krzyzewski was greeted by John Dubis, UNC class of 1990 and the operative assigned to guide and guard all opposing coaches. Dubis led the Duke party to its two locker rooms, one for the Blue Devils and one for the coaches, primarily Krzyzewski, who once inside took off his expensive suit jacket, hung it in a locker and spread the game plan out on one bench.

Krzyzewski didn't like the characterization that this was one of his better coaching jobs. With his ill or injured players missing a total of twenty-nine games, he had used ten different starting lineups. After losing at Maryland and Virginia Tech, he started walk-ons Patrick Davidson and Patrick Johnson against Wake Forest to send a message to his team because "these were the only two guys who believe in me." Krzyzewski was crazed that night, screaming at the officials from first minute of the game when Davidson committed a blatant foul on Wake's Chris Paul. Duke won the war 102–92 to snap the rare two-game losing streak.

Once considered a defensive coach whose teams were vulnerable when playing five-on-five half-court basketball, Krzyzewski had conceived an offense that got the ball inside easily to center Shelden Williams while relying on J. J. Redick's radar from the perimeter. Using the double-teaming attention paid to Redick, Duke still liked to run but also worked patiently to create open shots for Daniel Ewing and lefty Lee Melchionni as their third and fourth scoring options.

They had won their first 15 games, during which Krzyzewski reached 700 career victories, but 4 midseason losses, including 2 to Maryland, had locked the Blue Devils out of first place and rendered the finale with Carolina to rivalry-game status. It was a rivalry he had owned since a year after Smith retired in 1997.

His players went out to warm up with the assistant coaches while he remained in seclusion. They returned just before game time, and, after meeting with them briefly, Krzyzewski put his jacket back on and gathered his papers. He waited until they took the court before walking down the corridor by himself, trailing Dubis by a few feet. It was exactly the same routine he used every year Duke played in Chapel Hill. His pregame ritual was military to the minute.

Something else happened again, as it had without fail when the Duke coach entered the playing court and faced what Dubis called a "wave of hate, a blast of white noise that is really loud."

As Krzyzewski passed through the tunnel, a plastic baggie of cheese dangled on a string from the railing above. The coach Tar Heel fans called "Rat Face" for his pointy nose and narrow jaw was in the house.

He did not see the cheese, or anything else specifically, looking stone-faced and straight ahead as he strode purposefully along the baseline behind Dubis. His expression broke when he reached Williams. They chatted cheek-to-cheek; several photographers closed in to capture the moment. After the national anthem and lineup introductions, the starters shook hands around the center circle, the din rose again and the ball was in the air. The game college basketball fans, near and far, saw as the unofficial start of post-season was under way. Duke-Carolina on the last weekend.

Duke scored first against UNC's Senior Day lineup that started two walk-ons. Redick's first three-pointer gave the Blue Devils a 5–0 lead, his step-back jumper made it 16–9 and his second "three" from way out on the left opened Duke's biggest early lead at 19–11. Nervous noise rose whenever he touched the ball.

Playing without injured point guard Sean Dockery, Duke was using Redick and Ewing to handle the ball and get into its motion offense. The Blue Devils had the ability to look chaotic and organized in the same possession, but once Redick or Williams had the ball within range, it was going up.

Carolina's 8–0 run, ending with Manuel's breakaway flying dunk over two Dukies, evened the game after nine minutes. Freshman Marvin Williams's only basket of the half gave the Heels a five-point lead, but Redick's fourth three-ball from the right wing triggered a spurt that put his team back ahead at the last media timeout before halftime.

During the break, CBS aired a new American Express commercial featuring Krzyzewski.

I don't look at myself as a basketball coach. . . . I look at myself as a leader who happens to coach basketball.

When play resumed, those sitting along the scorer's table saw another side of him. After freshman DeMarcus Nelson couldn't get in the game, Krzyzewski glared at official scorer Mark Isley and screamed "Bullshit!" at the explanation that Nelson had arrived too late. Krzyzewski clapped mockingly at Isley after Ewing, the man Nelson was to replace, picked up a foul in the midst of a late 11–4 scoring run by the Tar Heels.

"Good job! Good job!" he yelled over sarcastically. "That one's on you!"

"Bullshit!" he yelled again at Isley while stalking off the court at the half, Duke down 47–41, to the jeers and catcalls of Carolina fans sitting near the tunnel.

Official Larry Rose stopped at the scorer's table to see what had happened. Rose was a veteran referee who over the years seemed to work a lot of Duke games and had the unflattering nickname around the ACC of "Duke's Sixth Man." Scott Williams, the twenty-eight-year-old son of Carolina's head coach, stood in his second-row seat and stared at Rose. "Larry Rose, be a man. Be a man, Coach K owns you!" Williams shouted.

Rose heard the taunt, looked up and told a UNC security guard to remove his heckler. The younger Williams went to the private box behind Section 127 where the rest of his family usually watched home games. His father was furious when he found out what happened before the second half began.

Carolina went ahead 49–41 and it looked for a moment like the team that *had* to win would win. Then Melchionni, who had missed all three of his attempts in the first half, hit two three-pointers. Manuel, having his most aggressive offensive game of the season, became Carolina's unlikely scoring star.

The Tar Heels had forgotten about center Sean May, who had already scored 23 points with jump hooks and offensive rebounds. They shot too quickly from the outside and made poor decisions with the ball during the most important part of the game. The anxious crowd groaned as one of UNC's worst stretches of the season unfolded painfully.

After Duke rallied to lead 64–62 on Melchionni's fourth three-pointer, a ball that hit the rim and backboard before falling through, Manuel scored his fifth field goal to forge a 64–64 tie on a fast break lob from Raymond Felton. Having been hammered on the glass and in the paint all afternoon, the Blue Devils gained strength from Carolina's confusion and sudden inability to get the ball to May, who was easily bettering his career averages of 17 points and 18 rebounds in 3 full games against them.

Three straight inside baskets by Shelden Williams built Duke's lead to six points with under four minutes to play. The Tar Heels came out of the timeout determined to go back inside, but Duke knew what they'd do and double-downed on May, slapping the ball off his knee out of bounds. Ewing began a drive from the left front court, circled along the right baseline toward the basket and whipped a pass to Melchionni in the left corner. As his fifth three-pointer rattled in, the bench area behind him erupted.

The Blue Devils led 73–64 with three minutes left. Their phalanx of assistant coaches and managers, all dressed in dark suits, were acting out like smug adolescents.

"SUB! SUB!" they yelled when one of their players reported to the scorer's table, then stood and clapped at Isley when the horn buzzed him in.

How unbelievable was Duke's run? The last of Redick's 17 points had come with three minutes left in the *first* half, and the ACC's leading scorer missed all six of his second-half shots. Carolina had also kept the most feared free-throw shooter in the country off the foul line. Forward Shavlik Randolph played only fifteen minutes with foul trouble, meaning his team had just about beaten Carolina with five players.

Jawad Williams tapped in a May miss to cut Duke's lead to 73–66 with 2:40 left in the game. The Tar Heels called a timeout as their fans sat stunned. In the huddle, Roy Williams promised if they played "every possession from here on" as hard as possible, they would have a chance at the end. Several empty faces stared back at him.

The Amex commercial ran again.

When they get into the workplace, they're armed not just with a jump shot or a dribble. I want you armed for life.

Along the media table between the benches, the Tar Heel Sports Network radio announcers were quiet, contemplating what was ahead. Color analyst

Mick Mixon wondered how he could ever find the words to explain yet another loss to Duke. "The specter of defeat has entered the building," he mumbled to himself.

Mixon could have said *re*-entered the building. Over the prior six years, the Tar Heels had lost 24 games at home compared to 18 during their first 12½ seasons in the Smith Center, which opened with a victory over Duke in January of 1986. Five of those two dozen defeats were to the Blue Devils.

The first year of Roy versus K restored competitive drama to the rivalry, and both coaches spent most of the season mad—but not at each other.

Despite his first Tar Heel team's 8–1 start that included a triple-overtime loss at home to Wake Forest, Williams's return to Carolina was not exactly triumphant. He looked more like he was homesick for Kansas than happy to be home. He was so upset after a half-hearted loss at Kentucky that he joked about jumping out of the plane on the way home and used the slang word "frickin'" so much that friends and UNC officials suggested he clean up his vocabulary.

Before they faced top-ranked Duke on February 5, 2004, the Tar Heels had fallen to 13–5, 3–4 in the ACC, and found themselves on the NCAA Tournament bubble. "We've got to play," Williams told the national media, which had requested a record three hundred credentials for the game. "If we don't really play, Duke is going to kick our rear ends so far back up state, we're going to think Chapel Hill is on the other side of Murphy."

The Tar Heels had one of their best stretches of the season, leading Duke by seven late in the second half before the Blue Devils ran off a 12–2 spurt to climb on top in the closing seconds. Jawad Williams's awkward three-pointer sent the game into overtime, and McCants seemingly forced a second overtime with a long "three" from the right wing. But Krzyzewski's philosophy of moving on to "the next play" caught Carolina celebrating. Chris Duhon took off down the court, and Williams explained later that his team "failed to build a wall" to stop Duhon's coast-to-coast drive for reverse layup and an 83–81 victory.

As his teammates swarmed Duhon on the floor, the rivalry appeared rejoined. Although the TV ratings were typically high, the results were all too familiar to the Tar Heel faithful. Williams had his next shot at Duke a month later after Krzyzewski had stolen the headlines.

The Blue Devils' 41-game winning streak at Cameron Indoor Stadium had been snapped by Georgia Tech, and Krzyzewski got nailed with a technical foul in the first half. Courtside observers said he should have been thrown out for his verbal and vulgar assault on officials Karl Hess and Ray Natili.

"His manners were deplorable, his language galling," wrote Ed Hardin of the Greensboro *News & Record* after covering the game from courtside. "If Krzyzewski didn't get thrown out against Georgia Tech, then what does it take to get thrown out of a game in this league?"

Twenty years had passed since Krzyzewski leveled his famous double-standard accusation about Smith, whom he had replaced as the preeminent college coach and the ACC's alleged privileged character. He claimed Smith, and consequently his teams, received preferential treatment from both the officials and the media after Smith, ironically, caused his own scene at the scorer's table when one of his players couldn't get into a game at Duke.

Krzyzewski said he "must have believed it then because I said it," but that time had changed his perspective. Acknowledging that his success was similar to Smith's, he understood his old adversary's position better and actually reminded old-timers of Smith in some ways. "But I don't think I get all the calls; I got a technical Wednesday night," Krzyzewski said, smiling.

Early Saturday evening, the Tar Heel bus snaked through the crowd and passed dozens of Dukies dressed in *Wizard of Oz* costumes to remind Williams he was no longer in Kansas. Inside swollen and sweltering Cameron, an overweight student in a tight-fitting UNC uniform with Sean May's number (42) carried a sign that said, "I ate Matt Doherty." Mocking May's puffy body, the Duke fatty feigned hunger and groveled on his hands and knees for a McDonald's Big Mac box bobbing from a fishing pole. The Crazies went nuts.

Cameron overflowed well beyond 9,314, the number Duke always put out as the official attendance when, truth was, many more bodies were usually crammed into the rock-covered Gothic hall. Unlike the twice-bigger Smith Center, where some tickets could generally be bought outside, scalpers struck out on this night. One celebrity that did get in was Donald Trump, who flew up from West Palm Beach and sat under the basket near the Carolina bench as a guest of Morgan Stanley CEO and Duke alumnus John Mack.

At halftime, with the Tar Heels ahead by three points, a local TV reporter stuck a camera and microphone in Trump's face. "I like number two," he said, referring to Duke freshman Luol Deng, who had rebounded from missing 14 of his 15 shots in the loss to Georgia Tech.

Carolina survived its own poor shooting and four Blue Devils in double figures (led by Deng's 25 points) to trail by only 3 with eighteen seconds remaining. Duhon had sprinted back on defense after making a perfect feed to Daniel Ewing on the other end for a shot that could have wrapped up the game. Ewing missed and Carolina recovered the long rebound.

The mercurial McCants had the ball and a chance to make good on his words earlier that week, when he had called Redick "not too much of a factor" on defense or anywhere else on the court if he weren't burying long bombs from behind the arc. Even the Duke *Chronicle* gave the nod to McCants in his matchup with Redick.

As Cameron droned like a jet engine, McCants flew across midcourt. With only five seconds left, he headed for his favorite spot in front of the UNC bench, driving into the double-team of Redick and Duhon. McCants crossed over, quick-dribbling the ball from his right side to his left. He hoped to freeze them momentarily, creating enough room to elevate and quiet the Cameron Crazies just as Williams had asked him and his teammates to do. Then, with the pressure on Duke in overtime, the Tar Heels would steal a win on Coach K Court and return the favor from Chapel Hill.

But McCants never completed his crossover. He had driven too far and had stepped over the three-point line. As he pulled his foot back, he lost control of the ball. Redick beat McCants to it and, like a linebacker stalking a fumble, dove on the ball and slid across the floor—calling a timeout as he did.

Two seconds remained, Duke had the ball and the game, beating Carolina at the buzzer again. Beating Carolina for the fourteenth time in the last sixteen meetings. Beating Carolina for the seventh time in its last eight visits to Cameron.

Afterward, Redick said nothing of McCants calling him out. The Blue Devils celebrated another win over the Tar Heels in the foyer of their new locker room—in front of a large photo on which the word DEFENSE began with the Gothic "D" logo. The picture was a Duke classic: All-American Shane Battier trailing UNC's Joseph Forte on a breakaway layup—and blocking Forte's shot from behind.

The coaches stayed mad as their teams faced two more opportunities for the third meeting in the postseason. Carolina blew its chance when it blew a late lead to Georgia Tech in the 2004 ACC Tournament in Greensboro after rallying from a first half that had Williams beside himself.

"I have no idea what offense we were running; some of the shots we took, you wouldn't see on the playground," he said after the game.

Duke welcomed another shot at Georgia Tech in the semifinals instead of facing UNC a third time, the second within a week. Hess officiated the game and hit Krzyzewski with an early technical foul that looked like a statement from the flak he had taken ten days earlier in Durham. It only energized and united the

Blue Devils, who turned a two-point deficit at halftime into a blowout win and moved on to the championship game against Maryland.

Duke squandered a 12-point lead to the Terrapins and eventually lost in overtime. As ACC regular-season champions, the Blue Devils' No. 1 seed in the NCAA Tournament was safe, but the weekend put Krzyzewski on the offensive after seeing how much of the Greensboro Coliseum rooted against his team.

At dinner Saturday night with his wife, daughter, and several Duke officials, Krzyzewski had asked, "How long have so many people hated us?" They reminded him it was part of being so successful, an obvious conclusion that had somehow escaped him.

"There were a lot of people happy that we lost," he said following the Maryland game. "The magnitude of it this year has been a surprise to me. I've never experienced that. It becomes cumulative. It really started going after we won our last national championship (2001), and the thing about how we get all the calls. I control the officials. Then all of a sudden, it's 'Yeah, that's how you win.' "

The controversy carried into the 2004 NCAA Tournament. Duke was the top seed and UNC seeded sixth in the Atlanta region and could meet for a third time if both won three games, the first time in twenty-five years they had been assigned to the same region. Krzyzewski remained embattled, comparing his program's dominant era versus Smith's at UNC but claiming the Tar Heels were never as hated as his teams because "they were never a minority" in the state.

"As good as they were, and are, and will be, and deserving of everything, there was no run like the run we just had in this conference," he said, referring to Duke's six regular-season championships and five ACC Tournament titles from 1997 to 2004.

Redick broke out of a late-season shooting slump in Duke's two easy wins over Alabama State and Seton Hall in Raleigh. In Denver, the Tar Heels took the court with shaved heads, a curious, late-season gesture of solidarity that prompted Williams to wonder, "Why weren't they unified earlier?" They rallied from a five-point halftime deficit to beat Air Force before falling to taller, tougher Texas in the second round. Williams spent a good part of the second half kneeling in front of his players on the bench, clapping in their faces and delivering an animated lecture on what they weren't doing on the court and what they needed to be playing beyond the second round.

Always disconsolate when the season "ends so suddenly," Williams did not cry like he had when Kansas got knocked out. He found himself dealing with several aspects of college basketball that he had managed to avoid at Kansas, having to "coach effort" for the first time in his career. Because he had consistently recruited tough-nosed kids to fit his system at KU, Williams was rendered inexperienced in several areas. And as the season wore on, it appeared more and more as if he wanted it to end sooner than later.

The players Williams inherited from Doherty turned out to be a selfish group more worried about individual achievement than team accomplishment. They had to be constantly prodded about playing hard, playing together and playing smart, the longtime mantra of Carolina basketball. Some had inflated opinions of their own abilities.

Williams spent much of the season wondering whether these guys would ever get it or if he needed to get new guys. His "Ol' Roy ain't that good" phrase amused early, but turned out to be right on the money. He called it his longest year in coaching and second-guessed himself more than ever before.

The Tar Heels went home with a 19–11 record, the same number of wins that Doherty had posted in his last season playing all but eight games without May, his starting freshman center. They had everyone returning for the 2005 season, plus Williams's first full recruiting class, but could they ever become a team in their new coach's image?

Duke's draw opened up favorably the next weekend in Atlanta, when the Blue Devils faced fifth-seed Illinois. Writers from the Midwest reacted to a recent story in the *Washington Post* by John Feinstein in which Krzyzewski claimed jealousy had spawned widespread hatred for his program and, more outrageously, that some people actually hoped his players got hurt on the court.

Redick, picking up the gauntlet from his coach, told the media the day before the Duke-Illinois game, "There's great level of hate for Duke." He pointed to some aggressive fouls on Deng, recounted an incident from seven weeks earlier when a Georgia Tech player came off the bench to pick a fight with him, and spoke of the rude and crude behavior of opposing fans. That, of course, got the least sympathy, since Cameron Indoor Stadium had set the inhospitable standard for college basketball.

An anti-Duke contingent filled the gigantic Georgia Dome, which had plenty to boo during the tense battle against thirteenth-ranked Illinois. The Illini coach, Bruce Weber, was already pissed off at Krzyzewski over the head-to-head recruitment of Shaun Livingston, a high school star from nearby Peoria. Weber had learned that the Duke coach said Illinois played for Big Ten championships while his team played for *national* championships.

Duke defeated the Illini by 10 points and then used a late spurt to hold off upstart and unranked Xavier to win its fourteenth of 16 Elite Eight games since

1963, the last 10 of 11 by Krzyzewski teams. Their only losses were to Purdue in 1980 and Kentucky in 1998.

The Blue Devils had not won an NCAA regional since 2001, and this was only their third in ten years, yet a perception existed that they made the Final Four every season. Carolina had actually been there four times since 1995, but Duke's ten trips in nineteen years left the more indelible impression.

They carried that burden to San Antonio. Another ho-hum Final Four, and unless Duke beat Connecticut in the semifinals and made it to Monday might there really wasn't anything to toast. Krzyzewski's task was to keep that attitude from infiltrating his squad, which faced its biggest challenge from a UConn team that was a consensus preseason No. 1 and, after recovering from a January swoon, playing its best basketball.

Carolina had a presence in San Antonio. Dean Smith and Mike Krzyzewski were in newspaper comparisons and on constant TV graphics: the most Final Fours, the most NCAA appearances, the most tournament victories. Krzyzewski's tenth trip was 1 behind Smith's 11 and 2 short of John Wooden's 12 at UCLA. His 4 NCAA Tournament wins in 2004 left him within 1 of Smith's record 65 victories, but he was still coaching, and passing the two retired legends was just a matter of time.

Krzyzewski was also trying to pass Bobby Knight in NCAA Championships. Both had 3, 1 short of Kentucky's Adolph Rupp and 6 behind Wooden's unreachable 10. Since Wooden retired in 1975, and the tournament began expanding toward its current sixty-five teams, just making the Final Four had become the equal of winning the national title in the days of twenty-five to thirty-two teams. Six victories were now required to take home the national championship, and the field was balanced geographically. So, who really had more postseason success, UCLA or Duke?

As the semifinal unfolded UConn's All-American center Emeka Okafor sitting out most of the first half with two fouls was remindful of Smith holding Michael Jordan out of the famous 1984 upset loss to Indiana. Krzyzewski kept his big men, Shelden Williams and Shavlik Randolph, in the game with two fouls. Both picked up their third before halftime, a key development, despite Duke's early dominance.

When the Blue Devils still led 75–67 with four minutes to play, the race against the clock began. Okafor had returned to take over the game, fouling out Williams, Randolph, and backup center Nick Horvath as UConn scored 12 straight points. Left to try to stop him was freshman Deng, who despite his strong postseason wasn't tough enough in the last minutes. He allowed Okafor to rip the ball out of his hands for the go-ahead basket. The Blue Devils needed one stop, one rebound, or one basket in the last six exchanges. Inexplicably, they stopped attacking on offense and played not to lose.

It came down to a missed three-pointer by Redick and his jump stop in the lane on the next possession, trying to draw a foul and the two free throws that could still pull out the victory. He didn't get the call and UConn came up with the loose ball.

"You killed us! You cheated us!" Krzyzewski screamed at official Ted Hillary with three seconds left and UConn up by an insurmountable four points. Like five years ago in St. Petersburg, Duke lost a Final Four game to Connecticut that it seemingly could not lose.

Duke left San Antonio with a 31–6 record but without the national championship and a fourth consecutive loss to UConn, which was later deemed by NCAA insiders as the worst-officiated game in Final Four history. At home, the meltdowns to UConn and Maryland in the ACC Tournament drew new attention to the list of big games Duke had frittered away, dating all the way back to blown leads against Louisville and Arkansas for the 1986 and 1994 NCAA championships.

Although Dukies reveled in calling Carolina and Smith "chokers" in their decades of dominance, harping on 1983 and '84 NCAA losses to Georgia and Indiana with Jordan on the roster, and the string of Final Four failures in the 1990s, their team had now bombed out more dramatically than Smith's Tar Heels. The Blue Devils led Seton Hall by 18 points in the 1989 Final Four, Kentucky by 17 points in the 1998 regional final, and Indiana by 18 points in the 2002 Sweet Sixteen before losing all three games. They suffered upsets to Kansas in 1988, Cal in 1993, and Florida in 2000.

During the spring of 2004, Duke and Carolina found themselves strange bedfellows again. They had united the summer before against ACC expansion, hoping the league would not kill the golden goose by bringing in new members that ended the league's traditional round robin in basketball and, especially, the cherished home-and-away games between the Big Four—Duke, UNC, N.C. State, and Wake Forest. They lost that battle, as the ACC took in Miami and Virginia Tech and eventually added a twelfth school, Boston College.

This time, the two programs found themselves losing important players, in three cases, before they ever enrolled.

At Duke, Deng wanted to stay for his sophomore season but pressure from his family in England to support their Dinka tribe back in the Sudan made him enter the NBA draft, where he was the seventh pick in the first round by Phoenix (and later traded to Chicago). The Blue Devils also lost Shaun Livingston, who had signed the previous fall but never put on a Duke uniform. The high school star, convinced by would-be agents that he was an early pick, entered the draft before the May deadline. He also went in the first round to the Clippers, leaving Krzyzewski miffed at the system.

Carolina's losses didn't seem so damaging, given the depth the Tar Heels had coming back. Citing a university policy to expel any athlete committing a felony, Roy Williams rescinded the scholarship offer to JamesOn Curry, the leading scorer in the history of North Carolina high school basketball who had signed with UNC after originally committing to Doherty. Curry had been caught in a sting operation at his school in nearby Burlington. After plea-bargaining his fifteen charges of drug trafficking and possession down to six, he received a suspended sentence and eventually signed a second-chance scholarship with Oklahoma State.

New Jersey high school star J. R. Smith, who was first recruited by Doherty and later befriended by Williams's assistant Joe Holladay, also opted for the NBA draft to help his blue-collar family. He went on the eighteenth pick to the New Orleans Hornets.

The attrition severely hurt Duke's chances of returning to the Final Four. With Deng and Livingston, the Blue Devils were a certain preseason pick to get back and win the NCAA Tournament, but Krzyzewski, who was once immune to NBA pillaging, had now lost eight players early in six years.

It led to wild speculation, and hand-wringing anxiety at Duke, over the July 4 weekend that Krzyzewski, himself, was leaving to coach the Los Angeles Lakers.

Mitch Kupchak, a former UNC player and general manager of the Lakers, had first talked with Krzyzewski in June and began pursuing him as a candidate to take over one of the most storied franchises in NBA history. Krzyzewski had moved between irritation and anger for the last year over expansion, negative reaction to his 2004 team, and finally the disheartening loss to UConn in the Final Four. After losing Deng and Livingston to the NBA, maybe it was time for him to take the money and run, too.

In June, Krzyzewski had walked into Cameron Indoor Stadium one night, while his basketball camp was in progress, and told small group, "Guess who just called? The Lakers want me to come out and coach them." They all laughed, but Krzyzewski's wheels were turning.

Kupchak targeted three other coaches besides Krzyzewski, starting with Roy Williams because of Kupchak's association with UNC. Williams had a chance to get involved with the Lakers after the 1992 season while still at Kansas (the Lakers eventually hired Randy Pfund) but insisted he was a college coach. He told Kupchak the same thing, and their conversation remained private.

The two others Kupchak called were one-time Lakers coach Pat Riley, who had retired to the front office of the Miami Heat and decided quickly he did not want to return to the sideline, and former Houston Rockets' coach Rudy Tomjanovich, who was considered the favorite throughout the process. Rudy T. was the Lakers' insurance policy and willing to wait until Kupchak covered all of his bases. He wanted the job but understood that Kupchak *had* to pursue Krzyzewski for several reasons.

The highest-profile coach in pro basketball, Phil Jackson, had resigned after six seasons and three World Championships. Lakers' owner Dr. Jerry Buss was obliged to try to bring another nationally known sports figure into the Los Angeles market. Kobe Bryant, the Lakers' superstar who was recruited by Duke before he jumped directly from high school to the NBA, had Krzyzewski on his personal preference list. Bryant had spoken to him, as well as to David Falk, Krzyzewski's high-powered Washington agent.

These factors helped offset an uncertainty over whether Krzyzewski's success could translate to the professional level. Of his eighteen first-round draft choices over the past twenty years, none were candidates to join him in the basketball Hall of Fame compared to three former UNC players already enshrined with Dean Smith (not yet including Michael Jordan) from his twenty-eight first-round picks. There was a feeling among NBA coaches and scouts that Duke players had inflated opinions about their own abilities, making their adjustments harder.

Just as Krzyzewski had done in 1994, within the first year of Nan Keohane's tenure, he forced new Duke President Richard Brodhead into the position of doing whatever it took to keep his renowned basketball coach. How could Brodhead, on the job less than a week, offset the $40 million contract over five years the Lakers had reportedly offered Krzyzewski?

Maybe the college game had changed enough for Krzyzewski to become disillusioned, and he was going to cash out, too, using the financial windfall to give his family of three daughters and grandchildren security for life. His annual income was estimated at $2 million, but $40 million was something he at least had to consider.

Krzyzewski went to dinner at Brodhead's home two nights before the Lakers' story broke and told him of the impending offer. He needed certain assurances in order to remain at Duke. Among them was a renewed commitment to build the practice facility that had been on the drawing board for several years.

Kupchak flew into Raleigh on Thursday, July 1, and met with Krzyzewski and his wife. He was encouraged, telling Lakers' assistant general manager Jim Buss by phone that "it's still a long shot but I think we have a chance to get him." The story made the Los Angeles media and a day later reached North Carolina. With rumors spreading, Duke Athletics Director Joe Alleva held a press conference on Friday afternoon to deter what he knew would be dozens of media inquiries over the holiday weekend.

Cynical fans and Duke critics called it another grandstand move. In '94, Krzyzewski had chewed on an offer from the Portland Trailblazers before meeting the press to say he was declining. This time, the petty speculation suggested he was not only demanding more from Duke but also wanted to upstage the national publicity Detroit Pistons coach and UNC alumnus Larry Brown had received for winning the 2004 NBA title "the Carolina way" with a team effort devoid of superstar performances.

Over July 4, as Krzyzewski huddled with his family at the beach, Duke students held vigil outside Cameron while fans flooded the basketball office with calls and e-mails. Krzyzewski was particularly moved by one e-mail from a student named Andrew Humphries that made him cry. Humphries said he had grown up dreaming of playing for Krzyzewski and, even though he wasn't good enough, he was still playing for Duke because the Cameron Crazies were the team's Sixth Man.

The story about the Lakers' pursuit received headline coverage across the country for four days on radio, television and in print. To many people, Krzyzewski was the national symbol of a sport that was flirting with disaster because of players and at least one high-profile coach (Stanford's Mike Montgomery) leaving for the NBA. One columnist likened Krzyzewski to the last guy out of the room turning out the light, suggesting that his leaving for the Lakers would flick the switch on college basketball.

By the time he held his own press conference on Monday July 5, reaffirming his commitment to Duke, the national feedback had become a focus group of the masses. Krzyzewski's advisors knew he was an icon in his own genre, but the reaction convinced them his influence and impact could be felt far beyond the athletic arena. They stepped up their plans to align him with selected "iconic" companies that were consistent with the image and message Duke wanted to convey.

David Falk and Mike Cragg, director of the Duke Legacy Fund that was already raising money to endow scholarships for his program, contacted representatives of American Express. Krzyzewski had smaller endorsement deals with Allstate Insurance and General Motors, plus his ongoing agreement with Nike, but his newest partnership proposal was for more comprehensive exposure.

Even though Amex had never used a basketball coach in any prior commercials, the financial giant thought Krzyzewski's strong leadership skills might fit well with the campaign it was planning to showcase personal stories of uniquely famous individuals.

Executives at American Express, and its various advertising and PR agencies in New York, debated how Krzyzewski would be received. He was unquestionably the most prominent college basketball coach in the country, the new face of the game, but because he coached at Duke, an elite university with snob appeal, and because his teams won so damn much, Krzyzewski was also a controversial figure.

Would his story be accepted like those of fellow endorsees Robert DeNiro, Ellen DeGeneres, and Tiger Woods and help strengthen Amex's market share, or would he be a divisive element that triggered more love-hate arguments over Duke and resulted in people cutting up their cards rather than increasing their credit lines?

The boardroom discussions considered the equally strong following of UNC's basketball program, constructed over thirty years by Smith, Krzyzewski's old adversary. Although the Tar Heels had fallen behind Duke during Smith's retirement, millions of Carolina fans still made up the next largest college basketball constituency. How would they, the economic equal of the Dukies, react to Amex aligning with Coach K?

Duke's defections left Carolina in the favorite's role because the Tar Heels had three seniors, four juniors, and one freshman who did come, Marvin Williams, as their top eight players for the 2004–05 season. Settling in as the odds-on favorite over the summer, they were eventually picked to win the ACC and capture the national championship by *Sports Illustrated,* Dick Vitale, and several major media polls.

Neither coach was on campus when their old and new players returned for the school year.

Krzyzewski was working the Jordan Senior Flight School at the Mirage hotel in Las Vegas, where he joined a dozen college and professional contemporaries in the four-day, $15,000-each adult fantasy camp run by MJ himself. Despite being the most successful active college coach there, Krzyzewski also took it the most seriously. He scouted campers carefully during the first day and selected the players he believed he could whip into a championship team. He invited past teams to games at Duke and to dinner at his home.

It became the model for his own $10,000-a-pop alumni camp and helped change Krzyzewski's opinion about his closest rival. He first met Jordan as an assistant coach with the Olympic Dream Team in 1992 and was amazed by the work ethic of the best player in the world. He used Jordan's example from then on with his own teams and in motivational speeches he delivered to corporate groups as a member of the Washington Speakers Bureau. His respect for UNC's program grew through relationships he formed with other ex-Tar Heels at Jordan's camp, which he rarely missed even though it often conflicted with the start of classes at Duke.

Williams was out of the country for six weeks in August and September as one of Larry Brown's assistants on the 2004 U.S.A. team at the Athens Olympics. That, too, was a mind-altering experience for Williams, who had spent a month with young millionaires like LeBron James and Carmelo Anthony. Comprised of only three members from the original squad that Brown and U.S.A. Basketball had selected the previous summer, the collection of NBA players had neither the time nor the inclination to become a unit capable of playing with European teams that had been together for years.

When he returned after the United States won a disappointing bronze medal in Athens, Williams said he was never so glad to have his feet back on American soil and joked that he was more anxious than ever to see McCants and some of the other kids who had made him so mad the previous season. He regarded the experience as on-the-job training under Brown, who had now won NBA and NCAA championships and who Williams regarded as the best active coach in basketball. He came home with new offensive and defensive wrinkles that he hoped to teach his second Tar Heel team.

UNC's season began with a discouraging loss at Santa Clara, with Raymond Felton sitting out a one-game suspension for playing in an unsanctioned summer league game. Furious that they looked like the same old Tar Heels, Williams put them through two days of boot camp practices for the Maui Invitational.

"Do I need to go get the damn Constitution of the United States to explain why I want things done a certain way?" he yelled during one stoppage. "I've won a few damn games, you know. Just do it like I say and quit loafing!"

Shocked out of their comfort zone, the Tar Heels swept through the Maui Invitational in such stunning fashion that basketball sports information director Matt Bowers boldly predicted they would be national champions come April. They went on to win 14 consecutive games, thrashing Kentucky in Chapel Hill and welcoming Virginia Tech to the ACC with a 34-point walloping in Blacksburg, before losing at third-ranked Wake Forest, unraveling under the pressure of their first true ACC road game.

Duke began its one hundredth basketball season ranked No. 11 and went 15–0 against a soft schedule that ACC officials admitted was back-loaded for TV so the Blue Devils played their biggest games during February sweeps.

They did beat Michigan State at home and Oklahoma in New York City around Krzyzewski's seven hundredth career win over Toledo. Duke also celebrated the sixty-fifth anniversary of Cameron Indoor Stadium by beating Princeton, which was the first opponent when the building opened on January 6, 1940.

Old nemesis Maryland upset Duke at Cameron for the third time in six years to break the unbeaten string. The Blue Devils were 17–2 after their second loss at Wake Forest and then returned home to defeat Georgia Tech on Saturday, February 5. Krzyzewski gave them Sunday off as mandated by the NCAA.

His day off from practice wasn't spent breaking down game tapes for Carolina's visit Wednesday night or making recruiting calls. A production crew hired by American Express was on campus to shoot a series of television commercials at Cameron and various locations. Krzyzewski had signed a lucrative contract with Amex to join its "my life, my card" advertising campaign.

The contract, worth seven figures, included a sizable donation to the Emily Krzyzewski Family Life Center in Durham, named for the coach's mother and one of his primary charities. The scripts were written and approved by all parties, including Duke and the NCAA. By February, they were ready to go into production.

The crew set up lights in Cameron to show a gleaming court and accent the brass and mahogany railings beneath the upper deck of seats. Footage of Krzyzewski was combined with cameos taken with a group of multiracial, attentive youngsters hired by Amex gazing up at the respected coach.

The producer for the video, which included cut-ins of Krzyzewski coaching, was a hall of famer in his own right. Errol Morris had won an Academy Award in 2004 for Best Documentary for *Fog Of War*. He shot the segments with Krzyzewski over nine hours on Sunday and returned to shoot campus scenes most of Monday when the team went back to practice for the Carolina game.

Krzyzewski held one of his two in-season press conferences on Tuesday. Once considered among the most accessible coaches in the ACC, he frustrated the local media that had supported him in his lean, losing years. In comparison, Williams met with the press almost weekly throughout the season and seemed much more approachable. When available, Krzyzewski was still candid and thoughtful, which made it all the more the shame. After getting sick in 1995, he decided something had to be cut out of his schedule. He chose regular meetings with sports reporters.

Ten years after Duke had bottomed out with a 13–18 season while he recuperated at home from a back injury and related stress, Krzyzewski said "it seems like that never happened. The time has gone so fast. I have a hard time believing it's been ten years . . . I have a hard time believing I'm fifty-eight." He acknowledged that reinventing his program after returning helped Duke regain dominance nationally and locally. The Blue Devils had been to three Final Fours and won a national championship in 2001, plus 11 assorted ACC titles. Their record against Carolina since 1996 was 16–5.

The Tar Heels arrived at Duke on February 9 ranked No. 2 and, for the first time in seven years, were considered to have the better team. The Blue Devils, after climbing to No. 2, were now No. 7 in the polls. They had played for a month without Randolph, who had mononucleosis, and worked reserve forward Lee Melchionni into a patchwork lineup that often consisted of four guards around Shelden Williams. That night they had Carolina at Cameron, where they had lost only seven times in the last eight years.

"You still have to beat Duke," Krzyzewski liked to say.

The Tar Heels were determined to do that and prove they had pulled even in what had become a lopsided rivalry. They weren't favored to win—a rarity for visiting teams in Cameron—but they were *expected* to win by many fans from both schools and most sportswriters. It just seemed like their turn.

UNC was tight early, trailed by seven at halftime and despite playing better in the second half remained down by nine with five minutes left. Only Sean May was on his game and kept them in it with his sixth double-double of the season as the Tar Heels dominated Duke on the boards. Felton, who had committed 8 of his team's 21 turnovers, scored 6 straight points to bring Carolina within reach.

The Blue Devils shot poorly most of the night but made their first 16 free throws to continually repel UNC rallies. Their late turnover and a missed jumper by freshman DeMarcus Nelson, playing his best college game to date, allowed Carolina to sneak back within a point on a driving layup by McCants. When Redick forced an airball as the shot clock expired, for the second straight year the Tar Heels had a chance to pull out a last-second victory at Cameron.

Duke clung to a one-point lead. Having seen Carolina run it before, Redick expected a play called Long Beach, which Williams had stolen from Long Beach State when he was at Kansas. Felton would attempt to penetrate from the top of the key and look first for McCants on the left wing rubbing off a high screen from May. As it turned out, the play wasn't even necessary.

When Felton crossed midcourt, Ewing went for the steal. Felton should have driven down the lane and taken the open fifteen-footer or fed the ball underneath to May or Marvin Williams. He didn't make the instinctive play, opting for the one his coach had called. Redick's defense foiled it again, and McCants failed to make a counter move. The clock ran out as the Tar Heels fumbled the ball, and the game, out of bounds.

The ESPN cameras caught Felton and McCants staring down each other. *Shit, man, we didn't even get a shot off for the second straight year.*

A month later, with the Tar Heels trailing Duke 73–66 in the game they *had* to win, CBS went to a commercial on an ominous out-cue from Jim Nantz, "Mike Krzyzewski is 6–1 against Roy Williams. Can he pull it off again?"

During the break, American Express sponsored a curious feature called "Defining Moments" about the Duke and Carolina programs and their great traditions. An attempt at political correctness for the massive following of both schools? Some UNC fans, faced with sure defeat, had already made note to call Amex in the morning.

Duke didn't need any more baskets, only to take care of the ball and get it into the hands of Redick, the leading free throw shooter in the country. Against a Carolina double team, however, Ewing threw the rock away and the Tar Heels took possession.

With the crowd coming to life, Felton missed a runner and Marvin Williams hauled in the offensive rebound. He went back up and was fouled by Shelden Williams. While Krzyzewski motioned for his team to "box out," UNC's Williams made both free throws. It was now a five-point game, 73–68, with two minutes to play.

The Blue Devils got to the foul line this time, but Nelson bricked the front end of a one-and-one, Duke's fourth straight failed free throw. Felton fed May, who hit the bottom of the rim with his power move, rebounded his own miss, and put it in as he was fouled. His three-point play reduced Duke's lead to two with 1:45 on the clock.

The Dean Dome was wild again. The lightheartedness on and behind the Duke bench had disappeared. Duke went back to the well with the play that had built its lead. Redick drove baseline and fed Melchionni in the left corner. His jumper was wide right. Shelden Williams recovered the rebound and found Redick in the opposite corner, wide open. His shot wasn't even close.

Duke still looked okay when Williams blocked his sixth shot of the game and the ball went out off Carolina. Fifty seconds remained as Ewing raced across midcourt looking for Redick. Trailing the play, UNC's David Noel reached around Ewing and flicked the ball away. In the scramble, Felton came up with it and got a timeout—a crucial call since Duke owned the possession arrow.

Felton wasn't waiting for the last shot this time, as he had at Cameron. He drove the lane and floated up a twelve-footer. Nelson collided with him for a two-shot foul.

Felton swished the first to cut Duke's lead to a point. He seemed to know his second shot was too long because he darted forward after releasing it. The ball hit back rim and came out, and he tapped it to his right side. Marvin Williams grabbed the ball and awkwardly went up in traffic. As he was bumped and fouled, his shot banked in.

Bedlam reigned while Roy Williams tried to contain his bench. Marvin made the free throw and the team that had been down by nine points less than three minutes earlier was now ahead 75–73. Duke, which had gone the entire stretch without scoring, called its last timeout. The play was going to Redick, who was still scoreless in the second half.

He ran off two screens and got open for a long three-pointer in front of Krzyzewski. The ball went halfway in before popping out. The rebound squirted out to Ewing, who had a last shot from the right wing. His hurried three-pointer was way off as the clock went to double zero and the fans flooded the floor.

Carolina had closed with an 11–0 run and won, despite shooting only 40 percent and going 1 of 11 from three-point range. May had 26 points and 24 rebounds and was a nonfactor for half of the second half, underscoring the greatest individual performance in the Duke-Carolina series since Charlie Scott's 40 points in the 1969 ACC Tournament.

"C'mon, 26 and 24 in a Duke-Carolina game," Krzyzewski said in a tight-lipped tribute to the junior center, who had posted eight straight double-doubles from Duke game to Duke game and turned superstar in a month's time.

"The moon was right," Roy Williams said of the comeback. He kept his team at the bench, called for the two tall ladders and waited for the students to clear the court. The Tar Heels cut down the nets as the undisputed ACC regular-season champions.

K versus Roy was officially under way. Like the ten years between the late 1980s and 1990s, the two giants of the college game were competing feverishly on the court and in recruiting. Krzyzewski, still without a hint of gray in his jet black hair, was now the most intimidating coach, talking to officials as if they were disobedient dogs—"Bad call! Bad, bad call!—and spending so much time chatting up refs on the sideline that it appeared they were justifying every whistle to him. Williams, three years younger and almost completely white-haired, spent more time imploring and cajoling his troops, often from a catcher's crouch with his fists clenched.

Williams was happy with the win but still peeved over his son getting thrown out for what he considered a mild transgression. He called the ACC office the next day and protested to Supervisor of Officiating Fred Barakat, who claimed Rose did not know it was Williams's kid and backed up his official for the ejection that involved no profanity.

Since pundits already said Krzyzewski owned the rivalry more than Smith ever had, the win was a must heading into postseason play. Losing to Duke again at home would have tarnished an otherwise great year. Instead, the dramatic victory drew Williams and Carolina closer to the Duke juggernaut and, in tangible terms, assured UNC a No. 1 seed in the NCAA Tournament.

Typically, the pendulum swung back after McCants returned from his illness to play in the 2005 ACC Tournament at the MCI Center in Washington, D.C. The Tar Heels barely survived the opener against ninth-seeded Clemson. Their sketchy play continued in the semifinal, giving up a record 35 points to Will Bynum and getting ousted by Georgia Tech for the second year in a row. Duke beat Virginia and, behind 35 points from Redick, repressed N.C. State to advance to its eighth consecutive ACC championship game, extending its amazing conference mark (Duke, UNC, and Wake Forest had all played in five straight title games previously).

The Blue Devils broke on top of Tech at the half but saw most of their 13-point lead dwindle in the closing seconds as foul trouble left them with a makeshift lineup. Krzyzewski was forced to go back with freshman David Mc-Clure, whom he had angrily banished to the end of the bench in the first half for mouthing off to Redick.

In what became known as the "phantom foul," Larry Rose called Jarrett Jack for holding Redick away from the ball. Since Redick was a 94-percent free-throw shooter, it was like giving the NCAA career leader two points to ice the game. He made them but Duke still needed Williams's tip-in to secure the 69–64 win. Tech coach Paul Hewitt complained bitterly about the Redick foul, and continued doing so on his radio show that week, drawing a reprimand from the ACC office.

Duke had cut down the ACC nets for a stunning sixth time in the last seven years, adding to another unmatched period of dominance by one program. The Blue Devils' ACC championship took the league's other top NCAA seed away from second-place Wake Forest, which had lost to N.C. State in the ACC quarterfinals with Chris Paul suspended for punching Julius Hodge in the groin during their regular-season game the weekend before. Duke got the No. 1 seed in the Austin (or South) Regional, its seventh in the last eight years, tying Kentucky with nine for the second most behind Carolina.

The Tar Heels, by virtue of winning the ACC race, were the No. 1 seed in the Syracuse (East) Regional, their first since 1998 and tenth since the NCAA began seeding teams in 1979. Roy Williams, however, was still ornery from a half-hearted effort in the ACC Tournament. He locked his players out of practice early in the week until, on Dean Smith's suggestion, they each signed a team pledge to rededicate themselves to the postseason where they were still favored to win the national championship.

Only once before, in 1998, had UNC and Duke been seeded No. 1 in the same season, but the pod placement caused the biggest stir.

The NCAA had planned to put two ACC teams in Charlotte, North Carolina, where they would practice and play in the same building. Besides both going to Charlotte, the Tar Heels and Blue Devils were also placed in the same side of the tournament bracket, setting them on a collision course for a national semifinal game in St. Louis on Saturday, April 2. That created another clear and present undercurrent as the archrivals arrived for their first-and second-round games.

The Dukies hadn't expected *this*.

They were going out to dinner in Charlotte the night before the first round of the NCAA Tournament. They had bussed from the nearby five-star Park Hotel to the Palm, the snobby steakhouse in the Galleria on the tony south side of the city.

Krzyzewski and his wife, Mickie, walked in first, their party of forty following politely behind. Before they reached their private room in the back of the restaurant, they suddenly, and a bit surprisingly, felt like visitors in their own state.

Charlotte was a "Carolina town." More alumni and supporters of UNC lived in Mecklenburg County than any other county, except for Wake County much closer to the Carolina campus. Most of the "Charlotte Mafia" headed by multi-millionaire developer Johnny Harris were Tar Heels. Hugh McColl, who had built tiny NCNB and merged it with Bank of America, began at UNC, as did Ken Thompson, CEO of warring Wachovia across Tryon and down Trade Streets. The world's most famous basketball player, also a Carolina grad, tried to save the city's first NBA franchise from unpopular ownership; if Michael Jordan had succeeded in buying the Hornets, they might have been moving into the $276 million "uptown arena" instead of the fledgling Bobcats.

Between 1956 and 2002, Carolina played at least one basketball game in Charlotte each season. Both Frank McGuire and Dean Smith liked to schedule a big-name opponent in the Queen City; sometimes Indiana, four times Notre Dame, three times Kentucky. The Tar Heels played "road games" against Clemson or South Carolina at the old coliseum on Independence Boulevard because its 11,666 seats brought in triple the money than the bandboxes in Clemson and

Columbia. Besides the "home" teams weren't going to win, no matter where the games were played.

The North-South Doubleheader began in 1959, with UNC and North Carolina State playing Clemson and South Carolina on Friday night, then swapping opponents on Saturday night. South Carolina dropped out when it quit the ACC in 1971 and Clemson soon followed. Carolina and State kept going down to face a variety of non-ACC teams through 1985 until Smith decided he'd rather play two more games in Chapel Hill. State, which had ridden on Carolina's coattails and took home half the net gate for more than twenty-five years, was bitter. Frank Weeden, the Wolfpack's bleeding red assistant athletics director, said Smith was not like the legendary Case, who brought big-time basketball to North Carolina.

"Everett was interested in promoting basketball," Weeden snipped. "Dean is interested in promoting *Carolina* basketball."

In 1988, when the twenty-three thousand-seat Charlotte Coliseum opened, locally owned TV syndicator Raycom (founded by UNC grad Rick Ray) invented the Tournament of Champions in which Carolina and N.C. State alternated hosting three intersectional teams every *other* year. Big crowds came only in the years when the Tar Heels played, and Raycom soon dropped State as a host. Smith stayed in the event until the contract ran out, and when he retired, Bill Guthridge refused to re-up. In sixty-five years of playing in Charlotte, Carolina had lost only 18 games, winning 159, and was an already perfect 5–0 when the NCAA Tournament was played there.

Charlotte had also been very good to the Dukies.

Hadn't they nearly won the national championship there with a rag-tag team taken on a magical ride by All-American Grant Hill in 1994? When they left the floor at the Charlotte Coliseum that April Monday night, they were cheered and applauded by an appreciative crowd that knew they had left every bit of sweat and energy behind.

Duke had more special moments in Charlotte and other "Carolina towns." The last two national championships for Krzyzewski's teams had begun with victories on Tar Heel soil. Their first ACC title and Final Four were hatched with five consecutive wins in Greensboro in 1986 before moving on to the East Regional in New Jersey, their "second home" that was always so ridiculed by the anti-Duke crowd. Just the previous year, they had begun another march to the Final Four with two wins at a sold-out RBC Center in Raleigh, where those rooting for the Blue Devils dwarfed fans from the Wake Forest team playing in the other half of Saturday's doubleheader.

Overall, Duke had a .770 winning percentage on neutral North Carolina courts under Krzyzewski. So the Blue Devils, who had won three ACC Tournaments and three NCAA Tournament games in Charlotte since beginning to dominate like no other program over the last eight years, should have felt at home there, as well.

Even this year, 2005.

That afternoon, in the Coliseum on Tyvola Road that was playing host to its last college basketball games before being razed in favor of the Bobcats' glitzy new downtown digs, Duke had worked out as the last of all eight teams in the Charlotte "pod."

When Iowa State came out for its open practice, about three hundred people were in the stands. When Carolina took the court two hours later, more than four thousand fans had filled much of the lower arena, and they sounded like ten thousand, especially when the Tar Heels put on their dunking exhibition during warm-ups.

About the same number of people, including several hundred UNC fans, were there for Duke's practice at six o'clock. While it was a heavily partisan gathering, a dozen teenage boys all wearing light blue shirts razzed the Blue Devils from behind one basket. In the press conference that followed, Krzyzewski said he didn't notice who was yelling what. "I'd rather have noise than no noise," he said.

The noise the Dukies walked into at the Palm was more a hum of excitement that Krzyzewski and the Blue Devils were actually there. Then came some good-natured heckling from a few people hunkered down at their mahogany booths and tables. A seven-year-old heard her parents say it was the Duke team, and she let out a little boo.

It was okay, all in good fun, a little buzz and a few barbs, but if the Tar Heels had come in, half the place would have been up and clapping with a few "Go, Heels!" bouncing off the expensive crystal.

About ten minutes after the Dukies had disappeared into the back room, Johnny Dawkins came out to hit the men's room. "Dawkins went to the bathroom and got heckled," Mike Cragg said, laughing, of the nice-guy assistant coach who hadn't suited up for twenty years.

The next morning, a young woman bussing tables while the Blue Devils ate breakfast at the Park Hotel gave them a hard time. By then, they already knew their visit to Charlotte was far different from the others to North Carolina's largest city.

Different from when they had played in Charlotte and only their fans came out to see them. In those years, the Carolina people had stayed home, watching their team play on TV in the family rooms of Myers Park or South Park or the bars at Quail Hollow and Piper Glen Country Clubs, or not watching at all.

This year the Tar Heels were also in Charlotte. They had been ranked among the top teams in the country throughout the 2005 season, and their light blue legion gobbled up thousands of tickets that were on sale for months. Because Wake Forest was in the top five consistently, the Deacons seemed most likely the second team in Charlotte. By the time the Blue Devils won the ACC Tournament the weekend before, the Charlotte Coliseum was sold out and thousands of *their* fans could not find a way in.

The four participating schools during each session received only 1,250 tickets apiece. So most of the atmosphere was being supplied by those who already had tickets in hand, gambling their team would be there. That team was Carolina.

It marked only the third time—the second in North Carolina—that Duke and UNC played in the same building during the NCAA Tournament. The most recent was in 1991, when they reached the Final Four in Indianapolis. The most glorious weekend in Duke basketball history was also the most painful ever for the Tar Heels, whose famous coach got thrown out late in a loss to Kansas, and Duke stunned unbeaten UNLV, then won its first national championship on Monday night. The other was Black Sunday in 1979, the infamous day when the Blue Devils and the Tar Heels played second-round games in the East Regional against Penn and St. John's in Raleigh. Duke was ranked sixth, Carolina third. They were heavily favored and well-supported by their fan base. However, both lost on the darkest day in ACC history.

The media recounted that story, as sportswriters reminisced and wrote about March 11, 1979. Krzyzewski was still coaching at Army and said he had heard about it many times since but, frankly, had no personal recollection of the two Eastern teams slaying ACC giants on one afternoon. Roy Williams was in his first year as Dean Smith's part-time assistant coach (part-time pay, full-time job, he liked to say) on Black Sunday.

"It was my first experience with how sudden, how swiftly it ends when you lose in the NCAA Tournament," he said. "I was sick over it. I was so poor I didn't even have a bicycle back then, so I had the bus driver drop me at my apartment at Glen Lennox on Route 54 on the way home from Raleigh."

Despite Carolina's first-round laugher against sixteenth-seed Oakland University, the sixty-fifth team in the field, brokers and hawkers were still getting at least twice face value ($50) for tickets. Although the Tar Heels had played 177 times in Charlotte, this was their first NCAA Tournament game there since 1987, when freshman J. R. Reid scored 27 points in a second-round win over Michigan. They shot 73 percent and led Oakland by 26 at the half, with Marvin

Williams's flying dunk awakening the crowd and several pro scouts in attendance, on the way to a 96–68 victory.

The atmosphere changed for Duke's seven o'clock game against a far better No. 16 seed, Delaware State. The Hornets' quickness bothered the Blue Devils early in the first half, and when they took a brief lead the coliseum was roaring with Tar Heels who had come back for the night session and impartial fans rooting for an upset. Krzyzewski was forced to pull his defense back under the basket and Delaware died, failing to score in the last five minutes of the first half and missing 25 of its last 32 shots. Duke didn't score a field goal in the last eight minutes, making the score closer than the game.

After the 57–46 win, which tied him with Smith for sixty-five NCAA Tournament victories, Krzyzewski joked about the negative reaction. "I've been in places where everyone was booing me," he said, "and then I walked out of my house."

When told that Mississippi State coach Rick Stansbury, whose team had defeated Stanford in the other first-round game, was soliciting support from Carolina fans for Sunday, Krzyzewski quipped, "Tell Rick not to bother. The votes are in, and, like Chicago, the people voted three or four times."

Their coach said "it's because we've won a lot," but the Blue Devil players were more disappointed by the reaction of the crowd. "There weren't as many Duke fans as we thought," Randolph said. "That's fine. A lot of people want us to lose. We're used to that."

During the respective press conferences after Saturday's practice sessions, the UNC and Duke players laughed, snickered, and stammered when asked if they were pulling for each other to survive and advance.

"We ain't pulling for anybody," McCants said, "'cause I'm sure nobody's pulling for us. We want every good team to lose to make it easier for us down the road."

The Dukies' press conference was more politically correct, if less sincere.

"You always want your conference to do well, even if you have a little grudge against a team," Ewing said.

Dockery, who had returned from his knee injury for the NCAA Tournament, interjected lightly, "What did they say about us?"

Krzyzewski got the first questions about his commercial TV time. American Express had stepped up its campaign featuring the Duke coach, and the ads ran during most first-round games Thursday and Friday. In Carolina's win over Oakland, Amex had chosen to run commercials featuring Tiger Woods and surfer Laird Hamilton, but Krzyzewski got plenty of exposure in the other games.

I want you to develop as a player, I want you to develop as a student, I want you to develop as a human being . . .

He was seen as promoting himself and his program far more than a credit card he couldn't leave home without, however. It was also a "dead period" in recruiting, when coaches were allowed no contact with prospects. As high school stars sat home and watched the NCAA Tournament, they saw Krzyzewski's face and message repeatedly during the commercial breaks.

The growing controversy helped turn Charlotte abuzz for the Carolina-Duke doubleheader Sunday afternoon. By now, lower level tickets were going for ten times the $50 face value. Unlike 1991, which was in the much bigger context of the Final Four in Indianapolis, the day reminded old-timers far more of Black Sunday in 1979, when both schools played at N.C. State's Reynolds Coliseum. A certain irony existed, as State's team was still alive and in the process of upsetting second-seeded Connecticut seven hundred miles away in Worcester, Massachusetts.

By the time the Tar Heels had jumped on and blown out Iowa State, the coliseum had filled save for a small section behind the Iowa State bench. That was also Duke's bench for the second game, and those closest to the Blue Devils couldn't stomach being in the arena while Carolina played. Cragg, who basically ran the noncoaching basketball operation, and Mickie Krzyzewski were among the Duke officials who hung out in the backstage press area while the Tar Heels finished off the ninth-seeded Cyclones 92–65 behind 24 points and 17 rebounds from Sean May.

The Duke-Mississippi State game was supposed to be much closer because of the Bulldogs' size, particularly center Lawrence Roberts, who had equaled Duke's Williams with 19 double-doubles on the season. As the Blue Devils took the court, their reception resonated through the arena—an ominous combination of cheering, booing, and awe, the fanfare of all heavy favorites. The Tar Heels once received just such a mixed welcome wherever they played. Now Duke did.

The coliseum crowd provided a subplot for the game on television, as well, where Billy Packer and Jim Nantz mentioned its reaction frequently from courtside during the CBS broadcast. The hypercritical Packer, so unpopular that he was summarily booed while receiving a meritorious award during the ACC Tournament the week before, was really an ACC homer at heart. He played for Wake Forest but almost attended Duke.

Packer, sixty-five, grew up in Bethlehem, Pennsylvania, and idolized two-sport Duke star Dick Groat, a Pittsburgh native who went on to be an all-star shortstop with the Pirates. Also a great high school baseball player, Packer wanted to follow Groat's path. However, Duke basketball coach Hal Bradley said he had only one scholarship left and had offered it to fellow Pennsylvanian Jack Mullen.

Bradley asked Packer to wait to see what Mullen would do.

Packer was cocky and had also been recruited by Horace "Bones" McKinney at Wake Forest. Against the wishes of his parents, who wanted him to go to Duke, Packer went to Wake and was a two-time All-ACC player, helping the Deacons reach the 1962 Final Four. He continued to live in North Carolina and built his broadcasting career regionally and eventually with NBC and CBS. He continued to work a handful of local ACC games each season. Because of his ties to Wake Forest and his outspoken, opinionated style, most fans from all over the ACC considered him overly critical.

This time, he seemed on Duke's side. Most of the fans favored Mississippi State, but Packer thought several key calls went against the Blue Devils late in a rough, defensive game in which both teams shot poorly and battled relentlessly for loose balls. Leading by 11 in the second half, Duke couldn't put the Bulldogs away because Redick didn't deliver the daggers that had made him the most feared shooter in college basketball. Against MSU guard Winsome Frazier's physical defense, Redick missed 12 of 17 shots and went 2 of 9 from three-point range. Duke's lead was suddenly down to two with 1:44 on the clock.

Shelden Williams had taken on Roberts and two other Bulldog big men all day and pulled down 15 rebounds. His biggest play was his third block of the game with forty-two seconds left, which Duke converted into a foul and two free throws by Lee Melchionni. The Blue Devils survived 63–55 and moved on to the Sweet Sixteen, their eighth straight and seventeenth overall (second to twenty for UNC and Kentucky) since 1975. That Krzyzewski passed Smith with his sixty-sixth NCAA win couldn't have meant as much to his current players, but they nevertheless tried to mess up his plastered hair in a brief locker room celebration.

In the end, was playing alongside Carolina in Charlotte an advantage for Duke, or would the Blue Devils have been better off in Nashville where their following would have been smaller but unchallenged? Krzyzewski didn't mind the crowd reaction.

"Some were cheering against us, but not as many as I thought," he said. "I thought it would be more like the Smith Center. Their fans appreciate good basketball, as ours do. They've got a great program. We've got a great program. I'm happy we have this going in this part of the country."

The rivals were headed in different directions, Duke to Austin and a rematch of an early season win over Michigan State, and Carolina to Syracuse, where in 1997 Smith's last team advanced to the Final Four. Both had to go home first, practice, meet the press, and prepare. They were each two wins away from a Final Four confrontation in St. Louis, which was now on everyone's front burner.

On Monday, Illinois coach Bruce Weber called Roy Williams to talk. Weber was edgy because his top-ranked and top-seeded Illini had managed only a pair of twelve-point wins in their first two games. He was also pissed over the Amex commercials. Weber was locked in a recruiting battle with Duke over 6' 6" Chicago-area player Jon Scheyer. He couldn't speak to Scheyer because of the dead period, but knew Duke's propaganda had gotten to him ad nauseam through Krzyzewski's Amex exposure.

"Bruce thought it was an unfair recruiting advantage," Williams said. "Coaches can do commercials. But it's not like Mike is telling everyone that he travels a lot and uses American Express when he does. This is different."

The same day, American Express executives met in New York. They were surprised to have seen Krzyzewski on ads for Allstate and General Motors during the NCAA Tournament. Also, excluding the Duke version of the campaign from the Carolina games hadn't done much to stem the criticism. They already had feedback from cardholders who were threatening to cancel their accounts.

On Tuesday, at Krzyzewski's NCAA press conference, a TV reporter said he had heard a lot of complaints about the Amex ads.

"I haven't heard anybody complain about it," Krzyzewski said, perturbed.

"I've heard people complaining," the reporter persisted.

"You must live in Chapel Hill," Krzyzewski said. "Is that where you live?"

With Duke, Carolina, and N.C. State all playing Sweet Sixteen games on the same day, Krzyzewski found another opportunity to pump up the ACC and its Tobacco Road rivalries. When the Blue Devils arrived at Raleigh-Durham Airport for their flight to Austin, two other chartered jets sat on the runway alongside theirs. The Tar Heels and Wolfpack were flying out at the same time.

"It's like we're either evacuating or we're all deploying," he said, using a couple of military terms. "That's why this region is such a hotbed; it's not just one school."

The last time NCAA regionals were held in Austin and Syracuse the same year (2000), Duke and Carolina were there, but at opposite sites from 2005.

The top-ranked Blue Devils had completed another spectacular ACC season, going 15–1 and winning their second of five consecutive tournament championships. They were the No. 1 seed at Syracuse and expected to cruise through Carrier Dome wins over fifth-seeded Florida and third-seeded Oklahoma State to reach the 2000 Final Four in Indianapolis.

The Tar Heels felt fortunate to be in Austin after a checkered season that had their program in turmoil. An eighth-seed with a 9–7 conference record that included two losses to Duke, they had rebounded from a dismal ACC Tournament defeat to Wake Forest, upset top-seeded Stanford in the South Region and found themselves the sentimental favorite at the Sweet Sixteen in Austin.

Their roles, as well as their venues, were now reversed.

Carolina was the heavy favorite in Syracuse, but had to get it done in Big East country where the ACC was seen as the villain that had torn one league apart to expand its own. The Heels had to face Villanova, their worst match-up because of the Wildcats' quick guards that could test UNC's resolve on defense. With its best big man, Curtis Sumpter, out with a blown knee from the second-round win over Florida, Villanova was "going small" with no pressure and nothing to lose.

There wasn't much to do in dark, dank Syracuse during March, except play basketball, and when Wisconsin coach Bo Ryan said as much in the Thursday press conference, the local sports columnist ripped Ryan the next morning.

"Let me get this straight," wrote Bud Poliquin in the *Post-Standard*, "we've got a guy in town from someplace where a fake wedge of cheese placed on one's head is considered high fashion, and he's busting our chops?"

There was far more action in Austin where, despite its No. 1 seed, Duke expected a dogfight from Michigan State. The Blue Devils had notched their fourth straight win over Coach Tom Izzo's team in December at Cameron, but that game was deceiving. It took 29-point efforts from both Redick and Ewing to hold off the Spartans, and this time Izzo was openly advocating "it's about time" they beat Duke.

The previous summer, when Krzyzewski contemplated the Lakers' offer, Izzo lamented the possible loss and called him the "soul of college basketball." In Austin, he continued to deify the Duke coach because of the Blue Devils' sustained success. "Not having been around for the John Wooden era, it's hard to top what Coach Krzyzewski has done," said Izzo, who is also regarded as one of the elite coaches in the game.

Izzo had lost to Duke twice in 1999, the second time in his first of three consecutive Final Four appearances. After his Spartans won the national championship the next season, he mentioned Duke as the model program he wanted his to emulate, but after two more losses to Krzyzewski, Izzo was ready to beat his hero. He agreed his feelings toward Krzyzewski had moved from awe to respect to frustration.

"I dreamed of having a program in the same area code, and now I think we do," Izzo said when he met the media the day before the game. "I'd like to get in the city limits—who I am kidding?—in the same damn building. Every other top team we've played, we've beaten at least once. Duke is the one that had eluded us."

Redick dominated the Duke press conference, confirming to the national press that he would return for his senior season.

"No question," he said.

Redick was also asked about his coach's career as TV pitchman and joked that on the bus ride last week from Durham to Charlotte, "We counted eight Coach K commercials in just over two hours."

Duke and Michigan State played the early game on Friday night, March 25, while unheralded N.C. State took on Wisconsin in Syracuse. Carolina fans in the Carrier Dome were more interested in Austin than the game played right in front of them. From the first PA announcement that the Blue Devils were in trouble, they eagerly awaited the next and kept their eyes on the electronic board updating other NCAA scores.

The college basketball world might have been relishing a Duke-Carolina game in St. Louis, but most Tar Heels fans wanted no part of it.

Even while Wisconsin rallied from nine down at the half to dominate N.C. State, a good portion of the North Carolina media in Syracuse stayed behind the blue curtain in the press area to watch the TV feed from Austin. When the Blue Devils went cold for six minutes in the second half, and Michigan State's nine-point lead was announced, the Carrier Dome went crazy. One Tar Heel fan raised a placard with a picture of Krzyzewski and the word AMEX with a large circle and slash through it.

With the game essentially over, Krzyzewski called a timeout in order to take Ewing out for the last time. The senior from nearby Missouri City, Texas, ended his career with the most wins (115) of any college basketball player in his class.

It was a different year, site, and team, but Duke's decline in 2005 was similar to its loss to Florida in Syracuse five years earlier. Despite a rigid conditioning program instituted by Dawkins, the Devils had little depth and lost their legs at the end of the season. Michigan State dominated the offensive glass in the second half and held on to win 78–68. From the outside, Redick shot 10 for 38 and missed 18 of his 24 attempted three-pointers in the three NCAA Tournament games. They flew home, the season over with a 27–6 record and their coach calling it a great year by his standard, the only one that counted. Duke had a quirky season, matching Krzyzewski's worst-shooting (1996) team but setting a new low for field-goal *defense*. Although Redick was the headliner, defense, rebounding, and blocked shots were the real stars. Williams broke the school mark he set in 2004 with 122 rejections.

Carolina was trying to avoid what would have been Black Friday, if the Tar Heels joined Duke and N.C. State as regional semifinal losers. They fought back from a 14-point deficit in the first half and eventually led Villanova by 10 when Felton fouled out with 2:13 to play. While the shaky Heels could barely pass and catch the ball in Felton's absence, the Wildcats rallied. Randy Foye and Kyle Lowry, who had accounted for 36 of Villanova's 54 points, led an 8–0 scoring run that made it a two-point game with forty seconds left.

Blowing his whistle and then hesitating, referee Tom O'Neill called Foye for traveling after a basket that would have tied the score. Boos continued to reign down from the Big East crowd as free throws from Melvin Scott and McCants saved Carolina, and the ACC, from an embarrassing night. Old-timers compared the questionable call to 1989, when official Rick Hartzell took the potential tying three-point play away from State's Chris Corchianni against Georgetown in the East Regional semifinals.

During the off day, Syracuse bars teemed with people watching the dramatic Louisville-West Virginia and Arizona-Illinois games. In the crowd, wearing a Duke sweatshirt, was Dave Paulus, whose son had signed to be the Blue Devils' next point guard. Paulus befriended some UNC fans and told them it was basically a coin flip between playing for Krzyzewski and Roy Williams and that, ironically, Duke's losing *football* program might have tipped the scales. Greg Paulus, also a high school All-American quarterback, wasn't sure if he would play college football, too, and considered Duke's program so low key that it didn't matter what he decided.

Having escaped Villanova and with the specter of another game with Duke now gone, the Tar Heels played better against Wisconsin until Felton fell back into foul trouble. McCants' quick shots and poor defense helped squander their early lead, igniting a Williams tirade in the locker room at halftime. McCants responded with the biggest plays on both ends, blocking a three-pointer by the Badgers' Clayton Hanson and then drilling a "three" from the top of the key with sixty-nine seconds left to essentially wrap up the 88–82 win, sending Carolina to the Final Four for the first time since surviving Austin in 2000.

The victory, finally, established an identity for the players who had disconnected with their fans during the Doherty debacle. They liked their new coaches but were tired of hearing about "Kansas and Nick Collison" from Williams and his staff. Assistant Steve Robinson wore his Jayhawks 2003 Final Four T-shirt to practice throughout the NCAA Tournament, irritating Sean May.

May, who had emerged as their leader and star, had told Robinson to lose the shirt if the Tar Heels got to their own Final Four. After putting up 29 points and 12 rebounds against Wisconsin, and donning his own St. Louis stuff, May cut up

Robinson's old rag in a raucous locker room celebration. Everyone laughed as May shredded the shirt with scissors. Only he wasn't joking around. These kids, who had become men at UNC, were one of three confluent forces at work as Carolina marched on to the arch.

Just as Carolina had a presence in San Antonio in 2004, Duke droppings were all over St. Louis. The Blue Devils were a part of the city's college basketball history, having lost to Kentucky in the last Final Four played there in 1978. That was in the long-gone St. Louis Arena, or Checkerdome, where in 1973 UCLA's Bill Walton hit 21 of 22 field goals and scored 44 points in the NCAA championship win over Memphis State. That was then, and Duke was also there now.

Redick, Ewing, and Duke Sports Information Director Jon Jackson checked into the Adam's Mark Hotel as the Tar Heel team party arrived on Wednesday night. Redick, who earlier won the Rupp Award as the nation's top player, was there as a nominee for the similar Naismith Award. Ewing was playing in the National Association of Basketball Coaches (NABC) annual all-star game for seniors at the Final Four. Jackson, who was not a Duke graduate and thought it okay to be quite friendly with his counterparts at UNC, was squiring the two Blue Devils.

Roy Williams was a guest at the Naismith banquet on Thursday and ran into Redick. The Dukie extended his hand and offered congratulations on the season. "You may find this hard to believe, but I'm really pulling for you guys," he said.

"You're right," Williams said with a half smile, "I find it hard to believe."

The Tar Heels practiced privately Thursday afternoon at St. Louis University and that night accompanied Williams to the NCAA Final Four Salute dinner with the other three teams. All the players wore suits of different styles and colors. Melvin Scott held his pants up with an illuminating belt that flashed FINAL FOUR. Later that night, former UNC football player and NFL star Dre' Bly picked up Felton, May, and McCants and took them to a club to meet rap singer Nelly, who was part owner of the NBA's Charlotte Bobcats.

More than thirty thousand people attended Friday's open workouts at the Edward Jones Dome, most of them orange-clad Illinois fans from the Midwest. Williams, coaching in his third Final Four in the last four years, loved Friday the best because several hundred of his envious coaching colleagues watched from the stands. The national media, so many that more than a hundred from smaller newspapers and radio stations were assigned to the football press box four hundred feet above the court, strutted around in their own celebrity.

Among those Williams spoke with was Bonnie Bernstein, the CBS reporter who had sent him Christmas cards since he ended her persistent questioning with a curse after the 2003 national championship game.

Packer and Nantz studied notes and game plans from their courtside broadcast location. That morning, a newspaper story on Packer and Dick Vitale reported that they had barely spoken over the past twenty-six years. In another story, Vitale was voted the ninth most influential person in college basketball. Packer, who stayed more in the background than the vivacious Vitale, was No. 26. Krzyzewski was ranked sixth, Williams eleventh, and Dean Smith thirty-first. CBS Sports President Sean McManus, the son of retired ABC broadcaster Jim McKay and a 1977 Duke graduate, was No. 2 behind Tom Jernstedt, the NCAA's executive vice president and the man who ran the men's basketball tournament, which was considered the top sports attraction of the year.

The so-called Duke influence, with McManus and Krzyzewski so prominent, filled the Final Four undercurrent beyond the American Express controversy. With so many Duke grads in high-profile positions, from CBS analyst Seth Davis to a broadcast lineup that included former Blue Devil players Jay Bilas, Mike Gminski, and Jim Spanarkel, a healthy paranoia existed among coaches, athletics directors and conference commissioners around the country. UNC had prominent alumni in the media, such as ESPN anchor Stuart Scott and former broadcaster Brad Daugherty, NBA analyst Kenny Smith, and national media stars Peter Gammons and Curry Kirkpatrick, but not nearly as many covering college basketball.

Critics believed that the ACC in general, and particularly Duke, got too much TV exposure from all of the networks at the expense of teams from the Midwest and especially the far West that played equally strong basketball.

Krzyzewski was in St. Louis for several coaches meetings but did not step inside the "Ed Dome" for either the practices or semifinal games. Neither did Kansas coach Bill Self, who was tied to the two favorites for the national championship. Top-ranked Illinois had made it there with the players Self recruited before taking over at Kansas when Williams left the Jayhawks. Self watched the semifinal games from a restaurant in downtown St. Louis, keeping a low profile on the unavoidable storyline that exploded after Illinois' easy win over Louisville in the first game.

Most of the external pressure fell on Williams, who was anointed the best coach to have never cut down the nets. His team played like it in the first half against Michigan State. In the locker room, trailing the Spartans by five points, he told the Tar Heels, "Of all my Final Four teams, you have just played the worst half of basketball. If you want to go home tomorrow, keep playing that way. If you want to play harder and together for twenty minutes, we have a chance to come back Monday night." Then he left the room.

At halftime, his mentor Dean Smith had to change seats in the cavernous dome. Deluged by autograph seekers after watching the first half from the stands, Smith was escorted to a private box. Following Carolina's second-half blitzkrieg and anticlimactic 87–71 victory, security guards stopped the seventy-four-year-old icon on his way to the locker room because he lacked a credential. That wouldn't happen Monday night, UNC officials promised him.

In North Carolina, as fans flooded Franklin Street feting their team's first visit to the NCAA championship game in twelve years, a bar mitzvah party was ending happily at the staid Washington Duke Inn in Durham. At first, the hotel refused to put the Final Four games on the television in the bar. After party guests kept complaining, the TV was turned on and about a hundred people screamed through the last ten minutes of the Tar Heels' win over Michigan State. That night, when the last guests had left the parking lot, the statue of James B. Duke out front wore a Carolina cap and Tar Heel T-shirt and was draped with light blue pompoms, plus a hand-written sign that said MAZL-TOV, HEELS!

By Sunday, Carolina's chances seemed good. On paper, the Tar Heels had finally met their match. They couldn't play partial games like they had against Villanova, Wisconsin, and Michigan State if they hoped to beat the top-ranked Illini. They were No. 2, the first time the top teams in the polls had met for the national championship since UCLA and Kentucky in 1975, and they could surely win the game—but they would have to have a forty-minute effort, or close to it.

Illinois fans had come across the Mississippi River by the thousands to buy tickets from scalpers now commanding $5,000 for a courtside seat. The crowd of 47,750 had been largely orange on Saturday, and would be much more so Monday night. Their team decided to stick with the same orange uniforms it had worn against Louisville, creating a dilemma for the Tar Heels and TV producers.

As the "second" No. 1 seed in the tournament, Carolina had brought along its blue uniforms and planned to wear them Monday night. That was fine with Williams, who liked the idea of the ultimate road game—us against the world, or at least the forty thousand Illinois fans who filled all four levels most of the way around the dome.

Orange and blue, however, made for bad contrast, especially on TV. When CBS raised the issue, Williams sent Media Relations Director Steve Kirschner to *tell* Illinois officials that the Heels would be wearing their home white. Weber, who had received a gaudy orange blazer from a prominent booster for Monday night, agreed.

The national championship crowd was seated early, in time to see the American bald eagle Challenger loosed during the dramatic national anthem. Except for Carolina's late first-half spurt, the contest everyone wanted to see was close all the way save for six minutes in the middle.

Behind 13 points at the half after going 5 of 19 from the three-point line, Illinois said, "what the hell," set more obvious moving screens on the perimeter, and kept firing. The Illini made five "threes" over four-and-a-half minutes to get back in the game and then capitalized on the Tar Heels going scoreless for six straight possessions.

May and UNC's inside game were still too much for Illinois. Center James Augustine went scoreless and fouled out after playing only nine minutes, leaving teammates Roger Powell and Jack Ingram (a combined 20 points and 21 rebounds) to battle May, who was on the way to his fifteenth double-double in the last 20 games.

As with most big games between evenly matched teams, it came down to made or missed shots, the bounce of the ball, and luck.

Felton's gutsy three-ball might have been a bad shot, given the Illini had just tied the score at 65–65 with a 10–0 run. But he had made big three-pointers for weeks and knocked this one down, too. Then came Melvin Scott's fifteen-footer seven seconds into the shot clock with a three-point lead and no one under the basket. It bricked, resulting in an Illinois fast break and the last tie of the game. Finally, McCants's ill-advised drive and wild reverse scoop shot missed everything, but Marvin Williams was there to tap it in for the Tar Heels' last lead and free McCants from potential goat horns.

The three possessions were as crucial as Duke's Deng not being able to control a rebound against UConn's Okafor the year before, Redick missing a three-pointer and then getting stripped in the lane when he was looking for the foul. Those plays did not go Duke's way, and these went Carolina's way in the 75–70 victory.

In the end, as Illinois' star guards missed four good looks from the three-point line in the last three minutes, luck prevailed with those confluent forces that had so badly splintered UNC basketball.

The first to hug Williams was assistant coach C. B. McGrath, the former Kansas player who personified how happy Williams's family and friends were that he finally won a national championship, no matter where.

The Tar Heel players, led by Final Four MOP May, had gone internal—some turning to prayer and becoming Born Again—during the disastrous Doherty years and felt vindicated about their own comeback and accomplishments.

The Carolina fans, in St. Louis and across the country, were more ecstatic that their *school* had returned to the top than they were for any coach or group of players. The next morning, they couldn't wait to look the nearest Dukie in the eye.

For all three entities, it meant the end of a long, frustrating stretch. Had there been only a singular cause, the chemistry might have been different, the pressure more concentrated and the result reversed.

Dean Smith had a pass to the locker room this time; his name was Jordan, who joined his old coach in the box and then accompanied him to shake hands and hug the players and coaches who returned glory to Smith's program and Michael's alma mater. The three generations were there, the man whom Frank McGuire brought to Carolina, the young man who had nailed down his coach's first national championship with a fifteen-footer from the left wing in 1982, and the current coach who had worked for one while mentoring the other and now had an NCAA title of his own.

As Williams entertained close friends in his hotel suite, Jordan took the entire team out for his own private party. Hundreds of happy Tar Heels jammed the lobby of the Adam's Mark till two in the morning as thousands of revelers crashed Franklin Street back in Chapel Hill, costing the town $165,000 for extra cops and clean-up. They all toasted the new national champions who finished with a 33–4 record.

In Durham, the streets were empty and at Duke the campus was quiet. The unofficial website of the Blue Devils, the *Duke Basketball Report* changed its background hue from royal blue to pitch black. Their consolation? Carolina kept Illinois (37–2) from breaking Duke's record for total wins in a season.

The national championship game drew the highest TV ratings since 1999, when the top-ranked Blue Devils lost to No. 3 UConn. UNC's victory was sure to swell the school's applicant pool and capital gifts, as it had after Duke's NCAA titles, and increase its already unprecedented sale of licensed, logoed apparel.

It also affected the Robertson Scholarship, a unique collaborative effort buried under the basketball publicity, funded by one of the many blue-blended families and mixed marriages that made the rivalry so intense, so personal, so much fun. Candidates to become the latest class of Robertson Scholars, who matriculated on both campuses, were interviewed over Final Four weekend in Chapel Hill. After they partied with thousands of Tar Heel fans, nineteen high school seniors who were also wooed by the likes of Harvard, Yale, and Princeton accepted scholarships, the highest number since the program began in 2000.

Just another way that Duke-Carolina, the co-brand, always seemed tied at the hyphenated hip no matter what each school accomplished on its own.

The Blue Devils have had their years, on and off the court, but 2005 belonged to the light blue in a rivalry that has changed colors, and champions, for going on sixty seasons . . . and counting.

RIVALRY FACTS
- Duke vs. Carolina since 1998: 15 wins, 3 losses
- Roy in the rivalry: 1 win over Duke, 3 losses
- Duke's 2004 trip to the Final Four was its tenth since 1986
- Carolina's 2005 NCAA championship was its third since 1982
- Duke is the preseason pick to win the 2006 NCAA title

K'S COACHING RECORDS
- Overall: 721–246 (.746)
- At Duke: 648–187 (.776)
- Vs. Carolina: 30–29 (missed 2 games in 1995)
- Vs. Roy Williams: 6–2 (.750)

ROY'S COACHING RECORDS
- Overall: 471–116 (.802)
- At Carolina: 53–15 (.779)
- Vs. Duke: 2–6 (.250)

NBA FIRST-ROUND DRAFT PICKS
- Carolina 35; Duke 25

PLAYERS (SEASONS OF ELIGIBILITY) LOST EARLY TO THE NBA
- Carolina 14 (19); Duke 7 (13)

PLAYERS IN THE NBA
- Current: Carolina 12; Duke 8
- All-time: Carolina 67; Duke 42

BEST QUOTE
"If we don't really play, Duke is going to kick our rear ends so far back up state, we're going to think Chapel Hill is on the other side of Murphy."

(Roy Williams, 2004)

2

THE FIGHTERS AND THE FIGHT

Frank McGuire settled into the front seat on the bus, a fancy fifty-seater from the Southern Coach Company. Since his University of North Carolina basketball team went undefeated and won the national championship in 1957, McGuire had rented the best busses he could find. Now a cult figure in the university town of Chapel Hill and his adopted state, the coach of the Tar Heels did pretty much as he wanted.

Looking out into the snowy February night of 1961, McGuire was glad he and his "fellas" no longer drove their cars to away games. In his early years at UNC, they jumped into three or four jalopies after meeting at Woollen Gymnasium, several of the players puffing on the free Lucky Strikes one of them had from selling cigarettes on campus. The "smoking car" was always last in line so McGuire wouldn't see what was going on. Those with written permission from home could smoke and drink beer, but not in his presence.

They never would have gotten out of town driving their old cars, McGuire thought, even if George Barclay had put chains on their tires. Barclay, the former football All-American and UNC's football coach for three losing seasons in the 1950s, owned a service station and was one of the local merchants that took care of McGuire's boys. Another was Spero Dorton, whose Goody Shop on Franklin Street fed the players before and after home games and local road trips like this one.

The Tar Heels—and their bigger-than-life coach—were on their way to Duke for a game that was being hyped as a real grudge match. McGuire, however, was more wound down than fired up. He looked out the window, and as his breath fogged his reflection his mind took off in reverse . . . the funeral he had attended just five days ago at the cemetery across the street, the bad news he had received the week before from the NCAA Infractions Committee. The recruit he had won and lost who made tonight's game extra special. His halcyon days at North

Carolina, why he left his native New York after a life of basketball there, and his block in Brooklyn where it all began.

The memories flooded his mind as the bus started up, hissed, snorted and rolled away from the curb, heading down the road toward Durham and a date with destiny.

McGuire had been a scrapper since his knickers-and-suspender days on East 10th Street in Brooklyn and later in the part of Manhattan they used to call Hell's Kitchen. He rolled marbles in the back alleys, flipped cards against the front stoops, and shot the eight ball into the side pocket as soon as he could see over the table.

He was a street kid who played pranks and might have wound up like "Shakes" Carcaterra and his boyhood buddies in *Sleepers,* but McGuire was smarter than those stupid punks who ran off with a hotdog cart and landed in reform school. He wasn't born with a silver spoon in his mouth; he just acted that way after getting good enough at basketball at St. Xavier High School to be recruited by St. John's University, where he was captain and high scorer the year he threatened to punch out the entire Pitt team after a game.

McGuire went on to coach at *both* his high school and college alma maters. At St. John's he was dubbed "the Irishman" for his dapper dress and New York City–sized persona. In 1952, the Redmen strutted into Reynolds Coliseum in Raleigh, North Carolina, and beat Everett Case's North Carolina State Wolfpack and Adolph Rupp's Kentucky Wildcats on successive nights in the NCAA East Regionals.

North Carolinians knew the name Frank McGuire long before his St. John's team made it all the way to the championship game of the 1952 NCAA Tournament against the University of Kansas. The Redmen lost to the Jayhawks, giving up 33 points and 17 rebounds to All-American forward Clyde Lovellette that March 26 night in Seattle. Kansas, coached by the erudite Dr. Forest "Phog" Allen, had junior Dean Smith on its roster, but the little-used reserve guard made just a token appearance in the title game against McGuire's Johnnies.

After that season, McGuire was hired away by the University of North Carolina, not for more money but more peace of mind for his invalid son, Frankie Jr., who was born with cerebral palsy.

Frankie Jr. was confined to a wheel chair, and McGuire wanted a warmer climate and cleaner air for Frankie to breathe. So Frank and Pat McGuire, who had been to Chapel Hill for Navy preflight school in 1943, packed up their Studebaker sedan and crossed the George Washington Bridge to begin their two-day trip South—down U.S. Route 1 through Baltimore and Washington and onto the rural roads of Virginia. The May day they reached their destination and drove up Franklin Street, past Brady's Restaurant, and into town, the sun was the only thing in the Carolina blue sky. The temperature was damn near 80 degrees.

The McGuires moved into a single-family brick home on Mason Farm Road, just across Highway 15-501 from the UNC campus. In New York, McGuire rarely got home to have lunch with Frankie. Here he could, every day, by making the five-minute drive from his office in Woollen Gym.

McGuire was hired to equalize the rivalries between UNC and the other three so-called Big Four schools: North Carolina State College, Duke University, and Wake Forest College. State, Duke, and UNC were located within a twenty-five-mile isosceles triangle in the contiguous cities and towns of Raleigh, Durham, and Chapel Hill; Wake Forest in the town with the same name was just a few miles north of Raleigh.

When McGuire arrived, UNC was fourth in the Big Four, having had consecutive 12–15 seasons that cost coach Tom Scott his job. The Tar Heels had lost 15 in a row to "State College" and Case, its reigning coaching giant whom McGuire had first met in the Navy. Case had been at N.C. State since 1946 and won six Southern Conference titles, advancing to the NCAA Tournament regional three straight years from 1950 to 1952.

UNC had also been swept in the 1952 season by Wake Forest and its star center Dickie Hemric, the league-leading scorer and first true big man in the South. Hemric, still only a junior, had taken the star mantle after Duke All-American Dick Groat ended his home career on February 29, 1952, by leading a 94–64 demolition of North Carolina. It was a leap year, and Groat leaped into the Duke record book with a single-game high of 48 points.

Case and Groat, in particular, typified the resentment their schools had for UNC, the state university with the mother lode of alumni, money, and influence in Raleigh, the capital city. For the blond, red-faced Case and the band of hurryin' Hoosiers he brought down from Indiana after a renowned high school and naval coaching career, 15 straight over the Tar Heels was just a start. For Groat, who had also scored 24 points against UNC as a junior to establish a Duke *season* scoring record, beating the reviled rival one last time was paramount; he couldn't sleep the night before his last home game and jimmied open a window in Duke Indoor Stadium at 3:00 A.M. to practice the overhead jump shot he helped introduce to college basketball.

After bowing out in grand style, Groat addressed the adoring crowd, apologized for losing five games the entire season, and was bawling as fans and teammates carried him off the court and into the locker room.

"Beating Carolina in my last game was the most important thing in my career," said Groat, who hailed from Pittsburgh and attended Duke on a baseball scholarship but earned more college fame in basketball. "Nothing else in my career would have mattered if we hadn't won that game."

So this was what McGuire walked into—an animosity in a region that manufactured the majority of cigarettes sold in the country and was appropriately called Tobacco Road—but McGuire wasn't intimidated. He had seen plenty of games in smoky Madison Square Garden; Case and Duke couldn't be worse than trying to survive the urban city game hit by the gambling scandals just the year before.

Frank McGuire, the city slicker, was ready to take on all the country bumpkins he could find in a South so quiet and dull that he used to say "at night you can hear the crickets fuck."

Physically, the Irishman appeared bigger than his six-foot frame. He had wavy, red hair parted smartly near the middle like his movie idol, Jimmy Cagney. His custom-made clothing featured shiny shoes and accessories like gold cufflinks that McGuire showed by "shooting" or tugging at his shirt sleeves.

McGuire brought basketball branding to North Carolina. His players traveled only in official team blazers, their faces had to be clean shaven and their hair trimmed neatly. If not, you did not even *practice* for McGuire. He wanted North Carolina to stand for something people would remember after they saw the Tar Heels play.

This was a formula that most people in the "Triangle Area" had never seen before—an ass-kicker with charm. McGuire's silver tongue could melt the girls, five to fifty, or cut down officials and opposing coaches like a surgeon's scalpel, without hardly ever raising his voice. He had charisma before the word was invented; and after he beat Case and eighth-ranked State College in Raleigh on his very first try (January 24, 1953), his reputation preceded him everywhere.

Although McGuire and Case got a feud going from that first year, it was as much bluster as belligerence. They were promoters at heart and occasionally dined together at Case's home in Raleigh, where he lived alone. They wanted to boost their game to match the interest in football, which was still the dominant sport on each campus. In fact, when seven schools from the Southern Conference met in May of 1953 to discuss seceding and setting up their own league, it was all for football and the money that could be made.

The old league was too big: sixteen members of different sizes and disparate academic philosophies that were formed from a ragged geography and were not nearly equal in their strength of teams and, consequently, scheduling. There were too many schools for a true round robin in any sport, and some accumulated stronger records by playing mostly weaker opponents. Besides the Big Four, there were George Washington, Maryland, Richmond, Virginia Military, Virginia Tech, Washington and Lee, and West Virginia to the North; Clemson, Davidson, Furman, South Carolina, and the Citadel down South.

The major disparity was in football, which some members saw as a source of increased revenue while others regarded it as a potential evil that had to be carefully controlled. Southern Conference members were divided on the issue of freshman teams. The so-called academic schools wanted them eliminated so first-year students could concentrate on their studies and the school could save some money. The bigger schools favored their continuation so freshmen who weren't good enough to play on the varsity would be properly trained to join the big team the next season.

Underscoring the commercial schism had been the 1950 vote to deny Clemson and Maryland the right to accept bowl bids. They both went anyway (Maryland defeated top-ranked Tennessee in the 1951 Sugar Bowl to finish 10–0), the first public indication that a split was coming.

To make the new league a reality, the basketball coaches had to agree, Case in particular. He had pushed N.C. State to finish rectangular Reynolds Coliseum, an on-campus gym that sat stuck like a steel skeleton since construction had stopped with America's entrance into World War II in 1942. The building with 12,400 seats, some of them a god-awful way behind the baskets, finally opened in December of 1949—just in time for the first Dixie Classic. This was Case's brainchild and was then a college basketball standard and huge money maker for the Big Four schools that engaged four outside teams in a three-day tournament each Christmas.

Case favored a new league and, football be damned, had visions of a postseason tournament much better than what had been held since 1922 in places from Atlanta to Raleigh to Durham. Because membership fluctuated between sixteen and twenty-eight over the years, only the top 8 basketball teams advanced to the Southern Conference Tournament. The rest stayed home, creating a class structure of hardwood haves and have-nots.

Case's idea was for an eight-team league where everyone played in the tournament. He also demanded another difference: that the tournament champion—not the team finishing first in the regular season—earned the only bid to the NCAA Tournament. McGuire, in only his first year, disliked rendering what happened in January and February meaningless but didn't have the juice to stop it and reluctantly went along.

The annual 1953 Southern Conference spring meeting on May 8 veered dramatically off course, breaking into closed session as the first order of business. The seven seceding schools—Clemson, Duke, Maryland, N.C. State, North Carolina, South Carolina, and Wake Forest—said they were forming a "playing league" and adopted the philosophy that all members would face each other on a regular basis.

At the inaugural meeting at the Sir Walter Hotel in Raleigh a month later, Wake Forest Athletics Director Jim Weaver was elected the spin-off conference's first commissioner. Among the names considered for the new league were Blue-Gray, Colonial, Confederate, Cotton, Dixie, East Coast, Mid-Atlantic. Mid-South, Piedmont, Seaboard, Shoreline, and Tobacco. Duke Athletics Director Eddie Cameron came up with the one that stuck.

When the Atlantic Coast Conference opened for business in the fall of 1953, Case, known as the "Old Gray Fox," and McGuire were two of its most dynamic coaches. Holding their own with powerful football figures such as Clemson coach and Athletics Director Frank Howard, Maryland coach Jim "Sunny" Tatum, and South Carolina AD Rex Enright, who had played for Knute Rockne at Notre Dame, they helped author a colorful and controversial era in the ACC, which was born for a contact sport played outside but would eventually be hailed as the best college basketball league in America.

Virginia, which had left the Southern Conference for independent status in 1936, became the eighth member in December of 1953, creating a chaotic first basketball season of scheduling in which the Cavaliers played only 5 conference games while others played between 8 and 12. A symmetrical fourteen-game round-robin schedule would be implemented for the 1955 season.

Duke's Cameron remained the most powerful man in the new conference because of his longevity and his close alliance with Commissioner Weaver. They personified their two smaller, private schools and shared an adversarial relationship with McGuire and Case, who had more money and less ethics and weren't afraid to use either.

The handsome Cameron, a football star at Washington and Lee, had come to Duke in 1926 as an assistant football coach. Although his secondary duties included coaching freshman basketball, he succeeded George Buckheit as varsity coach two years later. Cameron used the back of a matchbook cover to sketch out a new basketball gym, and Duke brought in the same architectural firm that conceived the Palestra in Philadelphia, which had opened in 1927 and hosted the first NCAA championship game in 1939.

Ironically, for a school that would be slow to integrate its athletic teams, Duke's new gym was designed by a young black man named Julian Abele, who had studied at the Ecole des Beaux Arts in Paris. Profits from the 1938 Rose Bowl, in which the previously unbeaten, untied, and unscored-upon Blue Devils lost to Southern Cal 7–3 on a late TD pass, were used to begin construction later that year.

When Duke Indoor Stadium opened in 1940, it was the biggest basketball arena south of the Palestra, but even better planned. Wooden bleachers for students ringed the floor. Upstairs, the balcony had six thousand theater-style seats reserved for season ticket holders, including alumni, faculty and staff. The change meant adults no longer had to sit through the freshman preliminary amongst rowdy students to get the best seats for the varsity game. As the popularity of Duke basketball grew, those upstairs seats became golden carrots for athletic fund-raising. The innovative seating division should have been used for every college arena built since then.

Cameron led the Blue Devils to a fourteen-year career record of 226–99, including three Southern Conference titles and a 19–14 record against UNC before turning it over to his assistant Gerry Gerard in 1942. He coached Duke *football* for four years while Wallace Wade served overseas in World War II. Cameron never lost to UNC (3–0–1) in football and beat Alabama in the 1945 Sugar Bowl. When Wade returned, Cameron remained as an assistant until Wade's retirement in 1950. Duke then named Bill Murray its new football coach and made Cameron the school's full-time director of athletics.

Gerard was diagnosed with cancer during the 1949 season. For three months, the next Duke coach looked to be Arnold "Red" Auerbach, who was hired that summer while Gerard's prognosis fluctuated. Auerbach, whose tiny office in Card Gym stayed full of cigar smoke, spent every day with Groat in the fall of '49, playing one-on-one and drilling him on defense before his varsity career began. Auerbach knew Groat played baseball, but told him his best sport was basketball.

Auerbach left Duke before the first game of the 1949–50 season. He didn't want to get a college coaching job because of someone else's misfortune and disdained "waiting around" to see if Gerard recovered. Auerbach turned to pro basketball and within two years began his Hall of Fame career with the Boston Celtics. Had Auerbach stayed, maybe all of those victory cigars would have been fired up at the Indoor Stadium instead of the Boston Garden.

Gerard coached through the 1950 season, when Duke dropped three more games to UNC to make it five losses in a row in the rivalry. His cancer returned that summer, and when he could not continue, Duke hired thirty-nine-year-old Harold Bradley from tiny Hartwick College in New York.

Between 1942 and 1953, Duke and Carolina played 28 basketball games. The

Blue Devils won 14 under Gerard and Bradley. The Tar Heels, coached by Bill Lange, Ben Carnevale, and Scott during that period, won 14. But they had not beaten Duke since 1951, mainly because the irrepressible Groat wouldn't let them. Groat never got to play in the ACC, which might have given him the exposure to make basketball his permanent pro career. He played briefly in the NBA before concentrating on baseball and ultimately earning MVP honors as an all-star shortstop with the Pittsburgh Pirates.

Duke went 9–1 to win the inaugural ACC regular season in 1954 with only one player, 6' 4" forward Ronnie Mayer, among the league's top 10 scorers and rebounders. The Blue Devils finished 22–6 and were ranked fifteenth by the Associated Press. N.C. State won the first ACC Tournament, largely because it was played in Reynolds Coliseum, the Wolfpack's on-campus home court that was known as the House That Case Built (or at least completed).

Case continued to act like it was the *league* he created. Not only a great innovator and promoter (he was the first coach to film games and hold regular luncheons for sportswriters), Case was also very creative when it came to recruiting. He played loose and easy with the rules, often holding illegal tryouts for prospects when they came on campus by throwing them into pickup games or scrimmages with his current players. In 1956, Case threw total caution to the wind while wooing Louisiana high-school hotshot Jackie Moreland, whom he illegally offered $1,000 in cash, $200 in new clothes each season, and seven-year college and medical scholarships for his girlfriend.

His competitors also recruiting Moreland blew the whistle on State, which received the stiffest penalty ever handed down in the history of organized college athletics—a four-year postseason ban in all sports. Moreland stayed one semester as a freshman at State and then transferred to Louisiana Tech, where he played three years of varsity basketball.

McGuire had a similar, if more subtle, recruiting machine, and while his rival scoured the schoolyards of Indiana, he was watching the playgrounds of New York City. He occasionally missed practice to go home to do his own scouting. When visiting with the families of Catholic youngsters he was recruiting, McGuire sometimes took along a priest to assure the parents their son would still attend Mass on Sundays in the Baptist South.

McGuire dressed and acted like a "Yankee" and was an easy target during his first two ACC seasons, when UNC compiled a 21–21 record while he searched for talent to build the same kind of powerhouse he had at St. John's. It took

McGuire five tries to finally defeat Duke and six more losses before beating State again.

The Duke students, clever even back then, mocked his shiny hair by slicking back theirs with Brylcreem. Several Duke players joined their fans in taunting McGuire as they ran by the bench. The UNC coach smiled but seethed silently and stored everything away.

Then, after a surprising 18–5 record in 1956 that ended at the hands of Wake Forest in the ACC Tournament, McGuire hatched his miracle season, thanks to a big delivery on the Underground Railroad, his mythical talent train immortalized in a New York *Daily News* cartoon that carried New York's best high school basketball players to North Carolina.

The starting five of Pete Brennan, Bobby Cunningham, Tommy Kearns, Joe Quigg, and All-American Lennie Rosenbluth—dubbed "Four Catholics and a Jew," all from the New York area, and all feisty, ferocious competitors—began the 1956–57 season with 11 straight wins, including victories over nationally ranked Utah, Duke, and Wake Forest in the Dixie Classic.

McGuire's cocky club survived one scare after another in the regular season, pulled out one game, then another, and another. The Tar Heels escaped overtime at South Carolina, NYU in Madison Square Garden, and double overtime at Maryland after McGuire had twice told them to "shake hands, be good sports, you can't win 'em all."

Their closest shave at home was against Duke, when the two schools played the first basketball game of any kind on television. The debut of "Broadvision," a telecast over the local public TV station with no audio that fans watched while listening to radio play-by-play, was the brainchild of UNC comptroller Billy Carmichael Jr. and Bill Friday, president of the state's Consolidated University system who correctly foresaw the TV age of college basketball matching what had begun in football.

Hours before the game, Carmichael and Friday, whose office was in Chapel Hill, were using hammers and picks to chisel a hole in the cinderblock wall behind the bleachers in Woollen Gym so they could fit the lens of the Broadvision camera. Curious viewers in the cities of Raleigh, Greensboro, and Charlotte settled in to watch a black-and-white telecast over WUNC-TV while the raspy voice of Ray Reeve described the action on the radio.

Carolina lost an eight-point lead in the last two minutes as Duke rallied to pull even on two steals by Bobby Joe Harris, a scrappy guard from King, North Carolina, who hated UNC because McGuire did not recruit him.

After his last basket, Harris began running back on defense and looked at the old hand-operated wooden scoreboard at the corner of the Carolina bench. It said "UNC 73, Duke 71." He was playing so hard, so instinctively, that he believed what he saw—that his team was still behind. The student manager operating the board was so caught up in the game he hadn't flipped over the "two" and "three" under VISITORS. The gaffe contributed to Carolina's luck that season.

Thinking the Blue Devils were still behind with just a few seconds left, Harris turned back and intentionally fouled Kearns, who made two free throws for the 75–73 win. The electronic scoreboard had it right, but the student manager inadvertently helped the Tar Heels stay unbeaten.

"I lost the game, and on purpose, but I didn't know it at the time," Harris said, mad and frustrated. "The scorekeeper was slow putting the points on the board. He cost us the game. They [UNC] didn't beat us. Their scorekeeper did. I wouldn't have fouled him if I knew the score was tied."

Carolina remained No. 1 in the polls and faced nationally ranked Wake Forest for a fourth time in the semifinals of the 1957 ACC Tournament. Recalling his club's loss to the Deacons the year before, McGuire had said through clenched teeth before sending his boys onto the court, "Don't let these sons-a-bitches spoil the season for you, like they did last time."

UNC edged Wake again on a late three-point play by Rosenbluth and kept the dream of winning the national championship alive by defeating South Carolina the next night for the ACC title and the league's only NCAA bid. The Tar Heels went home to McGuire's New York and clobbered Yale, then withstood potential upsets by Canisius and Syracuse in Philadelphia to carry a 30–0 record to the Final Four in Kansas City.

The largest media group in history assembled at Municipal Auditorium to cover the anticipated match-up between No. 1 North Carolina and No. 2 Kansas with its seven-foot center Wilt Chamberlain; it included an 11-station television network, 64 newspaper writers and live radio broadcasts on 73 stations in 11 states. Fittingly, for such hype, Carolina played into *triple* overtime on consecutive cold and drizzly nights as its Cinderella season continued. Meanwhile, throughout the weekend, a relationship was forming that proved just as memorable for UNC.

Dean Smith had graduated from Kansas in 1953 and, after two years in the Air Force, entered coaching as an assistant at the new Air Force Academy. His boss, Bob Spear, was a friend of McGuire's and they all shared a hotel suite in Kansas City. McGuire was looking for a young coach to replace his ailing, longtime assistant, Buck Freeman, and Spear had recommended Smith.

McGuire and Smith met briefly on Friday afternoon before the Tar Heels semifinal game against Michigan State and its All-American, Jumpin' Johnny

Green. Bookmakers had UNC as only a slight favorite because the eleventh-ranked Spartans were coming off a stunning upset of Kentucky in Lexington in the Mideast Region. The game with Carolina turned out to be dead even.

UNC and Michigan State each scored 29 points in both halves and were tied, 58–58, at the end of regulation. The Spartans had inched in front 64–62 with only a few seconds to play in the first overtime. At the foul line with a chance to ice the game, Green snickered before he shot, "thirty and one ain't so bad."

Green missed, Brennan grabbed the rebound and drove the length of the court to hit an off-balance jumper at the horn to tie the game again. Carolina finally won 74–70 in the third overtime. Rosenbluth finished with 31 points and Green only 11, as the Tar Heels advanced to play Kansas, an easy winner over San Francisco in the other semifinal.

Kansas featured college basketball's biggest sideshow, the towering and black Chamberlain and, despite being ranked behind Carolina for the last eight weeks, was a decided favorite to win the national championship in the Jayhawks' backyard. In the hotel suite on Saturday afternoon, McGuire asked Dean Smith who he would be pulling for that night.

"I'll have to go for the old alma mater," Smith said, swallowing hard. McGuire smiled and nodded his head.

Later that day Smith called his father, Alfred, a coach and teacher back in Topeka, and confessed that he might have blown his chances with McGuire. Alfred Smith assured him to the contrary, that his honesty and loyalty were trademarks McGuire admired.

McGuire and Chamberlain went on to have a close relationship in pro basketball, starting the night the gamesman coach sent Kearns, his 5' 11" lead guard, out to jump center against the skinny skyscraper. McGuire knew they couldn't win the opening tip but said he wanted to give Kansas something to think about. Kearns just stood there as the ball went up. Chamberlain took a funny little hop and tapped the ball to a teammate as Kearns backpedalled down the court.

Security wasn't very tight at the Final Four, and a few minutes into the game North Carolina Governor Luther Hodges emerged from the stands and sat down on the UNC bench. He changed his seat several times and, when the language got too salty, bailed out and returned to the stands.

Containing Chamberlain with a zone, Carolina led 29–22 at the half. Wilt broke out to rally the Jayhawks. When Rosenbluth fouled out with 20 points and 1:45 left in regulation, the Tar Heels found themselves behind. Bob Young, a senior who had rejoined the team in the spring semester after flunking out, saved them with a tying basket in the dying seconds.

As overtime began the tension hung as thick as the smoke in Municipal Auditorium, where most of the ten thousand people favored Kansas. Back on the East Coast, thousands more in North Carolina were watching only the second nationally televised college basketball game.

They were still tied 48–48 after one extra period and remained so when both teams failed to score a single point in the second overtime, each running off large chunks of time in the pre–shot clock era. UNC was in triple overtime for the second straight night.

With about ten seconds left in the third overtime, his team trailing 53–52, Carolina's Joe Quigg drove the right side of the key and had his shot blocked by Chamberlain. But official Joe Conway ran in to call a foul on another Jayhawk reaching in from behind, as the partisan crowd hooted.

Normally, Kansas coach Dick Harp would have called a timeout to "ice" Quigg, who was going to the line for two shots and a chance to win the national championship. McGuire beat him to it. He had a few things to discuss with his team and had complete confidence in Quigg. Rosenbluth, watching helplessly from the bench with his warm-up jacket slung over his shoulder, thought to himself, "I'm glad it's Joe taking the shots. Every kid pictures himself shooting free throws to win the national title. Joe lived for that."

McGuire told the Tar Heels that *when* Quigg makes the two shots they should drop back to half court and "Jesus Christ, no fouls!" He grabbed Kearns privately as the huddle broke and said if Quigg should miss them both, "Hack someone, anyone."

Quigg calmly walked to the line, flipped up the first shot with his two-handed release and tied the game. He did exactly the same thing to give UNC a 54–53 lead. The Tar Heels dropped back as McGuire had instructed and Quigg slapped away a long pass intended for Chamberlain. Kearns had the ball and heaved it skyward as the final seconds ran off the clock and the horn sounded.

Carolina's dream season was over, having captured the national championship with a flawless 32–0 record. After the awards ceremony on the court, the Tar Heels walked back to their hotel in their uniforms, unfazed by the cold drizzle.

Later that night, McGuire hosted a party of VIPs and his cronies in his suite at the team hotel. There wasn't enough room for all of the North Carolina sportswriters, so he asked Smith to take a group out to dinner and gave him a wad of cash. Smith chose the most expensive restaurant he could find, admitting later, "I was so mad we lost I wanted to stick it to North Carolina."

Up in the suite, McGuire ordered steak dinners for everyone. When they arrived, the salads did not have the Roquefort dressing he wanted. Chuck Erickson, the UNC athletics director and technically his boss, told him that the delicacy was just too expensive. McGuire cut him to pieces. "Damn it, Erickson, we just won the national championship!" he said, reaching into his baggy trousers for more cash. "I'll buy the damn Roquefort dressing!"

What happened in 1957 not only added to McGuire's legend, it jump-started the television era and in turn helped create the greatest fable in the history of ACC basketball. A broadcasting entrepreneur named C. D. Chesley had sent UNC's dramatic Final Four wins back to North Carolina on a grainy black-and-white television picture transmitted from tower to tower across fifteen-hundred miles of plains and mountains.

The next afternoon, thousands of fans wanted to see the Tar Heels in living color. They jammed the roads to Raleigh-Durham Airport and the runway as their plane landed just after four o'clock. Except for McGuire and Rosenbluth, who flew directly to New York to appear on the Ed Sullivan Show that night, the undefeated 1957 NCAA champions rode a wave of fans across the tarmac and to a team bus for the ride back to Chapel Hill, their feet barely touching the ground.

The storybook season made McGuire a deity in North Carolina. He made the list of the Ten Best Dressed Men in America. He drove a big Cadillac, given to him by appreciative Carolina alumni, and had open charge accounts all over town.

Almost overnight, "McGuire's Miracle" had turned the outspoken Irishman into a legend up and down the East Coast, from his native New York to his new North Carolina. His Tar Heels now set the gold standard in the ACC, loved by their own fans and, at first, the fascinating favorites on the road.

Soon they became the villains.

Although Rosenbluth had graduated, and Quigg broke his leg in preseason practice, McGuire's 1958 Tar Heels won 11 of their first 12 games, including the Dixie Classic championship by beating Duke and N.C. State. But Carolina lost 4 of its next 10, including a 16-point drubbing from the improving Blue Devils in Chapel Hill on February 8.

Duke had quietly built an 11-game winning streak under mild-mannered and gentlemanly coach Hal Bradley, who was underappreciated by his own fans and overshadowed in the media by McGuire and Case. (Duke beat State twice that season, once by 17 points in Raleigh, but Bradley still lost out to Case for ACC coach of the Year.) Ranked sixth, their highest ever in the polls, the Blue Devils entered their regular-season finale at home tied with UNC for first place in the ACC, both carrying 10–3 records into their third meeting of the season.

Duke had turned contender behind All-ACC seniors Jim Newcome, Paul Schmidt, and Bucky Allen, but had none of the league's top-10 scorers. The Blue Devils were unselfish and got it done with defense, rebounding, and aggressive play that excited the crowd at Duke Indoor Stadium, where raucous students surrounding the court were making a name for themselves.

They couldn't wait for the big, bad Tar Heels to arrive.

McGuire had long criticized fan behavior and taken steps to control rowdy crowds at Woollen Gym. During his first season at Carolina in 1953, he banned football players from standing behind the visiting bench and razzing opponents. McGuire's crusade might have backfired in the earlier loss to Duke in 1958 because he had pleaded with UNC fans to show better sportsmanship and not boo. With the home crowd calmer than usual, Carolina lost a first-half lead and eventually the game.

"Sure, that could have cost us a win over Duke," McGuire said later in the season. "I have received letters from people telling me that. It's time for students and fans to act like grown-ups and understand the principles of sportsmanship."

Because his Heels were big-headed and played ruggedly, McGuire was viewed as a hypocrite in some circles. It seemed whenever there was an ACC basketball controversy, McGuire was nearby. Since he had disciplined his own fans, however, McGuire had no problem taking on opposing crowds as well. He got a great opportunity to do so at the end of the 1958 game in Durham.

Duke's small lineup, which had three guards and no starter bigger than 6' 6", took an early lead and made the Tar Heels chase them most of the night. Plenty frustrated, McGuire objected when Bobby Joe Harris called a needless timeout with two seconds left in the game and the Blue Devils ahead 59–46. Harris wanted to stick it to Carolina after the scoreboard incident of the year before.

Duke students poured over the Carolina bench, and the refs ruled the game was over. As they lifted Coach Bradley onto their shoulders and paraded him around to celebrate their first-place finish in the ACC standings and a second straight defeat of their archrivals, McGuire kept his team huddled for twenty minutes and requested a police escort off the crowded court and into the locker room.

Bill Murray, in charge of the Indoor Stadium operations between football seasons, took offense at what he considered unnecessary grandstanding by the flamboyant Carolina coach and never responded. Even McGuire's own men thought it a bit over the top.

"It was ridiculous and unnecessary," Lee Shaffer, a sophomore that season, said years later. "That was Frank being Frank."

The UNC players eventually left the floor, and the building, without confrontation. Murray had a lot to say about it in the newspaper the following week, however.

"It was an uncalled-for demonstration," Murray told the Durham *Morning Herald*. "No athletic team will have trouble walking off this court. The Carolina team could have gone off the court without trouble. When the time comes that we need police protection to escort a team off the court, we should quit playing.

"In all my coaching experience, I have never seen a more obvious exhibition. It was the most revolting act by a college coach I've ever witnessed. The very idea of McGuire requiring police protection to go to his dressing room is absurd. He has created a monster in his publicity-seeking statements supposedly made to stop such things as this. I once admired him. Now I blame him."

McGuire responded in the same newspaper, drawing UNC's popular new football coach into the controversy. Jim Tatum, a UNC grad who coached the Tar Heels for one season in 1942, had returned to his alma mater where he and McGuire made up the most dynamic duo at any college in the country.

"I wish Murray had come to me with those remarks," McGuire said. "I'd tell him he has enough to worry about in Jim Tatum to keep him occupied. I'd tell him he'll never beat Carolina in football as long as Tatum's around." (Tatum had defeated Duke in his first try in 1957, but lost to the Blue Devils the next season and then died suddenly in the summer of 1959 from Rocky Mountain spotted fever.)

The Murray-McGuire controversy made the rivalry personal. It escalated further with a bitter recruiting battle over a player who had professed true love to both schools.

After losing the rest of his national championship class, McGuire was bent on getting more great players from New York, but, with Freeman too sick to continue as his chief assistant, he needed someone to run his program while he went recruiting.

He hired Dean Smith in the spring of 1958, selecting him over a young head coach at Belmont-Abbey College outside of Charlotte named Al McGuire, a fellow New Yorker but no relation. A different decision might have changed the course of history, because Al McGuire's Marquette Warriors defeated Dean Smith's UNC Tar Heels for the national championship in Atlanta almost twenty years later. Who knows? It could have been Al McGuire coaching Carolina and Smith coaching Kansas in 1977.

When Smith arrived in Chapel Hill, Frank McGuire drove him around town to look for a house while his wife, Ann, was back at the Air Force Academy with their two young daughters and pregnant with a third child. The two coaches ate three meals a day together, played golf, and began to understand their similarities and differences. They started building a bond that would last a lifetime of twists and turns for both men.

The biggest difference was how they regarded practice. Smith ran the players through intricate drills and preached fundamentals, while McGuire yelled at them through a megaphone as he entertained sportswriters and friends in the bleachers. Practice time was sacred to Smith, but McGuire didn't mind missing a day or two to go home and recruit high school players.

When he did, McGuire met with scouts in New York like the streetwise "Uncle Harry" Gotkin and businessman Mike Tynberg.

"New York is my personal territory," McGuire said. "Duke can scout in Philadelphia and North Carolina State can have the whole country. But if anyone wants to move into New York, they need a passport from me. All the people in New York are my friends. No one gets paid, but everyone looks out for me. The police department looks for players for me. So do the high school coaches, so do the brothers at the Catholic schools."

One player McGuire went to see several times during the 1958–59 season was Art Heyman, a 6' 5" wild bull of a forward from the south shore of Long Island. In December, Heyman's Oceanside High team played at Long Beach before a packed house pulling for an upset behind its small and clever senior guard Larry Brown.

Oceanside was a heavy favorite, but found itself in a tough game in a hostile gym. Brown was matching Heyman bucket for bucket and eventually outscored him. During the fourth quarter, the home crowd kept track of Brown's point total by chanting "38 . . . 38" and "42 . . . 42."

Long Beach won with Brown getting 45 points to Heyman's 29. As the game ended, Heyman hugged Brown and told him they should play together in college. That night, Long Beach coach Bob Gersten, a UNC graduate and captain of the 1942 Tar Heels, hosted a party at his home. Although Gersten was a full-time teacher and coach, he was essentially another scout for McGuire. At the party, McGuire and Heyman's stepfather, Bill, met for the first time. They didn't like each other.

Brown and Heyman weren't exactly birds of a feather on Long Island in the late 1950s. Both were Jewish and heard the same taunts and catcalls of "Kike" and "Sheenie." Both were also great basketball players, but that's where the comparisons ended.

Brown, a year older, was attractive and well-mannered, the vice president of his high school senior class. Heyman was a half foot taller, a pigeon-toed *schlep* and a real wisenheimer who envied Brown's popularity with girls. They had begun as friendly rivals from the nearby towns of Long Beach and Oceanside, kids with middle-class pasts who battled on the playgrounds during the spring and summer.

The nomadic coaching career for which Brown became famous began with his difficult childhood. The family had followed Milton Brown from Brooklyn to Pittsburgh, so the furniture salesman could peddle a better line and make more money. Traveling all week and seeing his wife and kids on weekends, Milton Brown grew weary and suffered a heart attack.

After her husband later succumbed to pneumonia and heart failure, Ann Brown moved Larry, seven, and his older brother Herb again and settled into three rooms above her father's bakery in Long Beach. There, she worked fourteen-hour days with her brother and cousins while watching her boys after school on the playground across the street.

Gersten first saw Brown as an eleven-year-old with "an intensity I thought was out of proportion then." Brown didn't grow very tall, but he developed Bob Cousy-like mastery of the ball and became somewhat of a local legend in the melting pot coastal town of well-to-do Jews, working class Protestants, and rowdy Irish Catholic beer drinkers.

Heyman was born Art Sondak. His father, Irving, also died when he was seven, perhaps making him and Brown kindred spirits, and he took the name of his mother's second husband, Bill Heyman, a draftsman and engineer from Rockville Centre. Since Art had started school in neighboring Oceanside, he was allowed to commute after his mother remarried.

He was an undefeated high-school soccer goalie and also a baseball player of note until his high school coach booted him off, but Heyman preferred basketball and practiced long hours year round. He shot by himself, played pickup with whomever was there, and participated in two or three summer leagues to the point, Heyman bragged, that at age sixteen he had taken ten thousand showers.

McGuire offered Brown a scholarship to UNC after the heroic performance against Oceanside. He also told Heyman he would have one for him the next year, and Oceanside went on to win the prestigious Nassau County Championship behind Heyman's double-double scoring and rebounding averages.

Bob Gersten visited Chapel Hill two or three times a year, and in the spring of 1958 offered to drive both Brown and Heyman to see the Carolina campus for themselves. Heyman's stepfather wouldn't let him go, and, as it turned out, Brown had to attend prep school in Virginia for one semester to beef up his grades. He returned home in January and took in several Oceanside games during Heyman's senior year.

By then, Heyman was a *Long Island* legend on his way to shattering the region's prep career record with more than 1,500 points, averaging 30 points and 25 rebounds as a senior, and surpassing another pretty good all-around athlete from Manhasset named Jim Brown.

In Chapel Hill, McGuire was hoping to have both Brown and Heyman in his program the next year. The 1959 Tar Heels were already pretty damn good, with sensational sophomores York Larese and Doug Moe joining junior Lee Shaffer on the ACC's biggest and best team. They won 17 of their first 18 games and were ranked No. 1 in the country, and McGuire chartered a luxury coach for their late February road trip to Maryland and Virginia. Besides the team, McGuire loaded the bus with sportswriters and friends for the five-day binge to play a pair of unranked ACC losers. At each stop to eat and drink, McGuire picked up the tab for the entourage, common behavior for the generous and free-wheeling coach.

On Saturday, Carolina dropped a 61–59 shocker at Maryland, which was .500 in the ACC and worse than that overall. The following Wednesday, after falling to No. 3 in the polls, they lost a one-pointer at Virginia, which had a *losing* ACC record. The writers in McGuire's pocket wrote that it was tougher than ever to win on the road; McGuire claimed the refs were out to get him since he won it all two years ago; his cronies kissed his ass and told him whatever he wanted to hear.

The road trip was a washout, but McGuire still figured he was headed back to the NCAA Tournament since the second-best team in the league, N.C. State, was on probation and couldn't go.

He was right, but McGuire did it his way. After Carolina advanced to the ACC Tournament championship game by beating Duke in the semifinals (UNC's third win over the Blue Devils in 1959), he "rested" his starters for more than twenty minutes against State because they had to travel to New York for a first-round game in the NCAA Tournament four nights later.

In reality, McGuire believed Case should have withdrawn from the ACC Tournament so he could not eliminate another team with a chance to earn the NCAA bid. McGuire's arrogant, obvious protest made a mockery of the title game and infuriated the rest of the ACC.

McGuire didn't care. He called Case and Duke's Cameron "cocksuckers" and referred to the do-or-die ACC Tournament he loathed as Russian roulette. After the Tar Heels lost their NCAA opener to Navy at Madison Square Garden, scuttling his "rest" strategy, McGuire stayed in New York and continued recruiting Heyman.

By then, Heyman had received more than seventy-five college offers (including $10,000 in cash a coach from a midwestern school dumped on his bed) and narrowed his choices to St. John's, NYU (where his father, Irving Sondak, was an All-American in the 1930s), and North Carolina.

Duke also recruited Heyman, using several players and assistant coach Fred Shabel to show him around campus. Their head coach, Bradley, had bolted for Texas after a disappointing 13–12 season, leaving Heyman so sure he wasn't going there that he cared less what he said to his hosts. Walking around the Gothic campus with several Duke players, Heyman wisecracked that he'd "like to get a few of you under the boards sometime."

When, a few weeks later, Heyman signed with UNC, the Duke players weren't all that upset and loved that they'd have a chance to get even with the loud-mouthed lout in a year or two.

On May 5, 1959, Duke called a press conference to introduce its new basketball coach. School officials had kept the appointment secret from curious newsmen who assembled on the stone walkway in front of the Duke Chapel. Eddie Cameron was looking for a certain type of coach: someone who could recruit good players to challenge N.C. State and UNC for supremacy in the ACC.

Duke had finished first in the ACC standings twice. But it hadn't won the ACC Tournament that Case had made such a focal point of the conference, and since Groat graduated, Duke had not boasted a star anywhere near his caliber. Meanwhile, State won four ACC championships and defeated Duke 10 of the last 14 times. Carolina captured the 1957 NCAA title in the midst of beating the Blue Devils 8 of the last 10.

So when Cameron heard that an assistant coach at N.C. State was interested in the Duke job, he figured the Case protégé at least had the pedigree Duke was looking for.

Victor Albert Bubas was the son of immigrant Yugoslavians who arrived in America unable to speak English and settled in the mill town of Gary, Indiana. At 6' 2" and a tenacious defender as a player, he was one of those Hurryin' Hoosiers recruited by Case to the old Southern Conference. After graduation, Bubas served six years on the State staff, where he helped recruit Jackie Moreland but was not implicated in the investigation or charges against Case.

He first interviewed at Clemson, where the ubiquitous Frank Howard balked at Bubas's request for more money and a bigger recruiting budget. "Son, if Clemson is going on probation," Howard grumbled to him, "it sure as hell won't be for basketball!"

Cameron had 125 applicants for the job, but after one meeting at the Raleigh-Durham Airport he knew he had the coach he wanted. Bubas agreed to an $8,500 salary, less than he made as an assistant at State.

"Don't you think it's time to go recruiting?" Cameron asked him as the press conference ended.

Bubas purposely shopped at different department stores, dry cleaners, and service stations to meet as many people as possible. He held basketball clinics for women, spoke to church groups, and kissed babies, trying to win over residents in a Durham so heavily populated with UNC alumni and fans.

No one was going to outwork him. A few weeks after taking the Duke job, Bubas joined a crowd of about fifty people watching a summer-league game on the Hickey playground in Rockville Centre, where Brown and Heyman were playing against each other.

Well aware that Art Heyman's stepfather disliked McGuire, Bubas stood behind Bill Heyman and grabbed his shoulder every time Art made one of his daring drives to the basket. "I love him! I gotta have him!" Bubas said into Bill Heyman's ear. The game ended with the friendly rivals pushing and shoving each other, and being separated, giving Bubas further hope that he could still get Heyman into a royal blue uniform.

A few weeks later, Heyman's stepfather drove him to Chapel Hill for pre-freshman orientation. Bill Heyman wasn't interested in talking with McGuire, but the coach showed up one night at the University Motel after Art had gone to the movies with Tar Heel player Danny Lotz.

Heyman's old man wanted to know if McGuire required strict class attendance and was serious about his players getting college degrees, not merely a basketball education. McGuire resented the questions, since he was used to parents putting their complete faith in him.

The conversation turned into an argument, then a loud shouting match. The younger Heyman returned to the motel room to find his stepfather and future coach nose to nose with fists clenched.

"I had to step between them," Heyman said when recounting the story. "My stepfather called Carolina a basketball factory and McGuire didn't like that. They were about to start swinging at each other."

According to ACC rules, Heyman's letter of intent to UNC was not binding until July 1. Bubas kept recruiting him, returning to New York and taking Bill and Charlotte Heyman to dinner at the Playbill Restaurant in the Manhattan Hotel, where he put the hard sell on the kid's parents.

"You're doggone right I went after him," Bubas said. "It's a good thing, too.

That season I didn't get anyone else. Art was one of the real plums. When he showed up at Duke as a freshman, he had played more basketball, against faster competition, than any senior I had."

"He [Bubas] convinced them I should go to Duke," Heyman said. "He charmed my mother and stepfather. They made me go to Duke. My friends from New York like Larry [Brown] and Doug Moe were at Carolina. If Duke hadn't picked me up at the airport, I would have just gone down the road and started school there [at UNC]."

Bill Heyman claimed McGuire's men, such as Gotkin, pressured him and that he never intended to send his stepson to UNC. "I signed the paper, but I did it to get Harry Gotkin off my back," he said. "I told him when I signed that the boy would never play at Carolina. When Mr. Bubas came up to see us, I was sold on him and Duke University and advised Arthur accordingly. What's so wrong with a seventeen-year-old boy changing his mind?"

So, instead of the package deal they had agreed to be, Heyman and Brown wound up heading for rival campuses in the fall of 1959.

"I can't believe Artie did that to me," Brown told his teammates.

Gersten, Brown's old coach, wrote a long letter to pro-Duke columnist Jack Horner of the *Durham Morning Herald,* defending McGuire's recruiting of Heyman and claiming Heyman's stepfather wanted more than what was legally allowed in a scholarship. Horner printed the letter in its entirety.

Bill Heyman considered getting a restraining order to prevent Gersten from further interference, but backed off.

Preparing for his trip to enroll at Duke, Heyman received hate mail with veiled threats about how difficult his life would be if he went through with his altered decision, suggesting that he go to another school in another conference. One arrived with a Chapel Hill postmark.

"Instead of being a good loser in this case," Horner wrote, "it seems Carolina's main desire is to have the boy go outside the ACC. However, Mr. Heyman and young Art are more determined than ever he enter Duke where the schoolboy cage sensation will get a shot at Carolina."

"Mr. Cameron told me never to go to Chapel Hill," Heyman said, "because McGuire hated Duke with a passion. I remembered that after I visited UNC, we were going to drive to Durham to see Duke, and McGuire didn't want us to do that. The word was after I committed to Duke, they [UNC] hired a private eye to follow me around and get me in trouble."

There was no ESPN at the time, and only scant coverage of recruiting in the newspapers. So while this was a big story, most Duke and Carolina fans didn't know many of the details, only the important one: that a high school star from New York had committed to Carolina and then defected to Duke. That was enough to agitate a festering rivalry.

That Heyman first had a season of freshman ball only increased the apprehension. Had he been able to play for the varsity right away, everything would have been out on the table. As it was, the tension had a full year to grow before some old friends from New York became bitter antagonists, cursing and spitting at each other during games.

Making matters worse, the Bubas-Heyman period at Duke began as a dark cloud hovered over college basketball in the South. The threat of punches and point shaving was as much a part of the game as shots and rebounds. It was a nasty, uncontrollable era when coaches, players, fans, and even sportswriters wore their affiliations on their sleeves, as well as their sweaters, and weren't afraid to take sides and swings. Hacks used words like "crucified" in their columns, and coaches claimed that their enemies were "out to get me . . . shooting at me" in their postgame quotes.

Fans threw apple cores and coins from the stands. Fights interrupted and, in some cases, stopped games. In 1959 a scuffle occurred near the end of UNC's 75–66 win at Wake Forest. Wake coach Bones McKinney, also an ordained minister because he couldn't make ends meet as a coach, got decked by a fan sitting behind the Carolina bench. Officials sent the starters from both teams to the locker rooms while the subs mopped up. The brawl caused Weaver to move the game to Greensboro the following year.

At the same time, gamblers preyed on the poor kids who played the game, some married with young children, trying to get through college. Wearing dark suits and hats and packing pistols, they roamed the hallways of Reynolds Coliseum or approached players in the shadows outside their apartments. They bribed the most vulnerable to "arrange" games by altering the final score so it would wind up on the correct side of the point spread.

None of this was new to McGuire, who swore if he ever encountered one of these leeches, he would beat his ass himself. He kept a scrapbook of newspaper articles from the point-shaving scandals that had rocked New York City in the early 1950s. Before each season, he made his new players read the stories and sign pledges they wouldn't cheat or take bribes.

During the 1959–60 regular season, Heyman and Brown starred for their respective freshmen teams, which had become a pretty big deal. From its inception, the ACC had eliminated varsity eligibility for freshmen so athletes could get accustomed to academic demands and college life for a year. Prior to that, there were still freshman teams, but the better players could spend all four years with the varsity.

Freshman basketball now previewed and showcased the recruited players who were on scholarship. They joined a team that was filled out by walk-ons who tried out from the student body, creating the essence of college athletics— students of all backgrounds playing together.

The freshmen had their own head coach, usually a seasoned assistant entrusted with preparing the scholarship players for active duty with the varsity and maybe finding a hidden talent or two who would eventually earn a scholarship. They wore hand-me-down uniforms and even went by underling nicknames such as the Blue Imps and Tar Babies. They usually practiced just before or after the big team, sometimes traveled with the varsity to road games, and were treated like fraternity pledges or Army plebes by the upperclassmen.

Their schedules were shorter and localized so they could adjust to the first year of college academics. Thus, schools with the greatest proximity played several times a season. Heyman's freshman team faced Brown's in a home-and-home series and then played a third game in Siler City about twenty miles southwest of Chapel Hill.

Due to the notoriety of his recruitment, Heyman drew big crowds to freshman games and remained in the news off the court. He was homesick a lot, got scared by a few threatening letters he received from Ku Klux Klansmen, and told friends he was thinking about leaving school. For most of the season, he fought off rumors fueled by Carolina fans that he was transferring to NYU.

Though McGuire always denied holding a grudge—"I've never said a bad word about Art Heyman; I wish I had him," McGuire insisted—there were signs to the contrary. He refused to mention Heyman by name on his weekly TV show and in most interviews, and many believed McGuire ordered a "hit" on Heyman during the freshman game at Siler City, where it could be witnessed by fewer fans and might somehow escape closer scrutiny by the two universities.

In an era when "PC" meant privileged character to most kids, no taunts were taboo for some players. Several Carolina freshmen called Heyman "Christ killer" and other anti-Semitic names almost from the opening tip. While this seemed odd, considering Larry Brown was also Jewish, ethnic jokes were an accepted part of the environment McGuire created.

"He called me 'Jew Bastard' so often I began to think that was my first name," Brown said.

"I coach nationalities," McGuire said. "There are ways to motivate Jewish players and Italian players. I know how to get them mad and get the most out of them."

Slurring Heyman was the Carolina strategy, hoping to unnerve the Duke star and perhaps entice a fight. When Heyman began to react early in the game at Siler City, Bucky Waters, Duke's freshman coach, called a timeout and sat his high-strung star down for a pep talk.

"He was shaking and you could see he was just about to go off," Waters recalled. "I said, 'Art, this is the start of a great career, young man. But you have to understand one thing. If you're a .350 hitter they throw it up under your chin; they throw it up under your belt. If you're a .250 hitter, they throw it right down the middle. You're a .350 hitter. You are going to be the focus, not just with Carolina but everybody. Get ready for it. It goes with the territory. It goes with talent. It goes with your reputation.' "

Heyman managed to keep his cool and eventually scored 34 points in Duke's one-sided romp. Late in the game, UNC forward Dieter "Killer" Krause went after Heyman with more than words.

"At the top of the key, Art came out to get the ball," Waters said. "Right behind him was Krause with his fist clenched, like he had a javelin but somebody had taken the javelin out of his hand. Art never saw him, and Dieter just drilled him."

While Heyman was taken off the court to Siler City Hospital for six stitches in his mouth, Waters had an ugly, physical confrontation with UNC freshman coach Ken Rosemond, grabbing him by the jacket lapels and pushing him against the scorer's table so hard that the lights on the gymnasium scoreboard began blinking wildly.

Duke complained bitterly, but because freshman games weren't under the jurisdiction of the ACC, Krause received no punishment. McGuire brushed off the incident, saying it was just another fight in a basketball game.

Afterward, however, rumors circulated that Krause's father was a German heavyweight-boxing champion. "Unfortunately, the German-Jewish thing became an issue," Waters said. "It was the opening round of a career in which Art had problems in the games against Carolina."

Meanwhile, the varsities were also in contrast. Bubas's first Duke team struggled to win more games than it lost. The Blue Devils had one all-conference player, Howard Hurt, who got the fewest votes on the second team. Hurt was the tenth-leading scorer in the ACC and 6' 6" center Carroll Youngkin was the ninth-best rebounder. They finished 7–7, fourth in the ACC, and carried a modest 12–10 record into the 1960 ACC Tournament in Raleigh, pretty much biding their time until Heyman moved up the next season.

McGuire's juggernaut looked capable of winning his second national championship. He had almost everyone back from his 1959 NCAA Tournament team, boasting talent and toughness. Shaffer, an athletic senior, and junior marksman

Larese were All-ACC players. Moe, a junior, sat out the first semester in academic trouble but came back in January to average 17 points and 11 rebounds. The Tar Heels were deep enough to overcome losing junior center Dick Kepley to a broken ankle during preseason practice.

They lost only four times before February 20, all to nationally ranked opponents: Kentucky, St. Louis, and twice to Wake Forest, once in the championship game of the Dixie Classic. Then they went to Charlotte to play Clemson and South Carolina, schools that couldn't care less about basketball in those days and were considered "sure wins" by the ACC powers. N.C. State was also in the annual North-South Doubleheader weekend, with the Wolfpack and Tar Heels switching opponents on Friday and Saturday night.

Heavily favored UNC, which had stomped both in earlier meetings, barely beat Clemson by five points and then lost to South Carolina by four the following night. It was a curious weekend that even had some of the participating players wondering what had happened.

UNC rebounded and tied Wake Forest for first in the conference with a 12–2 record, blowing out Virginia, Maryland and Duke over the last five days of the regular season to enter the ACC Tournament as the favorite to take the title and earn the NCAA bid. The win in Durham was Carolina's third over the Blue Devils that season by at least 22 points and its sixth straight in two years.

Duke and Carolina both won first-round tournament games, the Blue Devils holding off 10–16 South Carolina and the Tar Heels routing last-place Virginia for the second time in a week. Facing a fourth meeting with Duke in the semifinals, the UNC players thought they could name the final score.

"There was no way they could beat us," said Shaffer, who averaged more than 18 points and 11 rebounds that season. "We knew it, and they knew it."

But, with Shaffer in early foul trouble, Duke built a 35–19 edge to lead by 12 at the break. Shaffer got his fourth foul right after halftime and had to play behind Youngkin, who shot over him for a career-high 30 points to stave off one Tar Heel comeback after another.

As an upset became a possibility, the overflow crowd of nearly thirteen thousand in smoky Reynolds Coliseum roared like an aluminum wind tunnel. Hundreds of slat chairs behind the baskets vibrated on sloped wooden platforms while fans stood and sat, stood and sat, as the final minutes elapsed.

Despite 25 points from Larese and 21 from Shaffer, Duke hung on to win 71–69 on four free throws by Hurt and John Frye. The Blue Devil reserves leaped off the bench and swarmed their teammates on the court. Bubas and his assistant coaches Waters and Shabel sat stunned momentarily before they too joined the celebration.

The Tar Heels walked off the court in a daze, realizing they were out of the ACC Tournament and not going to the NCAA Tournament–done for the season with an 18–6 record.

"It's hard to beat a team four times," McGuire said, shrugging.

The next morning in New York City, while sipping his coffee, district attorney Frank Hogan scanned the sports pages of the *Daily News*. He saw the Duke-Carolina score and knew North Carolina had beaten Duke badly in three previous meetings. He picked up the *New York Post* to see if there wasn't a misprint. When he found the same score, Hogan wrote a note to himself about the game, "3/4/60, Duke-UNC, +15"—the last number representing how many points Carolina had been favored by to win.

After giving Bubas his first victory over Carolina, Duke advanced to the ACC Championship game the next night against eighteenth-ranked but distracted Wake Forest led by All-ACC stars Len Chappell, Dave Budd, and Billy Packer, who went on to be a prominent television basketball analyst.

Budd, a muscular senior forward already on probation for fighting, had been thrown out of the semifinal against N.C. State for tangling with the Wolfpack's Anton "Dutch" Muehlbauer. Wake hung on to win, 71–66 (which also did not beat the point spread), and ACC Commissioner Weaver suspended Budd for the championship game.

Wake Forest appealed, claiming Muehlbauer started the fight and that State sacrificed him to get Budd tossed out, a trade-off that hurt the Deacons far more and one in which Muehlbauer may have had an ulterior motive. Wake was favored by eight points and without Budd in the game, the Deacons would have a hard time "covering."

The ACC's executive committee overturned the suspension late Saturday afternoon a few hours before the tip-off, clearing Budd to go against Duke. The sky-high Blue Devils played their five starters all but two minutes and used a 1-3-1 zone that had 5' 11" Jack Mullen in the middle to pester the 6' 8" Chappell and Budd. Wake Forest wound up missing 49 of its 74 shots (Packer was 2–11). Doug Kistler led four Duke players in double figures with 22 points, including the go-ahead basket with 1:40 left in the game. The 63–59 win gave Bubas a completely unexpected ACC title in his first season as a head coach.

"It was like Christmas in March," he said.

Duke shot to No. 18 in the polls and won two games in the NCAA Tournament, pounding Princeton in New York and edging St. Joseph's in Charlotte. One game from the Final Four, the Blue Devils lost to NYU (led by All-American Barry Kramer and Tom "Satch" Sanders) to finish their once-mediocre season 17–11.

At thirty-three, Bubas became a coaching legend overnight, a magical springboard to his own honored career. Duke basketball, in the shadow of its football program and the State-Carolina rivalry, had instant credibility—and the Blue Devils had Heyman coming up the next season.

McGuire, meanwhile, had become the ACC's most controversial coach and divided even his own school with his arrogance and his team's combativeness on the court. He stonewalled the NCAA Infractions Committee in Kansas City in the spring of 1960, calling it a kangaroo court and hoping to keep the Tar Heels eligible for the NCAA Tournament the following season.

The investigation, in part, involved travel expenses from that 1959 road trip to Maryland and Virginia for which McGuire kept no detailed records. He maintained he was buying meals for sportswriters and his friends, but the NCAA Council was unconvinced, believing the money funded recruiting payoffs by talent scouts like Gotkin and Tynberg in New York. That McGuire recruited Heyman at the time was not lost on investigators.

McGuire countercharged that the chairman of the Infractions Committee, who was Dean of the graduate school at Columbia, had it in for him since his days at St. John's, when the Redmen ruled New York City basketball and their coach was a big shot.

After McGuire refused to answer most of the questions during the hearing, UNC basketball was cited for excessive expenditures, specifically while entertaining recruits and their families. When UNC Chancellor Bill Aycock received the formal charges, he gave a copy to McGuire and asked him straight away, "Are they true?" The Irishman said they were a bunch of malarkey.

"Frank, for your sake, and the sake of the university, we've got to gather information to refute these charges," Aycock said.

McGuire had neither the time nor the paper trail that the NCAA needed, but he did have Dean Smith, his bright, second-year assistant coach. Smith had been on the trip and spent hours getting affidavits from those who traveled in McGuire's party. He split time between the basketball office and the Chancellor's suite in South Building.

In the fall of 1960, Smith and Aycock flew to San Francisco to appeal the case in front of the NCAA Council, cramming into the coach cabin because it was a state policy that university administrators could not fly first class. Smith hadn't been on many recruiting trips with McGuire, but he booked a lot of his airplane reservations.

"You know," Smith said to Aycock, "Coach McGuire would never ride tourist class." The men shared a smile.

That was the only hint of criticism Aycock had ever heard from Smith, even though it was clear McGuire had made a mess of things. As Smith untangled an Agatha Christie tale of what McGuire spent and on whom he spent it, Aycock developed a deep respect and admiration for the young coach.

He began thinking to himself, "If I ever had to hire another coach, this is the kind of man I would want."

Largely because of the documentation they presented to the NCAA Council, the charges were sent back to the infractions committee for a second look. McGuire was happy to hear the news but was more concerned with getting his team ready for the 1960–61 season.

Sophomore Larry Brown started at point guard with junior Yogi Poteet in the backcourt. Shaffer was gone, but All-ACC seniors Moe and Larese were back, and Kepley had recovered from his injury. Krause and Kenny "Moose" McComb came off the bench as McGuire's enforcers.

Heyman was the only scholarship sophomore playing for the Blue Devils, joining four returning starters in the lineup and immediately establishing himself as one of the best and boldest players in the ACC. In Heyman's first varsity game, he quickly demonstrated no one man could stop him by taking the ball and driving past four LSU defenders and barreling over the fifth for a layup.

Carolina, however, remained the team to beat in the ACC.

The Blue Devils were still getting comfortable with newcomer Heyman when they faced UNC in the championship game of the Dixie Classic on New Year's Eve. Moe, the best defender in the ACC, frustrated Heyman and held him to five points in the final thirty-five minutes as the Tar Heels held on to win 76–71. The next morning, Heyman tore Moe's picture out of the Durham *Morning Herald* and taped it to the wall in his dorm room.

Five days later, forty-eight hours before Carolina's game against Notre Dame in Charlotte on January 7, 1961, the NCAA summoned McGuire to a final hearing in Pittsburgh. His team hadn't played in a week since beating Duke; why couldn't they have called him a few days earlier? He was perturbed by having to take off in the middle of the season and, when questioned, wise-mouthed the committee again. The NCAA promptly placed UNC on probation for one year, making the Tar Heels ineligible for the 1961 NCAA Tournament.

"Those cocksuckers," McGuire told Erickson, using his favorite expletive, "they were out to get me and weren't gonna stop until they did."

McGuire hated the ACC Tournament, anyway, so he talked Erickson and the faculty council into pulling the Tar Heels out of it. Although he used the same rationale for which he criticized Case back in 1959, McGuire's move was really a selfish stunt so he could publicly protest the probation.

Why UNC allowed him to deprive his players of three more games and a chance to cut down a net said more about McGuire's misplaced power at the school than the so-called reason for the move. By then even many of McGuire's own fans had grown weary of his histrionics.

Even though Carolina was winning and had climbed to No. 5 in the rankings, Heyman and Duke were now the bigger story. The Blue Devils were on their own run, unbeaten since their loss to the Tar Heels with their highest ranking in history—No. 4 in the AP poll.

Suddenly, Duke-Carolina was *the* game everyone anticipated, eclipsing State-Carolina. McGuire's machinations aside, the heated home-and-home series was about to begin. The February 4 rematch at Duke Indoor Stadium marked the first time both teams had played while nationally ranked in the top 5—but it's not like these were old pals who just got competitive.

Hard feelings dated back five years. UNC had dominated the series since 1956, Duke winning only twice. Then came the Murray-McGuire feud of '58, which deepened in antipathy when Carolina's football team pasted Duke 50–0 in the fall of '59. Three months later came the Blue Devils' shocking upset of the heavily favored Heels in the 1960 ACC Tournament.

Heyman's arrival on the varsity threw fuel on the fire that still burned from Duke killing Carolina's national championship hopes the year before, a humiliating loss that grated on McGuire and his returning players.

After backing down against the vengeful Tar Heels in the Dixie Classic for their only loss of the new season, the Blue Devils itched to pay them back. Heyman had Moe's picture to remind him on a daily basis.

Now McGuire had the probation that made him even surlier and turned his boys into testy young men.

Duke (15–1) warmed up for UNC by beating South Carolina Tuesday night in Columbia. Before the game, midterm grades came out and the Blue Devils learned that starter Jack Mullen would be ineligible for the spring semester. Mullen was a key defender who was expected to guard Larese, the Tar Heels' hot-shooting guard who averaged more than 23 points a game.

Carolina (14–2) handled Maryland at home on Thursday night for its twelfth straight win. Besides the game account, two local newspapers reported the presence of a quiet high-school graduate named Billy Cunningham, who once scored 61 points in a game for Brooklyn's (New York) Erasmus Hall and would be a UNC freshman the next fall. The spindly, 6' 6" lefty, who later won

NBA championships as a player and coach with the Philadelphia 76ers, was spending a year in Chapel Hill working out and studying with a private tutor.

As a Nor'easter paralyzed much of the state, the week leading up to the game remained hotter than hell.

Heavy snow and freezing temperatures postponed most high school basketball, but not the big college battle scheduled for regional TV on Saturday night. Even in 1961, television affected the starting times of games and created jealousies among competing schools.

Duke's Cameron had turned down a request from one of the national networks to play the game in the afternoon because he didn't want to inconvenience alumni coming in from out of town. Besides, he knew C. D. Chesley was planning to show the game as far North as Pennsylvania, which was Duke's prime recruiting area. Except that Wake Forest, which was hosting Maryland, complained that a local telecast of the game would hurt its own home gate, so Cameron agreed to push the tip-off back one hour to 8:30.

Meanwhile, Erickson had to refute a report in *Sports Illustrated* that the recruiting violations and probation were pulling McGuire toward the NBA to coach the New York Knickerbockers. The years of rumor and innuendo about McGuire and his entourage were finally catching up with him, and he found himself sad as well as mad at the state of things at UNC.

He had actually wept at the graveside ceremony for Billy Carmichael Jr. who was only fourteen years his elder when he was buried on Monday at the Chapel Hill Cemetery at age sixty-one. McGuire felt guilty for giving the university's chief financial officer so much guff about the leaks in Woollen Gym. On one rainy night, Carmichael had seated a state legislator directly under the hole in the roof.

"Are we ever going to get a new gym?" McGuire had scolded Carmichael on more than one occasion. "We've won a goddamn national championship here, you know!"

Frank McGuire was an ass kicker, all right.

Nevertheless, on this snowy night in 1961, he sat on the team bus wondering if they were all about to get *their* asses kicked. He worried that he had gotten too big for his silk britches and the off-court controversies and on-court shenanigans had finally caught up with them all.

In Durham, Art Heyman was ready to walk across the icy street from his Gothic dormitory to Duke Indoor Stadium. He hung out in his room a little longer than usual, staring at the picture of Moe, another New Yorker who had shut him down and spit at him in his first varsity game against the team he was once sure he'd play for. He put on his Navy blue CPO jacket and walked into the winter dusk. There was another basketball game that night, one of hundreds he would play before his career ended.

While he knew it was a big one, shadowed by the recruiting saga that had engulfed his family, two universities, two coaches, and thousands of fans he would never meet, Heyman could not have fathomed how big, nor how this particular game would change the course of an entire athletic conference and help turn what was a neighborhood rivalry into a national phenomenon.

The Tar Heels rode their bus in the snow to Durham, angry over the probation and mad at McGuire for yanking them from the ACC Tournament.

Although the Tar Heels could still beat Duke and win the 1961 ACC regular season, McGuire wasn't sure how his tough guys would react once they got inside the hostile hotbox at Duke. Would they play hard and keep their heads? Or would they be combative and out of control?

When they arrived, McGuire stepped off the bus and into a slush puddle. Suddenly, he wished he had taken his wife Pat's advice as he left her and Frankie at the house.

"Put on your rubbers," she had said.

McGuire had shrugged her off, not wanting those ugly black elastics stretched over his expensive alligator shoes and showing under his wool overcoat, which covered his favorite silk suit purchased in New York on his last recruiting trip.

He knew the doormen at every arena in the ACC, such as Sheriff John Baker at Reynolds Coliseum and gentleman Howard Blalock at Duke. McGuire shook hands quickly with Blalock at the side entrance of Duke Indoor Stadium, winking knowingly, not wanting him to get in trouble with his bosses, Cameron and Murray, for being too friendly to the Carolina coach.

McGuire was a marked man at Duke. The ill will from the 1958 game turned into bad blood with the Heyman recruiting rancor and became a full-fledged feud when the UNC and Duke freshmen fought and Krause laid Heyman out. The hostility had caused the Durham police chief to send over some extra men.

Inside, most of the eighty-eight hundred fans had packed in to see the freshman preliminary. Behind touted recruits Jeff Mullins and Jay Buckley, the Blue Imps were expected to crush the Tar Babies who had on their roster, among others, future Charlotte mayor and gubernatorial candidate Richard Vinroot. And Duke did, 79–52, as Mullins scored 20.

The freshman game was a physical foreshadowing of the main event and ended with only three Carolina players on the court. Five from both teams fouled out and three more were ejected for fighting, including UNC's Jimmy Siceloff, who tackled a Duke player on a breakaway layup.

Fans were in a fervor when the varsity teams came out to warm up. McGuire's grand entrance had become a focal point, home and away. He never went out early with his players, remaining in the locker room to visit with sportswriters and well-wishers until just before tip-off. When he finally emerged, it was to a full house and crazed crowd watching his every move, like Elvis or another rock star taking the stage.

Among the spectators was Footsie Knight, the ACC Director of Officials who lived in Durham. He was there to see how the refs he had assigned, Charlie Eckman and Joe Mills, handled what the local media was calling a collision of "collegiate basketball giants."

Compared to the brawls on an NBA court in Detroit and a football field in Clemson on one regrettable weekend nearly thirty-four years later, this looked like a bad B movie. Kids from warring neighborhoods, with crew cuts and greasy pompadours, squaring off like Jets and Sharks in a white *West Side Story*.

In the first half, Moe threw an elbow that barely missed Heyman's nose and they stared each other down as Eckman and Mills broke it up. Duke's Kistler also stepped between them, but Heyman said it wasn't Moe's elbow that incited him.

"He spit on me," Heyman said. "Every time I took a shot he spit at me, and I told him I wasn't going to take that. I said to Doug (Moe), 'I've got a cold, so the next time you do it, you get it back right in the face.'"

Krause came off the bench to challenge Kistler and Duke trainer Jim Cunningham ran out to push Krause away, causing McGuire to complain to the refs and anyone else who would listen to his unsavory speech. It didn't matter to McGuire that Cunningham had gone to high school with Krause and thought he could help prevent a repeat of what happened in Siler City.

Heyman had a big night and needed almost every one of his baskets to keep Duke in the game. He started fast and hit 9 of his first 11 shots, many on power moves in the lane. Moe couldn't stop him this time. Carolina led 35–34 at the half, and the players left the court through the same narrow runway. UNC cheerleader Albert Roper patted the Tar Heels on the backside and mistakenly did the same to Heyman as he ran by. Heyman turned back, shoved Roper and kept running.

(Durham lawyer and UNC alumnus Blackwell "Dog" Brogden was at the game and saw what happened from the stands. He decided to file an assault charge against Heyman, but Roper refused to testify against Heyman and on Monday morning the case was thrown out within ten minutes.)

Moe had no better luck on offense than he did defending Heyman, scoring only 11 points after missing 12 of his 14 shots from the floor and fouling out with seven minutes to play. But Larese and Brown were brilliant and had the Tar Heels in position to win in the closing moments.

Carolina led the tense game 73–70 with three minutes remaining. Then Duke's Frye hit a free throw, and Heyman scored five straight points for a 76–73 lead. Every possession from that point resulted in a foul, and Heyman's two free throws with fifteen seconds on the clock stretched Duke's lead to a secure 80–75.

Brown took the inbound pass as Duke dropped back into a zone. He wheeled and headed for the corner in front of the UNC bench, driving the baseline behind the zone. Heyman, stationed in the middle, ran down the lane to grab Brown over the shoulders as he went up to shoot, bear-hugging him to prevent a clean shot. Eckman blew his whistle for a foul just as Brown broke free, threw the ball at Heyman and began swinging.

Heyman swung back at Brown, which turned the place to bedlam in front of the UNC bench. Carolina's Donnie Walsh jumped in and hit Heyman from behind, knocking him and Brown down as several other Tar Heels piled on. Heyman claimed alligator shoes were kicking him, but films later showed McGuire briefly trying to hold some students back and then walking to mid-court buttoning his suit jacket, pulling on his cuffs.

The ten Durham policemen on hand struggled to restore order. Heyman fought to his feet and went looking for Walsh, who had backed out of the conflict. Moe was tangling with Duke students and fans and had his jersey ripped. Mills joined the police in trying to break up the melee; ref Eckman hid behind the basket support, which gave Weaver, Knight, and other ACC officials a big laugh when they watched the film a few days later.

After about ten minutes, the court was cleared and players ushered back to their benches, students into the bleachers. McGuire and Bubas met the officials at the scorer's table and exchanged more heated words about who started it. Heyman was ejected for allegedly throwing the first punch, even though he had fouled out on the play, and spent the last few seconds of the game crying to Bubas on the Duke bench.

"I was hit three times and spit at during the whole game before I started to fight," Heyman said afterward.

Amazingly, Brown was not thrown out and made two free throws. Duke's

Buzz Mewhort added one in the final seconds to make the final score 81–77, and both teams left the court without further incident.

"Duke won the game but lost the fight," Horner wrote the next morning. "There must have been forty or fifty individuals on the floor, swinging wildly in all directions at the height of the fisticuffs."

Bubas said in another story, "Heyman left the game on his fifth foul. A punch? We were ahead. He had no reason to throw a punch."

A two-month controversy ensued. Weaver began by reviewing films of the game from both schools and the telecast. Eckman, upon seeing the film, admitted that he was wrong and that it was Brown, not Heyman, who swung first. While they awaited Weaver's ruling, McGuire, Bubas, and Cameron waged a war of words in various North Carolina newspapers and magazines.

Heyman was scheduled to speak at the Durham Sports Club Monday, and he showed up with a projector and reel of film he had taken from the Duke basketball office. He wanted to prove that Brown had thrown the first punch and really started the melee.

Duke held a news conference Wednesday and played the fight film for forty reporters, attempting to exonerate its coach and players. The grainy, sixteen-millimeter movie shot from the catwalk above the Indoor Stadium showed no other Blue Devil besides Heyman involved. Bubas manned the projector; he made no comment but his intentions were clear.

McGuire called the Duke press conference a "set up" and predicted a "bloodbath" at the rematch in Chapel Hill three weeks later. "I'm afraid the situation might get worse; we might have to call out the National Guard," McGuire said in typical hyperbole.

UNC braced for bad news from the ACC's investigation. Weaver had censured McGuire and Lee Shaffer two years earlier when the Tar Heels were in a similar scrap at Wake Forest, Weaver's old school.

"Weaver's out to get me," McGuire charged, claiming the animosity started after he wrote a letter to UNC alumni the year before calling Weaver a puppet and saying Duke really ran the ACC.

Cameron countered with his own snide comment.

"We're terribly sorry this happened, but there is a common factor in these basketball fights we've had in the ACC during the last few years," he said, referring to McGuire and Carolina.

The press was just as opinionated. Various columnists said the next game scheduled for February 25 should be cancelled or moved to a neutral site. One writer suggested the schools suspend play in basketball as they did in football sixty-seven years earlier. Others took sides.

Homer Horner wondered whether "McGuire gives his boys boxing lessons." Greensboro *News & Record* sports editor Smith Barrier, whose office was a few miles from ACC headquarters, defended the conference and commissioner against attacks from McGuire. In Charlotte, *Observer* sports editor and UNC grad Bob Quincy and columnist Ron Green, a golf buddy of Dean Smith, were sympathetic to the Tar Heels and McGuire's claims that Duke should have controlled its home crowd better.

As Weaver continued his probe, the hangover affected the rivals. Heyman scored only 14 points in Duke's loss at N.C. State, while Carolina dropped its second straight game by losing at South Carolina. Heyman rebounded to score 31 in Duke's home win over Wake Forest on February 9.

Weaver called a press conference for February 14, the date of Duke's second game against Wake Forest. The Blue Devils and Tar Heels, along with the rest of the ACC, waited anxiously to hear the results of his ten-day investigation.

On Valentine's Day, Weaver hardly had flowers and candy waiting for the culprits. He suspended Heyman and also Brown and Walsh for their remaining conference games, which ended the season for the Carolina combo because McGuire had pulled the Tar Heels out of the ACC Tournament.

That McGuire had originally lured all three players from New York wasn't lost on many Southerners who saw him as a disruptive influence on the game. Those fans still supporting McGuire—and not all of them did—called the most severe critics "Yankee-haters," further inflaming the rivalry.

Weaver's statement, waxing eloquent in some sentences, blamed Brown for starting the fight but also held Heyman and Walsh accountable for the roles they played. Conference commissioners since then have avoided such public detail, certainly without the prolific prose.

"It is true that had Heyman not fouled Brown, there would have been no reason for the fight," Weaver said. "But this was not a disqualifying foul and players must learn to accept the fact that such fouls may occur. Had Brown not struck Heyman, there would have been no fight, so Brown must accept responsibility for initiating what followed.

"Furthermore, had Walsh not engaged in his 'hit-and-run' tactics, the fight would have been of short duration. Consequently, Walsh must assume his share of responsibility for the prolongation of the fight. Had Heyman not charged Walsh, the near riot which followed might have been averted.

"I do not hold Heyman altogether to blame for striking Brown, for this retaliatory action was almost instinctive. However, he must be held responsible for the subsequent attack on Walsh who had indicated by retreating a few steps that he had withdrawn from the fray."

Duke immediately appealed Heyman's suspension to the ACC Faculty Chairmen, which allowed him to play in the game at Wake Forest that night. He again scored 31 points but this time the third-ranked Blue Devils lost to the Deacons 103–89, a 24-point turnaround from their home win five days earlier. The next morning, the ACC upheld Weaver's decision. "Do you know what they suspended Heyman for?" asked Bubas. "For continuing the fight. For *continuing* it, understand? Not for starting it. What in the world did they expect him to do? Lie there with people walking up and down his spine?"

Carolina did not appeal, using only five players for all forty minutes to beat N.C. State at home the night of February 15.

Heyman got to play twice more in the regular season, road wins at nonconference Navy and Seton Hall, but he stayed in Durham for the eagerly anticipated regular-season finale on February 25 in Chapel Hill, which was played under heavy security at Woollen Gym, including guardrails in front of the bleachers and chains at the bottom of each aisle.

Brown and Walsh watched in street clothes from the end of the UNC bench. Some Carolina fans booed McGuire, who was now more than ever rumored to be on the way out. Carolina defeated Duke 69–66 in overtime as the regionally televised rematch went off without trouble, largely because the chief antagonists were benched and the rest of the players were on their best behavior. The Tar Heels won the ACC race with a 12–2 record, but with no ACC Tournament participation their season ended abruptly at 19–4.

UNC's chance to win another national championship died with the NCAA probation.

Duke was dead, as well, because it couldn't work Heyman back into the lineup effectively enough. He made the All-ACC Tournament team, but Wake Forest beat the Blue Devils in the championship game, as Chappell and Packer avenged the loss of a year before. Duke was 22–6 and Heyman finished second to Chappell in the ACC scoring race, averaging 25 points and 11 rebounds. He was also the first sophomore in college basketball to make third team All-American in both wire-service polls.

After the season, the second college point-shaving scandal in ten years exploded. Two UNC players were eventually implicated, Moe and Lou Brown, a benchwarmer from New York who was no relation to Larry Brown but knew players all over the ACC.

Brown admitted to being the gamblers' go-between and under immunity testified against Aaron "the Bagman" Wagman, a New Yorker charged with thirty-seven counts of corruption and one charge of conspiracy. Over the next year, dozens of players were busted, but most made similar deals to help nail Wagman and his cohorts.

Four N.C. State players admitted shaving points against Wake Forest, Duke, Georgia Tech, Maryland, and South Carolina. Muehlbauer, Stan Niewierowski, Terry Litchfield, and Don Gallagher said they accepted money to influence the final scores of games, cooperating to avoid indictment.

They testified that players who took bribes in fixed contests made at least $1,000 a game. The gamblers and bookies stood to make a lot more by laying bets on teams to either lose games or win by less than they were favored. Culminating an investigation that had lasted three years, Hogan, the New York DA, convicted Wagman and three others for hiring players to shave the points. Wagman went to jail for doling out bribes of almost to $30,000 in two years.

Lou Brown's first-person account in *LOOK* magazine, told to Raleigh sportswriter Dick Herbert, fingered himself and Moe, the four State players and several from other schools in the East. Brown said the police had a tapped phone conversation in which Wagman offered him $1,000 and Moe $1,500 to fix the UNC-Clemson game in Charlotte in 1960, which heavily favored and nineteenth-ranked Carolina had won, but only by five points.

Moe admitted accepting $75 from one of the fixers but denied shaving points in any game and was never charged. He was still banned from playing in the NBA for his part in the scandal.

"I didn't see anything wrong in taking the money from Wagman for doing nothing," Moe told *LOOK* magazine. "But I guess I was involved, wasn't I?"

Most of the players involved went on to be law-abiding adults, remorseful for their wrongdoings. They were all impressionable kids at the time who made poor judgments, persuaded by the fixers that they weren't actually "dumping" games, only affecting final scores.

UNC's shocking ACC Tournament loss to Duke in 1960 was the perfect point-shaving game because the Tar Heels were so heavily favored they could have still won without covering the large point spread. But Brown wasn't blowing the whistle on any of his teammates, and the New York prosecutor stayed focused on the N.C. State players Brown had implicated. The game escaped scrutiny, and no UNC player ever admitted taking a bribe to try to hold down the score.

In the spring of 1961, McGuire's support was waning. Chancellor William Aycock gave him the famous ultimatum that getting off probation would determine whether UNC renewed his contract the year before it expired in 1963.

Despite his angelic face, Aycock was tough enough to stand up to McGuire and the relatively few well-heeled alumni who still sided with the controversial coach no matter how hot his water.

Aycock had once taken on the fat cats when McGuire was still king. One evening in 1960, with the investigation into McGuire's program under way, Aycock and his wife Grace walked from the chancellor's residence to have dinner at the Carolina Inn. Passing the old Pine Room Lounge off the main lobby, Aycock noticed a small group of prominent Rams Club boosters huddled around the bar. Aycock knew two of the men, Judge Carlisle Higgins and Fred Huffman, and walked in to say hello.

"We're holding a meeting and we're going to fire Chuck Erickson," Huffman told the chancellor, referring to the athletics director who was McGuire's boss and nemesis. "We believe he's the cause of McGuire's problems, and we don't want to lose our basketball coach."

Aycock nodded and suggested they all come by his office the next morning to discuss the matter further. The vigilantes arrived at the appointed hour to find chairs set up in front of Aycock's desk and reading material on each chair.

"Please take your time and go through this material," Aycock said, heading for the door of his office. "I think you'll find that McGuire's problems are not all because of Chuck Erickson."

The report included certain NCAA allegations, such as paying scouts to help recruit kids in New York City, plus UNC's own charges of poor sportsmanship, profanity, and bad bench behavior that led to fights in games against Wake Forest the last two seasons. When Aycock returned, the group had been forced into checkmate. None of the men could argue that rules and public appearances weren't important, and they left Aycock's office never to be heard from again about firing Erickson.

So when it came time to discipline McGuire a year later, Aycock had no problem penning the letter of April 28, 1961.

"In an effort to be absolutely fair to you, I inform you now that my decision will rest largely on the unfolding events during the next twelve months," Aycock wrote to McGuire. "The number of games won or lost during the next season will not be a material factor in my recommendation. All of us desire to help you in every way to avoid the many mistakes that have been made this year and to have a basketball program which will reflect the highest credit on the university."

For most of the summer things were quiet in Chapel Hill and also in Durham, where Bubas already had McGuire-like status. Their protagonists, Larry Brown and Art Heyman, were in Israel, where they settled their differences enough to cocaptain the U.S.A. team to a gold medal in the sixth annual Maccabiah Games, the Jewish Olympics.

In August, after denying reports all summer that he was heading to the NBA, McGuire quit to coach Wilt Chamberlain and the Philadelphia Warriors. He claimed that he stepped down with the stipulation that Smith get the job, but Aycock had made up his mind long before then that he wanted Smith. He said UNC needed a different kind of coach.

Thus, when Aycock eventually promoted Smith, it came with three mandates, and winning games was not among them.

"I told him not to worry about wins and losses," Aycock said, "just to run the program correctly, keep the university out of trouble, and make us proud of our student-athletes."

Smith remembered a couple of other specific orders Aycock gave him. "Make sure your players graduate, no problems with gambling, and no recruiting violations."

A new era of UNC basketball began under the thirty-one-year-old with no head-coaching experience and some big Irish shoes to fill. For the first time in years, Carolina found itself looking up at Duke.

RIVALRY RECORD IN THE 1950s
• Duke won 14; Carolina won 14

HOW THEY DID IN THE DECADE
• Duke 182–93 (.662); Carolina 168–90 (.651)

ACC CHAMPIONSHIPS
• Duke none; Carolina 1957

NCAA CHAMPIONSHIPS
• Duke none; Carolina 1957

RIVALRY RECORDS
• Tom Scott vs. Duke: 9–6
• Frank McGuire vs. Duke: 15–11
• Gerry Gerard vs. Carolina: 7–13
• Hal Bradley vs. Carolina: 14–11
• Dick Groat vs. Carolina: 5–4

BIGGEST UPSET
• Duke 71, Carolina 69, March 8, 1960

BEST QUOTE
"This is like Christmas in March."
(Vic Bubas)

3

DOMINATE, THEN INTEGRATE

Even Frank McGuire's departure and the sanctions that doomed Dean Smith's early teams couldn't dull the rivalry, largely because Art Heyman remained at Duke to remind Carolina of what it had lost. In retrospect, the blizzard of 1961 probably helped by immortalizing the fight that Heyman and Larry Brown started the night of February 4.

The game was on TV across five states, one of the earliest regional telecasts in the ACC. Thousands of viewers were holed up in the snowstorm watching the Blue Devils and Tar Heels tangle in the final minutes of Duke's 81–77 victory. Just as Carolina's 1957 televised national championship win over Kansas had made an indelible impression, the Brown-Heyman brouhaha lived on in ACC folklore.

If snatching Heyman away from Carolina, then knocking the Tar Heels out of the 1960 ACC Tournament, was Vic Bubas's Gettysburg, losing two potential starters to academics and severe recruiting restrictions were Smith's Waterloo after he had been named coach by UNC chancellor William Aycock.

Bill Friday, president of the Consolidated University of North Carolina, laid down the hammer on unethical conduct that he would wield over college sports for fifty more years in various watchdog capacities. Beyond the NCAA probation levied on McGuire's last team, Friday saw a far more insidious enemy plaguing college basketball in the South.

Because of the gambling scandals that had migrated from the Northeast, Friday abolished the Dixie Classic Christmas tournament, where according to testimony a lot of the point-shaving deals were made. He also imposed institutional penalties on N.C. State and UNC that reined in recruiting and limited their schedules to sixteen regular-season games in 1962.

Everett Case was the veteran Wolfpack coach who had already been on probation twice. Smith had inherited McGuire's team that was coming off NCAA sanctions in 1961. Friday restricted both to recruiting no more than two players from outside of the ACC region, figuring this would lessen the influence scouts and flesh peddlers from Indiana and New York had on the two programs. It hurt the unknown Smith far more than Case, whose recruiting network was well established and kept his name alive.

While Bubas had Heyman, and added sensational sophomore Jeff Mullins and 6' 10" Jay Buckley—Duke's tallest player ever—to his varsity, Smith began his head-coaching career with a thin squad that had lost 5 of McGuire's top 8 from the year before. Gone were All-ACC stars York Larese and Doug Moe, fellow senior Dick Kepley, and two guys who had flunked out, Yogi Poteet and Kenny "Moose" McComb. Another talented and tough New Yorker recruited by McGuire, Bill Galantai, lost his eligibility for a second straight year after the NCAA discovered he had played for a semipro team one summer.

The losses were devastating for UNC. Freshmen weren't eligible in 1961, so that kind of attrition could not be remedied by simply signing up some high school hotshots to play the next season. Juniors Larry Brown, Donnie Walsh, and Dieter Krause were the only experienced players; all of them had been involved in fights with Duke the last two years and helped keep their new coach in McGuire's shadow.

Smith posed an uncomfortable contrast to his predecessor. With a large nose and angular face, he was homelier than the handsome McGuire and shied away from the spotlight. He spoke in a high-pitched, nasal voice and said so few inflammatory things that one local editorial noted, "The successor to Frank McGuire, one of the most dynamic men in sports, is not overpowering in personality."

He was smart as a whip, though, and quick of mind and tongue when he had to be. UNC Athletics Director Chuck Erickson, who was still sore that Aycock hadn't consulted him on hiring McGuire's successor, called Smith on the carpet one day to question how much time he spent on the telephone.

"Your phone bill is higher than mine and the chancellor's," said Erickson, who was picking on Smith because of criticism from alumni who had wanted a bigger-name coach.

"I should hope so," countered Smith, "You and the chancellor aren't trying to recruit basketball players."

Smith grew up as a three-sport athlete in Emporia, Kansas, where his family attended two Baptist church services each Sunday and one on Wednesday night. Competition was part of his life from an early age, when he played in table tennis tournaments. His parents also set report card goals and paid Smith and his sister an extra allowance if they made good enough grades.

His mother was a teacher and superintendent, his father a teacher and coach who had been the first to integrate Kansas high school basketball. The Kansas state coaches association wanted Alfred Smith to cut Paul Terry, a black player at Emporia High School. Alfred Smith refused, offering to resign his position. Terry stayed on the team and the board backed down.

That obviously made an impression on young Dean Smith, a lifelong liberal Democrat who took public stands on a number of sensitive issues, speaking for integration and a nuclear freeze and against the death penalty. He got hooked on coaching by hanging out on the field and at the gym with his father at Emporia and later Topeka High and doodling plays for his dad to look at after practice. He earned an academic scholarship to Kansas and warmed the bench for Dr. Forrest "Phog" Allen, giving him plenty of idle time to think about strategies, substitutions, and how to treat his players.

After graduation and a year helping to coach the KU freshmen, Smith joined the Air Force and served in Germany, where he was a player-coach for the base basketball team and met his first boss, Bob Spear. When Spear started up basketball at the Air Force Academy, he lured Smith back from Europe and arranged for him to finish out his military commitment as an assistant coach. Smith was still there when he attended the 1957 Final Four in Kansas City and met McGuire.

Earning a salary of $9,100 a year, Smith admitted all he wanted to do was coach basketball and follow Aycock's mandate to rebuild the UNC program. But he had to learn the hard way from Bubas, who had already contacted many of the high school players that Smith tried to recruit. He noticed that Bubas always seemed to recruit players in the Midwest while his assistants were assigned to other regions of the country. One recruit's mother showed him several handwritten notes she had received from the Duke coach.

Smith wanted to recruit nationally and, like Bubas, segmented the country and compiled his own detailed files on each prospect. He was to get even better than Bubas about sending birthday cards to the prospects, their siblings and parents, plus Christmas cards.

Smith wasn't as organized with his first team, failing to bring out a game ball for his head-coaching debut on December 2, 1961, against Virginia and then totally forgetting the first innovation he had put in during preseason practice. Players could take themselves out of the game by raising a fist, then put themselves back in when they were rested. This system was to insure maximum effort while they were on the court, but Larry Brown found himself futilely thrusting a fist at Smith, who jumped up, pumped a fist back at Brown and yelled, "Way to go, Larry!"

The Tar Heels finished 8–9 in Smith's first season, losing by 22 points at Duke when the Blue Devils were ranked sixth in the country and playing them closer at home in an 82–74 loss. They barely lost to South Carolina in the ACC Tournament, giving Smith what would be his only losing record in 36 seasons as a head coach.

Duke won 14 of its first 16 games in the 1961–62 season and finished second to Wake Forest in the ACC race, losing to the unranked Deacons at home with Heyman sidelined by a severely sprained ankle. He missed a total of four games during the season and was still hobbling during the ACC Tournament. The Blue Devils beat Maryland in the first game but were stunned by sixth-place Clemson in the semifinals, sending the 12–14 Tigers into their only ACC championship game ever. An embarrassed Heyman promised sportswriters afterward that the 1963 season would be a lot better for him and his team.

Wake Forest, with guard Billy Packer and All-American forward Len Chappell, won the 1962 ACC Championship and reached the Final Four for the only time in its history. The Deacons lost in Louisville to Ohio State and a couple of guys named John Havlicek and Jerry Lucas. The Buckeyes in turn lost to Cincinnati, which became the third team (after Oklahoma State in 1945 and '46 and San Francisco ten years later) to win back-to-back national championships.

Wake edged UCLA 82–80 in the third-place game and helped the ACC finally earn a first-round bye in the NCAA Tournament. Byes were awarded to leagues with the best cumulative NCAA record. UNC's 1957 national championship, on its own, was not enough. Duke and Wake Forest making the regional final in 1960 and '61 got the ACC close. Wake's victory over UCLA (which was the last NCAA loss for John Wooden and his Bruins until 1974) gave the ACC a 13–5 mark over the past five years, promising the 1963 champion a bye and much-needed rest after its own grueling tournament.

In Smith's second season, there was still not a shot clock in college basketball. On December 17, 1962, the Tar Heels visited Kentucky two days after having been blown out at Indiana by the Hoosiers and ballyhooed Van Ardsdale brothers. They dressed in the bowels of Memorial Gym during the freshman game as the crowd stomped and shook the ceiling of the old bandbox right above their heads. Larry Brown got so nervous that he broke out in hives. Smith walked in, saw the red blotches on Brown's face and called the players together. He had to try something to keep his team from getting blown out again.

"Let's pretend that the uniforms they're wearing tonight say TENNESSEE," he said of the Southeastern Conference school that wasn't much of a basketball power. The players laughed and seemed to loosen up.

Smith then said that they were going to test Kentucky with a stall offense that "we've fooled around with" in practice the last few weeks.

"Larry," he said to Brown, his senior point guard, "when we have the ball, you hold it out near midcourt and let's see what they do on defense."

"Yogi," he said to Poteet, who had returned to school and become Carolina's best defensive player, "you shadow Nash wherever he goes, try to keep the ball out of his hands."

Nash was Cotton Nash, the latest Kentucky All-American who became so frustrated with Poteet's face-guarding defense that he stopped moving and spent much of the game on the bench being cursed at by his coach, Adolph Rupp, the famed Baron of the Bluegrass.

Brown's stalling tactics made the Wildcats spread out and chase the Tar Heels, who scored easily on weaves and cuts to the basket. When they missed, sophomore leaper Billy Cunningham grabbed one of his 17 rebounds. Nash missed 9 of his 12 shots and wound up standing off to the side, covered by Poteet, watching everyone else go four-on-four.

Carolina led most of the second half and, feeding off the frustrated Kentucky crowd, held on to win 68–66. The players carried Smith off the court, several yelling something about Tennessee. After speaking with the few North Carolina sportswriters who made the trip to Lexington—while the throng of Kentucky reporters sought Rupp's explanation—Smith and trainer John Lacey walked the two miles back to the team hotel, savoring the win in virtual privacy.

The spread offense produced so much teamwork and so many high-percentage shots—both Smith trademarks—that he kept the maneuver as a regular part of practice each day. Then, one afternoon in Woollen Gym the following January, Brown accidentally invented the offense that would become the bane of opponents for years to come.

Standing under the basket, quietly talking to his defense, Smith called for a switch from zone to man-to-man to see if Brown recognized the change. Brown did not, saw what he thought was a breakdown in the zone and drove the lane for a layup. Smith blew his whistle and walked out onto the court.

"Larry!" he shouted, "run that again."

This time, Smith motioned for Cunningham to stand in the corner and break toward the basket when Brown made his move. Smith told one of the defenders to block Brown's drive down the lane. When he did, Brown saw Cunningham cutting for the goal and fed him a perfect bounce pass.

"Run it again!" Smith shouted in his Kansas twang.

They ran it over and over, each time with Brown making a move past one player, getting picked up by another and hitting the uncovered teammate for a layup. Afterward, Brown was so tired he asked Smith if it was a conditioning drill as punishment for missing the change in defenses at the beginning of practice.

"No," Smith said, "we just invented a new offense."

The Four Corners offense wasn't enough to beat Duke in 1963, mainly because Heyman was having a monster senior season and wouldn't let any opponent get the lead and hold the ball on the Blue Devils, who became the second team (after UNC in 1957) to go 14–0 in the ACC.

Duke not only had Heyman, who fulfilled his promise from the end of the last season by leading the league in scoring, and Mullins, but Bubas had also put together the tallest team in college basketball while keeping the lethal fast break going that he had learned under Case at N.C. State.

Buckley was backed up by another 6' 10" player, sophomore Hack Tison. Led by Heyman, Mullins and Buckley, all among the top 10 rebounders in the ACC, the Blue Devils played eight guys and literally ran opponents off the court with so many fast breaks they wound up setting a school record by making 51 percent of their field goals.

Duke had beaten a damn good Carolina team by eight points in Chapel Hill and long ago clinched first place in the ACC when Heyman's last home game arrived. Turned loose by Bubas, he scored a career-high of 40 points, and pulled down 24 rebounds, in a 106–93 thrashing of the Tar Heels and received a three-minute standing ovation when he walked off the Duke Indoor Stadium court with twenty-two seconds left.

"First time I've ever given a player completely free reign," Bubas said. "It was a gamble but it worked out. Everyone talks about how great Dick Groat was. Groat was a great basketball player. I guarded him and he is a good friend of mine. But Heyman is bigger and stronger. He's got to be the best player who ever put on a Duke uniform."

A near-unanimous pick for conference player of the year, Heyman averaged 25 points and 11 rebounds against every defense imaginable. Smith threw the kitchen sink at him to no avail.

"We doubled and tripled him in the lane because he was such a great scorer—and we knew he wasn't going to pass the ball back out," Smith said. "We had two of the best defensive players in the conference on him, Larry Brown and Yogi Poteet, but he kept making baskets."

Of all of his accomplishments, Heyman was proudest that, after the 1960

Dixie Classic in his sophomore year, Duke did not lose another game to the Tar Heels in which he played, ending his career 5–1 against UNC.

Heyman then won his first and only ACC Tournament title, rallying the Blue Devils from 8 points down by scoring 15 of Duke's 20 points in the decisive stretch to unseat two-time defending champ Wake Forest 68–57 in the championship game. As the horn sounded, Heyman grabbed Bubas and shouted, "We waited four years for this, baby! We did it, we did it!"

Bubas said winning the ACC championship had become an obsession with Heyman. "It was the only thing left. Art talked about it a lot. He didn't want to be like Oscar Robertson and Wilt Chamberlain—player of the year in the nation, All-American and all that, but without a title."

Thanks to the prior success of UNC and Wake Forest, Duke was the first ACC team to have a bye in the NCAA Tournament. Despite entering the East Regional on such a high note, Heyman had two subpar games against NYU and St. Joe's, missing 26 of his 35 shots. Thankfully, All-ACC Mullins, the league's third leading scorer behind Heyman and Cunningham, bailed him out and led the Blue Devils to victories over both and their first Final Four, the third ACC team to reach the promised land.

Duke faced a Loyola (Chicago) team on Friday night, March 22 in Louisville that started four black players—Vic Rouse, Les Hunter, Ron Miller, and Jerry Harkness joined Johnny Egan, the white starter. The Ramblers led by 13 points at the half and 17 in the second before Heyman sparked a desperation rally that cut the deficit to 3 with four and a half minutes left, but the Blue Devils were spent, scored only one more point the rest of the game and lost 94–75. Heyman and Mullins combined for 50 points and 23 rebounds.

All five Loyola starters scored in double figures and the next night denied Cincinnati and its incredible trio of Ron Bonham, Tom Thacker, and George Wilson a third straight national championship. Loyola won its only NCAA title but, more importantly, continued changing the color of the Final Four and the character of college basketball from mostly white kids taking jump shots to a more athletic game played above the rim.

Despite not making the championship game, Heyman was still named Final Four Most Outstanding Player (MOP) after leading Duke's 85–63 romp over Oregon in the third-place game. He was the first pick in the 1963 NBA draft by the New York Knicks but after making all-rookie in 1964 bombed out as an oft-injured journeyman pro, blaming it on the fact that he could never find another coach he loved as much as Bubas.

Heyman was a contradiction, on the court the prototype of a Duke villain thirty years later named Christian Laettner and off the floor a jokester who liked to tease his teammates and give them unflattering nicknames like Needle Nose and Baldy.

He was a great basketball player, but not a gifted natural athlete; a great scorer but not a pure shooter; a ferocious rebounder but not a particularly high jumper. He had a nose for the ball and uncanny instincts for the game. Bubas turned out to be the perfect coach for him, a father figure and disciplinarian who put the ball in Heyman's hands.

The publicly cool Bubas was a firebrand privately, getting Heyman ready to play by slamming him against lockers before the game. Heyman loved the motivational ploy and Bubas' Svengali-like spell over him. He often answered Bubas' commands by irreverently saying, "Yes, *Mein Führer!*"

Heyman prided himself in always playing hard and, off the court, played hard, too. He stayed in trouble throughout his career. As a senior, he won a highly publicized legal battle after almost taking out the eye of another Duke student in a dorm fight. In return, his own teammates nicknamed him "The Pest."

He visited local hospitals but was the last candidate for Boy Scout. Heyman had a car, a white Grand Prix convertible, until Bubas made him give it up after he was seen driving around town at all hours of the night. On his last weekend with the car, Heyman took a Duke coed to Myrtle Beach, South Carolina, and checked into a motel under the name of Mr. and Mrs. Oscar Robertson, the black All-American. He couldn't hide and didn't want to.

"A weaker person would have left," said Heyman, who was also questioned during the point-shaving scandals because several kids he had played with in New York were under investigation at various colleges in North Carolina and Pennsylvania.

"I was so oblivious to the notoriety. I lived in my own little world. I did what I wanted to do. But I never drank, never smoked and always took care of myself. I went down there as a kid and came out a man. You had to be a man to survive all the crap I went through."

Bubas reloaded with an endless line of stars—including Mullins, Jack Marin, Steve Vacendak and Bob Verga, and just missing on Bill Bradley when the future Rhodes Scholar opted for Princeton at the last minute (just as another future politician, Tom McMillen, would jilt Carolina for Maryland five years later). Two other players that Bubas barely missed on were West Virginia All-American Rod Thorn and Fred Hetzel, who was the foundation of Lefty Driesell's program at Davidson.

. . .

Even with Bradley, it was hard to imagine how Duke could have been any stronger on paper in 1964. Mullins, whom Bubas plucked from Lexington, Kentucky, right under Rupp's nose, was the best player in the ACC, averaging 25 points and taking more than twice as many shots as any other Blue Devil. Nonetheless, he had a great supporting cast, eight deep with fellow senior Buzzy Harrison and two terrific sophomores from Bubas's recruiting bailiwick of Pennsylvania, Marin and Vacendak.

Marin, a 6' 6" southpaw distinguishable by his blond hair, fair skin, and large purple birthmark on his shooting shoulder, turned into one of the most versatile players in the country, scoring inside and out and often roaming the top of the Duke zone to bother the opponent's outside shooters.

Vacendak, a self-assured and selfless 6' 1" guard from the schoolyards of Scranton, gradually became Duke's leader. Rather than hunting his own shot, Vacendak set up the array of scorers Bubas brought into the program. He did not start as a sophomore but was usually in the game at the end as the Blue Devils tried to prove they could be as successful in the ACC and go further in the postseason without Heyman.

In mid-December, Duke dropped an overtime game at unranked Vanderbilt and ten days later got blown out at Michigan by the third-ranked Wolverines and their star, "Jazzy" Cazzie Russell. A third loss in their first ten games came against No. 1 Kentucky in the Sugar Bowl Tournament on New Year's Eve. Bubas couldn't figure out whether his team was overrated or overscheduled. The Blue Devils then won ten straight that included a 20-point win at home against struggling Carolina.

The Tar Heels, who came off a 15–6 season in which they lost to Wake Forest by a point in the 1963 ACC Tournament semifinals, graduated five seniors and were left with All-ACC star Cunningham and a roster of seventeen other players. Smith had re-recruited Cunningham, who was signed by McGuire, and may have felt like he owed the junior jumping jack a chance to be a star. Instead, he made him a one-man team.

"My worst coaching job," Smith lamented. "I couldn't settle on a lineup, I used so many different combinations and relied too much on Cunningham. It was Billy, get the rebound, Billy, bring it up against the press. It was also the first time I ever let a player rest at half court on a fast break if he had gotten the rebound."

As the season teetered on the brink of disaster, Smith felt the heat of alumni for the first time and no longer had Aycock, who had stepped down as chancellor, to protect him. With Cunningham leading the ACC in scoring and rebounding, critics felt the team should be doing better than a .500 record. Smith turned to his interest in theology and read a book given to him by his sister, *Beyond Ourselves,* by Peter and Catherine Marshall. He particularly hung on the chapter entitled "The Power of Helplessness" on learning to not worry about what one cannot control.

The book also convinced Smith to review his goals and philosophies and to decide that the mistake he made with Cunningham was a sign that he had veered off course. He vowed that, as long as he coached, he would adhere to what he always believed, that basketball was a team game and should be played unselfishly. It was too late to salvage the current season, however, which ended with five losses in Carolina's last six games, fifth place in the ACC and a 12–12 record overall.

Duke, meanwhile, had pulled it together. The Blue Devils concluded their ten-game streak with a pulsating 82–75 win over Davidson, whose coach Driesell was a Duke grad and felt disrespected by his alma mater. Driesell had the fourth-ranked team in the country and wanted a home-and-home series, one game in Durham and the next year at the Charlotte Coliseum. After Bubas refused, he nevertheless agreed to play at Duke Indoor Stadium to get the exposure for his program and the chance at an upset.

To motivate his players, Driesell reminded them that Bubas had given his last scholarship to Buckley over his own star, Hetzel, who was having a much better career. Buckley got word and was spurred to outplay Hetzel. The game stayed close throughout and came down to the last few possessions before the Blue Devils pulled it out 82–75. Incensed by several calls that he felt cost his team the win he so badly wanted, Driesell ill-advisedly called Bubas a coward for not giving him a return match. The remark would come back to kill his chances to take over the Duke program.

Despite a one-point loss at Wake Forest, which snapped their 28-game ACC winning streak, the 1964 Blue Devils ran away with another regular-season race by four games and finished 13–1, capped by a 35-point rout at Carolina that had the crowd in Woollen Gym booing and then bolting early. They beat UNC for a third time six days later and cruised to a second consecutive ACC Tournament title with an average victory margin of 23 points. They handled Villanova in the East Regional semifinal and then demolished Connecticut, coached by Bubas's former assistant Fred Shabel (who had recruited Heyman in 1959 when Duke was without a head coach) to advance to their second straight Final Four.

The site was Kansas City, which apparently didn't know the difference between the basketball team that had won the 1957 national championship there and another from the state of North Carolina. As the Blue Devils arrived at the hotel next to Municipal Auditorium, a sign read "Welcome Tar Heels." Predictably, it both amused and angered them.

This time Duke defeated Michigan to reach the national championship, avenging the loss in December in Ann Arbor. Buckley, who had been badly outplayed by Michigan center Bill Buntin in the first game, continued his hot streak and had his career game with 25 points and 14 rebounds. Tison added 13 rebounds. Mullins' scored 21 points as Duke put five players in double figures to offset 31 by Russell.

Playing for its first national championship in any sport, Duke faced a small-and-quick opponent the next night called UCLA. The Bruins had had a nice program in the early sixties and were also looking for their first NCAA title under coach John Wooden. They were led by a pair of All-American guards, Gail Goodrich and Walt Hazzard, but sophomore Kenny Washington from Beaufort, South Carolina, who would be focal point in the escalating Duke-UCLA series because of his race and home region, became the unsung hero.

Mullins, Marin, and Buckley combined for 56 points, but a whopping 29 turnovers against Wooden's zone press helped UCLA win 98–83—the highest-scoring national championship game to that date—and begin its string of ten titles over the next twelve years. Had Bradley been in the Duke lineup instead of dominating the inferior Ivy League, perhaps he would have helped offset 27 points by Goodrich and 11 from Hazzard, the Final Four MOP. The real shocker was Washington, who was averaging 4 points a game but came off the bench to contribute 26 and a team-high 12 rebounds.

With Cincinnati and Ohio State fading, Duke had become a dominant program in college basketball by playing in back-to-back Final Fours even though it had not won a national championship.

Besides Mullins, who averaged 22 points and 9 rebounds for his career, Buckley and Harrison also graduated. Bubas, however, had added sensational shooter Bob Verga and forward Bob Riedy to a lineup that still had Tison, Marin, and Vacendak. He also had young assistant coaches Bucky Waters and Chuck Daly, two names to remember.

Smith worked hard at recruiting, too, and finally had his first player of note moving up to the varsity. Bob Lewis, a skinny 6' 3" shooting guard from Washington, D.C., had first seen Carolina play on television in 1963 when the Tar Heels upset Notre Dame in South Bend. Lewis pulled a box of recruiting letters out from under his bed and found the one from North Carolina, which he hadn't opened previously.

Smith borrowed one of McGuire's old traits, charming the mother on Lewis's official visit to Chapel Hill and asking her directly if she would let him take care of her son over the next four years. She liked Smith and when interviewed by Charlotte *Observer* columnist Ronald Green, one of Smith's pals, she said that she was sending her son to UNC.

Smith celebrated the recruiting victory but wasn't sure the skinny Lewis could handle bigger, stronger college players. As Lewis wowed large crowds at 1964 freshman games with his double-digit scoring, Smith went right into Duke's prime recruiting territory to chase the one player he *knew* could play as a collegian.

Making sure he matched wits with Bubas, Smith battled the Blue Devils for Larry Miller, a highly coveted high school star from Western Pennsylvania. Carolina assistant coach Ken Rosemond spent a year befriending Miller's father, a third-shift factory worker. In the days of unlimited recruiting visits, Rosemond spent numerous afternoons sitting with Miller's father on the front porch of their home in blue-collar Catasauqua, forcing himself to drink the Pabst Blue Ribbon beer he hated and talking while they waited for Larry to get home from school.

One afternoon, Rosemond told the younger Miller, "You know, Larry, the saddest thing is that if you went to Duke you'd be going all that way and you'd still be five minutes from heaven." Miller, a strapping 6' 4" who lifted weights before it was fashionable for basketball players to do so, was expected to fall in line and join Duke's stable of stars.

Up until then, Bubas had owned the Pennsylvania-Ohio corridor, using Dick Groat's legacy and his help in recruiting stars Marin, Vacendak, and Mullins from contiguous Kentucky. Groat had gone on to be the National League MVP for the Pittsburgh Pirates in 1960, the year they won the World Series, but always said he liked basketball better and was still considered Duke's greatest player ever.

In 1964, there was no "early signing period" and most high school stars waited until after their senior seasons to chose a college. Bubas and Waters met Miller and his parents at the Holiday Inn in Allentown, Pennsylvania, in May. Miller had tears in his eyes as Bubas took the folded grant-in-aid from his inside jacket pocket and handed it to him with a ballpoint pen. They weren't the tears of joy Bubas had expected.

"I was crying because Vic Bubas was a wonderful person and I really liked Bucky Waters, too," Miller said of his refusal to sign. "It was really emotional; I couldn't decide between Duke and Carolina."

The week before, he had visited Chapel Hill and hopped fraternities with Cunningham and Lewis. Smokey Robinson and the Miracles played a concert on campus during Jubilee Weekend. "They asked me if I wanted to go to the movies or to a party," Miller recalled. "I said, 'Are you kidding?'"

Despite Duke's emergence as a national power with consecutive trips to the Final Four, Miller was confident that whatever school he picked would have a winning team and actually liked the idea of being the player around whom Smith rebuilt UNC basketball. Miller was a two-hundred-pound man-child who had given up teenage gangs to concentrate on getting a scholarship. He always won in high school and played against semipros twice his age in the old Eastern League during the summer.

Finally, Miller told Bubas and Smith that he would invite the college coach of his choice to his high school graduation in June. Smith was conducting his summer camp in sweltering Woollen Gym when a secretary ran in to tell him his wife had called with the good news. Miller wanted him to be in Pennsylvania the next night.

Still, Miller would have to play his year of freshman ball first, waiting to join the varsity and a chance to bail out his beleaguered head coach.

Bubas got some bad news in December of 1964, when Case, his old coach at N.C. State, stepped down after two games into the new season because of failing health. After forty-one years of coaching high school, naval, and college teams, Case's overall record was 1,159–214, an incredible .844 winning percentage. His State teams won six Southern Conference titles and four ACC crowns. Bubas visited his mentor at his Raleigh home and spent an hour reminiscing about old times. Case was succeeded by assistant Press Maravich, whose sensational son Pete was tearing up opponents at Raleigh Broughton High School while already wearing his future trademark floppy socks.

There was an irony to Case's retirement. It coincided with the return of his old adversary, Frank McGuire, who had been hired by *South* Carolina to energize a basketball program that never had a winning ACC record in the eleven-year history of the league. McGuire was gone from North Carolina only three years, and had been coaching Wilt Chamberlain and the Philadelphia Warriors of the NBA. When the franchise moved to San Francisco, McGuire refused to leave his East Coast comfort zone and connections.

It wasn't long before McGuire ran afoul of his old enemies in the ACC, Duke Athletics Director Eddie Cameron and Commissioner Jim Weaver. Having inherited a terrible team, McGuire recruited more than coached that first year; he was busy laying a new set of tracks for his Underground Railroad from New

York. Only one player remained at North Carolina from McGuire's old glory days there. He had left without ever getting a chance to coach Billy Cunningham, who was now the best player in the ACC.

By 1965, Cunningham was a senior who was leading the league in scoring and rebounding for the second straight season. With the high-scoring Bobby Lewis moving up to the varsity, UNC still lost four consecutive games in late December and January. Upon returning from the fourth straight at Wake Forest, the team bus rolled to a stop in front of Woollen Gym. An effigy of Smith hung from a tree.

Cunningham jumped off the bus, pulled down the dummy and ran off the few students who had the guts to stick around and wait for the team bus. Smith claimed he didn't know exactly what happened, but nevertheless spent a disconsolate evening at the home of friends Lou and Florence Vine, whom he had known since the McGuire days.

"Dean came over and was so depressed," said Lou Vine, a local veterinarian. "We sat around, had a few drinks and Dean finally said, 'Maybe I'm in the wrong business.' He never doubted his ability to coach, but the criticism was getting to him. Florence and I both told him, 'You've got to stick it out at least another year.'"

Next up on the schedule was a trip to Durham on Saturday, January 9, and sixth-ranked Duke, which Smith had not defeated in seven games as a head coach dating back to 1962. The local newspapers noted that UNC entered the game with 837 all-time victories, just one ahead of Duke. A win for the Blue Devils would pull them even.

Bubas made a name for himself by shocking Carolina in his first season, but Smith was now in his fourth year as a head coach. News of the hanging made him wonder what his team thought, and how it would react at Duke. He held individual meetings with every player the next day, something he had never done during the season, and found out they were all upset by the student prank. Confident that his squad was solidly behind him, Smith tried to channel its emotion by saying at practice that afternoon, "That's behind us, now let's go on from here."

He planned to substitute less than usual against Duke; the starters would play until one of them gave him the fist, or tired signal. Smith instructed them to spread the court, keep passing and keep moving for as long as it took before someone broke open for a good shot, hoping to wear Duke down.

Precision, more than motivation, gave them an early lead on the favored Blue Devils, who had won eight of their first nine games. It wasn't a full-blown stall, but more an exercise in execution to methodically work the offense until they got high-percentage shots close to the basket. That's how Smith differentiated himself—as a coach whose teams patiently passed the ball around the key and eventually to their two top scorers.

Duke, with superior personnel, tried to speed up the game by shooting quickly and crashing the boards. Dogged on defense by Cunningham, Marin could not get the ball and attempted only nine shots. The Blue Devils hit less than 40 percent and allowed the Tar Heels to be a two-man team. Cunningham finished with 22 points, Lewis with 21, and Carolina triumphed 65–62.

Smith's first win over Duke did not settle the natives. Students hung him in effigy again four days later, while someone played "Taps" on a trumpet, following a home loss to N.C. State by the exact 65–62 score. After a rare two-week break in the middle of the season, Carolina lost again at home to Maryland. But beating Duke had given his critics pause, and when UNC won six straight games Smith finally seemed safe from the lynch mob.

In the finale in Chapel Hill, the same slowdown strategy worked against the now No. 5 Blue Devils, with Cunningham and Lewis this time combining for 45 points and 25 rebounds. The Tar Heels won their seventh in a row 71–66 and finished 10–4 in the ACC, in a three-way tie for second place. They were 15–8 overall and thought they could be 1965 ACC champions, but Cunningham turned ice cold in the second half and they got hammered by Wake Forest in the opening round of the 1965 ACC Tournament.

Cunningham ended his career as Carolina's all-time leading rebounder and second-leading scorer behind Lennie Rosenbluth; he led the ACC in both categories his last two years and as a senior won conference Player of the Year. He only made second- and third-team All-American because he never participated in the NCAA Tournament and showcased his talents on a national stage, missing the college recognition of his Duke counterparts.

In the 1965 ACC title game, N.C. State reserve Larry Worsley came off the bench to score 30 points on 14 of 19 shooting, as the unranked Wolfpack defeated Duke to deny the Blue Devils a third consecutive NCAA bid, which in 1965 still went only to the ACC Tournament champion. Worsley won the tourney MVP, renamed that year in honor of Case, who was gravely ill but managed to both present the award and join his last team in the tradition he began, cutting down the nets.

Happy for his fading mentor, Bubas believed that playing the tournament at Reynolds Coliseum gave State too much of an edge. His team had won the regular season and thought it should have also been ACC champions—and would have been on a neutral floor. The 1965 Blue Devils won 20 games (20–5) and ended ranked in the top 10 in both wire-service polls, but still sat home. State got a first-round bye and six-day layoff before its East Regional opener.

Princeton, on the other hand, had a warm-up game by beating Penn State on March 8 and, behind All-American Bill Bradley, routed State in the regional semifinal at College Park, Maryland, to join the highest-scoring Final Four in history. The Ivy League champ Tigers lost to Michigan, then Bradley set an NCAA Tournament record that still stands with 58 points in a third-place romp over Wichita State. UCLA won its second straight national championship, defeating Michigan 91–80 in another wide open title game. Gail Goodrich had 42 points and Cazzie Russell 28, but the Final Four MOP still went to Bradley as a parting tribute to his college career. Like Heyman two years earlier, his performance in the consolation game counted heavily in the voting of courtside reporters.

Just after the 1965 Final Four, UCLA and Duke agreed to an unusual and historic two-year series. The Bruins would visit Durham and Charlotte for back-to-back games against the Blue Devils early the next season, and then play two more games at UCLA on consecutive days the following year.

Duke was anxious to use the UCLA games in December of 1965 as a barometer for the new season, but the week before, the Blue Devils got caught looking ahead and were ambushed in Columbia by an improved South Carolina team. McGuire had already stocked it with six surly sophomores from the New York area, just as he had done at the other Carolina.

The game was rough and nasty; McGuire had new punks, with different uniforms, and several times the teams had to be separated. Much of the bad blood stemmed from McGuire's accusation that Duke's Eddie Cameron had wielded his power the year before to keep tall and talented recruit Mike Grosso from playing for South Carolina. After Grosso failed to make the 800 on his SATs required by the ACC for a scholarship, McGuire claimed a rich uncle was paying his way as a freshman. Several schools complained to the conference office. The ACC's investigation rebuked the rich uncle theory and concluded that someone else was funding Grosso's scholarship. He was banned from the league and wound up at Louisville. South Carolina and McGuire escaped retribution other than losing Grosso.

Duke rebounded from the 73–71 loss in a big way, defeating two-time defending national champion UCLA on consecutive days, victories that brought the school tremendous national publicity and not all of it good. The sweep was featured in a *Sports Illustrated* story that used the line "blood on the Carolina

'rank McGuire and the 1958 team started a feud when his team refused to leave the court after a loss at Duke.
Left to right) Bob Cunningham, Joe Quigg (who broke his leg and missed the season), ACC Player of the Year
'ete Brennan, and Harvey Salz. *(Courtesy of the University of North Carolina)*

Vic Bubas (lower right) and his 1960 team flamed the feud by shocking Carolina in the ACC semifinals after having lost three lopsided games to the Tar Heels that season. Carroll Youngkin (last player on right, top row) had 30 points and 17 rebounds. *(Courtesy of Duke University)*

A brawl breaks out after Art Heyman grabbed Larry Brown, resulting in the suspension of Heyman and UNC players Brown and Donnie Walsh. *(Courtesy of Harold Moore)*

McGuire resigned under pressure after the 1961 season and was succeeded by his thirty-year-old assistant, Dean Smith, who McGuire had brought to UNC. *(Courtesy of the University of North Carolina)*

Suspended Brown, left, and Walsh sat out practice before the rematch with Duke, which Carolina won in overtime. *(Courtesy of Mike Ronman)*

Vic Bubas had put together a juggernaut in 1962: (left to right) Fred Schmidt, Jeff Mullins, Jay Buckley (the ACC's first 6' 10" player), Art Heyman, and Buzzy Harrison. *(Courtesy of Duke University)*

Five Tar Heels guarding Heyman couldn't keep him from scoring 40 points and grabbing 24 rebounds in his last home game at Duke on February 23, 1963. *(Courtesy of Duke University)*

Mike Lewis sinks the decisive free throw in a pressure-packed 21–20 slowdown over Carolina in the 1966 ACC Tournament semifinals. "The rim looked as big as a dime," Lewis said. *(Courtesy of Harold Moore)*

Bubas and Steve Vacendak, 1966 ACC Tournament MVP and Player of the Year, snip nets after Duke defeated N.C. State the next night to win Bubas's last ACC championship. *(Courtesy of Harold Moore)*

The changing of the guard was completed in 1967 when UNC's sterling sophomore class moved up to the varsity. Dean Smith celebrates his first ACC championship with the team—after Carolina's third win over Duke that season. *(Courtesy of John Page)*

Duke assistant coaches Hubie Brown, left, and Chuck Daly, center, went on to their own standout careers when neither was named to succeed their boss, Vic Bubas, in 1969. *(Courtesy of Duke University)*

UNC broke the color barrier in 1968 with star guard Charlie Scott, who joined the ACC champs and Final Four line-up of Bill Bunting, Dick Grubar, Rusty Clark, and Larry Miller. Scott's 40 points would be the difference in Carolina's 1969 ACC title win over Duke. *(Courtesy of the University of North Carolina)*

Phil Ford ran the famous Four Corners offense for four years and also became UNC's all-time leading scorer. *(Courtesy of Sally Sather)*

Kenny Dennard celebrates the Blue Devils' 1978 ACC Championship and Final Four run with a raucous dunk against Villanova in the NCAA Tournament. *(Courtesy of Thomas McGuire)*

After taking over Duke in 1980 and rebuilding the program, Mike Krzyzewski's last key recruit was point guard Tom Amaker (4) who joined a lineup of Mark Alarie, Jay Bilas, Johnny Dawkins, and David Henderson. *(Courtesy of Duke University)*

Tar Heel seniors Pete Chilcutt, King Rice, and Rick Fox celebrate the blowout of Duke in the 1991 ACC Tournament. *(Courtesy of Hugh Morton)*

Carolina followed Duke's back-to-back titles with the 1993 national championship and took extra pleasure in receiving the trophy from Duke's Tom Butters, chairman of the NCAA Basketball Committee. *(Courtesy of Scott Sharpe)*

In 1996 Krzyzewski returned from his back illness, after missing most of the 1995 season, and coached his last game against Smith in 1997. "I loved competing against him," he said of the retiring legend. *(Courtesy of Hugh Morton)*

moon" and related how certain fans at Duke Indoor Stadium taunted the family of Kenny Washington sitting behind the UCLA bench with racial slurs.

Home-court disadvantage aside, the Bruins had dropped a notch after graduating Goodrich and Hazard. They were waiting for a talented freshman class, led by skinny, seven-foot center Lew Alcindor, to move up to the varsity and would eventually lose their Pac-8 Conference title to Oregon State, missing the 1966 NCAA Tournament altogether.

Duke, on the other hand, was vastly improved. Bubas replaced the 6' 10" Hack Tison with a rugged center from Missoula, Montana, who would lead the ACC in rebounding as a sophomore. Growing up two thousand miles away, Mike Lewis was Bubas's first player from West of the Mississippi and the earliest symbol of his national recruiting scope. The sister of Lewis's high school teammate was at Duke and tipped off the coaching staff. Waters flew to Chicago and then to Billings, and quickly learned it would be one of his easiest recruiting jobs. Lewis wanted to attend school in the East and play for a great basketball program. Duke fit the criteria, having been to two consecutive Final Fours when Lewis was in high school. Done deal.

Meanwhile, the Tar Heels had moved into a brand new nine thousand-seat arena named for UNC's former CFO Billy Carmichael Jr. whom McGuire had given such a hard time over the leaks in Woollen Gym. Dubbed "Blue Heaven," Carmichael Auditorium was a three-sided structure attached to Woollen because the state legislature only approved funding for the "expansion and renovation" of an existing building. On December 16, 1965, junior Bobby Lewis scored 49 points against Florida State to set the UNC single-game record.

Ignited by the back-to-back wins over UCLA, Duke took over the No. 1 ranking and won 13 consecutive games before stumbling at unranked West Virginia. The Mountaineers' new coach was twenty-nine-year-old Bucky Waters, whose familiarity with Bubas' style of play helped them run the Blue Devils right out of their hillbilly hall 94–90.

Duke recovered from the loss, won five of its last six ACC games, including the tense rematch with McGuire's Gamecocks in Durham. The players nearly fought several more times and McGuire was pelted by fans with the apples they bought at concession stands. Just five years removed from his days at UNC, he still knew the local sportswriters and held court with them after the 41–38 loss.

"Some people in this conference didn't want me back in it," McGuire said, "and they know who they are. They also don't want South Carolina to be any good in basketball. But we're pretty good now and will be better."

Besides a heart-stopping 99–98 loss at Wake Forest, which dropped Duke to

No. 2 in the polls, the Blue Devils still led the 1966 ACC race comfortably entering the regular-season finale against Carolina, the last home game for Marin and
Vacendak. Duke won easily to finish first in the league standings for the fourth
year in a row (a string that would stand until Mike Krzyzewski's teams won five
straight regular-season titles from 1997–2001.) and, in the process, surpassed
the Tar Heels in all-time victories.

Smith was more concerned with the here and now, having lost to Bubas's
team twice by a combined 25 points while placing third in the ACC. It caused
him to contemplate an extreme strategy if they met again at the ACC Tournament in Raleigh. He knew, if that happened, the full-fledged Four Corners offense was coming out of the closet.

UNC had five touted freshmen in waiting, led by center Rusty Clark, forward
Bill Bunting, and guard Dick Grubar. They had defeated the varsity in a preseason scrimmage, the last time Carolina was to ever practice that way because it so
divided the younger players from the upperclassmen. In his later years, Smith
had his entire squad sit on the same bench during the annual Blue-White intra-
squad game, force-feeding unity.

In 1966 only two Tar Heel varsity players were of Duke's caliber, Larry Miller
and Bobby Lewis, who had gone on to be the ACC's leading scorer with a 27-
point average. When Duke blasted Wake Forest by 30 points and Carolina edged
Maryland and advanced to the 1966 ACC Tournament semifinals, Smith decided
not to take on Bubas's sagging defense. Still without a shot clock in college basketball, the Tar Heels stalled the game by placing one man in each corner of the
front court and a ball handler in the middle playing keep-away.

The Blue Devils stayed camped under the basket, waiting for Carolina to
shoot or at least *do something* as minutes ran off the clock. The crowd in
Reynolds Coliseum greeted the slowdown by yelling and throwing trash at the
UNC bench, and several balled-up paper cups hit the coaches.

Larry Brown had joined UNC's staff for the 1966 season after playing semipro ball for a couple of years. He said he preferred being on the court in the middle of Four Corners than watching it with Smith on the bench.

"We're sitting there, and he's coaching like usual and people are yelling,
'C'mon, Smith, play ball!' and throwing things at the bench," Brown said. "At one
point, I wanted to turn around and say, 'He's the head coach; if you're going to
throw anything, hit him!'"

Smith's move worked perfectly early on, as Carolina led 7–5 at the half and
17–12 late in the game before a couple of missed shots and mistakes allowed the
Blue Devils to rally and tie the game, 20–20, on Vacendak's basket with less than
a minute to play.

The Tar Heels held the ball for what they hoped was the game-winner, but they missed. Duke rebounded and set up for the last shot. Mike Lewis drove and got fouled with four seconds remaining. He had two free throws to keep his team's NCAA Tournament chances alive. Lewis was so nervous when he stepped to the foul line and took his stance that the rim looked the size of a dime. He clanged the first free throw.

Carolina had won over the once-hostile crowd, which was now cheering for the upset as the ball went back to Lewis for his second shot. This time, he felt his knees knocking as he dribbled twice and prepared to shoot.

Somehow, the ball went in cleanly and, after Carolina threw the inbound pass away, the Blue Devils survived 21–20. Despite losing, the game helped establish Smith as a daring young coach and strategist.

"It was within the rules," said Vacendak, who was Duke's high scorer in the game with six points. "We wouldn't come out and play very far. We weren't chasing them. We took their best shot. They used the rules to the maximum of their ability, and we still won."

Duke played N.C. State for its third ACC title in four years. After the drama of the semifinals, and facing the Wolfpack in its own building, Bubas called the pressure of the ACC Tournament greater than in the NCAAs, especially for the regular-season winner.

"No words can describe the pressure on the top-seeded team . . . which has a national ranking and does not have the home-court advantage," he said. "I've been to the NCAA Tournament, but this is where you live."

Marin, Lewis, and Riedy combined for 41 rebounds, and all five starters scored in double figures, but Duke still needed a clutch basket by Vacendak with less than four minutes remaining to offset 22 points from State junior Eddie Biedenbach and take the lead for good. Vacendak led five Blue Devils in double figures with 18 points and won tournament MVP, plus ACC Player of the Year, even though he had made only second-team all-conference in that voting completed the week before.

The tense 71–66 win put Duke back in the NCAA Tournament, but did little to change Bubas's mind about moving the tournament from Raleigh. He remained staunchly opposed to playing on N.C. State's home court and lobbied the press for another poll of ACC coaches like the one the Charlotte *Observer* had conducted in 1960, when only Everett Case said he favored keeping the tournament in Reynolds Coliseum because its seating capacity of 12,400 meant the most money for the ACC. With Case gone, the other coaches had a louder voice and a change of venue was inevitable.

Duke returned to Reynolds the following week and, ironically, had mostly

Duke fans in the stands while edging St. Joe's and Syracuse to win the East Regional and reach another Final Four. Although Bubas had used a zone defense to shut down Syracuse star Dave Bing, the Orangemen stayed close behind Bing's bespectacled backcourt mate, Jim Boeheim.

Duke had parlayed the last three of its ACC championships into Final Fours, and Bubas believed that the pressure was now off: a third time would be the charm for the NCAA title, especially with UCLA not even in the tournament. The Blue Devils were small and quick in the backcourt, the 6' 1" Vacendak joined by junior long-range bomber Bob Verga, who could help his team from anywhere on the floor, but off they marched to a different drummer.

Verga was a deadly shooter who slingshot the ball from behind his head and, similar to future Duke star J. J. Redick, would fire when ready from anywhere. He was a loner, a '60s greaser from the Jersey Shore. "He was Springsteen before there was a Springsteen," said Duke alumnus and Durham PR man Tom Drew.

The moody Verga didn't talk to some of his teammates and had a two-year personality clash with Marin, who was more outgoing. In 1966, they both averaged 18-plus points, and it was left to point guard Vacendak to diplomatically get them the ball in equal dosages.

When Verga went off by himself, his favorite spot was the Stallion Club, a black lounge on Cornwallis Road that featured famous groups like Ike and Tina Turner. Verga loved the music and atmosphere and played a real life version of the scene from *Animal House* when the Deltas were the only white guys in the bar listening to Otis Day and the Nights.

Besides being quick on the perimeter with players who could score from outside or drive the basketball, the 1966 Blue Devils were also athletic and beefy inside. The bruising Mike Lewis, who wrestled steers as a kid in his native Montana, gave Duke its most dominating presence under the basket.

The Final Four was played in College Park, Maryland, a familiar ACC court to the now second-ranked Devils. Their semifinal opponent was No. 1 Kentucky, led by Pat Riley, Larry Conley and Louie Dampier. Most pundits predicted that the survivor of this semifinal matchup would go on to win the national championship the next night.

The game had drama before it started, when Verga arrived weakened by something that resembled strep throat or tonsillitis. Reporters told Kentucky coach Adolph Rupp about it, and the Baron snorted that Conley was sick, too, and actually checked him into the hospital the night before the game. Years later, Rupp admitted it was a scheme to keep Duke from any psychological advantage, born out by the fact that Conley "recovered" to play most of the game and score 10 points.

Marin scored 29 but, with Verga playing sparingly and held to 4 points on 2 of 7 shooting, the Blue Devils could not hold a 42–41 halftime lead. Riedy's late layup rolled off the rim and Kentucky hung on to win 83–79. Rupp was all but handed his fifth national championship against the reputed renegades from Texas Western College (now UTEP). That ground-breaking game symbolized the racial inequality in sports of the 1960s, and Kentucky represented the lily-white side.

By 1966, race in college basketball had become a major issue. Even though he had coached black players at an Illinois high school in the 1920s, Rupp's reluctance to integrate his roster at Kentucky made him a bigot in the minds of those who regarded all-black colleges akin to the old Negro Leagues in professional baseball. Texas Western had a white coach, Don Haskins, and several whites on its roster, but the Miners' five best players were black, and Haskins started them all.

Their all-black lineup set the game apart from other NCAA Tournaments. San Francisco had started three blacks eleven years earlier in 1955, two of them named Bill Russell and K. C. Jones of the future Celtics dynasty. Cincinnati had at least three black stars during its dynasty run in the early 1960s. In 1962, the Bearcats started four blacks when they won their second straight national title. Loyola beat Duke with four black starters in 1963, and played them all forty-five minutes in dethroning Cincy in overtime the next night.

Perhaps because it was Kentucky, where Rupp used "nigger" openly for years, that made the 1966 title game so historic. Neither San Francisco, Cincinnati, nor Loyola were in the South. Texas Western had a helluva team that was hard to handle for Kentucky, both figuratively and literally.

Bobby Joe Hill, David Lattin, and Orsten Artis combined for 51 points and 20 rebounds, outplaying the celebrated Kentucky stars and cementing the 72–65 win by making 28 of 34 at the free-throw line. Rupp was furious about their 23 fouls compared to Texas Western's 12, but the Wildcats were left chasing the quicker Miners. It was that contrast—five whites versus five blacks—and Rupp's reputation that made it a milestone game.

Kentucky people have always believed it was happenstance that their program got tagged as racist. What, they wondered, if Duke's all-white team had played Texas Western? Bubas—a master politician—did not have the reputation that dogged the aged Rupp. Perhaps the presence of black walk-on C. B. Claiborne on the Duke freshman team that year would have defused some of the controversy and dulled the comparison.

Maryland had begun ACC integration in 1965 by signing freshmen Billy Jones and Pete Johnson. Although he had one of the ACC's first black players in

Claiborne, who had a naval ROTC scholarship, Bubas knew that by the mid-1960s other schools could admit minority athletes more easily than Duke, which had stiffened its entrance requirements to Ivy League standards under President Doug Knight.

"The black athlete was more afraid of Duke than Duke was afraid of the black athlete," said Waters, Bubas's freshman coach through 1965. "The recruiters would go in there and say, 'What are you going to study? Prelaw? Premed?'

"It was a difficult time for those kids, anyway, and to be thrown into what was purported to them to be an impossible jump academically . . . 'You're not even going to be eligible.' No matter how hard you tried, they were being told, 'What are you going to do for your race—you're going to flunk out.'

"And these were the brightest and best [black high school stars] from New York and New Jersey. Whether or not it was real, it was very difficult to overcome. We couldn't say you don't have to work at Duke or we had an easy curriculum at Duke. We just couldn't say that."

UNC, in contrast, was determined to integrate its program. McGuire had told Smith about student body president Eli Evans from Durham coming to his office in 1958 and asking him to sign a black player. McGuire told Evans that he had recruited Wilt Chamberlain out of Philadelphia, but that the Stilt didn't have the combined 800 SAT scores required then by the ACC.

Smith remembered his father refusing to cut Paul Terry thirty years earlier and, as McGuire's assistant coach at UNC in 1959, had helped integrate the restaurant where the basketball team always ate pregame meals. Smith had become a charter member of Binkley Baptist Church, a liberal spin-off in Chapel Hill. He agreed to accompany his minister, Bob Seymour, and a black theology student to the Pines for dinner. All three were allowed to stay and eat, and the Pines fed blacks from that point forward.

When Smith succeeded McGuire in 1961, he told close friends that one of his biggest goals was to find a qualified black student-athlete. In 1964, Smith offered a full scholarship to Willie Cooper, who had made the freshman team as a walk-on and would have been the first black player in the ACC, but Cooper failed an economics test and decided to concentrate on his studies (his daughter, Tanya Cooper, was a scholarship player for the UNC women in 1993–96). Smith recruited Greensboro's Lou Hudson, who also didn't have 800 on his SAT and went to Minnesota in the already-integrated Big Ten.

Then, in in 1966, Smith learned of a 6' 6" black athlete who was turning heads at Laurinburg (North Carolina) Institute prep school about two hours south of Chapel Hill.

Following his junior year at Laurinburg, Charlie Scott had made a nonbinding verbal commitment to play for Davidson and the national power being built by Lefty Driesell. As an excellent student, Scott was a perfect candidate to break the color barrier for athletes at UNC.

Larry Brown first went to see Scott in 1966. On the recommendation of Charlotte broadcaster Bill Currie, UNC's play-by-play announcer, Smith told Brown to stop in Laurinburg on the way home from a recruiting visit to Lebanon, Indiana, high school legend Rick Mount, who was featured in *Sports Illustrated.*

Brown flew into Charlotte, picked up a rental car, and wound his way down old Route 74 to the hamlet of Laurinburg. He watched Scott practice and grew so excited he couldn't wait to get back to Chapel Hill and called Smith from a pay phone.

"Coach, he's better than Rick Mount," Brown said.

"No, no," Smith said.

"Coach, he's better."

Smith soon learned that Scott was upset because the black coach at Laurinburg, Frank McDuffie, had been denied service at a Davidson restaurant when taken there by Terry Holland, Driesell's assistant. Smith invited Scott to Chapel Hill for Jubilee that spring. This time, both Smokey Robinson *and* the Temptations entertained.

"After seeing this, they have a good shot at getting me," Scott said.

When they met privately for the first time, Smith asked Scott what he wanted to be called. "Charles," Scott said of the name his family used with him. From that point on, Smith always referred to Scott as Charles, pushing dignity on those who might have seen only skin color.

Smith also took Scott to church Sunday morning at Binkley, which had a mixed congregation, something Scott always remembered. "It showed me that if I went to Carolina I'd just be one of the guys," he told *Sports Illustrated* in 1997. "That's what makes you comfortable when you're afraid. And make no mistake, I was scared about what I was doing."

Bubas was watching all this transpire and thought he needed to get involved. Scott was a good enough student to be recruited by Duke and his visit there was hosted by Vacendak, who had just completed his career. "I told Coach Bubas that Charlie had a great time," Vacendak said, "and that if he didn't come it was his fault, not mine."

It was neither. With a small black student enrollment, Duke drew little consideration from Scott. He loved his weekend at Carolina, where Smith had him meet with Howard Lee, who would become Chapel Hill's first black mayor, and several black faculty members and friends. Lee and his wife Lillian, a high school teacher, offered Scott a room in their home if he didn't want to live in the dorm as a freshman.

Scott felt very comfortable at Carolina, returned to Laurinburg and decided he'd be better off there than at Davidson.

The next day, Scott called the Davidson basketball office and learned Driesell was hunting in Texas. He got the number where Driesell was staying, made the call and delivered the bad news. Lefty was angrier than a rattlesnake, believing Scott was the key to his winning the national championship some day.

"Hell, Charlie, I want to see you when I get back," he drawled.

A week later, Scott and Smith were walking the Laurinburg campus when Driesell surprised them by stepping out from behind a bush. A former player at Duke, the 6' 4" Driesell towered menacingly over the 5' 10" Smith. And he was pissed. The story has become legendary in ACC annals.

Apparently, with arms flailing, Driesell accused Smith of stealing his player and threatened to whip his ass right there before Scott cut him off and stepped between the two men.

He had known Driesell longer and even called him "Lefty" since they first met his sophomore year at Laurinburg. He said what had happened to Coach McDuffie at the restaurant in Davidson got him to thinking that maybe UNC was a better place for a colored boy from New York to go to college.

"Charlie, they didn't mean nothin' in that place, I've already straightened that mess out."

Driesell pleaded, but the look on Scott's face told him it was too late.

Smith told Driesell he, too, was sorry and walked off with his newest recruit. In the spring of 1966, he signed Charles Scott to be the first black scholarship athlete at the University of North Carolina.

In Raleigh, the N.C. State campus sat vigil to await the imminent death of Case, who had one last surprise after he succumbed to melanoma on April 31, 1966. He had revised his will to split $69,525 of his estate among several of his former players. Bubas, still a close friend but by then a prosperous head coach, was not among them.

Following the 1966 season, with his son's academics and SAT scores in question, N.C. State coach Press Maravich accepted a big offer from LSU, denying the ACC and Tobacco Road a chance to see his son play. Imagine what it would have been like: Duke, the reigning king, and Carolina, the team of the future—and

Pistol Pete Maravich working his court magic for State. Norman Sloan, who played for Everett Case in the 1940s, left Florida to take over the program, and the Maraviches moved to the Southeastern Conference. Instead of shaking Reynolds Coliseum from its steel girders, the Pistol drew capacity crowds to LSU's "Ag Center," a livestock barn that turned into a smelly basketball gym a couple of times a week.

Also imagine how McGuire's cocky kids would have defended Maravich. Due to near fights in their two games the previous season, Duke and South Carolina agreed not to schedule each other in 1967, giving that rivalry a chance to simmer. Most people blamed McGuire, whose style of confrontational basketball was back in force. As North Carolina fans had done, South Carolinians fell in love with the Irishman because his bad boys won and stood down anyone who dared to challenge them.

For the first time, Bubas was having some trouble within his own program. Verga was a senior and leading the ACC in scoring (his 26.1 points a game has remained a Duke record). But after losing their opener to Virginia Tech in Charlotte and getting blown out twice in their rematches at UCLA, the Blue Devils were 3–4 after seven games. A narrow win over a bad Wake Forest team didn't do much to ease Bubas's frustration.

Before they played Penn State on January 3, 1967, Bubas suspended Mike Lewis and six other players for violating curfew at a fraternity party on New Year's Eve. Verga wasn't with them and had to carry the team. Although Bubas started a makeshift lineup and had only two subs dressed out on the bench, Duke still won 89–84.

Despite Verga's scoring and Lewis improving his rebounding average to 12.3 as a junior, Duke was in jeopardy of not wining 20 games for the first time since 1960, at the same time the arch rival down the road had finally caught up. When Verga capped his career with 39 points against Wake Forest in his last home game, the Blue Devils were behind UNC in the ACC standings by two wins. They hadn't played the full complement of conference games due to the two cancellations against South Carolina.

Smith was finally winning big behind Bob Lewis, Miller, and a tall, talented sophomore class (Clark was 6' 11", Bunting 6' 8" and Grubar a 6' 4" point guard). It completed a lineup that allowed Lewis and Miller, who had played inside the previous season, to return to their natural perimeter positions and become the new one-two punch in the ACC.

The ACC's star combo was called the "L&M Boys" in reference to the Liggett & Meyers (L&M) Tobacco Company that was headquartered in North Carolina.

"The sophomores were put in the best possible position because they were join-ing two fabulous players and didn't have to be the stars right away," Larry Brown said after coaching them as freshmen in 1966.

Lewis and Miller led the Tar Heels to a dramatic win at Duke, a 59–56 victory that Miller won by driving the length of the court while Smith frantically tried to stop play. "It's a good thing no one saw me signaling for a time out," Smith said. Bubas saw the game as a changing of the guard in the ACC. Referring to Smith being hung in effigy at UNC just two years before, Bubas said, "If you hang me, do it close to the library. It's more academic that way."

By Bubas schmoozing sportswriters and winning so much, his Blue Devils had earned their status as media darlings. This was an era when coaches still in-vited local sportswriters to fly on team planes, because getting to places like Clemson, South Carolina, and Charlottesville, Virginia, were not easy trips by car. So, despite a 13-point loss in the rematch at UNC, they were still the senti-mental favorites to win the ACC Tournament, which through bullying by Bubas and other coaches was moved to Greensboro even though it had three thousand fewer seats than Reynolds Coliseum.

With a 21–4 record and having dominated the regular season, the Tar Heels faced the pressure to win what was still a do-or-die tournament and gain the ACC's only NCAA bid. And to validate that it was the best team.

At practice that Monday, the players arrived to find a volleyball net set up on the Carmichael Auditorium basketball court. It was a diversionary tactic by Smith, who played in the volleyball game himself by joining Clark's side because it had the obvious advantage of size.

Smith Barrier, the widely respected sports editor of the *Greensboro Daily News*, wrote a column that week saying that Carolina was better but Duke had the experience and would win the ACC Tournament again. Miller tore the article out and taped it to his locker.

The following Saturday night, after both survived close games in the Friday semifinals, they met for the ACC championship. Smoking was allowed in the old Greensboro Coliseum, which packed more than nine thousand spectators under its low roof that seemed to trap the cigarette smoke. The air was also thick with tension, as the heavily pro-Carolina crowd nervously awaited the 8:00 P.M. tip-off.

It was arguable which was more important to them—taking the ACC title away from Duke or being the only team to gain the NCAA Tournament bid. In the 1960s, when college basketball was still very much a regional sport, few peo-ple outside of North Carolina cared about the Duke-UNC rivalry. So ruling To-bacco Road meant more to most ACC fans than a deep run toward the *national* championship.

"People today don't understand what kind of pressure that was," Miller said, echoing Bubas from the year before. "You had to win three games in three days or you weren't called the champion, no matter what you did during the regular season. I couldn't eat, I couldn't sleep. My stomach was in knots. I had to tell my parents not to come down for the tournament."

Smith always scoffed at that particular comment, knowing Miller's fierce competitiveness and his connections on campus. "I'm sure Larry told his parents to stay home so he could sell his tournament tickets," Smith said of his left-handed superstar who could score from anywhere on the court.

Duke broke out to a nine-point lead in the first half before Miller triggered an 18–3 run that opened a 40–34 halftime edge for Carolina. The Blue Devils were in foul trouble, losing three starters in the second half, but sophomore Dave Golden came off the bench to hit six of seven shots and push Duke into a late 70–65 lead. Smith began to panic on the sideline.

"Coach, don't worry, we've got it," Miller told him as he dribbled by the bench. He and Bobby Lewis combined for 58 points, as the Tar Heels sprinted to victory 82–73 and Smith's first ACC title. The players lifted both Smith and Brown on their shoulders and paraded them around the court before they all took turns cutting down the nets. Miller put one around his neck.

To cap a dominating junior year in which he averaged 22 points and 9 rebounds, won ACC Player of the Year and tournament MVP, he hit 13 of his 14 shots in the championship game. While slicking back his pompadour after the game, Miller told sportswriters that he thought the one shot he missed—a jumper from the corner—was going in, too. He also showed them Barrier's article, which he had folded and put in his sneaker before the game.

The NCAA Tournament field had fluctuated between 22 and 25 teams since 1953, during which time the National Invitation Tournament remained prominent and, in the Northeast, actually bigger. In 1950, City College of New York had won the NCAA Championship and because it was the home-town school was also invited to the NIT. CCNY won that title, too, the only time one team won both tournaments in the same year.

The ACC, however, had an unwritten rule stemming from the point-shaving scandals of the last two decades that it would not send teams to the NIT. Bubas requested that policy be changed in 1967, and it was.

Duke accepted the ACC's first-ever bid to the NIT, which invited the next-best sixteen teams after the NCAA selected its field. All four rounds were played in New York's Madison Square Garden. The Blue Devils trekked to New York forty-eight hours after the grueling three-game ACC Tournament and lost their opening game to eventual champion Southern Illinois. The Salukis' Walt Frazier went on to win MVP of the NIT and used the exposure as a springboard for "Clyde" Frazier to launch his storied pro career with the New York Knicks. Duke went home with an 18–9 record.

The Tar Heels moved on to defeat fifth-ranked Princeton and No. 9 Boston College, coached by former Celtics great Bob Cousy, in the NCAA East Regional in College Park to reach the Final Four in Louisville, Smith's first as a coach. On the tenth anniversary of McGuire's Miracle, signs popped up all over Chapel Hill with the slogan, "Remember '57 in '67!"

Dayton All-American Donnie May shredded the Tar Heels for 34 points and the unranked Flyers ruined UNC's return to the Final Four 76–62. After Houston and Elvin Hayes won the third-place game by 22 points, Carolina fans still chanted "We're No. 4." They were just happy to have beaten Duke and be back in the running after ten years.

Following such a successful season, Smith and Brown believed they had a great high school backcourt tandem locked up. Dick DeVenzio was a shifty southpaw guard from Ambridge, Pennsylvania, and Austin Carr, a smooth shooting swingman from Washington, D.C., (Carr, ironically, had been born at Duke Hospital when his parents were moving from South Carolina and his mother went into labor passing through Durham). Smith had sent Brown to see them often during the season, and now they planned to sign both recruits in one swoop into the Northeast. They soon found out rival coaches had also been working hard while the Tar Heels were at the Final Four.

They flew into Washington and rented the biggest car they could find because Smith believed that impressed eighteen-year-olds. Nevertheless, they couldn't find Carr, whose family or friends didn't know where he was. After he eventually signed with Notre Dame, they learned Carr had been spirited away to a hotel by Irish coach Johnny Dee and kept there until Smith and Brown left town.

At the same time, Bubas and Waters were with DeVenzio, convincing him that Carolina had Grubar and two other point guards and that he would never play for the Tar Heels. When Smith and Brown arrived at DeVenzio's house the following night for their scheduled visit, the family was gone. DeVenzio opened the door and was crying. "I'm going to Duke, I'm going to Duke," he said and closed the door.

DeVenzio, also heavily recruited by Wooden at UCLA and Driesell at Davidson, joined Bubas's last great recruiting class. Randy Denton, a 6' 10" center from Raleigh, and Durham's Brad Evans, also a star football quarterback (whom Alabama's Bear Bryant wanted so badly that he offered Evans's best friend a scholarship, too), both picked the Blue Devils and started as sophomores. They were the last in-state players Duke beat Carolina for until Shavlik Randolph, thirty-five years later.

The curly-haired Denton was the only Duke player besides Heyman to lead the team in scoring and rebounding for three consecutive years. He hit 55 percent from the floor his last two seasons. Denton was always a favorite of Smith's, the kind of center highly coveted by the Carolina coach, and often left him uttering, "We really wanted him."

As the NCAA contemplated freshman eligibility, Duke and Carolina staged some of the last classic freshman games in 1968. Duke had a perfectly balanced team: Denton at center, Steve Litz at power forward, Rick Katherman at small forward, Evans at shooting guard and DeVenzio at the point. They appeared unbeatable, but they lost an early stunner at Davidson and found the far-less-heralded UNC class hard to handle.

The Tar Babies were coached by Bill Guthridge, who had just joined Smith's staff after twenty-seven-year-old Larry Brown left to play with the red, white, and blue ball of the fledgling American Basketball Association. Guthridge did not have a highly recruited team; Lee Dedmon, a gawky big man, was the only scholarship freshman who would later start for the varsity.

Carolina won the first meeting on a neutral court, but Duke rallied in the rematch in dramatic fashion at a jam-packed Carmichael Auditorium. The game was tied with seconds left when DeVenzio hit a shot from his own foul-line (seventy-five feet away), which remained a bit of folklore in the rivalry.

The big teams were still the biggest news. The nationally third-ranked UNC varsity, without the graduated Bobby Lewis, was even better in 1968 because the sensational Scott had moved up to join Miller and the junior class. The Tar Heels won 22 of their first 23 games.

After a hard-fought 75–72 defeat in Chapel Hill in January, Duke's fourth loss in a row to Carolina, Bubas was desperate. Referring to UNC's newest duo, he moaned, "We're doing a pretty good job of containing Miller, and Scott is tearing us apart. I'm thinking we've got Superman covered and Zorro is killing us."

Carolina so dominated that it was 12–0 in the ACC and wrapped up a second consecutive first-place finish by the last week of the regular season. The Tar Heels lost at home to McGuire's South Carolina team in Larry Miller's final home game and went to Durham with nothing more than pride on the line. Duke had climbed into the rankings with an eight-game winning streak in February and was No. 10 in the polls for UNC's weekend visit.

On Friday night, March 1, came the freshman rubber match for the Big Four championship. UNC dominated, establishing the then-fiery Guthridge as an outstanding young coach. The Duke frosh, coached by Tom Carmody, finished 12–4 with supposedly the greatest recruiting class in ACC history.

The varsity game was played the next afternoon, a balmy Saturday, before a capacity crowd at Duke Indoor Stadium that was pent up for Mike Lewis' last home appearance.

Lewis was leading the ACC in rebounding with 14-plus per game but fouled out with 3:54 left in the second half of a tight game. Bubas sent in junior bench jockey Fred Lind, a 6' 8" reserve forward who scored only 11 points in 6 games as a sophomore and 29 points in 13 games that season. The night before, Bubas had warned him he might play against Carolina because regular back-up center Warren Chapman was out with sore knees. Lind had already spelled Lewis briefly in the first half.

Writing himself into the history books, Lind played the rest of regulation and hit two free throws that sent the game into overtime. He scored a field goal to force a second overtime. After the game stretched into a third extra period, Lind began a fast break leading to Steve Vandenberg's layup and, ultimately, Duke's 87–86 upset of the favored Tar Heels.

Lind scored 16 points, easily his career high, grabbed 9 rebounds and wound up in the middle of a wild celebration. After leaving the Indoor Stadium, a mob of students picked Lind up and carried him halfway to the Duke Chapel before he managed to get down—a moment in time that endeared him to alumni and fans forever because, after all, he beat Carolina.

If the Blue Devils had the momentum Bubas wanted heading into the ACC Tournament, they did not fight very hard to keep it during the most bizarre game in ACC history.

The tournament had moved to Charlotte and the old coliseum on Independence Boulevard that had 11,666 seats, about 2,000 more than Greensboro. The event was so popular that tickets were no longer sold to the general public. Booster clubs from the eight ACC schools used all of them as fund-raising carrots.

Duke had moved up to No. 6 in the polls and was facing slowdowns from almost every inferior team it played. Clemson took the air out of the ball in the opening round and stayed close the entire game before falling short 43–40. The Blue Devils moved on to face an N.C. State team that had a 15–9 record, finished 9–5 in the ACC, and played two competitive games against them during the season.

State's Norman Sloan used the same slowdown strategy against Duke, refusing to play from the opening tip of the semifinal game if Bubas kept his defense below the foul line.

Large chunks of time ran off the clock while Duke again refused to come out and chase. Bill Currie, broadcasting the game from courtside, called what was, or wasn't, happening in front of him "as exciting as artificial insemination." TV actually broke for commercials while the nonaction continued, and Duke led the unbearably boring game at the half 4–2.

Duke still led 9–8 with two minutes remaining when both teams decided to play for real. Nine timeouts were called in the last two minutes, which took longer than the first thirty-eight. Dick Braucher's put-back of a missed free throw gave State its last lead and Duke missed on the other end.

State's stunning 12–10 victory marked Duke's lowest point output since 1909 when it was still called Trinity College and lost to Wake Forest 30–5.

UNC survived the other semifinal in overtime against South Carolina, avenging the loss during the last week of the regular season, and faced State in the final. The Wolfpack played it straight and lost by 27 points, the biggest blowout in ACC Tournament championship game history until Duke beat State by 30 in 2002.

After the 1968 ACC Tournament, UNC and Duke were tied with 913 all-time wins. While the fourth-ranked Tar Heels, who had now taken home two straight ACC regular-season and tournament titles, earned another NCAA bid, the Blue Devils were fading. They went back to the NIT and were involved in two shockers. In their opener, they were beating Oklahoma City so badly that the Indians' outrageous coach, Abe Lemons, kept his team on the court at halftime and scrimmaged "shirts and skins" to the amazement of the Madison Square Garden crowd. Then Duke got shocked, itself, by tiny St. Peters in the second round to finish the season 22–6.

Carolina's 1968 team proved to be Smith's strongest to date, the best in the country that year besides UCLA. In the East Regional in Raleigh, they routed third-ranked and previously unbeaten St. Bonaventure with seven-foot Bob Lanier and then defeated Driesell's eighth-ranked Davidson Wildcats, reaching their second straight Final Four at the Los Angeles Sports Arena.

Smith wanted to avoid a repeat of the previous year, when he felt the Tar Heels had looked past Dayton to UCLA and the national championship game. This time, they focused on the semifinals and beat Ohio State and advanced to the title game Saturday night. Eleven years after McGuire's 1957 Tar Heels had stunned Kansas in triple overtime in Kansas City, UNC was playing for the NCAA crown again; more importantly, Carolina had replaced Duke as the ACC's best program.

Before the game, however, the Tar Heels received some news from their coach that divided them.

Smith had scouted the other semifinal in which UCLA, with the lineup of Lew Alcindor, Mike Lynn, Lynn Shackelford, Lucius Allen, and Mike Warren, had demolished Houston and Elvin Hayes 101–69 in the much-hyped rematch between the two teams. Houston had upset the Bruins in the first nationally televised college basketball game the previous December at the Astrodome. Smith doubted Carolina could stay in the game playing a normal tempo, so he told his star players they were up against the greatest college basketball team ever assembled on what amounted to its home court across town from the UCLA campus.

Miller and Scott disagreed and debated his inclination to use Four Corners; after several meetings with Smith the afternoon of the game they decided to play one half each way. Trailing 32–22 at the break, Carolina went back to a normal tempo and got booted into the record book. Alcindor, who later took the Muslim name of Kareem Abdul-Jabbar, had 34 points and 16 rebounds in the 78–55 romp, the largest margin in a championship game ever—an ignominious mark that stood until UNLV beat Duke by 30 points in 1990.

Appreciative UNC fans still gave Smith a Carolina-blue Cadillac convertible after the 1968 season, delivering it to him outside his office at Carmichael Auditorium. Smith was happier over having signed a class that would help replace Miller, his cornerstone recruit who had graduated and was on his way to stardom with the Los Angeles Stars of the old ABA.

During the season, Smith had gone back to Pittsburgh to recruit Dennis Wuycik, a rugged forward who, like Duke's DeVenzio, was also from Ambridge, and guard Steve Previs from nearby Bethel Park. Bubas was again UNC's chief competition, and he thought he had both locked up. He had taken Groat, the former All-Star shortstop with the Pittsburgh Pirates who had recently retired after a fourteen-year Major League career, and Heyman to see both recruits. What could be better than Duke's two greatest players ever?

Smith, however, won this battle, adding Wuycik and Previs to a 1969 freshman class that included New York forward Bill Chamberlain, the second scholarship black player to join the Tar Heels. Smith later learned from the recruits that his cause was aided by Heyman talking so incessantly about how UNC was winning *in spite* of Smith.

Landing Wuycik, who was in the mold of Miller, was a coup for Carolina because he played for Ambridge coach Dave DeVenzio, the father of the Duke point guard. Smith still loved Dick DeVenzio and always wished he wore Carolina blue. DeVenzio wound up wishing the same thing.

Midway through DeVenzio's sophomore year, 1969, Bubas announced he would retire after the season. The Blue Devils lost four consecutive games for the first time in his tenure and limped into the regular-season finale with a

12–12 record. The forty-two-year-old coach found himself under fire from his own fans.

"Toward the end, I took longer to dress for practice," Bubas said. "You wonder, should you see one more film, one more kid? At the end, I didn't. It wasn't fair to the team. You owe your recruits the best chance to win the championship. I was starting to slip. I had to weigh it all—and I found myself losing interest. I had done it for eighteen years, how about something else?"

Bubas' last home game was also the senior game for Fred Lind, the unsung hero of the 1968 triple-overtime win. During warm-ups, a UNC manager told Lind that Smith asked to speak to him. Smith wanted him to play in a post-season all-star game he was coaching in Hawaii. The gesture endeared Smith to Lind, who scored 18 points and grabbed 10 rebounds that day as Duke upset fourth-ranked Carolina for the second straight year. (Lind played for Smith in Hawaii and later worked several summers at the UNC basketball camp.)

After the game, Smith praised Lind and Vandenberg's career-high 33 points but gave DeVenzio the ultimate compliment. Intimating that DeVenzio's defense and floor game were most responsible for the 87–81 loss, Smith said, "You could say the outcome was decided two years ago when DeVenzio picked Duke over Carolina."

Clearly, however, it wasn't the same Duke program DeVenzio had joined. The Blue Devils were falling and had relinquished their role as chief *challenger* to the Tar Heels. Upstart South Carolina had emerged as a new, burgeoning power in the ACC on the way to its first 20-win season in the school's history. After five years of rebuilding the Gamecocks, Frank McGuire, their new coach, had put them on the college basketball map.

McGuire had recruited an even bigger brand of New York wisenheimers than those he once pipelined to Chapel Hill. Sophomores John Roche and Tom Owens brought savvy, size, and skill to the South Carolina lineup but more of an edge and cynicism than any of his former players. Though they were grade-schoolers when McGuire last won big, the newest Northern transplants gave the "us-against-the-world" philosophy new life in Columbia, extending the battle on Tobacco Road to a war between the states.

The more the Gamecocks won, the more belligerent McGuire became. Early in the 1969 season, they fought against Virginia and Davidson. Then, losing a late January game at Florida State, which was not yet in the ACC, McGuire pulled his players off the court with less than two minutes remaining, complaining that the refs were allowing them to get physically abused.

Because of the rivalry between the two schools and the relationship between McGuire and Smith, all North Carolina-South Carolina games drew enormous interest and were sold out, with tickets being scalped outside for three and four times the face value ($10). One of the most memorable was the 1969 North-South Doubleheader in Charlotte, when UNC and N.C. State played Clemson and South Carolina for two nights.

South Carolina, with four sophomores and a junior guard named Bobby Cremins, played all five starters forty minutes and upset once-beaten and second-ranked UNC 68–66. Sophomore sensation Roche scored 30 points, and McGuire used his timeouts carefully to give his five iron men enough rest to re-buff the Tar Heels' repeated comebacks.

The rematch came twelve days later in Columbia. After South Carolina had pulled within two points, the game came down to a bang-bang call as Roche drove the lane and crashed into UNC's Rusty Clark. The whistle blew as twelve thousand people at Carolina Coliseum held their breath. The call was charging on Roche! The Tar Heels hung on to win 68–62 and avenged their earlier loss.

Fans from both schools eagerly anticipated a third meeting at the 1969 ACC Tournament in Charlotte. Duke caught the Gamecocks looking ahead in the semifinals and pulled off the 68–59 upset in a game without a single substitution—all ten starters played forty minutes. DeVenzio, Lind, Vandenberg, and Golden, who had five straight baskets at the end of the game, all scored in double figures. Denton had 9 points and 10 rebounds.

Bubas's final hour as Duke's coach proved apropos to the new face of ACC bas-ketball. His Blue Devils led the championship game by 9 points at halftime and 11 in the second half. Grubar, UNC's senior point guard, was gone with a torn knee ligament, and the Tar Heels were unraveling. Several Duke cheerleaders sit-ting along the baseline talked about how they would get to Maryland, site of the NCAA East Regional, the next weekend.

"I looked down at the Carolina bench and everyone looked like the game was over," Bubas said. "Everyone except Charlie Scott; he was on the court yelling, 'Give me the ball! Give me the ball! I'll win the game!' "

The ACC's first black superstar took over.

Scott began scoring on drives, jump shots, and at least 10 long bombs to pour in 28 second-half points and finish with 40. Had there been a three-point line, Scott might have scored 50 because half of his 17 field goals were from way out-side. He rallied the Tar Heels to their third straight conference title and, tri-umphantly, back into the NCAA Tournament with the ACC's only invitation. "In the final minutes of a game, he was like Arnold Palmer birdieing 17 and 18," Smith said of Scott.

Scott's explosion proved a pivotal moment in the history of ACC basketball. Not only was it the greatest individual performance of the Duke-Carolina rivalry, considering its stage, it foreshadowed the future of the sport at the two schools with full integration on the way.

His fabulous feat proved the black player could and would change the game like no other—a spectacular statement that couldn't be ignored. While several schools had integrated with blacks who weren't outstanding players, the first *great* one had arrived. The ACC had to deal with it.

Unwittingly, Scott also laid down the gauntlet to Duke that it would fall further behind Carolina unless it started recruiting black stars.

Off the court, the ACC now had to confront the issue of prejudice among the old guard. Scott was clearly one of the two or three best players in the conference and deserved the same spoils as any similarly deserving white player. Only he didn't get them.

Carolina went to the regional in College Park angered by obvious bigotry in the All-ACC voting that came out just before the tournament. Somehow, five voters had left Scott off their ballots. The best player on the ACC champions and, unquestionably, one of the five best players in the league, Scott's omission was for only one reason—his race.

Scott was never in trouble at UNC; to the contrary, he was an Academic All-American who had represented the United States at the 1968 Olympics in Mexico City, where black athletes Tommie Smith and John Carlos protested but Scott stayed out of the controversy. This time, he did not.

Asked about it following Carolina's 79–78 win over Duquesne in the Sweet Sixteen, Scott said, "A player wants to be appreciated. I wasn't picked unanimously for the all-conference team. They put a guy ahead of me because I'm not white. That was the first time I ever felt racially slurred. It was my best year, and we were the only team to go to the NCAA Tournament."

With Smith leaving the decision in his hands, Scott considered boycotting the East Regional championship game against Davidson. But, with the help of assistant coach John Lotz, Scott's best friend and confidante, he decided the strongest statement he could make to alumni and fans who had supported him as a pioneer for future black athletes was to play. For that, as much as his ability on the court, he would be voted ACC Athlete of the Year.

Scott would not have had the same impact had he gone to Davidson instead of UNC, a state school like Alabama and Mississippi so identified with Civil Rights and education. How ironic that Scott taking center stage came at the expense of the school and coach he had jilted in 1966. Driesell had already missed one chance to win the NCAA title by losing to the Tar Heels in 1968.

BLUE BLOOD

"I'd rather die than lose to North Carolina again," screamed the *Washington Post* sports headline the morning of the 1969 East Regional championship game.

Playing with a patchwork backcourt because of the injury to Grubar, Carolina stayed close to Davidson until the final minute, when reserve guard Gerald Tuttle drew a charge to give the Tar Heels the ball with the score tied 85–85. Smith called timeout and told the Tar Heels to "find Charles" with the inbound pass. They did and Scott hit a high-arcing jumper from the top of the key as time expired for a 87–85 win and a third straight trip to the Final Four.

Louisville was again the site (as it was for Smith's first Final Four in 1967), but the NCAA had changed the Friday-Saturday format to Thursday night semifinals and a Saturday afternoon championship game. Still without Grubar and worn down by the long season of hot contests and hotter controversies, Carolina faced Purdue and All-American Rick Mount, the player Larry Brown once said was not as good as Scott. Mount's backcourt mate, Winston-Salem native Herm Gilliam, had his own motivation, not being able to play in the ACC because he, too, hadn't made 800 on his SATs.

Mount outplayed and outscored Scott, pouring in 36 points on mostly long jumpers as the Boilermakers blew out to a big lead and routed the Heels 92–65. Scott scored 35 in an anticlimactic 20-point defeat to Drake in the third-place game. UCLA and Alcindor won their third straight title, the fifth national championship of the decade for John Wooden's teams.

Together, Duke and Carolina made six trips to the final Four in the 1960s but, largely due to the Bruins, went home to become trivia questions in the NCAA record book. In their own backyard, however, they took turns dominating the decade with nine first-place finishes in the ACC and seven tournament championships. From 1963–69, only one year passed (1965) without either reaching the Final Four. Coincidentally, they each played in only one championship game in their "middle" Final Fours and both suffered lopsided losses to UCLA. Accordingly, Bubas won respect earlier than Smith.

Considered a dominant coach at Duke long before Krzyzewski, Bubas compiled a 213–67 record in ten years, including winning 87 of 100 home games. Only Wooden had a better record in the 1960s. Bubas's Blue Devils won 77 percent of their ACC games, placed first four times in the regular season and won four conference championships for the highest winning percentage in the ACC Tournament (.777) of any coach before or since. Under Bubas, Duke finished in the top 10 for six consecutive seasons. In addition to the three Final Fours, two more of his teams made the NIT in the days when it meant they were among the best forty in the country.

Bubas brought big-time college basketball to Duke, setting the national recruiting pace in the ACC and introducing mobile forwards to the fast-break game he learned from Everett Case. He loved the spirit and atmosphere surrounding the West Coast schools and started the Duke dancing girls to emulate UCLA's cheerleaders, as well as dressing the Duke pep band in straw hats and striped shirts after Cal-Berkeley's band. He put his players' names on the backs of their uniforms to familiarize them with fans watching on TV and in person, another staple of the future.

Bubas wanted everyone to follow the Blue Devils, so he introduced preferred parking for boosters and hired smiling coeds to check their coats at the Indoor Stadium; he started a family section in the end zone, where season tickets sold for $10, and was among the first to have ball boys under the basket. He made sure the women had clean rest rooms and encouraged them to mingle with the players after games, get autographs, and have their pictures taken with them. He was way ahead of his time.

Bubas's battles with Smith were eventually overshadowed by Krzyzewski, but the Duke-Carolina rivalry of the twenty-first century was fostered, if not founded, by two Midwestern gentlemen who were terrific teachers, championship coaches, and modern motivators, and all the while devoted family men. Bubas often brought his wife, Tootie, and children on road trips and opened his home to his team. Like Krzyzewski, Bubas raised three daughters to be involved with the program. His oldest, Sandy, married one of his players, Stu Yarborough, and his second, Vikki, was a Duke cheerleader.

Beyond his accomplishments on the court, twenty-nine of the thirty-three players who played for him graduated. Bubas said spearheading a drive to build a student union was his greatest achievement at Duke. "It took a lot of hard work, but the Bryan Center will stand there as long as there is a Duke University."

As the 1960s drew to a close, however, Bubas knew Duke could not keep pace with ongoing integration in college basketball. Public education had left black students behind, and a private school in the South like Duke was moving more slowly than most of the competition in admitting them. UNC fans believed Bubas quit because he couldn't compete with Smith and Carolina; that was only true with regard to integrating his program.

In February of 1969, Bubas's last year, Duke lost for the second time at West Virginia, where Bucky Waters was in his fourth season as head coach. Bubas told his former assistant and fellow N.C. State alum that he would recommend him as his successor—but it came with a couple of warnings.

"The black athlete is coming into the league," Bubas said. "Carolina is loaded. None of these things are good for Duke."

Bubas stayed at Duke, moving to the Allen Building as a Vice President for six years before being named commissioner of the new Sun Belt Conference. He did not meddle, but remained interested in those who had supported him. Durham *Morning Herald* sports editor Elton Casey, who had broken the story of Bubas's retirement in 1969, was an alcoholic always on the verge of getting fired. When the newspaper essentially booted him upstairs, Bubas acknowledged the need for change but implored management to "be gentle" with the move.

Dean Smith, interestingly, was also sympathetic toward Casey, encouraging him to stop drinking and even loaning him large sums of money to get out of debt. Compassion was one of many traits shared by Smith and Bubas, gentlemen off the court who never cursed in public and brought civility back to the Duke-Carolina rivalry. The 1970s would not go as smoothly.

RIVALRY RECORD IN THE 1960s
- Duke won 14; Carolina won 12

HOW THEY DID IN THE DECADE
- Duke 213–67 (.760); Carolina 184–72 (.719)

ACC CHAMPIONSHIPS
- Duke 1960, 1963, 1964, 1966; Carolina 1967, 1968, 1969

FINAL FOURS
- Duke 1963, 1964, 1966; Carolina 1967, 1968, 1969

RIVALRY FACTS
- Vic Bubas vs. Carolina: 14–13
- Art Heyman vs. Carolina: 5–1 (missed 1 game)
- Most Famous Game: Duke 21–20, March 4, 1966

BIGGEST HEROES
- Fred Lind, Duke 87, Carolina 86 (3 OT), March 2, 1968
- Charlie Scott, Carolina 85, Duke 74, March 8, 1969

BEST QUOTE
"In the final minutes of a game, he was like Arnold Palmer birdieing 17 and 18."

(Dean Smith on Charlie Scott)

4

CATCH US IF YOU CAN

As ridiculous as it sounded, the rumor persisted that Adolph Rupp was coming out of retirement to coach Duke.

Bucky Waters, who had succeeded Vic Bubas, quit suddenly a month before practice began for the 1973–74 season, leaving the school scrambling to find his replacement. No head coach at another major university would leave his job after classes had started. Duke was desperate to restore the reverence and respect it had lost during Waters' turbulent tenure.

Following the 1972 season, Rupp was banished from the bench by Kentucky's mandatory retirement age of seventy. He didn't want to go, but the university refused to fight the state law to retain the Baron of the Bluegrass. So he was put out to pasture, literally, retreating to his five hundred-acre cattle farm in Lexington.

In Durham, North Carolina, however, the resurrection rumor would not die.

Rupp remained in mind, even in Atlanta, where old hacks always used him to play one particular prank on new reporters. They told their youngest colleagues, as impossible as it seemed, to try to get an interview with the living legend. Here's his number—he probably won't take your call, but you must try. It was protocol at the *Journal-Constitution*.

Cub reporters dialed the number apprehensively. After thirty minutes of listening to Rupp ramble about basketball, birds, and farming, they turned around to see the hacks across the newsroom, doubled over with laughter. *Anyone* could get Rupp on the phone, and no one could get him off. Their initiation was complete.

The new sports editor in Durham remembered, having fallen victim to the ploy when he started at the paper in Atlanta. He also remembered that Rupp's number was still written in his black address book, so he dialed up the coach with the most wins in the history of college basketball. Rupp answered.

"Coach, I'm calling from Durham, North Carolina, and . . ."

Rupp interrupted. "Son, do you know Carl James?" he asked, naming the athletics director at Duke.

"Yes, sir, I do."

"Can you call him for me?" Rupp continued. "We've had an electrical storm here and my phone doesn't call out. I don't know how you got through. Can you call Carl James for me?"

"Yes, sir, I can. What do you want me to tell him?"

"Tell him not to send that plane for me. Tell him I can't be at the press conference on Thursday because my farm manager, Carl Yazell, dropped dead this afternoon. And I have to stay here. Will you call him for me?"

"Yes, sir, I will," the sports editor said. And he did, delivering the news to James and getting a hesitant thank you.

After that, he wrote the biggest story of his young career. Adolph Rupp *was* coming to Duke. Then he wasn't.

How had Duke basketball sunk to the level where it needed to try what amounted to a publicity stunt—coaxing an aging icon out of retirement to attract attention and trump the top 10 programs at neighboring North Carolina and N.C. State? It took some undoing, for sure.

The hiring of Waters in 1969 had been delayed by squabbling between Eddie Cameron and insiders favoring alumnus Lefty Driesell, who had turned Davidson College into a national power after the small school outside of Charlotte took a chance on the candid high school coach from Norfolk. When he interviewed with Davidson President Grier Martin to replace former UNC coach Tom Scott in 1960, Driesell promised he wouldn't use it as a stepping stone unless he had a chance to go back to Duke.

"I would have to do that, be the coach at Duke," Driesell said.

His first team upset nationally ranked Wake Forest with Len Chappell and Billy Packer, giving Driesell instant credibility that he parlayed into recruiting success. He chased high school players literally around the clock, sometimes sleeping in his car overnight outside a particular recruit's house to show how much he wanted him.

Driesell always resented that an N.C. State man, Bubas, was coaching at his alma mater, and it was his public slap at Bubas after the loss at Duke in 1964 that cost him the position he always wanted when it opened up in 1969.

Despite having followed the same path as Bubas, Waters was still seen by many Dukies as an N.C. State graduate with rough edges. He had been at Duke for six seasons before going to West Virginia in 1965 as the nation's youngest head coach at twenty-nine. His first three teams each finished 19–9 and he twice beat the Blue Devils before, but his fourth slumped to 12–13 (ironically, Bubas's last team also had 13 losses). Meanwhile, Driesell had led Davidson to the NCAA East Regional title game for the last two years, losing to UNC both times, and left for the University of Maryland, vowing to make it the "UCLA of the East."

Chuck Daly, another Bubas assistant who had been on the staff since the 1964 season, also wanted the job badly. When he didn't get it, Daly succeeded Bob Cousy at Boston College and later coached Penn in the Ivy League before going to the NBA. The second assistant, thirty-six-year-old Hubie Brown, had been with Bubas only one year and drew little consideration. He remained as Waters's right-hand man.

How might Duke's past have been rewritten had either Driesell or Daly—or even Brown—followed Bubas rather than the embattled Waters, who was never the popular choice?

As the new decade began, Waters and Dean Smith tried to maintain the levels their programs had reached in the last decade, but times were changing and so were college basketball players. The head coaches had to change with them or they wouldn't make it.

That was easier for Smith, who had already struggled through integration off and on the court. One night at South Carolina, a redneck fan called Charlie Scott a "black baboon" and Smith was ready to punch the racist jerk before being restrained. He felt parental toward Scott, whom he had squired through his pioneer role at UNC, and was disappointed when he let Scott shoot too much during his senior season of 1970 and Carolina lost more games (nine) than it had in five years.

Smith referred to himself as a benevolent dictator within the confines of his program. When his players were on their own, he preferred that they be guided by the rules of society and hoped they would adhere to his belief that "the disciplined person is the truly free person. We give our players discipline to make them free." With sticky issues like the Vietnam War, which was still tearing apart campuses with protests all over the country, Smith supported freedom of expression but asked them to consider their basketball family before they got involved publicly.

He also asked them to be totally unselfish for the 1971 season. Smith had allowed Scott to shoot so much because he felt it gave the other players their best chance in the big games. Sans Scott, Smith again went back to the total-team concept. He promised these Tar Heels that if they did exactly what he said, they would win, prognosticators be damned (some had picked them as low as sixth in the ACC).

Junior guard Steve Previs, a prolific scorer in high school, bought in completely and turned sacrificial lamb. He gave up chippies to make an extra pass so someone else could score. He was the floor-slapping defender long before Duke started doing it and, from his prowling position, would have easily led the ACC in steals if official statistics were kept in that category. It was Smith's incessant defensive praise of Previs and, later, Bobby Jones that eventually led the conference and college basketball to begin officially recording steals in 1980.

Waters had less of his team's respect and attention but, frankly, was at a tougher place to coach. At West Virginia, he made players who didn't give maximum effort wear practice shorts with frilly laces. He tried the same thing at Duke, and it did not play nearly as well with Northern kids who wore their hair long and were proud to be student activists with other left-wing causes beyond opposing the war in Southeast Asia.

With his own head shaved into the flat top of an army private, Waters insisted his players trim back so they wouldn't "lose the ball while their hair was in their eyes" and bragged "we're not a team that carries hair dryers around with us on the road." He was known for other laughable lines such as, "This game was like two hours in a dentist's chair" and "We cannot play in tuxedos."

He had early success in recruiting, signing up high school standouts Jim Fitzsimmons, Jeff Dawson, Richie O'Connor, Gary Melchionni, and Alan Shaw, all of whom thought they were coming to play for a Vic Bubas protégé. Fitzsimmons transferred to Harvard (where he eventually led the Ivy League in scoring) at midsemester of his freshman year, giving the bug to some of the others. After the 1970 season, Waters lost two important sophomores. Two-sport star Brad Evans decided to play football instead. Don Blackman, Duke's first black scholarship basketball player, also quit and transferred to Rhode Island.

Meanwhile, some critics were calling Dean Smith a flash in the pan who had lucked out by signing Larry Miller and the recruiting class of 1969 that won three straight ACC championships. It was reminiscent of a favorite Smith saying, "You start the way you finish." Beginning in anonymity, without respect and in the shadow of the flashy Frank McGuire, he still hadn't won enough to satisfy everyone.

By heeding their coach, the Tar Heels turned that criticism around in 1971. They upset second-ranked South Carolina with a slowdown strategy in Chapel Hill and finished first in the ACC by a full game over the Gamecocks. However, they were devastated by a last-second loss to McGuire's team in the ACC Tournament championship game at Greensboro, when 6' 3" Kevin Joyce beat 6' 10" Lee Dedmon for the decisive jump ball that led to the winning basket.

Thus, Carolina and Duke became strange bedfellows at the end of the 1971 season. Both were invited to the NIT, which was still a big enough deal in those days for some schools (such as Marquette in 1970) to accept a bid over the NCAA Tournament. To the Tar Heels and Blue Devils, it meant they hadn't won the ACC title, so they commiserated together.

Between its early exit from the ACC Tournament and the NIT opener, Duke did not have a game for more than a week, and Waters feared his players would tire of practicing against each other. He called Smith and asked if he could bring them to Chapel Hill to work out with his team.

From where the rivalry had been, and what it has become since, the suggestion of such a cooperative practice was extraordinary. That could not, or would not, happen today—but it happened in 1971.

Smith needed something to help his players get over the crushing ACC Tournament loss, a game they blew with missed free throws and a last-second screw-up on the jump ball. Maybe this could help them move beyond their disappointment and refocus on the NIT. Smith told Waters if it was okay with the ACC office, it was okay with him.

Duke and Carolina players who considered themselves arch enemies got acquainted, and several formed lifelong friendships from their afternoon together in Carmichael Auditorium. They ran offensive and defensive sets against each other, and when they met in the NIT semifinals it resulted in a predictably sloppy game.

On the Madison Square Garden court, the Blue Devils and Tar Heels joked about knowing exactly what each of them was doing. When one called a play, the other was waiting in perfect defensive position. "What took you so long to get here," they kidded each other throughout the ugly encounter that featured poor shooting and plenty of turnovers.

The Tar Heels won 73–67, their third victory over Duke that season, and beat Georgia Tech for the NIT championship behind MVP Bill Chamberlain two days later to end their season at 26–6. Duke finished 20–10, but the Blue Devils were losing the last great recruiting class from the Bubas era, namely Randy Denton and Dick DeVenzio.

DeVenzio, barely 5' 10" and quick, much preferred Bubas's open floor game over Waters's low-post sets and methodical half-court offense. As he fell deeper into the new coach's dog house, his shooting and scoring dropped steadily his last two seasons. He hung out in Chapel Hill with Previs and Dennis Wuycik, Carolina players from Pittsburgh, as much as he did with his own teammates. After he graduated, DeVenzio revealed that he had advised George Karl, another Pennsylvanian, to go to UNC on his recruiting visit to Duke. He remained closer to UNC basketball then for thirty years until his death in 2001 from intestinal cancer at age fifty-two.

. . .

Dean Smith's watershed season came in 1971, when he became more than a coach to his players. In the 1960s, some of the Tar Heels figured their talent was winning and the coach they irreverently referred to as "Smitty" went along for the ride. Smith even agreed, allowing, "After 1971, no one ever questioned anything I said again."

That they all wept together in pain after losing the ACC Tournament to South Carolina, and then again with joy after sweeping the NIT, made Smith human to his players. From that point on, they considered him both a father figure and friend, sniping at sports writers who described Smith even in the least unfavorable manner. That kind of loyalty begot more recruiting success.

It was a stunning contrast with what was happening at Duke. Dissatisfaction with Waters's nit-picking discipline and slower style of offense helped cause widely reported dissension and continued the rash of unprecedented defections. A total of seven players left early, draining the Blue Devils' talent pool and the patience of alumni who longed for the good old days under Bubas. Duke's 1972 team had some talent, but little togetherness.

All the transfers told a bigger story about college life in the '70s, the greatest period of self-examination and change in American history. Students went from short hair to long, clean shaven to beards, khakis to jeans, and chugging beer to toking joints. Winning teams became only one of the peer pressures for students. At UCLA, John Wooden had a helluva time keeping Bill Walton in line and out of demonstrations on the streets of Westwood.

So what happened at Duke was typical of college campuses all over the country. What made it worse was the basketball team, once a unifying cause celebre, was going down the tubes. Players were leaving, students were protesting or at least acting out. What was a losing coach to do?

Carolina, fortunately, was bolstered by the return of four starters from their NIT title team and made most preseason polls in 1972, given a reasonable shot at dethroning UCLA, by now the five-time defending national champion. Smith had a lot more reason to keep the Tar Heels in line.

They responded by winning 12 of their first 13 games and were ranked No. 3 going to Duke on January 22. It was the day the school officially renamed Duke Indoor Stadium for Eddie Cameron, the former basketball and football coach who was retiring as athletics director. Already inducted into the National Football, Duke, North Carolina, and Virginia Halls of Fame, Cameron called it his "most cherished honor."

However, the halftime ceremony was a mixture of standing ovation and student protest. Cameron had hired the unpopular Waters, and several hecklers who blamed him for the collapse of Duke basketball disrupted the speeches by yelling, "Stop, don't do it!"

Despite a mediocre 7–6 record, the Blue Devils were playing one of their best games and gave their fans more reason to cheer in the second half.

With the clock running out and the score tied 74–74, Carolina turned the ball over near midcourt. Senior reserve guard Robby West, who was averaging five points a game and shooting 39 percent, carved his name into Duke lore when he dribbled to the foul line and sank a fifteen-footer that stunned the Tar Heels. Angry that they had looked ahead to a hyped match-up with Maryland, Smith praised Duke's effort over that of his own players.

Driesell had recruited Maryland into ACC contention, landing Pennsylvania high school All-American Tom McMillen at the last minute after McMillen had committed to Carolina. Smith had no trouble getting the Tar Heels up for McMillen's first visit to Chapel Hill, as they overcame his 20 points and 13 rebounds to post their one-thousandth all-time victory with a 92–72 romp on national television.

The following week, at its January convention, the NCAA restored freshman eligibility after years of schools complaining that they could not afford to field separate teams, travel, uniforms and coaches for players who were ready to compete on the college level right out of high school. Smith opposed the move because he believed freshmen, no matter how good they were in basketball, needed one year to get acclimated to academic and college life, but UNC was wealthier than most and *could* afford it.

His rivals disagreed, particularly N.C. State coach Norman Sloan who had the best player to ever come out of North Carolina, a 6' 4" sky-walking forward named David Thompson who had originally committed to Smith before signing with State. Sloan lobbied self-servingly on his weekly television show for the NCAA to render freshmen eligible immediately, so Thompson could join his varsity right away. The vote passed, but effective for the 1972–73 season.

Without Thompson moving up, unranked N.C. State still managed to upset the No. 5 Tar Heels the last week of the regular season.

"How much you think we'll beat Duke by?" UNC's George Karl snapped as he left Reynolds Coliseum, referring to the rematch with the Blue Devils on Saturday. Still angry, they blasted the Blue Devils by 24 points to go 9–3 and finish first in the ACC for the second straight year.

Duke tied for fourth at 6–6 and won one game in the ACC Tournament before losing to Carolina again, going home with a 14–12 record amidst renewed criticism of Waters. UNC routed Maryland for the ACC title and the next week got a chance for sweet revenge in the Sweet Sixteen.

South Carolina, which had bolted from the ACC in 1971 to be an independent, earned an at-large bid to the NCAA East Regional in Morgantown, West Virginia. The Tar Heels drubbed the Gamecocks 92–69 and beat Penn two days later to qualify for the Final Four in Los Angeles. High in the rafters, their pep band struck up "California, Here I Come" as the game ended.

Looming was a national championship test against mighty, undefeated UCLA and All-American Bill Walton. Second-ranked Carolina was distracted by Chamberlain showing up late for the pregame meal and violating a team rule. With Chamberlain losing his starting position to sophomore Bobby Jones, UNC got blindsided by unheralded and uncontainable Florida State, which was also an independent in 1972. Falling behind the Seminoles and super-quick guard Otto Petty by 12 points at the half and 23 in the second half, the Tar Heels staged a rally that fell short by 4 points.

UCLA's Wooden put Smith and his regional program in their proper place after the semifinals when he told the throng of sportswriters, "I don't know much about Florida State because all of you assured me we'd be playing North Carolina." The Tar Heels were left to whip Louisville in the third-place game before UCLA won its sixth straight national title over FSU.

They were hardly disconsolate on the cross-country flight home. Led by Previs, an aspiring actor and most quotable Heel, they played cards and kibitzed in the back of the plane. The Final Four had not yet grown into a national spectacle and to many coaches, players and fans held less prestige than winning their own conference championship. Carolina had returned to the top of the ACC, claiming dominance over their closest neighbor and reestablishing Smith's program with a 26–5 season.

Duke basketball looked bad when compared to how Smith had finally garnered complete support from his team and fans. Two more Blue Devils transferred before the 1972–73 season, hastening their decline. Even worse was the one-year NCAA probation Duke received in the recruitment of N.C. State's Thompson. Both Duke and State were cited for illegal inducements (a Duke fan had given Thompson a sports jacket and trousers and taken him to the 1971 ACC Tournament) and banned from postseason play in 1973.

The Duke students, unified against Waters, held up FIRE BUCKY! signs at games until they were confiscated. The *Chronicle* student newspaper ended an editorial lamenting the ruin of basketball with the phrase, "Can the coach." Not even an upset of fourth-ranked Maryland helped Waters, because Duke fans thought he'd let local Durham legend and Terrapins' freshman star John Lucas get away. The Blue Devils faded to fourth in a seven-team league then dominated by N.C. State, UNC, and Maryland.

They lost three more times to UNC that season, blowing a late lead at Cameron in the regular-season finale that heightened the cry for a coaching change as the painful season went on. The 12–14 finish was Duke's first losing record in twenty-three years and only its third ever.

The night of the official team banquet, *Chronicle* sports editor Bob Heller sponsored an anti-Waters dinner at the Ranch House restaurant in Chapel Hill. The evening included a telephone hook-up with the disgruntled former player Dick DeVenzio, who was launching his career as an activist against big-time college athletics. To be fair, Heller allowed pro-Bucky speakers, but they were badly outnumbered.

Waters still asked for a vote of confidence and a contract extension to stave off rumors of his imminent demise. He received neither and resigned with a 63–45 career record on September 12, just thirty-three days before practice started for the 1973–74 season. He took a fund-raising position at the Duke Medical Center, brazenly going to work for a few influential doctors who had remained supportive. Critics claimed Waters waited as long as he did to screw Duke for refusing to support him, leaving Carl James, the new athletics director, in the lurch.

Unable to get a sitting coach at such a late date, James needed something to get back in the game with N.C. State and Carolina and couldn't wait a year for a new coach to come in, pick up the pieces and rebuild the program. He convinced himself that he could turn the eyes of college basketball back on Duke by bringing in Adolph Rupp as a figurehead coach; what national publicity it would create!

After the surprise press conference, national newspapers, magazines, and networks would descend upon Duke. The once-banished Baron would impart on his new players whatever wisdom he could conjure up while assistant coach Neil McGeachy ran the daily operation. Despite a lousy team, Duke would still get plenty of TV exposure. Was it a desperate measure, because Duke was desperate, or was it out-of-box brilliance by an athletics director looking to jump-start a ravaged basketball program?

The answer was never known because Rupp bailed out. James rebuffed any public debate over the idea by categorically insisting he never offered Rupp the job, barely acknowledging they had even spoken. The prospect seemed so outrageous that most Duke fans believed him and blamed the local newspaper for fabricating such an outrageous story. What fun it would have been had Rupp's farm manager not dropped dead, and he had taken the job.

BLUE BLOOD

What if Rupp had coached at Duke and renewed his rivalry with Smith, who surpassed his career record of 876 victories in 1997? Like Smith, Rupp was a Kansas graduate and had mentored the young coach early in his career. Smith's record against Rupp was 5–2, winning four straight at one stretch, and they had remained friends through the years although Smith privately denounced Rupp's reluctance to integrate his program.

James angrily rebuked the newspaper story when he instead introduced Neil McGeachy, an assistant on Waters's staff for two years, as Duke's "interim" head coach at the press conference that had been scheduled for Rupp. The thirty-one-year-old former three-sport star at Lenoir-Rhyne College (where he has since returned as athletics director) received a one-year contract and coached two of the most memorable games ever with Carolina.

The orphaned Blue Devils were 6–5 on January 19, 1974, when the fifth-ranked Tar Heels (11–1) visited Cameron and their coach showed up with a new look. The once short-haired, slicked-back Dean Smith wore a thick crop with side-burns. As it turned out, several of his former players were behind the makeover, buying him his first hair dryer.

Duke was the same old Duke, despite its new interim coach, but as the rivalry has proven so many times, the records did not matter. The underdog Devils out-played Carolina for virtually forty minutes and had possession out of bounds with the score tied in the final seconds. At worst, the game was going to overtime.

Duke sophomore Paul Fox inbounded the ball from the UNC bench area. Intended for teammate Bob Fleischer, Fox's cross-court pass was picked off by Bobby Jones, now a senior All-American, who drove in for the winning layup, as the once-hysterical Cameron crowd gasped. Jones celebrated momentarily on the floor, and then disappeared into the locker room.

Between the UNC games of 1974, Duke posted the school's one thousandth victory (88–78 over Virginia on February 13th) in a season, ironically, the Blue Devils were to record the fewest wins in thirty-five years.

Their next meeting with the Tar Heels was either famous or infamous, depending on one's shade of blue. It came on the last day of the regular season in Chapel Hill, where Jones was closing out his home career. Duke had skidded to 10–14, beaten down from seven defeats in its last nine games and the constant speculation over who would replace McGeachy after the season. The players liked McGeachy and wanted to save his job with an upset at Carolina, and they again outplayed their heavily favored hosts.

The Tar Heels, ranked fourth, were feeling sorry for themselves after 11-point losses at No. 6 Maryland and No. 1 N.C. State. Without a proven point guard, Carolina relied too much on the first freshman to ever start under Smith, Walter Davis, for its outside scoring. As it turned out, Davis was asked to score from *way* outside.

The Blue Devils played like champs for virtually forty minutes, spurred on by a cast of veterans that didn't want a third coach in three years, and led 86–78 with seventeen seconds remaining. The game was essentially over, and much of the unhappy Carolina crowd had already started up or down the aisles of Carmichael Auditorium.

In Rocky Mount, North Carolina, a high school star named Phil Ford turned off the TV and went outside to wash the family car. His favorite college team was dead, trailing by "eight points with seventeen seconds" left to play after his favorite college coach had called a timeout.

"Let's do the things we practiced, and we can still win," Smith said in the huddle. "After Bobby makes these free throws, go fifty-four defense, trap the first pass in."

Jones was going to the free throw line for two shots, but it didn't matter. All Duke needed to win the game was a successful inbound pass, which McGeachy emphasized to the Blue Devils in their huddle.

After Jones indeed made both foul shots, Duke couldn't handle the double team in the corner. The ball got loose, and UNC's John Kuester laid it in to make the score 86–82. Thirteen seconds remained, and Carolina called another timeout to set the defense. Again Duke fumbled the inbound pass, losing it over the end line. The Tar Heels actually missed twice before Jones's put-back made it 86–84 with six seconds to play. All five of them signaled timeout, their next-to-last. Smith always saved them just for situations like this.

Hundreds of people scrambled back to their seats or stopped to watch from the narrow walkway separating the upper and lower seats at Carmichael. Dozens of sportswriters coming down from the catwalk press area were stuck on the steel staircase, straining to see what was unfolding below. UNC students in the bleachers behind both benches stood, stomped and screamed all at once.

Duke finally got the ball in to Pete Kramer, a left-handed junior and 77 percent career foul shooter whom Smith knew was making only 58 percent of his free throws that season. Kuester grabbed him immediately. Kramer had a one-and-one with four seconds left. Though he usually waved off fans distracting the opposing foul shooter, Smith was powerless to stop the hysterical home crowd trying to *will* a miss.

Kramer hit back rim, Ed Stahl clutched the rebound and Carolina called its final timeout with three seconds left. Smith knelt at the front of the huddle; the players leaned in more closely to drown out the din.

"Wouldn't it be fun to catch up after being so far behind?" Smith said, smiling. Outside of the closed Carolina huddle, it was mayhem with the Carolina pep band blaring and the crowd roaring.

College basketball had yet to add the three-point shot, so the best the Tar Heels could do was tie the game and win in overtime. Most coaches would have had a blackboard and chalk out diagramming a play, but Smith drilled these situations every day, and his team knew exactly what the call would be.

"513, skip the 1," Smith said. "Walter, you have enough time to get a good shot."

Sophomore center Mitch Kupchak was the "5" man in the 513. There wasn't enough time to hit the "1" man or point guard with a short pass, so Kupchak had to "skip the 1" and throw a long pass directly to Davis, the "3" man curling toward the sideline at half court. With no timeouts, Davis was to get as close as he could and fire.

The play worked imperfectly.

Kupchak, who became an NBA star and general manager of the Los Angeles Lakers, hit Davis in the hands. Instead of driving hard to the basket, as Smith had told him, Davis took two long dribbles and launched a twenty-eight-footer that had little chance to go in. The ball was off to the right but long enough to hit the backboard. It slammed against the glass and, from that angle, ricocheted right through the hoop for the tying field goal. The hum over Blue Heaven during the ball's flight exploded into a collective yell of "Yes!" as hundreds of fans flooded the floor to celebrate the tie.

Davis admitted he wasn't trying to bank the shot, and in practice two days later Smith had the Tar Heels run the same play. Davis missed everything as they erupted in laughter. For Duke, the eventual 96–92 loss in overtime was no laughing matter. The wife of Sports Information Director Richard Giannini sat behind the Duke bench and was trampled by Carolina students after Davis's shot went in. She suffered a separated shoulder, and when Duke officials told her husband she had been taken to the hospital, he kicked the Carmichael bleachers so hard he broke his foot.

McGeachy remained bitter over the loss and his treatment by Duke, refusing to discuss it for more than ten years. Finally, at the school's one hundredth anniversary of basketball celebration in 2005, he was able to poke fun at the game that got away.

Even had Duke hung on to win, McGeachy would not have been retained because Carl James was already in private conversations with other head coaches, among them Southern Cal's Bob Boyd, Memphis State's Gene Bartow, Providence's Dave Gavitt, Utah's Bill Foster, and Eddie Sutton, who was at Creighton before going to Arkansas, Kentucky, and Oklahoma State.

Foster, a Pennsylvanian who said, "I'm an Eastern guy," was introduced as Duke's new coach on March 28, two days after his Runnin' Utes finished second in the 1974 NIT. Foster previously coached at Bloomsburg (Pennsylvania) State and Rutgers, but his biggest Eastern tie was to retired Temple coach Harry Litwack and the basketball camp they owned and operated together in the Pocono Mountains.

At forty-three, Bill Foster was exactly Dean Smith's age, and was just as smart, just as well read, and far more outgoing—he loved going to country music concerts. Foster was determined to coexist with Smith and N.C. State's Norman Sloan, whose Wolfpack had won the 1974 ACC and NCAA championships. He used his wry sense of humor to deal with what was left of the rivalry as he tried to rebuild a once-proud program ravaged by dissension and defeat.

Foster inherited an average team that was also dysfunctional from so many coaching changes. Seniors Kevin Billerman, Bob Fleischer, and Pete Kramer, junior Willie Hodge and sophomore Tate Armstrong started. The sixth man was twenty-seven-year-old George Moses, a black juco transfer Foster took because he needed another warm body. Aptly named, Moses looked forty years old, played a mean game of chess and couldn't jump. He reminded Foster of Casey Stengel's old joke about how the Yankees finally got him a black player named Elston Howard, who turned out to be one of the slowest guys on the team.

Foster's first game against Carolina came in the 1975 Big Four Tournament, an annual two-day event in Greensboro that began when the coliseum expanded to 15,836 seats in 1971. The coaches did not want to play each other a third time, but the schools saw the format as a big money-maker in the college basketball dog days of December.

They were right, and by 1975 the Big Four's popularity was a close second to the ACC Tournament. Because tickets were split only four ways, more fans from each school could attend. It became a miniversion of the old Dixie Classic, a neighborhood brawl without any outsiders.

When Duke arrived for the Friday night doubleheader, Foster had never seen anything like it in the middle of the season: Fans from Duke, Carolina, N.C. State, and Wake Forest had lost the Christmas spirit and were fired up like it was March. But his Blue Devils had seen it and were ready to play, sick of having lost eight straight to Carolina.

The Tar Heels were ranked eighth and favored but, frankly, more concerned with breaking in their freshman point guard, Phil Ford. Ford had signed with UNC in the spring, and was so bad early in the season that a sportswriter called him an Edsel.

He wasn't much better in the Big Four Tournament, and Duke's veterans made the big plays in the closing minutes to pull off the 99–96 upset in overtime. Foster was 1–0 in the rivalry and joked with his assistant coaches after the game about quitting right there and then.

Mainly because of Ford's arrival, Duke and Carolina were moving in opposite directions. While Foster tried to figure out how to construct an ACC contender, Ford saved Smith from recurring criticism about too much regimentation compared to the free-wheeling, run-and-shoot style of N.C. State and its exciting superstars, David Thompson, 5' 7" point guard Monte Towe, and center Tom Burleson, the first seven-footer to play in the ACC. State had gone unbeaten in the league for two years, relegating the Tar Heels to the NIT in 1973 and '74.

As Ford improved, he became a big hit. He was an Energizer Bunny at point guard. He dribbled, passed, and shot with an abandon that endeared him to Carolina fans and converted thousands more. Though he was a poor defender who forced Smith to protect him with more zone than he liked to play, Ford elevated every other part of UNC's game. He was the first point guard Smith gave the green light to shoot from anywhere, a major departure for someone criticized for turning high-scoring high school guards into careful floor leaders whose main job was to get the ball inside.

Duke lost its next two games with Carolina on the way to last place in the ACC, as reality set in for Foster. The Blue Devils would watch the Tar Heels dethrone N.C. State at the 1975 ACC Tournament behind Phil Ford, the first freshman to win the tourney MVP, and regain the recruiting advantage they owned before State and Thompson took over briefly. Smith and his staff were already working the blue-collar neighborhoods of Jersey City for a funny and flamboyant forward named Mike O'Koren, who boasted with pride that he came from the "upper lower class."

Foster thought he had inroads with O'Koren, having signed his teammate at Hudson Catholic High school the year before. In comparison, Jim Spanarkel was lightly recruited, but he and O'Koren were friends and Duke hoped that bond would reunite them in Durham—but Carolina was in better.

Assistant coach Eddie Fogler, who was from Queens across the Hudson River, spent hours with O'Koren's rowdy crowd in the bars of Jersey City, setting up Dean Smith's visit to the projects of Jersey City. By the time Smith arrived,

Rosie O'Koren had prepared a baked ziti dinner and was recruiting the Carolina coach to show her son a better life. It was all over but the signing.

Although Duke kept trying and thought it was a two-horse race, Notre Dame actually wound up O'Koren's second choice. He liked Spanarkel okay, but wanted to play for a winning program, and when the 1976 Tar Heels dominated the ACC by four games O'Koren knew where he was going. Duke, meanwhile, had a losing record (13–14) and finished dead last in the league.

Besides getting continually thumped by the Heels, who regarded N.C. State and Maryland as more worthy rivals, the Blue Devils had plenty more to be mad about. They were getting little credit for improved play that resulted in hard-fought, narrow defeats. In 1976, they lost eight games by 10 points or less behind the emergence of Tate Armstrong, a lightly recruited junior from Houston who turned into a great shooter and averaged 24 points a game.

Smith had been named U.S.A. Olympic coach for Montreal in 1976 and in-vited Armstrong to try out in the spring at N.C. State's Carmichael Gym. There was supposedly a selection committee, but Smith basically hand-picked a roster heavy with ACC and UNC players. Tate Armstrong, Maryland forward Steve Sheppard, and emerging State star Kenny Carr joined four Tar Heels: Phil Ford, 1976 ACC Player of the Year Mitch Kupchak, Walter Davis, and Tom LaGarde. Smith drew widespread criticism for the squad's local flavor, but he reasoned that his own players and those who knew him would be happier as substitutes than stars and starters from far-away schools.

The strategy and chemistry worked for the regulars, and the U.S.A. won the gold medal with all college players. However, Armstrong languished at the end of the bench, exacerbating the Duke-UNC rivalry. Armstrong had impressed Smith the least of all the reserves during practice. Saying the right things publicly, he vowed privately to beat Carolina his senior year to get even with his Olympic coach.

Foster had also vowed not to get sucked in by the rivalry, but he too was furi-ous about the slight to one of his hardest-working players. Plus, a Duke guy sit-ting on the bench while four UNC players collected their Olympic minutes only raised Smith's and Carolina's profile when the coaches hit the recruiting trail again in the fall of 1976.

Years later, Armstrong had a different perspective. "I was just fortunate to be on that team, and he told me that," Armstrong said of Smith. "To this day, look-ing back, I was one of the luckiest guys in the world. No question, I wanted to play more, and it provided a little edge when we played North Carolina, but it was always there anyway."

To save face, Foster laughed along with those who poked fun at the derivative nickname he had chosen, the Runnin' Dukes, from his Runnin' Utes at Utah.

They were slow, but the Blue Devils ran and ran and sometimes even looked like they allowed the opposition to score to speed the tempo. The close losses hurt, but Foster figured it would be easier to recruit better players if he fielded a high-scoring team.

His great sense of humor aside, he agonized over his own tough luck and occasionally blew up, once drop-kicking the locker room door open after another last-minute loss. Foster took defeat so hard that his players worried about his health, and his staff put in longer hours to console him, even going along to see the Oak Ridge Boys in concert, his favorite diversion.

They all continued recruiting tirelessly, looking for secondary players with potential and using Foster's extensive contacts through all levels of basketball to get in with the high school stars that had not looked at Duke for years. Their breakthrough recruit turned out to be 6' 11" Connecticut high school *junior* Mike Gminski, who had taken so many advanced courses that he was eligible to graduate a year early.

Carolina was the first to recruit Gminski when he averaged 40 points and 20 rebounds his last year in high school, but mistakenly judged him too slow to be an ACC impact player. After an unofficial visit to Chapel Hill early in his junior year, Gminski received a letter from Bill Guthridge, Dean Smith's chief assistant, telling him that pursuing UNC wasn't in his best interest.

"I wanted to play a lot as a freshman, and I think that played a part in it," said Gminski, who signed with Duke, got his high school diploma and arrived in Durham as a seventeen-year-old bushy haired behemoth.

"He's here," Foster said, giddily, "the big guy's here."

Gminski knew little of the rivalry with Carolina when he arrived in Durham, but it didn't take him long to understand the animosity between fans of the two schools, if not the players. "We got to know the Carolina players and had a decent relationship with them," Gminski said, "but our fans didn't like that. They thought we should have nothing to do with them."

The 1976–77 Blue Devils sprinted to a 10–1 start and were looking not only like an ACC contender but Duke's first NCAA Tournament team in eleven years. Then, after a competitive loss at Carolina that left Armstrong bitterly disappointed, their season effectively ended when Armstrong broke his wrist against Virginia, a game in which he managed to finish and score 33 points.

UNC was also hit by injuries. Even without senior center Tom LaGarde, who tore an ACL at mid-season, the Tar Heels managed to finish first, win the ACC Tournament and advance to the East Regional final at Maryland, where Foster was recruiting and took in the marquee match-up with Kentucky.

Walter Davis had come back from a broken finger and Ford was doubtful with a sprained elbow from the semifinal win over Notre Dame. Smith knew his wounded band could not beat Kentucky over forty normal minutes. With a lead early in the second half, and figuring it was his only chance to win, Smith sent Carolina into Four Corners with senior John Kuester (in place of Ford) in the middle. Foster, watching from the stands at Cole Field House, got up and left. He abhorred Smith's stalling strategy, which the Tar Heels used to freeze away a 79–72 win over the thirteenth-ranked Wildcats.

Ford also played hurt at the Final Four in Atlanta. Again using Four Corners for much of the second half, Carolina upset fourth-ranked UNLV behind 38 points from rambunctious freshman O'Koren to make the Monday night final against Marquette and their kooky head coach, Al McGuire, who had announced in January that the 1977 season would be his last. The team of destiny was meeting the sentimental favorite.

Marquette, ironically, was probably the weakest opponent Carolina had played to that point in the NCAA Tournament, having squeezed into the field and owning the most losses (seven) of any team that had reached the Final Four. The Warriors were talented, all right, but had a bunch of characters who sometimes listened to Al McGuire and sometimes did not. Bo Ellis was their All-American forward and Butch Lee their standout playmaker, but their rock was second guard Jimmy Boylan, a tough Jersey kid who had known O'Koren from the schoolyards and wanted a scholarship to UNC. Smith already had too many guards and recommended Boylan to McGuire at Marquette.

Al McGuire, who nineteen years earlier nearly went to UNC as an assistant to his no-relation namesake Frank McGuire, coached by feel and instinct, and never more so than when Smith called for Four Corners with the game tied midway through the second half. Using hand signals like a sideline maestro, McGuire had Lee and Boylan passively pressure the Tar Heels but still kept Ellis and the big men underneath guarding the basket.

McGuire wanted to keep the game going and the clock moving because he saw O'Koren sitting at the scorer's table, waiting to come in.

O'Koren was Carolina's first option off Four Corners, a backdoor artist who could get free for Ford's passes, but Smith refused to use one of his precious timeouts to sub him in for senior reserve Bruce Buckley. The Tar Heels lived by that loyalty and died by it that night when Buckley's layup was blocked by Ellis, and the Warriors regained the lead on the other end.

The 67–59 win was McGuire's coaching swan song, as he left the court in tears, saying his next move would be to ride his motorcycle out West. He retired with a national championship and the next season joined NBC as an entertaining commentator on college basketball broadcasts.

. . .

Overall, Duke suffered 40 defeats in Foster's first three seasons (while Carolina won 76 games and built another 8-game winning streak against the Blue Devils), but the wide-shouldered, 240-pound Gminski was the great white hope. He earned ACC Rookie of the Year in 1977 by averaging 15 points and 11 rebounds and brought an exuberance that helped lay the groundwork for Duke's spectacular worst-to-first season.

Foster was more comfortable rebuilding than trying to maintain a winning program when he got it there. Duke turned out to be the perfect challenge for the turnaround specialist. Still emerging from its 1950s and '60s provincialism, trying to become an elite private university with only 8,000 undergraduates and a disengaged alumni, Duke's glory days in athletics were considered dead and buried.

Its football team had not been to a bowl game since 1960, a year *after* head coach Mike McGee won the Outland Trophy as the nation's best lineman. McGee had returned to his alma mater in 1971 at thirty-one with dreams of resurrecting Bill Murray's Blue Devils of the 1960s. However, he found heightened academic standards and a fear of athletic emphasis pushed by eccentric faculty members under President Doug Knight.

Duke began growing into a prestigious national university when former North Carolina governor (and UNC alumnus) Terry Sanford took over as president in 1970. As a student at Carolina and lifetime resident of the state, Sanford idolized former UNC President Frank Porter Graham and tried to recreate much of the warmer Chapel Hill atmosphere at Duke. Just as "Doctor Frank" had done on a then-smaller UNC campus, Sanford had breakfast at the same time at the same table each morning in the Duke cafeteria, welcoming any student or faculty member who wanted to join him.

Duke's student body was largely from outside North Carolina, and most graduates went home with their degrees. Compared to Carolina's mushrooming enrollment and expanding graduate school, Duke remained in the shadow of the state university in the most visible sense, athletics, which required fan attendance for its financial support in the 1970s. TV had yet to become the ACC's cash cow or fund-raising a big business in college sports.

With a small local alumni fan base, Duke drew poorly in football and lived in financial crisis. The athletics department survived on an annual university subsidy, and employees joked about their next paychecks bouncing. Several of McGee's assistant coaches earned only $10,000 a year, and their recruiting budget was paltry compared to bigger, richer ACC schools.

Change began when Tom Butters, director of the Iron Dukes booster club, replaced Carl James as athletics director in 1977. The previous year, Butters had been named special assistant to Duke president Sanford, who expanded Butters's fund-raising duties beyond athletics. Some people saw the move as separation from James, who was eventually ousted in favor of Butters in a dual-role capacity.

Duke then had an athletics director and chief fund-raiser who actually answered, instead of dodged, questions about the Blue Devils' basketball and football futures. Among the first to accept life-insurance policies, and then borrow against the amounts bequeathed, Butters raised money easily because he was both a convincing salesman and a tough, shrewd leader. Still tight with the dollar, he had a grand plan and vision admired by alumni and fans.

The strapping Butters was a promising pitcher with the Pittsburgh Pirates when his career was curtailed by an automobile accident. He had an alluring personality and spoke dynamically. He made Duke supporters believe they could be big winners again, and, unlike James, had the full support of the administration in the Allen Building and the coaches in his department, as well as the Iron Dukes boosters to whom he was already connected.

Coincidentally or not, in Butters's first full year in charge, Foster's fourth Duke team parlayed Gminski, a pair of freshmen forwards and a junior journeyman who was becoming one of the best all-around players in the ACC into a team capable of winning a championship.

With the kind of contacts coaches need to pull off a recruiting coup, Foster had landed flamboyant Philadelphia forward Gene Banks, considered the best player from the City of Brotherly Love since Wilt Chamberlain. UNC also recruited Banks but couldn't even get him to visit because he was essentially blocked by Foster's people in Philly.

Foster's good fortune was that Joey Goldenberg, Banks's high school coach, worked at his summer camp. An engaging, articulate youngster, Banks had good grades but horrid SAT scores. Foster had clashed with the Duke admissions office on other recruits who did not meet the school's entrance standards, but he wasn't about to lose a program-turning talent. When Banks wanted to commit to Duke, Foster suggested he hold a press conference at his high school and essentially dared Duke to not admit him.

During this infighting, Banks's commitment wavered, largely because Notre Dame coach Digger Phelps wouldn't leave him alone. After his high school team played in Washington, D.C., in March of 1977, Banks went into seclusion for fifteen minutes with Phelps. "All I can do is go by what the kid tells me," Phelps said, "and he hasn't told me to stop recruiting him." Foster was around, too; it was the weekend he walked out of the UNC-Kentucky game.

Finally, Duke gave in and agreed to admit Banks, but the admissions office needed assurance that this would not happen again. And it didn't under Foster, who the next year could not get talented guard Wes Matthews past the front door. Matthews went on to star at Wisconsin and play in the NBA.

Foster was proud of Banks, his first top 10 signee and the highest-profile black player ever to attend Duke who was in the same class with superstar recruits Albert King of Maryland and Ervin "Magic" Johnson of Michigan State. He wanted to promote him immediately—unlike Smith, who shielded freshmen from interviews until after their first game. Duke scheduled a press conference when Banks came to Durham for summer orientation. Foster had to cancel it because Banks was not yet enrolled in school, but he encouraged writers to watch Banks play pick-up in Card Gym and talk him to there.

All the hoopla helped Duke, whose attendance had dwindled in the early 1970s, sell out season tickets within forty-eight hours after Banks committed. From that point on, in fact, only Iron Duke members could buy them. Banks was preseason second-team All-ACC and Rookie of the Year, both of which he eventually earned for real by averaging more than 17 points and 8 rebounds as one of the fresh faces who helped transform the 1977–78 Blue Devils.

Foster also signed underrated forward Kenny Dennard from rural King, North Carolina, whom Smith didn't recruit very hard because he already had the colorful O'Koren at his position. One of Smith's biggest tenets was to never "recruit over" an underclassmen because it showed a lack of confidence in the incumbent.

Gene Banks and Kenny Dennard joined pigeon-toed junior Jim Spanarkel, a one-time overweight after-thought who had become a solid player. Driven by the success of O'Koren, his higher-profile rival at Carolina, Spanarkel had worked relentlessly to reshape his body and garnered All-ACC honors and All-American mention as a sophomore. Four starters were in place for Foster's restoration; missing was a quality point guard.

Signs of greatness were emerging, symbolized by a $650,000 renovation of Cameron that included a new floor and student bleachers and carefully engineered baskets suspended from the baffle-lined ceiling of the thirty-eight-year-old gym, Foster's reward for finally selling out the place.

The Blue Devils lost to UNC in the Big Four Tournament in December, but upset No. 18 Wake Forest for third place. They proved they could play on the road in an overtime loss at Southern Cal, where security guards threw obnoxious brothers and Duke fans Mack and Vint Fountain out of the LA Sports Arena after a call that was so bad Foster got a letter of apology from the old Pac 8 director of officiating.

Duke would finish December 7–2, still virtually unnoticed but with clearly its strongest team in years.

Duke had used Carolina as the benchmark while putting together a championship-caliber club. Gminski tried to emulate the Tar Heels' emotion on the court, hugging and high-fiving teammates after big plays. Spanarkel was finally escaping O'Koren's shadow, averaging 21 points a game; Dennard still resented not having been recruited more seriously by his state university; and Banks just wanted Duke to win the way UNC had seemingly done forever.

Foster and his staff, none of whom had grown up in North Carolina, wondered whether the Tar Heels would ever have a down period. After all, he was used to rebuilding programs and experiencing good year, bad year, good year, bad year. Soon it dawned on them that with Dean Smith in the saddle and with UNC's resources no such swoon was coming. Duke had to raise its game to the same level.

Bob Bender, a transfer guard from Indiana's 1976 national champs, turned eligible after the first semester. Along with fellow sophomore John Harrell, a transfer from North Carolina Central in Durham, they were catalysts for Duke to turn the corner. Bobby Knight's program at Indiana University knew how to win in tough situations, and Bender, the son of a hard-nosed high school coach from the Hoosier State, brought that mentality with him to Durham. Harrell earned the starting point guard spot and played so well that Bender had to come off the bench when he became eligible.

At long last came the measuring stick, the home game with Carolina and its celebrated senior point guard, Phil Ford. A few dozen students camped out the night before to get the best seats once the doors opened. Alumni, fans, and sportswriters were anxious to see if the Blue Devils could break the latest losing streak to the team called the "Tar Holes" in the *Chronicle,* the program that had owned the series since the late '60s by winning 26 of the last 32 games.

Failing to stay above the rivalry, Foster and his staff believed the popular theory that Smith got all the big calls. They also thought college superstars such as Ford were treated like their NBA counterparts and subject to a different standard by officials whose job it was to keep them in the game for as long as possible so fans could get their money's worth.

Ford had a spectacular game, but Duke's combination gelled on a frigid winter Saturday afternoon in sizzling Cameron. Gminski led the team effort with 29 points and 10 rebounds as Duke's 66 percent shooting repeatedly foiled Carolina's pressure and turned Ford into a one-man gang. The unranked Blue Devils ran off with an impressive 92–84 win in front of a wild home crowd that infuriated Smith for the insulting way it treated one of his players.

He criticized courtside placards poking fun at O'Koren's facial acne, saying the personal attack crossed the line and beginning his two-decade joust with Duke students. At the very moment of Smith's harangue to the media, some delirious Dukies were actually cutting down the nets in Cameron to celebrate the win and taking over first place in the ACC. Smith did credit his vanquisher, calling Bender's 11 points and 4 assists the difference between this team and the Duke of old.

The Blue Devils soon cracked the rankings after a seven-year absence, but because of their newness to the national scene remained on Carolina's heels in the polls through most of February, despite having fewer losses. They didn't care, basking in their sudden glory and keeping on with silly superstitions and rituals actually inspired by their quirky coach.

On one hand, Foster was a born promoter. He would consider any goofy idea to bring publicity to his program. He liked billboards on the highway that showed a player dunking with the slogan DUKE BASKETBALL IS REALLY BIG STUFF! He hammered out his own letters and promotional flyers on a portable typewriter while players shot around in the gym. He carefully watched the rival down the road, amused and irritated by its omnipotence across the state and locally.

Foster wondered why the Durham *Morning Herald* and *Sun* covered the Tar Heels so closely. "They have their own newspaper in Chapel Hill," he said, only half-kidding. Foster once threw a local reporter, a UNC graduate, out of his locker room for not having clearance to enter after a practice. He was in the right, but couldn't help turning the knife about Smith's overprotected program. "You can't do this at Carolina, can you?"

After three losing seasons as an ACC also-ran and UNC's punching bag, anything that kept their success going was okay with Foster.

Banks carried a stuffed dog with him to every game and left it in his locker. He also wore the same pair of socks all season. Dennard was the team flake, and always brushed his teeth just before taking the court. Bender shot the last layup in warm-ups. While the rest of the team wore colorful clothes with wide lapels and wild ties, Foster stuck with one brown suit during a five-game winning streak in February. He had it on again for the regular-season finale in Chapel Hill, when the irrepressible Dukies had a chance to complete their improbable journey from last place in the ACC.

The rivals entered the rematch tied for first in the standings with 8–3 records. Duke had climbed to No. 11 in the poll, its highest ranking in ten years. Though still eighth-ranked, Carolina was reeling, riddled with injuries to Ford and

O'Koren and having split the last four games. Ford's final home appearance, however, was the X-factor.

The poised and confident Blue Devils, clearly the better team by that point in the season, stayed ahead and in control most of the game. Ford, who had recently become UNC's all-time leading scorer, played with a sprained left wrist numbed by adrenaline. His brilliance kept the Tar Heels close enough for a late rally, and his 34 points finally offset the 69 scored by Banks, Gminski, and Spanarkel in Carolina's dramatic 87–83 win.

"He was not only inspired, he was just taking it down and spinning it off his feet or under his legs or hooking it," Foster said, jokingly, adding truthfully, "We didn't have any defense for him."

Duke felt miserable enough about losing, but the outcome provided further concern. By finishing first, Carolina wrapped up one of the ACC's two NCAA bids. The other now belonged to the ACC Tournament champion, unless UNC won that, too. Duke could get invited by playing the Tar Heels in the final, but under any other scenario would have to win the tourney title.

The ACC Tournament had not changed since its inception in 1954. First-round games were played on Thursday, the semifinals on Friday night and the championship game Saturday night. At first, TV rights holder C. D. Chesley and sponsor Jefferson Pilot provided coverage of the semifinals and championship game to the four-state footprint. Once the public sale of tickets ended in the 1960s, and most of the ACC schools used them as fund-raising incentives with their booster clubs, Chesley began showing all seven games. Public school attendance dipped dramatically on the first Thursday in March, as thousands of kids played hooky to watch the afternoon sessions of *the tournament.*

For years, the ACC was happy with its regional coverage and refused any inquiries or offers to change, but, in the spring of 1977, the conference received an offer it couldn't refuse.

ABC had proposed to broadcast the 1978 ACC championship game on Saturday afternoon, March 3, on its popular *Wide World of Sports* show and guaranteed several hundred thousand dollars above the league's annual TV take from Chesley. ABC was preparing to bid for the rights to the NCAA Tournament, held by NBC through 1981, and wanted to demonstrate it could produce quality national basketball telecasts.

ABC, however, did not want a sloppy title game between tired opponents that had played the night before. The tournament schedule was changed to begin on Wednesday and have an off-day Friday, during which the finalists would practice around a major press conference. That game, ABC hoped, would be a rematch of the classic in Chapel Hill the week before.

Carolina had a first-round bye because there were still only seven teams in the ACC. Duke and Wake Forest won their first-round games comfortably, but Maryland needed three overtimes and almost three hours to oust N.C. State. As the game ended late Wednesday, snow was already falling in Greensboro.

Although schools closed and traffic snarled, a full house made it to the Greensboro Coliseum for Thursday night's semifinals. Duke defeated Driesell's tired Terrapins to reach its first championship game since Bubas's last year in 1969. Wake Forest then upset UNC in the second game, killing ABC's plans. Usually happy to see Carolina go down, the Blue Devils were now under added pressure to win the ACC Tournament and get the other NCAA bid.

Foster was the ACC's funniest coach, and at Friday's press conference he was in the rare spotlight and full of quips.

"They said it would be a snowy day in Greensboro before Duke played in the ACC finals," he began. "We usually lose and I go home. In the past, I've packed a handkerchief and that's about it. But this time I packed for the whole weekend and so did the team."

The weather cleared and a capacity crowd of nearly 16,000 jammed the coliseum for the historic final. NBA legend Bill Russell handled color commentary for ABC and UNC graduate Jim Lampley called the play-by-play. Nervous Duke fell behind by five points at the half to hot-shooting Wake Forest, led by 1977 ACC Player of the Year Rod Griffin and fellow senior Leroy McDonald.

Foster cracked a couple of jokes in the locker room, trying to loosen up his atypically uptight team. It must have worked. Behind Gminski's 25 points and 16 rebounds, 22 points from Banks, and 20 from Spanarkel, the tourney MVP, the Blue Devils rallied in the second half and ran away from the Deacons to win the ACC title and an NCAA ticket, touching off a wild celebration on the court.

"I felt I had let the university down the last three years," Foster said after clipping part of the net and as the uncontainable "Tinkerbell" Banks ran around waving the Duke mascot's pitchfork so enthusiastically that he nearly fainted.

"This is the greatest thing that has ever happened to me in basketball, because I never thought we'd get there," Foster said, wearing one of the nets.

Besides the unprecedented exposure on ABC, the cover of *Sports Illustrated* that week carried a picture of Banks under the headline DUKE BREAKS LOOSE. It all helped to captivate the country when the Blue Devils began play in their first NCAA Tournament since 1966.

Mike Krzyzewski has been credited with making the NCAA Tournament more significant for Duke and Carolina than what happened during the regular season, but that shift really began in 1978.

While UNC fans never forgot Ford's grand home finale, it was also his last shining moment. The Tar Heels followed their quick exit from the ACC Tournament by losing in the West Regional to Bill Cartwright and nineteenth-ranked San Francisco, an unfair draw for the ACC regular-season winners. His career dashed with two straight defeats, Ford wept in the locker room as he took off his Carolina uniform for the last time.

Guthridge, Smith's assistant for eleven years, grew so emotional that he changed his mind about taking the head-coaching job at Penn State. He was scheduled to be introduced at University Park on Monday, on the way home from Phoenix, but Guthridge rerouted his bags to Raleigh when they caught a connection in Chicago. He couldn't leave on such a losing note.

The Tar Heels finished with a 23–8 record and a thud. For the first time in twelve years, they sat home while Duke played on. The Blue Devils were placed in the East Regional and faced a second-round game against Rhode Island in Charlotte the night after Carolina's season ended.

Ford was the ACC Player of the Year, but Gminski was easily the most valuable. Without the gentle giant, Duke would have been one and done. His two free throws and blocked shot in the final seconds allowed the Blue Devils to edge Rhode Island. Then, in the Sweet Sixteen, his three straight blocks sparked an 18–2 run that overcame quicker Ivy League champion Penn in Providence. Before the game, snow began to fall. The Dukies saw it as another omen and figured they now had it made.

They got some other unexpected help from the two Philly teams in the East Regional.

Despite losing, Penn coach Bob Weinhauer and star guard Bobby Willis, who had turned down a scholarship offer from Duke, called the Blue Devils too slow to beat Villanova, their Big Five brethren, in the regional championship game.

"I see Villanova winning by six," Weinhauer said in the post-game press conference. He earlier had been critical of how much TV time Duke got in Philadelphia during the season.

The next night, Villanova coach Rollie Massimino was dining at a Providence restaurant and carrying on with friends when several sportswriters overheard him predict that his much-quicker Wildcats would have no problem against the bigger, slower "elephants" from Duke.

By the time the teams took the court, Massimino's boast was all over the news and the Providence Civic Center. Called slow afoot in print and inspired by the criticism, the bigger team was also the faster team, blowing out to a 21–6 lead that grew to 21 by the end of the half. The Blue Devils made 65 percent of their shots and literally ran Villanova out of the building, capped by Dennard's raucous 360 dunk in the closing seconds.

A few hours later, a tipsy Foster joked of the 90–72 win, "I guess the elephants stampeded!" His first Final Four was also Duke's first since Bubas's last in 1966. Out of nowhere, the team time had forgotten was back in the spotlight, namely the Checker Dome in St. Louis, joining the stud field of Notre Dame, Arkansas, and Kentucky.

Duke faced a Notre Dame team so beefy across the front line that it gave Foster his next one-liner, "I'm back coaching football."

The Devils, however, were faster and led Phelps's only Final Four team by 14 points at halftime. Delirious Dukies in the stands and watching on TV had to pinch themselves. After more than ten years of being overshadowed by Carolina, they were on the verge of playing for the national championship.

Then Notre Dame rallied behind its front court of Kelly Tripucka, Dave Batton, and Bill Laimbeer, and the outside shooting of Donald "Duck" Williams, cutting the 14-point deficit to only 4 late in the game. Irish fans in the Checker Dome, who had been vocal and frustrated because their team had rolled to three easy victories in the Midwest Region, began roaring with the prospect of a late victory.

However, Notre Dame had committed too many fouls and repeatedly put Duke back on the free throw line. Gminski's 13 of 17 and 12 straight by Spanarkel salted away the 90–86 win, sending the relieved Blue Devils to their second national championship game ever. The first was against UCLA in 1964 and resulted in the start of John Wooden's reign; the second would be against Kentucky, whose coach, Joe B. Hall, was still chasing an NCAA title.

The bluegrass Wildcats had beaten Arkansas in the other semifinal, and in the locker room the wacky Dennard, the most outspoken of the delightfully candid Devils, spoke to sportswriters wearing a plastic Hog's hat. While top-ranked Kentucky was a grim, decided favorite with all the pressure, the Dukies had become the adored media darling for their personalities and candor off the court, as well as their success on it.

Foster was now a fixture during the month of March Madness. So was his new wardrobe of a blue blazer, white shirt, and plaid tie and pants. He wore the gaudy, good luck combo through seven straight ACC and NCAA Tournament wins and put it on one last time Monday night when the Blue Devils took college basketball's biggest stage in prime time.

Duke was still regarded as more of a Cinderella than a legit challenger by the cocky Kentucky fans. "We'll win because we have a damn Philadelphia lawyer in the backcourt," one blue-clad booster chirped on the way into the Checker Dome, referring to slick senior point guard Kyle Macy.

Kentucky got into early foul trouble, and indeed Macy helped negotiate the Wildcats out of it. They spread the court against Foster's 1–3–1 zone, the defense that had carried Duke to the last game of the college basketball season. Foster stayed with it, even after Macy continued finding forward Jack "Goose" Givens in the seams for open midrange shots. Givens scored his team's last 16 points of the first half and had 23 when Kentucky went to the locker room ahead, 45–38.

Givens returned just as hot, once making a shot after it grazed the side of the backboard, but Foster refused to come out of the 1–3–1. With thirteen minutes left, Duke was down by 16 points and the Kentucky crowd began celebrating. Hall even loosened up and took his starters out early enough to allow Duke to rally and make the 94–88 final score closer than the actual contest.

Givens wound up with 41 points, the third highest in championship game history behind UCLA's Bill Walton (44) and Gail Goodrich (42). Hall escaped Rupp's ubiquitous shadow with the Wildcats' first NCAA title in twenty years. Until his team stripped the nets, the stoic Hall had called it "a season without celebration."

Duke did not win but celebrated nonetheless when welcomed home by a screaming crowd at Cameron. Gminski, Spanarkel, and Banks, who had combined for 63 points against Kentucky, were all coming back the next season. The Blue Devils had made a remarkable turnaround from last place in the ACC each of the prior three years, going 27–7 and tying Art Heyman's senior team in 1963 for the most wins in school history.

Following the 1978 season of renewed prominence, Duke inducted Heyman into its Sports Hall of Fame. He had not been back to campus much in fifteen years, still miffed over not having his No. 25 jersey retired. Before the banquet, he clowned with Spanarkel, to whom he was compared as a limited athlete that made himself a great basketball player.

The weekend spawned another movement by alumni and media old-timers to hoist Heyman's jersey to the rafters of Cameron. He had met all of the criteria—first-team All-American and national player of the year in 1963—but his controversial career as a troublemaker on and off the court had seemingly denied him the highest honor in Duke basketball.

Acknowledging that he lived and played outside of the so-called Duke image, Heyman quipped in his Hall of Fame induction speech, "I was the only player that they had to keep a lawyer on retainer for."

The true jersey issue was Eddie Cameron's rule that Dick Groat's No. 10 be the only one in the rafters. He had rejected Bubas's original request to hang Heyman's jersey, but Cameron was now retired and Butters didn't give a damn about his archaic view. Heyman decided to move to Durham and open a hair replacement business with his wife. Soon the crevices of Cameron began filling up with retired jerseys and eventually championship banners.

Larry Brown also went back to his roots in 1978, when he quit as coach of the Denver Nuggets after fifty-three games.

College basketball was Brown's first love. He spent his first years after college flip-flopping between the amateur and professional game, playing semipro and for the 1964 U.S.A. Olympic Gold Medalists in Tokyo. After serving on Dean Smith's staff for two years in 1965, he returned to star in the new American Basketball Association.

In 1969, when Driesell went to Maryland, Brown was named head coach at Davidson but quit a few weeks later because he said the school reneged on some promises. He began his pro coaching career with the old Carolina Cougars of the ABA, went to Denver when the Cougars folded, and remained through the merger of the pro leagues. After three years as an NBA coach, Brown wanted to give college basketball another try.

UCLA was looking to replace Gary Cunningham (who had replaced Gene Bartow, who had succeeded John Wooden). Athletics Director J. D. Morgan tried to lure Smith to the West Coast, aware that Smith had been remarried to a psychiatrist from Southern California. Smith turned Morgan down but told him that Brown was tired of pro ball and said he was actually better suited to teach the college game.

Brown coached the Bruins for two seasons, leading them to the 1980 NCAA championship game behind All-American Kiki Vandeweghe before losing to Louisville and Darrell Griffith in Indianapolis. Frustrated with how UCLA lived in the past and refused to upgrade coaching salaries and facilities, Brown resigned and went back to the big NBA money with New Jersey.

A year later, UCLA received a one-year probation from the NCAA for recruiting violations committed during Brown's coaching tenure. Brown was not directly involved in illegal gifts players received from alumni and boosters, but he was cited for failing to properly monitor his program.

Heyman and Brown had been out of college for more than fifteen years, during which time the provincial game they boosted to another level with their famous fight had exploded into a national sports phenomenon. The local rivalry they personified was, once again, hotter than hell.

After Ford graduated and went second in the NBA draft to Kansas City, Carolina found itself reading more about Duke's togetherness on and off the court. Without Ford, the Tar Heels looked like they might revert to Smith's starless, passé system that supposedly suppressed individual talent. The bolder Blue Devils were the new "in" team, and Smith faced one more decision about his career.

Two days before practice began, on Friday the thirteenth of October, 1978, Smith was in New York to see the third game of the World Series between the Yankees and Dodgers. He was the guest of Yankees vice president and longtime friend Clyde King, who was from Goldsboro, North Carolina. Smith watched all-star pitcher Ron Guidry beat the Dodgers 5–1 from King's box, but he also thought about the meeting he had had that morning in the executive suite of Madison Square Garden.

Impresario Sonny Werblin had recently taken over as president of the Garden and was essentially running the struggling New York Knicks franchise. Werblin wanted to fire second-year head coach Willis Reed, the former Knicks star, and sought Smith to replace him—starting immediately, as the 1978–79 season was about to open.

Werblin had won the bidding war for rookie quarterback Joe Namath with an unprecedented $400,000 contract in 1967 when he owned the New York Jets. He slid a blank check across the conference table in his posh office on 34th Street in midtown Manhattan.

"Fill in a number, Dean, whatever it takes," Werblin said.

Smith smiled and said nothing for the moment, collecting his thoughts. Sure, he was content at UNC, but Ford was gone and maybe it was a good time to leave. Plenty of quality players remained in Chapel Hill, and quitting just before practice began assured that Guthridge would succeed him. Guthridge would be an excellent head coach and was ready for the challenge, having let emotion cause his about-face with Penn State.

"I'm flattered, Sonny, I really am," Smith said. "But I'm more cut out to be a college coach. And I love Chapel Hill."

Werblin asked him if he could change his mind. Smith shook his head and then shook Werblin's hand. Fourteen games into the new season, after they opened with 6–8 record, the Knicks fired Reed and replaced him with Red Holzman, who had previously coached them for ten years and to the franchise's two NBA titles.

By then, Smith was readying for another season, and, after thinking about

UCLA the year before and the NBA most recently, he decided he was at UNC to stay. So did Guthridge, who had been offered the Arkansas, Auburn, and Colorado jobs, as well as Penn State, but would never interview for another head-coaching position.

Foster wasn't nearly as entrenched. Duke's rebirth put the forty-seven-year-old coach in a new spotlight and made him edgier than when he was the lovable loser. His players began the 1979 season less affected, unanimously voted preseason No. 1, and exuding the same confidence and bravado as the year before. They won their first six games, including a ten-point victory over Carolina in the Big Four Tournament championship game.

Then they hit New York City over Christmas for the Holiday Festival at the Garden against a field of unranked opponents looking to knock off the odds-on favorites to win the national championship. *Sports Illustrated* was planning to release a story that called Banks, Gminski, and Spanarkel the three best players at their positions in college basketball.

In the opening game against Ohio State, Duke led comfortably at halftime. Then, as if they forgot what had made them a great team, the Blue Devils began missing shots and making bad plays. They lost to the Buckeyes and, the next night, blew another enormous lead to St. John's.

Monday morning, *SI* scrubbed the story amidst critical columns in the local papers about how Duke blew both games. Nothing was easy for Foster's team after that, as the Blue Devils hit a prolonged shooting slump, transforming them from loose and easy to a testy and joyless bunch.

Dennard personified the skid into 1979 and the new year. He partied too much, let his weight balloon and stopped working hard in practice. His field goal and free throw percentages plummeted, along with his scoring, rebounding, and assist averages. His happy-go-lucky manner on the court turned surly and confrontational with officials. He sat for long stretches as Foster broke freshman Vince Taylor into the lineup.

Harrell was also unhappy, believing he had been unjustly replaced in the starting lineup by Bender for no apparent reason. Harrell had started over Bender throughout Duke's Final Four season and their statistics were almost dead even, except that he had 28 fewer assists in 12 more games. Harrell stopped working as hard in practice, letting his game and weight slip.

After losing at third-ranked Carolina on January 13, Duke dropped to No. 8 in the polls. The teams stayed within a game of each other in the ACC race through February and were actually tied for first heading into the last week of the regular season. Then the Blue Devils lost badly at Clemson on Wednesday night and the Tar Heels beat N.C. State at home on Thursday.

The game on February 24 was the last at Cameron for Spanarkel, by then a svelte senior and a personable, popular player. Duke had to beat Carolina to get even and force a coin flip for the first-round bye in the seven-team ACC Tournament the next week. Clemson's 21-point upset of the Blue Devils not only guaranteed UNC a share of first place, how the Tigers spread the floor against Duke also gave Dean Smith an idea.

Smith always considered winning on an opponent's Senior Day (especially when it had an outstanding senior) one of the tougher tasks in college basketball. The Tar Heels had proven it the year before when Ford put them on his back in his final home game. Smith worried most about Duke's menacing zone, anchored by the imposing Gminski, the leading candidate for ACC Player of the Year whose favorite lyrics that season were Randy Newman's "Short people got no reason to live."

How could Carolina handle the G-man, silence the raucous Cameron crowd, and open up Duke's defense so Smith's freelance passing game could out-quick the bigger, slower Blue Devils? Smith took a page from Clemson but did not tell the players what he was thinking until they met a few hours before the bus ride to Durham.

"Okay," Smith said, as he knelt in front of them in the pregame huddle, "you know what to do."

Duke controlled the opening tip and Gminski, against tight defense, short-armed a jumper from the foul line. Three Tar Heels had the lane covered, but the ball barely hit the rim and Vince Taylor slipped inside to convert the awkward carom for a 2–0 lead. The Blue Devils retreated into their regular zone defense. UNC point guard Dave Colescott crossed midcourt and started passing the ball around. He also stopped the game.

Smith sat back on the bench and crossed his legs. Duke sat back near the basket and didn't come out. It was 1966 all over again.

"We didn't want to play against their zone," Smith said later.

"We had the lead," Foster countered.

The Duke crowd booed and hissed the Tar Heels, who ran more than twelve minutes off the clock in the cat-and-mouse game. Occasionally testing both sides of the Duke zone, Carolina eventually got impatient and fed the ball to center Rich Yonakor on the left baseline. He took one dribble and fired anxiously. His left-handed shot flew over the basket, missing everything.

"Air-ball! Air-ball!" yelled a few creative Duke students, an impromptu cheer that became a part of basketball in every gym on every level. The Blue Devils grabbed the rebound, went down and scored for a 4–0 lead. Carolina continued to hold the ball, and Yonakor again missed everything. That's when AIR-BALL!

really took hold. After Colescott's last-second heave fell way short, Duke led 7–0 at halftime. The Heels left the floor to bombastic chants of AIR-BALL! Not only shut out, they hadn't even hit the rim!

The teams played normally in the second half, and each scored 40 points. Late in the game, with Duke leading and Carolina trying to put the Blue Devils on the foul line, Gminski kayoed UNC's Al Wood with an elbow that left the teams pushing and shoving each other and sent Smith onto the court after Gminski. The 5' 11" coach tried to get in the 6' 11" center's face, but had to settle for looking up and yelling.

"You knew what we were trying to do!" Smith said. "We were trying to stop the clock. There's no need to play like that."

Gminski retorted, "Hey, they're not calling any fouls. I'm just trying to protect myself."

The argument was interrupted by the officials coming over to eject Gminski for the only time in his college career, which in turn brought Gminski's high-strung father, Joe, out of his seat cursing at Smith.

Duke was particularly sore that Smith's slowdown ruined half of Senior Night and that the strategy dominated the next day's headlines over Spanarkel's remarkable, self-made career. Averaging more than 16 points, 4 assists and 3 rebounds a game, Spanarkel personified Duke's rise which Foster himself labeled as "outhouse to penthouse."

Of course, Smith defended his decision to hold the ball; his plan failed due to impatience and poor execution. "What I did was *so* sound," he said after the 47–40 loss that left UNC and Duke deadlocked for first place. The coin flip at ACC headquarters Sunday morning was critical, because the winner would have to play only one game to reach the ACC Tournament final, the loser two games.

The local radio station in Chapel Hill, WCHL, went to Greensboro to "cover" the coin flip. A few overzealous UNC fans also showed up and began screaming, "We got the bye!" over the radio when ACC Assistant Commissioner Skeeter Francis came out to make the announcement to the attending media.

Foster said he didn't care about losing the bye, which gave Carolina an enormous advantage of having to play one less game. "Our kids like to play," Foster said sarcastically on his radio show Sunday night. He was more intent on chiding Smith's strategy in the game twenty-four hours earlier.

"If this is what's happened to the game, maybe it's time for me to do something else," he said. During a break in the show, Foster first used his famous pun. "I thought *Naismith* invented basketball, not Deansmith."

To read between the lines, Foster's frustration showed how tired he was of competing with Carolina and their fans off the court. He had beaten Smith at his own game, the slowdown strategy that Foster loathed. When he should have been laughing with satisfaction, however, Foster couldn't enjoy it.

Criticism of the slowdown echoed from every corner, and was not limited to the media and opposing fans. O'Koren questioned the move in the Durham *Morning Herald,* saying he wanted to play all out against Duke. The public lack of loyalty incensed Smith, who Monday called O'Koren onto the Carolina blue carpet in his office where he chain-smoked a pack a day.

O'Koren said it was like the voice of God speaking to him from behind a cloud.

"Michael," Smith said with clenched teeth, holding a cigarette in one hand and the article in the other, "You play, I'll coach."

That afternoon, O'Koren ran the stairs of Carmichael, wearing a weighted vest. God had spoken.

The ridicule the Tar Heels took served as incentive for the ACC Tournament the next week. They ripped Maryland in the semifinals to return to the championship game for the fourth time in five years. Duke was dragging as it edged Wake Forest and N.C. State, surviving the Wolfpack on Bob Bender's best college performance. He scored 16 points to help set up a fourth meeting of the season with UNC in the title game, which had returned to Saturday night.

Bender awoke early Saturday morning with sharp stomach pains. He was rushed back to Durham and, after being diagnosed with acute appendicitis, was already out of surgery at Duke Hospital by the time the ACC final tipped off at 7:30 in the Greensboro Coliseum. He was replaced in the lineup by Harrell, who had sulked most of the season and was not in the best physical shape either.

Carolina jumped on Duke, challenging the zone with drives, penetration, and pull-up jump shots and took a 31–25 lead at halftime. Late in the second half with the score still close came the play of the game from the player least expected to make it.

Dudley Bradley was UNC's long-armed senior guard nicknamed the Secretary of Defense. He earned the moniker on the way to becoming UNC's all-time leader in steals. In January, he had made a last-second swipe from N.C. State's Clyde Austin and slammed the ball home for a 70–69 win in Raleigh to stun a crazed crowd of Wolfpack fans.

Still, the last thing Bradley was known for was offense. He owned a career scoring average of 4.4 points and had never made the all-conference team. Maybe for that reason, Bradley posed little threat to the giant Gminski when he got the ball on the baseline to the right of the basket. Far better offensive players than Bradley didn't dare test the G-man, the 1979 ACC Player of the Year, on his way to 19 points and 16 rebounds in the title game.

Expected to pass it back out or, at the very most, fire his flat jump shot from in front of his face, Bradley instead drove the baseline, then crossed over toward the middle, catching Gminski flat-footed. Bradley kept going and slam-dunked the ball over the front of the rim.

The play, which became folklore for UNC fans, was symbolic because it defined Carolina's aggressiveness one week after the Tar Heels had seemingly backed down from Duke. Smith insisted that he had stalled at Cameron because the odds were against his team that night, but that it would have no effect on how a subsequent game might be played.

The Tar Heels' 71–63 win for the ACC championship bore that out, although Duke felt screwed because it had to play one more game in the ACC Tournament and the final without Bender. Bradley scored a season-high 16 points, had 7 steals and was named tournament MVP.

The rivals awaited the NCAA Tournament pairings and where they would be playing the next week, figuring they had seen the last of each other. The selection committee, though, had other plans, as it often did when a juicy rematch could be arranged for TV.

The field had increased to forty teams for one year before expanding to forty-eight with no limit on how many bids a league could receive. Another reason the 1979 tournament was memorable: the entire East Region was scheduled for North Carolina, with the first two rounds in Raleigh and the Sweet Sixteen back in Greensboro.

As if the selection committee could not decide, or was trying to avoid a protest by one of the schools, it placed *both* UNC and Duke in the East. Seeded No. 1 and No. 2, they had first-round byes and needed to win two games to meet for a *fifth* time in the regional final in Greensboro, where they had already played twice.

A dream doubleheader that had fans in a frenzy became one of the most infamous days in college basketball history. A highly partisan crowd filled Reynolds Coliseum to watch Carolina take on two-time Ivy League champion Penn, and its ACC-critic of a coach, Bob Weinhauer, followed by Duke's second game of the season against St. John's.

The Tar Heels had suffered their share of NCAA tough luck in recent years, what with the injuries to Phil Ford, Walter Davis, and Tom LaGarde and the heart-breaking loss to Marquette. They had no excuses this time; they were healthy and playing well and had a huge, highly partisan crowd backing them on N.C. State's home court.

Smith kept the team in Chapel Hill, as was his custom for games less than ninety minutes away. He liked his players to sleep in their own beds, but several of them roamed the Franklin Street bars Saturday night before turning in. They bussed to Raleigh and took the underrated Quakers too lightly, suffering an inexplicable 72–71 loss that ended their season and seemingly cleared the way for the Blue Devils to reach the Sweet Sixteen.

Hard-luck Duke was without Bender and Dennard, who had sprained his ankle at mid-week horsing around in Cameron with a bunch of inebriated football players. Plus, Gminski had eaten some bad pizza the night before and was heaving into a bucket by the bench during timeouts, as his crippled team tried desperately to hang on.

After leading the Johnnies most of the game, as they had the previous December in New York, the Devils let it slip away in the last few minutes. The worst part of their 80–78 loss was that Bender and Dennard were expected back the next week and Gminski, of course, would have stopped throwing up by then. Like the strangest bedfellows, they joined the Tar Heels at home while thousands of people tore up their tickets to Greensboro.

Players and fans from both teams wandered around their respective campuses and towns, uncomfortable with their inactivity after holding such high expectations. Carolina had finished 23–6 and ranked ninth; Duke 22–8 and No. 11. Weinhauer and Penn got the last laugh by advancing to Greensboro, as the Blue Devils and Tar Heels shared a strange, symbiotic sorrow over the agony of what became known as Black Sunday.

Although only one of them could have survived the region and moved on to Salt Lake City, where Magic Johnson and Michigan State beat Larry Bird and Indiana State for the national championship, they found common ground in their disappointment and embarrassment.

Without Bradley and Spanarkel, the thirteenth and sixteenth picks in the 1979 NBA draft, the rivals played four more times during the 1980 season.

Duke opened by beating second-ranked Kentucky and then edged Wake Forest and sixth-ranked Carolina to win the Big Four Tournament for the second straight year. The Blue Devils streaked to twelve consecutive victories and the No. 1 ranking. Carolina struggled early trying to find a place for 6' 8" freshman star James Worthy, who started at one post position and moved O'Koren to small forward. The Tar Heels upset fifth-ranked Indiana in Bloomington but then lost their first two ACC games at Clemson and Virginia. After holding off an average Wake Forest team, they were installed as a 21-point underdog against top-ranked Duke the following Saturday.

With Worthy breaking out, at one point spinning and dunking over a dazed

Dennard, Carolina stunned the Blue Devils by 15 points in a disquieted Cameron. Smith didn't like it when one sportswriter told him that his team "covered the spread" by thirty-six, having begun to lobby publicly against newspapers carrying the betting lines of college games.

That loss spiraled Duke to a disastrous 5–7 stretch and down to No. 16 in the polls, frustrating Foster, who was linked to the coaching vacancy at South Carolina and bugged daily by the media on his future. Foster hadn't signed up another star player since Vince Taylor and the rumor mill transformed him from approachable to sarcastic and short.

UNC was playing far better basketball and continued to do so even after losing Worthy with a broken ankle against Maryland in late January. By the February 23 rematch in Chapel Hill, the Blue Devils were dispirited and in disarray and, predictably, got blown out by 25 points in O'Koren's last home game.

The Tar Heels had adjusted to playing without Worthy and finished tied for second in the ACC, two games behind Maryland. The Blue Devils, distracted and down by persistent reports of Foster's departure, could finish no better than 7–7 and tied for fifth with Virginia in the new eight-team league that had admitted Georgia Tech in 1979. Duke lost the tie-breaker and wound up seeded sixth and in UNC's bracket for the ACC Tournament.

Six days later they played again, their eighth meeting in two years. Duke completed the 39-point turnaround in their semifinal game by blowing out the Tar Heels in the second half. The 75–61 win, dominated by Gminski's 24 points and 19 rebounds, restarted the Blue Devils. They upset Maryland for the ACC championship the next night, as a blizzard blanketed the state and only eight thousand people could get to the game.

"Another snowy day in North Carolina," Foster quipped, referring to two years earlier.

The snow cleared and Foster decided to clear out. He knew he was leaving and stopped recruiting. His boss, Butters, spent two weeks skiing in Vail and did little to keep him before Foster made a clandestine deal with South Carolina. Duke's cupboard would be bare after Banks and Dennard played their senior year for a new coach.

Finally, Foster confirmed widespread speculation that he was resigning, and his team seemed relieved. The Blue Devils played hard and fast in the NCAA Tournament, advancing to the Mideast Regional where they stunned top-seeded Kentucky on its home court.

Two days later, with Foster looking bewildered on the bench, they lost to Joe Barry Carroll and Purdue 68–60 in the round of eight. Despite the dramatic tournament run, Foster was a wreck after the game, barely coherent with the media and near tears in the locker room. He wanted to go out with another Final Four, maybe to stick it up Duke's ass or maybe because he knew how hard it would be to do it somewhere else.

Foster might have stayed if Duke had given him everything he asked for and avoided his thorny relationship with tightwad Butters. However, Foster's leaving had probably more to do with the makeup of the man. He had not been anywhere beyond eight years, and Duke turned out to be no exception.

After one Final Four and two ACC championships in his last three seasons, he had had enough of Smith, UNC, and Duke basketball. Succeeding the ousted Frank McGuire at South Carolina, which was still an independent, Foster traded the bitterness of a local rivalry for a school where he could schedule nationally and enjoy life more.

"I guess it was just time to leave, I don't know," Foster said a few years later. "Those were my most memorable days in coaching. But I never did enjoy it. I don't know what it was. It didn't really sink in and that's my own fault. I don't blame anybody for that. I certainly don't blame Duke. I just never relaxed."

Smith's sustained run overshadowed what Foster accomplished at Duke, a 113–64 record and those two ACC titles. He talked about UNC fans razzing his daughters at school, and getting needled himself at the local grocery store. He hated how whatever Smith said was taken as gospel.

They were once on a plane together, when the sun burst through the clouds so brightly that Smith said it reminded him of Chapel Hill on a summer day. After a drought caused a water shortage in Smith's university town, Foster had to zing him with a note about what "too much of that Chapel Hill sunshine" can do.

Gminski, his breakthrough recruit who graduated the same year Foster left, wasn't surprised by his coach's departure. "The incestuousness of the whole thing," he said. "We're, what, six miles apart [actually eight]? It's so concentrated that you never get away from it. There's never a waking moment when you're away from it. I think that played a big role in why Foster left."

Foster coached thirteen more seasons at South Carolina and Northwestern, never getting back to the NCAA Tournament. After retiring from the bench, he remained in basketball as supervisor of officials for the Big 12 and Western Athletic Conference and stayed active with the coaches' association he once chaired and as an NBA scout.

Though short, Foster's tenure revived the Blue Devils and prevented Carolina from dominating the rivalry for fifteen years between Duke's two greatest coaches, Bubas and Krzyzewski. It also helped continue to rebuild the mutual respect that had grown since the fight-scarred 1960s.

RIVALRY RECORD IN THE 1970s
- Carolina won 23; Duke won 8

HOW THEY DID IN THE DECADE
- Carolina 239–65 (.786); Duke 162–116 (.582)

ACC CHAMPIONSHIPS
- Carolina 1972, 1975, 1977, 1979; Duke 1978

FINAL FOURS
- Carolina 1972, 1977; Duke 1978

COACHING RECORDS
- Bucky Waters vs. Carolina: 3–9
- Neil McGeachy vs. Carolina: 0–3
- Bill Foster vs. Carolina: 6–13

BIGGEST UPSET
- Duke 76, Carolina 74, January 22, 1972

MOST FAMOUS GAME
- Carolina 96, Duke 92 (OT), March 2, 1974

BIGGEST TURNAROUND
- Carolina 96, Duke 71, February 23, 1980
- Duke 75, Carolina 61, February 29, 1980

BEST QUOTE
"I thought Naismith invented basketball, not Deansmith."

(Bill Foster)

5

BLUE BLOOD BITTERNESS

Mike Krzyzewski jumped off the bench, reacting to the hard contact under the basket. "Hey, 42, that was a dirty foul!" he shouted at UNC center Scott Williams.

On the opposite bench, Dean Smith pulled himself up, clapped his hands and screamed at his adversary, "Don't talk to my players!"

Coach K glared down the sideline, crinkling his nose and forehead in anger.

"Hey, Dean!" he yelled back. "Fuck you!"

The infamous nine-word exchange between Dean Smith and Mike Krzyzewski during the 1989 ACC championship game in Atlanta spoke volumes about where they had been, where they stood, and where they were headed as caretakers of the Carolina-Duke rivalry.

UNC fans who heard (about) it were furious that their legendary coach, seventeen years older and in the league nearly two decades longer, could be treated so disrespectfully by the Duke upstart. Where did Krzyzewski get off cursing the coach who never cursed?

Who was he to complain about another team's physicality? In his first decade at Duke, he had introduced such ferocious defense that other ACC coaches now complained about a new "double standard" from the one Krzyzewski had accused Smith and his program of enjoying only five years before.

Conversely, the ABC (Anybody But Carolina) crowd had a field day with the public dissing of someone they considered a long-time hypocrite. Wasn't it Smith who stormed onto the court during the 1977 NCAA Tournament when he thought the Kentucky players were roughing up his own and called Wildcats' center Rick Robey a son of a bitch?

Eerily, the career patterns of these antagonists followed one another roughly twenty years apart.

An unknown, if not unpopular choice, the young coach quickly lost his anonymity, barely escaped alumni henchmen who scoffed at his strategy, and begrudgingly earned the respect of his players. He then began winning so rapidly that the cynics turned supporters virtually overnight, and he retreated to the trust of his family and a few close friends.

Sound familiar?

Who would have guessed that the professional life of the thin, profanity-spewing coach with jet black hair had paralleled that of the theology-reading paunchy, graying pooh-bah so closely?

But it did. They shared more than Midwestern nasal voices and large noses.

Both faced periods of unrest that were almost fatal, both insisted on playing basketball their way and to hell with the critics, and both had their breakthrough games against the other's programs, if not teams.

Also, both won their first championships at the exact same mileposts of their coaching careers.

When Tom Butters, Duke's athletics director, began looking for a new basketball coach in March of 1980, he used one standard. North Carolina had just completed a decade in which it won 242 games and lost only 64, took home ten assorted ACC championships and fought off challenges from South Carolina, N.C. State, Maryland, and Duke, and remained a consistent force.

Dean Smith, the Tar Heels' forty-nine-year-old coach, had gone from a shy Midwesterner wearing conservative suits and slicked-back hair to a somewhat flashier, nationally known sports figure who had led the 1976 U.S.A. Olympic team to a Gold Medal, a controversial innovator whose players loved him and whose fans hung on every one of his often rambling, fragmented sentences.

"We sat in the middle of the ACC, a small school trying to figure out how to compete in the changing world of college basketball," Butters said. "Eight miles away sat a legend, perhaps the greatest coach of all time. He cared about his school and his kids, and he kicked ass every day. I was inundated with thoughts of beating Dean Smith. If we couldn't beat him, we could never get to what we were thinking about."

Butters was a self-confessed college basketball junkie. He loved the game and the personalities who made it so popular in the South, if not across the nation. As the man charged with upholding Duke's legacy, he kept a private list of coaches whom he thought would be good candidates for jobs not only at his school but at others as well. He believed winning basketball began with defense, so the first coach he called was Bobby Knight at Indiana.

Knight was already an icon, bigger even than Smith. His Hoosiers had won the 1976 NCAA championship with an undefeated (32–0) record and a style that could be best described as basketball boot camp. Indiana's success began and ended with defense, and that's what Butters wanted for Duke. Although Bill Foster's last three teams had been fun to watch, defense was not their forte.

Butters asked Knight if he would consider leaving Indiana for Duke, knowing the answer but wanting to set the bar for his next question.

Who then would Knight recommend of his protégés, men of his ilk who could coach the same kind of man-to-man defense for Duke?

Knight mentioned his former assistants who had gone on to be head coaches, Dave Bliss at SMU, Bob Weltlich at Ole Miss, and Don DeVoe at Tennessee, three names Butters already had on his list.

"What about the guy at Army?" Butters said.

Before Indiana, Knight had been head coach of the U.S. Military Academy team at West Point for six years. The then Army coach, Mike Krzyzewski, played for Knight, worked under him for a year at Indiana and was one of his guys, as well, but at thirty-three the youngest and least known.

Butters knew about Krzyzewski from Steve Vacendak, the former Duke player he had just hired as his assistant. Butters respected Vacendak because he was a contrarian; they often disagreed, but Butters always listened to him.

Vacendak had lived in Annapolis, Maryland, while working for the Converse shoe company, and his territory was the Northeast. Navy and Army were two of his accounts. He told Butters that Krzyzewski could really coach.

"Oh, him," Knight said of Krzyzewski. "He has all of my good qualities, and none of the bad ones."

Butters asked Knight to elaborate and did some checking on his own.

Krzyzewski grew up in a two-story house filled with relatives in the working-class section of Chicago. After the mean streets, he learned life and basketball tough-guy style from Knight, who helped him through the death of his father during his senior year at West Point and inspired him to coach.

He then served five years active duty and rose to captain while coaching service teams and at a military prep school until his discharge in 1974. Krzyzewski rejoined Knight for one graduate assistant season at Indiana, and after that was named head coach at Army at the age of twenty-eight.

He made a name in Eastern basketball by leading the Cadets to a 20–8 record and into the ECAC playoffs, winning district coach of the year honors in his second season. In 1978, Army finished 19–9 and played in the NIT, a rarity for service academies. The Cadets went 14–11 in 1979 and then slumped to 9–17, taking Krzyzewski off the radar screen and, in the here-and-now of college basketball, made him an improbable candidate for an ACC school.

Foster had announced he was leaving Duke after the 1980 ACC Tournament, which the Blue Devils won to gain an automatic NCAA berth. Butters began calling and interviewing candidates while the Blue Devils were still playing. Because Army's season had ended, Krzyzewski was able to visit Durham right away. He knew Duke was in North Carolina but hadn't been aware it was so close to UNC and Smith's program.

The first meeting went well, as Butters and Krzyzewski spent several hours together away from campus getting to know each other.

Butters invited him back the next week for a second visit, this time with the search committee. The local media was still more concerned with Foster's last team, which beat Pennsylvania in West Lafayette, Indiana, and moved on to the Sweet Sixteen in Lexington, Kentucky. Butters called Krzyzewski and asked if he could meet him for a third time that weekend in Lexington.

"He said they had twelve inches of snow on the ground, but he'd find a way to get there," Butters said. "That impressed me."

Krzyzewski made it, watched the Blue Devils lose to Purdue in the Mideast Regional championship game and went back to upstate New York, unsure of where he stood with Duke.

He went to a second interview at Iowa State, which was offering him a good salary and two Cadillacs. That was the old Big 8, next door to Krzyzewski's native Chicago, his mother and older brother. He said he was going home to think about it.

Iowa State Assistant Athletics Director Max Urich, a classmate of Butters's at Ohio Wesleyan who had been on the Duke football staff in the 1970s, called Butters. "Are you going to hire Mike?" Urich asked. "Because if you're not, we are."

Urich was wrong. Krzyzewski turned down Iowa State and decided to roll the dice on Duke. But could the school risk hiring a coach coming off a losing season at Army?

Vacendak was pushing for Krzyzewski, whom had he gotten to know by trying to peddle Converse sneakers to his team.

"I went to a pregame meeting before they played Navy one year," Vacendak said. "I was impressed with how he had everything organized. I watched him coach. It was just good basketball, really good basketball. He was in control.

"When we interviewed him the first time, he was very clear in how he thought about things; not forceful, but articulate and straightforward. He was conveying himself, not just talking to impress us so he could get the job."

Butters spent the next month considering other candidates, including Weltlich,

Old Dominion's Paul Webb, and Bob Wenzel, one of Foster's assistants. The search committee liked all four and gave Butters the green light to hire any one of them to replace Foster, a popular coach who had won 73 games and made the NCAA Tournament his last three years.

Butters told the story repeatedly that he knew the hiring of Krzyzewski would elicit a strong reaction but "there was something about Mike . . . I kept going back to him . . . I couldn't get him off my mind. All the credentials he had, quite aside from basketball coaching, made sense to me.

"I wasn't trying to hire Dean Smith, I was trying to hire someone with the same qualities. It was the only chance that a small university like ours had."

In late April, Butters asked Vacendak who Duke should hire.

"We *should* hire the Army coach," Vacendak said, "but I don't think you have the nuts to do it."

The first week in May, Butters brought all four candidates back in for final interviews, purposely scheduling Krzyzewski last. While waiting for the others to end, Krzyzewski walked the Duke campus with his wife. "Don't screw this up," Mickie Krzyzewski told her husband.

Mickie stayed on campus while Mike went to the home of Vice President Chuck Huestis, who controlled all of Duke's money. The meeting went well but, again, no offer was made. They all shook hands and Krzyzewski and his wife left for the airport.

Butters, Vacendak and Huestis were all sitting around the dining room table in Huestis's home, when Butters said, "Steve, go get him back."

"Which one?" Vacendak said.

"Mike," Butters responded.

"God, Tom, you're not going to interview him *again,* are you?"

"No," Butters said, "I'm going to *hire* him."

Vacendak's jaw dropped. He went to the phone, called the airport and paged Krzyzewski. "Don't leave," he said. "I'm coming to pick you up."

Mickie flew home and Krzyzewski had soon joined the three men at the dining room table at Huestis's house.

"Do you want to ask me a question?" Krzyzewski said.

"I want to know whether you will be our basketball coach," Butters said.

"I accept," Krzyzewski answered.

"But we haven't even discussed your salary," Butters said.

"I don't care. I know you'll be fair."

They drove back to campus to Butters's office and began making plans to have a contract drawn up and a press conference scheduled the next day. Late that afternoon, Krzyzewski called his wife after she had arrived home.

"Mickie, I got the job," he said.

"Good, what's your salary?" she asked.

"I don't know. We didn't discuss it."

Krzyzewski's name had not been mentioned a single time by the local and state media dogging the story. On May 4, 1980, the Durham *Morning Herald* reported Duke was introducing its new coach that day and promised his last name would begin with a "W"—Webb, Weltlich, or Wenzel. When he walked in with Krzyzewski, Butters seemed as delighted that he had snookered the press as he was in finding a new coach.

Later that week, Vacendak walked down to Wallace Wade Stadium, where light stanchions were being installed for the 1980 football season. Vacendak asked the foreman if he could borrow two lug nuts the size of a fist from the scrap heap.

When Butters arrived at his office, he found them sitting on his desk with a note that read, "It took someone with nuts this big to make the right hire." He laughed out loud.

Taking over a proud-but-wounded Duke program, Krzyzewski was a virtual unknown to the casual basketball fan—an odd-looking young man with straight hair he wore across his forehead. He gave reporters a quick pronunciation lesson of his name (sha-SHEF-skee) and said his players at Army called him Coach K, which seemed like a cutesy, sophomoric nickname.

He was perceived as a bargain-hire because Duke was in a well-documented financial crisis. At one point in Foster's career, he had complained, among other things, that the athletics department was too cheap to pave the muddy lot where he and his assistants parked their cars every day. Butters denied that was ever an issue, but it was such a funny and popular story that it stuck as the main reason Foster fled.

As expected, Krzyzewski's modest 73–59 coaching record prompted speculation that Duke hired a no-name coach it could afford. Truth was, money meant very little to him, and the small annual salary of $48,000 Duke paid him was enough to support two young daughters, nine and one.

A history buff, he may have gained solace from the fact that he went to Duke with more head-coaching experience than the thirty-year-old Smith had when he took over at UNC in 1961. Old-timers told him that many UNC fans wanted Smith fired in his early years, which Krzyzewski found hard to believe. Now he had his own obstacles to overcome.

"Who's He" Krzyzewski—as he was called by some sarcastic fans—had to replace All-American center Mike Gminski and starting point guard Bob Bender off Duke's 1980 ACC championship team. He inherited only three ACC-caliber players, two of them seniors, Gene Banks and Kenny Dennard.

Bent on setting a standard for the future, Krzyzewski's rigid, military-trained style was so at odds with his likeable, laugh-a-minute predecessor that the returning Blue Devils joked about being in boot camp. Players who knew they had fallen into the new coach's doghouse irreverently barked in the shower after practice.

A week into Krzyzewski's maiden season, Duke played UNC in the last Big Four Tournament before it was vetoed by the coaches who no longer wanted an extra game against each other. The Blue Devils trailed most of the way but showed true grit and wound up losing by only two points. Their new coach noticed that some fans applauded as they left the court.

"They did not believe a team with a coach named Sha-shef-ski could give Carolina a game," he said. "We lost but they were still happy."

They played another competitive game in Chapel Hill before losing again and faced the eleventh-ranked Tar Heels for the third time in Durham on February 28, the last day of the 1981 regular season. Duke students expected another loss and some were more excited about a charter bus trip that night to see superstar rocker Bruce Springsteen in concert at the Greensboro Coliseum.

It was Krzyzewski's first game against Carolina in Cameron Indoor Stadium and Senior Day for Banks and Dennard, the colorful duo that had shown so much promise as freshmen forwards on Duke's 1978 Final Four team. During player introductions, Banks dramatically threw four red roses into the crowd and bear-hugged Dennard at mid-court.

Spurred by the emotion and absence of injured UNC star forward James Worthy, Duke hung around the entire game and after Carolina's Sam Perkins made a pair of free throws trailed 58–56 with two seconds remaining. The Blue Devils threw the ball to midcourt for a timeout; one tick remained. In the huddle, Krzyzewski drew up several options, but Dennard knew what to do.

Banks rubbed off a screen at the top of the key, caught the inbound pass from Dennard and, in what Smith later termed "a very long second," turned and fired a high archer over Perkins's outstretched, forty-two-inch arm. The ball was slightly tipped but stayed on course like a Scud missile. When it fell through the net, Cameron erupted. Overtime. Springsteen could wait.

Banks was under the basket in the final seconds of overtime with Duke behind by a point. Teammate Vince Taylor missed, the rebound fell to Banks and he laid it in, a far easier shot than the equalizer a few minutes earlier. The last two of Banks's game-high 25 points sealed the 66–65 win and sent him, arms thrust high, into wild celebration with the fans.

Taking the microphone for his Senior Day speech, Banks beckoned to his mother in the stands to c'mon down as if she were on *The Price is Right*. The royal blue sea of fans parted, and the two embraced like in a scene from *Rocky* or some other wonderfully sappy movie.

Krzyzewski, pretty stiff in his first few years, may not have liked all the showmanship, but, after all, these weren't his players and they did beat Carolina in his first season on what was an even more memorable day for him. Later, he had a romantic evening with Mickie and has since claimed that his youngest daughter Jamie was conceived that night (making him the third Duke coach, after Vic Bubas and Foster, to have three girls).

Duke students also celebrated but considered the win another reason to party (and enjoy Springsteen, the Boss, who like many of them was from New Jersey), rather than the start of a new era. They remained in awe of the All-Americans and future all-pros that Smith brought over on UNC's annual visit to Cameron, yelling humorous asides to their own players like, "Don't make them mad!" His team was the gold standard in the ACC.

Smith was proud and protective of his program's image. In a long analysis of Carolina's success, the Durham *Sun* reported the Tar Heels offered a scholarship to the highly sought Sam Perkins even though he was an academic risk from the projects of Brooklyn. The next time Smith saw the sportswriter who wrote the story, he said pointedly, "Duke recruited Perkins, too!"

Smith commanded so much respect that, no matter how highly recruited, his freshmen always knew their place. They carried the equipment, the old sixteen-millimeter projector and films Smith still used on road trips, plus the upper classmen's bags when they were asked to. Also, his teaching was so intricate that he could always find a reason to keep a freshman on the bench if need be.

After another Durham reporter had written a column in 1981 saying that freshman Perkins should be starting over journeyman senior Pete Budko at center, Smith snapped at the scribe one night, "Budko plays much better defense!"

As Carolina won the 1981 ACC championship and strengthened its hold on the rivalry, Duke earned an NIT bid and an opening-round game at home against North Carolina A&T. Banks had broken his arm in practice and was out, so he wore a tuxedo to his Cameron encore. The Blue Devils won a couple of NIT games before their season ended against Purdue for the second straight year. Krzyzewski's first team finished 17–13, a respectable start, but life for the new coach got a lot worse before it got better.

By 1982, Duke had little going with only senior Vince Taylor, the ACC's leading scorer and the second quality guard (after Jeff Mullins) that Duke had snatched out of Lexington, Kentucky. Taylor, an athletic 6' 5" and the school's next black star, was the last blue-chipper Foster signed before rumors of his departure killed his recruiting. After Banks and Dennard graduated, the quiet and well-spoken Taylor was left leading a truly terrible team.

Krzyzewski had to play no-names like Mike Tissaw, Chip Engelland, Tom Emma, and two freshmen from his first recruiting class, Greg Wendt and Dan Meagher. This was a far worse group of players than what Foster began with in 1974, exaggerated by Krzyzewski's failure to land high school stars such as Chris Mullin in his first full year on the job.

The chasm in the rivalry was never greater; Duke dropped four of its first five games in 1982 while the veteran, top-ranked Tar Heels won their first six including a 13-point victory over No. 2 Kentucky. The Blue Devils faded from respectability, as their old arch rival looked to Virginia and towering Ralph Sampson as a more important opponent. When they paid any attention to Duke, the UNC coaches poked fun at Krzyzewski's overuse of the word *positive* regarding his program. "There were a lot of positive things that came out of the game," Krzyzewski would say of a double-digit loss. They didn't see much positive about a team that stood 4–9 after the disinterested Tar Heels handled them easily in Cameron on January 16.

Krzyzewski had a hard time just existing. His oldest daughter Debbie came home crying from grade school after being cruelly razzed by Carolina fans, at least once by a teacher who was a UNC alumnus. "I feel like I'm behind enemy lines," he said to his wife.

He was at an early crossroad. Basketball insiders regarded him a great teacher and a superb floor coach who would get the best out of his players, someone who, if successful, could change the way the ACC played defense with his aggressive man-to-man. On the other hand, he came from Army where the players were appointed to the Academy; could he recruit at the ACC level? Except for his graduate assistant year at Indiana, he had never had to deal with the kind of kids he would need to win at Duke.

In retrospect, he probably cast too wide of a recruiting net his first year and was ridiculed for the first freshman class he did get—an innocuous group that included Todd Anderson, Jay Bryan, Greg Wendt, and Dan Meagher. Duke graduate John Feinstein, who went on to be a best-selling author, actually wrote a story for *Sport Magazine* detailing the recruiting failures. Krzyzewski had yet to develop credibility as a head coach, got started too late on most of the prospects and, despite working his ass off, could not close on any of them. He needed more lead time and more luck.

During the dismal 1982 season, as Krzyzewski struggled with the least-talented

Duke team in history, he secured a verbal commitment from a top player in Illinois, Welden Williams, reportedly someone Knight wanted. That raised eyebrows, and a month later, in late December, Duke landed lefty Bill Jackman, a multiskilled 6' 9" white star from Nebraska touted as the next Larry Bird. Duke was picking recruiting pockets where the local schools lacked basketball tradition and coaches from established powers weren't spending a lot of time.

As critics questioned Krzyzewski's credentials and coaching skills, the commitments by Williams and Jackman meant something. The class got even better right after the New Year when 6' 8" Californian Jay Bilas took a gamble on the unproven coach and committed to Duke. Thus, Krzyzewski was already perceived as having recruiting success *before* he tried to close on three guys who could make a great class.

Duke ended its 1982 season with a blowout loss to Wake Forest in the ACC Tournament. Only a few thousand people remained in the Greensboro Coliseum for the last quarterfinal game of the long day. When Taylor came out in the closing minute, he received a prolonged standing ovation from those still left in the building—a combination of appreciation and sympathy for such a fine player having had to squander his senior year on a 10–17 team—Duke's worst record ever.

The postseason belonged to the better teams and players, such as Carolina's Worthy and Virginia's Sampson—the next short-term rivalry to remember in the ACC. The Tar Heels and Cavaliers had already played several epic games, including a third meeting of the 1981 season in the Final Four semis in Philadelphia, when Al Wood scored 39 points at the old Spectrum in Philadelphia and UNC students painted "39" on sidewalks and buildings all over Chapel Hill.

Carolina's ultimate goal was to uphold the '81 team's pledge after losing the NCAA title game to Indiana on the day Ronald Reagan was shot. Smith had been so upset by the attempt on Reagan's life by John Hinckley that he wanted the game postponed until the President was out of danger. When NBC and the NCAA decided to play on, UNC Dean of Students Don Boulton, a minister who was in Philadelphia, was asked to write and deliver the pregame invocation about Reagan.

The Tar Heels squandered an early lead and lost to the Hoosiers 63–50. At a team breakfast the next morning, they vowed to return in 1982 and win it all. Only Wood graduated and was replaced by a freshman from Wilmington, North Carolina, named "Mike" Jordan, a cocky and competitive athlete who turned heads from the moment he stepped on campus. One day in early September of 1981, assistant coach Roy Williams stopped by Carmichael Auditorium, where the UNC players were in a full-court pickup game.

"The best 6' 4" player I've ever seen in my life is out in the gym," Williams told fellow coaches Bill Guthridge and Eddie Fogler a few minutes later, referring to Jordan who was raw and still growing.

Worthy, who was the MVP of Carolina's ACC Tournament and NCAA East Regional championships, led the Tar Heels back to their second straight Final Four in 1982. He had the decisive dunk over a young Akeem (later changed to Hakeem) Olajuwon as UNC beat Houston and Clyde Drexler on semifinal Saturday in the Louisiana Superdome, putting Carolina into the 1982 championship game against sixth-ranked Georgetown and freshman center Patrick Ewing on Monday night, March 29.

Hoyas' coach John Thompson was a close friend of Smith's, having sent his adopted son, Donald Washington, to play at UNC in 1971 before Washington flunked out as a sophomore. Smith had encouraged Thompson to jump from high school coaching to the college game, spent hours in person and on the phone with Thompson helping him make the transition and named him one of his assistants on the 1976 U.S.A. Olympic team.

The 6' 10,", 250-pound Thompson, a former NBA center, was a fiercely proud and competitive African-American widely respected in the black community. He built a small, predominantly white university into a basketball power with black players, some disadvantaged and others who had been in trouble. Intimidation was Georgetown's game with an aggressive, hand-checking defense and menacing, towel-and-tongue-flapping bench. Friendship aside, it was no different against Carolina.

Thompson instructed Ewing to try to block any shot in close by the Tar Heels in the early minutes, hoping he could at least deter their inside game. Ewing gave UNC five early baskets on goaltending calls. Failing to be intimidated, Worthy kept his team close or in a narrow lead and had scored 28 points on 13 of 17 shooting by the final, pulsating minute of the game.

Matt Doherty missed a chance to put Carolina up by three points when he clanged the front end of a one-and-one. Georgetown's Eric "Sleepy" Floyd sent the Hoyas ahead 62–61 with a short jumper that hit the rim and bounced over. Senior point guard Jimmy Black came across midcourt with the ball, looked confused and, after Smith jumped off the bench making the "T" sign with his hands, called a timeout with thirty-two seconds remaining.

Smith knew Thompson wouldn't let Carolina beat him inside with yet another basket by Worthy or Perkins. Thus, Smith also knew that against Georgetown's sagging defense there would be an open perimeter shot if the Tar Heels ran their zone offense or "T-game" correctly. Of Black, Doherty, and Jordan, the freshman was by far the best outside shooter. He had been a role player but one Smith gave more responsibility to as the season progressed; he had damn near become the team's best man-to-man defender in one year.

After telling them to look inside first, then to the weak side, Smith said "everybody get on the board!" He said if the shot missed and Georgetown got the rebound, foul right away. There was still enough time for another possession. Smith put his right fist in the middle of the huddle for the traditional ritual. They all touched his hand and began to get up. As they did, Smith tapped Jordan on the knee and said, "Knock it in, Michael."

Smith figured it would come down to an outside shot, that at one point Jordan would have the ball in his hands with a good look. He wanted to make sure the eighteen-year-old youngster knew it was okay for him to fire the potential game-winner and not force another pass to a less-capable shooter.

The Tar Heels tried to run their low-high set with Perkins going from block to block. Worthy flashed to the high post, couldn't get the ball and went back underneath. Now Doherty had it at the top of the key. The Hoyas blocked the lane and Doherty went back out to Black, whose skip pass over the zone found Jordan alone for a moment on the left wing. The Superdome clock showed seventeen seconds.

With Smith saying "Shoot it, Michael" to himself, Jordan went straight up, stuck his tongue out and released a shot from his right finger tips. As the ball spun toward the basket, Jordan shut his eyes to complete the dream he had had the night before of making the winning shot. He never saw it go in.

Georgetown still had fifteen seconds to counter and Floyd raced the ball up court, passing to teammate Fred Brown on the right side. The Hoyas bench was up, some of them waving towels and all of them yelling different instructions to Brown. He picked up his dribble and saw somebody flash by him, clear across his passing lane on the right.

Admittedly making "the worst defensive play of my career," Worthy had overrun Brown's pump fake and was now behind the ball, the last place a defender should be. He was so far out of position that Brown thought he was a teammate and threw him the ball. Worthy could have run the floor and thunderdunked for his thirtieth point but instead bailed out to the left corner where he was fouled. He missed both free throws, but the only people mad were those who had taken the Tar Heels to cover the point-and-a-half spread. Carolina had its second NCAA title, and Smith's first, by a 63–62 score.

Smith, who had warmed the bench on Kansas's 1952 national champs, got the symbolic monkey off his back that everyone seemed to care about more than him. He was just happy his Tar Heels had won the last game of the college basketball season for the first time, uncharacteristically hugging players and coaches and even a couple of sportswriters. At this press conference, he had to jab former Charlotte *Observer* columnist Frank Barrows about a story he had written predicting Smith would never win the national championship because his teams were *too* consistent, never emotional enough to go on a six-game tournament run.

The Tar Heels returned home to a triumphant parade down Franklin Street and a pep rally in Kenan Stadium. Worthy, a junior, was likely going pro (which he did to the Lakers as the No. 1 pick) and Black was graduating, but three other starters were returning and Smith had signed another good recruiting class, preserving Carolina's place in the college hoops hierarchy and the stark contrast with its one-time rival in Durham.

Krzyzewski kept recruiting like crazy to complete his next freshman class, but retained his sense of humor in his situation. In the spring of 1982, he was in the living room of Marc Acres, a 6' 8" center from Oklahoma, who wasn't showing much interest in anything he said. Halfway through his recruiting pitch, Krzyzewski *knew* he wasn't getting this kid and brought the visit to a close by asking his mother if she had any more questions.

"No, I just want Marc to go somewhere he'll be close to God," she said.

Krzyzewski felt the edges of his mouth turn up as he debated whether to say it. *Oh, what the fuck.*

"Well, Mrs. Acres, if Mark comes to Duke he'll be only eight miles from God," he said, referring to Smith.

Duke was luckier with 6' 8" Mark Alarie, because Lute Olsen had yet to change jobs from Iowa to Arizona in Alarie's native state, allowing Krzyzewski to steal his first great inside-outside big man. Though others got more publicity, Alarie was the early poster child for Duke's resurgence—a smart and handsome young man with an absolutely gorgeous sister who often sat behind the Duke bench and eventually got a lot of TV face time.

Johnny Dawkins's recruitment was the key. Krzyzewski wanted the 6' 2" guard badly, but after his near-misses the year before couldn't afford to pin all his hopes on one player. So he also recruited another great guard named Jo Jo Buchanan and promised to take whichever one committed first. Luckily, Buchanan picked Notre Dame (which was also recruiting Dawkins) and soon afterward Krzyzewski's first great player chose Duke.

Signing David Henderson was also lucky, because it came after Duke lost Durham Southern star Curtis Hunter to Dean Smith and the Tar Heels. Krzyzewski had been planning to ask the 6' 5" Henderson to attend prep school before N.C. State's Jim Valvano offered him a scholarship. On the verge of losing Henderson, Krzyzewski convinced the admissions office to take a gamble and Duke admitted him as an academic exception.

Dawkins and Henderson were Krzyzewski's first two great black players. Foster had recruited Banks and Taylor, and Duke had to reestablish its recruiting balance under a new coach hoping to erase all the problems of the late 1960s and '70s. Otherwise, Duke was never moving up in the ACC.

Besides trying to compete with its neighboring national champions, Krzyzewski now faced a real live icon. In April of 1982, Smith donned a hard-hat and shovel for the ground breaking of UNC's new Student Activities Center. Though reticent about asking people for money, he and the late Hargrove "Skipper" Bowles, the father of former White House Chief of Staff and U.S. Senatorial candidate Erskine Bowles, spearheaded a Rams Club drive to raise $36 million over the next four years.

The following September, Smith was nominated for the Naismith Hall of Fame. At fifty-two, he was in the prime of his career and in the small, esteemed echelon of college coaches that included Bobby Knight and Louisville's Denny Crum. It was a given that the Tar Heels would be among the top teams in the country, no matter who left school or who was coming in. Carolina was a constant.

Early in Krzyzewski's third year, influential Duke alumni began meeting secretly to oust the struggling coach. Prominent boosters who went on to be his biggest supporters were in those meetings, although they refused to admit it in later years. Krzyzewski knew who they were but bided his time.

"They called themselves the Concerned Iron Dukes," Krzyzewski said years later. "What the hell were they concerned about? That I couldn't do the job. Well, they were wrong, and where are those people today?"

"He was enormously optimistic and upbeat in those days," said Donna Keane, Krzyzewski's administrative assistant from 1981 though 1995. "He knew he would eventually turn it around and had a great attitude about it. He ignored all of the negative stuff and did not let it impede him."

Duke's breakthrough freshman class of 1983—Alarie, Bilas, Dawkins, and Henderson—experienced its own disastrous season that included losing at home to tiny Wagner College. Although Krzyzewski had played some zone the previous year with an untalented team, especially down the stretch of close games, he refused to in 1983 and heard about it constantly.

With the players he hoped would be the foundation of his program, Krzyzewski was determined to implement his defensive principles. He pushed and prodded them, molding a team that gave him far less push-back than the malcontents he inherited. These were *his* kids and he was determined that their success started with man-to-man defense akin to hand-to-hand combat.

Krzyzewski was establishing a sort of civilian military, treating his players like student soldiers. The message was becoming clear: I'll lay down my life for you, if you will do the same for me. Be men; I may curse you, but I love you. We'll go to war together and return victorious, but you must do what I say or face the consequences.

For the first time since he coached at Army, Krzyzewski was getting a complete buy-in from his team. He was building something, a college program that could be pretty good if everyone stayed the course. Ninth-ranked Louisville played at Cameron on January 12, 1983. The Doctors of Dunk, who had been to two Final Fours in the last three years, had their hands full for a stretch of the game. The Blue Devils matched the high-flying Cardinals in a free-flowing spurt that had the crowd going crazy. The Dukies couldn't sustain it and Louisville won easily, but fans left dazzled by their potential.

They also ran out of gas at the end of several games trying to play their man-to-man defense. They collapsed at Cameron against Wake and let a sure win get away. They faded at N.C. State, lost at Georgia Tech by a point, at home to Maryland by 11 and at Wake Forest by 6. As the losses mounted and it became clear Duke didn't have the depth to keep up the defensive pressure, more fans criticized Krzyzewski for stubbornly refusing to play at least *some* zone.

Unfair criticism incensed Krzyzewski, especially when he thought it came from the Carolina machine that he likened to IBM for its omnipotence. He spoke at the Raleigh Sports Club one Wednesday afternoon, armed with a copy of a speculative newsletter published by former UNC basketball player Dennis Wuycik that had been particularly hard on him and his struggling program.

"What is this?" he asked the group, waving a copy of *The Poop Sheet* to the crowd. "What is this and where does this come from?"

The 1983 season ended with a 43-point loss to Virginia in the ACC Tournament in Atlanta, a game that was actually close (50–41) at halftime. Krzyzewski was angry at the Cavaliers for running up the score and accusing Duke of dirty play, when it was Sampson who got a late intentional foul for throwing a flagrant elbow. The frustrated Sampson would end his college career without winning the ACC championship.

At a Denny's restaurant outside of Atlanta later that night, Duke sports information director Johnny Moore raised a water glass and said, "Here's to forgetting what happened tonight." Krzyzewski snapped back, "Here's to *never* forgetting what happened tonight."

Terry Holland, who retired as Virginia's coach in 1990, has heard the accusation about that ACC Tournament game but never discussed it with Krzyzewski.

"Running up the score? I went back and checked the final box, and none of our guys played more than twenty-two minutes," he said. "Ralph was asked about it, and he said they [Duke players] were pulling the hair on his legs and grabbing his jock strap. The writers asked him if he thought that was dirty tactics, and Ralph said they could decide for themselves."

After twenty years, Krzyzewski hasn't said much about that game, Duke's largest margin of defeat since the ACC was formed. "There was a lot of anger," he admitted. "But it was both bad and good anger. It propelled us, gave us impetus to build on something."

Besides the motivation and experience Duke derived from its 11–17 season, the Blue Devils still needed to develop depth. It came with the signing of Tommy Amaker, who was from suburban Washington, D.C., and the final piece of Krzyzewski's puzzle.

Amaker was a magnificent defender who on offense freed Dawkins to roam on the wing, where he turned into a multifaceted scorer. By the time the next season began, the still-unheralded Blue Devils were not only loaded for bear they were a bear of a team to handle.

The next game with Virginia was on January 7, 1984, in Charlottesville. Before boarding the bus, they practiced in Cameron with the scoreboard reading 109–66 for the entire two hours as a terse reminder of the ACC Tournament debacle. Duke upset the twentieth-ranked Cavaliers 78–72 and would not lose to Virginia for seven years, winning 16 straight and only once by fewer than 5 points.

The Blue Devils were still in the shadow of the ACC's three best teams, Maryland, Wake Forest, and top-ranked UNC, and they didn't do much to escape it when they lost at home to the No. 5 Terrapins and by 31 points to the twelfth ranked Deacons in Winston-Salem. Despite an improved team and record, the wolves were still baying at Krzyzewski's door.

Butters stopped by the basketball office the morning after the blowout loss at Wake Forest. Krzyzewski had yet to arrive.

"Tell him I want to see him in my office when he gets in," Butters told Keane.

"In your office?" Keane said.

"In my office."

Those who worked with Krzyzewski could always tell when he was tense because his mouth got so tight that his thin lips almost disappeared. When he walked into Butters's office, the area between his nose and chin looked recessed by six inches. He thought he was getting fired.

"Sit down," Butters said.

"Mike, we've got a public that doesn't know what kind of a coach we have. We have a press that's too dumb to report what kind of a coach we have. And, right now, I'm not sure we even have a coach who knows what kind of coach we have."

Always given to the dramatic, Butters opened his top drawer and pulled out a document. It was a new five-year contract, and he slid it across the desk.

"Only thing," Butters said, "I want you to announce it."

In Butters's own words, all hell broke loose after that. Within a week, he had received three death threats. The last was when he and his wife Lynn were out to dinner and came home to find their teenage daughter, Jill, in tears.

"Dad, are you going to Atlanta tomorrow?" she asked.

"Yes," Butters said.

"A man called tonight and said, 'Tell your father not to be on that plane to Atlanta in the morning.'"

Butters shook his head and told both his wife and daughter that it was a bad joke, but a joke nonetheless.

After Jill went upstairs, Lynn Butters said, "Do you believe that?"

"Not for a minute," Butters said, beginning to feel a smile coming on. "But would you do me a favor when you get up in the morning?"

"What's that?" Lynn said.

"Will you go out and start my car?"

The rivalry between Krzyzewski and Smith changed on Saturday night of January 21, 1984. Carolina was 13–0 and had been ranked No. 1 all the way back to every preseason poll, including one from *Sports Illustrated*, which featured Jordan and Perkins on the cover wagging index fingers in a "We're No. 1" gesture. The blowup poster made it into every bar in Chapel Hill.

Smith didn't mind that cover, because Jordan was a junior who might turn pro after the season and Perkins was a senior on his way to becoming another NBA first-round draft choice and the school's all-time rebounding leader. He had no problem promoting players who had earned publicity, and long lobbied for the stars of winning teams to receive the most credit.

Two years earlier, Smith had rejected a request from *SI* basketball editor and UNC graduate Larry Keith to put Jordan, a projected starter as a freshman, on the cover of the preseason college issue with the four returning veterans from the 1981 Final Four team. Smith posed with Perkins, Worthy, Black, and Doherty. "You haven't proven that you deserve it," Smith told Jordan after refusing Keith.

This time, Smith could not keep Keith and the magazine from featuring freshman Kenny Smith in an article on the Tar Heels before the Duke game. Nicknamed "Jet," Kenny Smith had won a starting point guard position from Coach Smith with his quickness on defense, but he was still a freshman, which in Carolina nomenclature was synonymous with buck private or entry level.

Smith was already looking for something, *anything*, to back down his cocky and unbeaten team. He had been so mad at Jordan's showboat jam at the end of a 74–62 win at fifth-ranked Maryland the week before that he instructed Tar Heel broadcaster Woody Durham to leave it out of the highlights on his weekly coach's show. He also didn't like that assistant coach Eddie Fogler had said to a *Washington Post* reporter after the game, "I'll give it a 10.1."

The article on Kenny Smith came out in *SI* on Monday before the game at Duke, and UNC's upperclassmen rode their frosh point guard all week. The team considered the most talented in Carolina history wasn't much concerned with the next opponent. Perkins and Doherty were the only starters who had ever lost to Duke, so none of them really understood that the Blue Devils had gotten pretty damn good.

Plus, everyone at Duke was upset over what had happened the week before when Maryland visited Cameron.

Maryland's Herman Veal had been accused of sexual misconduct and his coach, Lefty Driesell, of calling the woman and trying to talk her out of filing charges against his senior forward. Both player and coach were reprimanded by Maryland, but neither was formally charged. Duke students pelted Veal with condoms before the game and chanted "rape . . . rape" throughout, growing frustrated as the fifth-ranked Terps held on to win by six points.

Duke caught a firestorm of national media for its crowd behavior, and the school went into damage control. President Terry Sanford wrote his famous "avuncular" letter in the Duke *Chronicle* telling the students to clean up their act. Krzyzewski visited several fraternities and then talked to those camping out for UNC passes, asking them to cheer "for Duke" and not against an opponent.

The students capitulated, arriving for the Carolina game wearing halos made out of coat hangers and covered with aluminum foil. They yelled, "We beg to differ" rather than "Bullshit" at the refs. Krzyzewski was lit up because the Blue Devils had lost two straight games and, during one early timeout, stared down the refs for thirty seconds.

Carolina turned the ball over repeatedly trying to get it inside against Duke's aggressive defense. The Tar Heels hit 16 of their 29 shots but still trailed 40–39 at halftime, frustrating Smith and his staff. Bill Guthridge chased officials Hank Nichols, John Moreau, and Mike Moser off the floor, screaming about a call. In the locker room, Guthridge yelled that they had "to beat all *eight* of those guys," and Smith was so angry he could barely talk to the team.

He was looking for a reason to go off in the second half. At one point, when a Carolina sub wasn't buzzed in quick enough, Smith walked over shouting "Hey!" in his nasal voice and banged the scorer's table, causing the control panel to jump and add 20 points to UNC's total on the scoreboard.

"We always make sure play is stopped before we blow the horn," said Tommy Hunt, the ACC's supervisor of football officials and Durham resident who has run the basketball clock at Duke home games for thirty years. "Dean wanted to get a sub into the game, but play resumed before we could blow him in. He came over and banged the table, but there was nothing we could do about it at that point."

Smith worked the refs relentlessly, managing to avoid a technical foul, but was still mad that center Brad Daugherty rarely touched the ball and failed to take a single shot in the game. Jordan scored 18 points in only twenty-nine minutes, as Smith kept taking him out in favor of sophomore Steve Hale, who had 13 points in nineteen minutes. The Tar Heels eventually pulled it out 78–73, a final score aided by a technical on Krzyzewski with five seconds remaining. Still peeved after the game, Smith had harsh words for the crowd and little sympathy for his own team. He was particularly tough on Kenny Smith, who hadn't scored and committed five turnovers for the first thirty-five minutes of the game, but exploded for 10 points in the last five minutes. It wasn't redemption enough for his coach.

"I guess they've been reading their press clippings," Smith said afterward, not singling out an individual but clearly referring to his freshman namesake.

In his own press conference, Krzyzewski altered his relationship with Smith forever. Drained and angry from his third straight loss, and fifth in a row to the Tar Heels, he admonished the media while making his famous accusation about Smith and Carolina, turning peaceful coexistence into open hostility.

"There was not a person on our bench who was pointing at officials or banging the scorer's table," Krzyzewski said. "So let's get some things straight around here and quit the double standard that sometimes exists in this league."

In light of how his own school and program had been blasted the week after the Maryland game, Krzyzewski challenged what he believed to be a Carolina-biased press in the state to, as coaches like to say, call it both ways and not treat Smith with the traditional kid gloves.

Krzyzewski's record at Duke was only 52–51 at the time, and while his tirade against Smith was applauded by alumni and fans, it did little to change their feeling that Butters had hired the wrong man for the job. Cameron was still not selling out; there were almost a thousand empty seats for the UNC game.

Six weeks later, the Blue Devils went to Chapel Hill for the rematch, hoping to snap an eighteen-year losing streak in Carmichael Auditorium. They led most of the way before Carolina scored late to send the game into overtime, where Duke still clung to a two-point lead with only seconds to play. Matt Doherty drove down the lane and hit a runner to force a second overtime and keep his Senior Day, as well as that of Sam Perkins, from going down the tubes along with the Tar Heels' undefeated record in the ACC.

In the second overtime, Carolina broke it open and won 96–83. A relieved Smith said Duke handled his scrambling defense better than anyone had all season. The game was the Tar Heels' second with Kenny Smith back from a broken wrist he had suffered against LSU a month earlier. Dean Smith took a calculated gamble by playing him with a half-cast on his left hand. Hale didn't have the same speed and quickness but had played well in Smith's absence.

After their perfect ACC regular season (14–0) locked up the No. 1 seed in the NCAA East Region, Carolina met Duke again in the semifinals of the conference tournament in Greensboro. Several Tar Heels fussed over their tournament tickets before the game, and they played that way against an opponent still seething from two narrow defeats to UNC during the season.

Duke opened hot from the outside and led 40–32 at the half. Steamed in the locker room, Smith told his players they had been out-hustled and given up too many offensive rebounds to a smaller opponent—a cardinal sin at Carolina. When they began the second half with a 16–5 spurt and took the lead on Jordan's slam dunk, it appeared order had been restored.

The Blue Devils, however, proved Duke was different by scoring 14 points in seven key possessions, culminated by Dawkins' tip-in that gave them a 69–67 lead. When Dawkins scored again, the vaunted Tar Heels were left chasing and fouling. Henderson's four free throws secured the 77–75 win.

Late in the game, a comparison between the coaches emerged, one that Krzyzewski would subtly promote. When Duke needed a crucial basket, Dawkins took the ball to the open court, trying to draw the defense and create an advantage. Carolina countered in the final seconds with more regimentation: Pass the ball to half court, take a timeout, and set up another play. Krzyzewski drew an analogy from his favorite hobby, gardening. He compared a plant growing inside a jar to one growing unimpeded. Before 1984, it was coaching babble. The upset of Carolina gave him some literary license.

Duke celebrated and couldn't come back to Earth in the championship game against Maryland. The Blue Devils led 30–27 at the half but were spent emotionally and physically and did not finish the job. Driesell won his only ACC title after five tough losses in the finals, gaining a measure of satisfaction by beating his alma mater. Duke earned its first NCAA Tournament bid under Krzyzewski, but the season ended in the first game to Washington and Detleff Schremp when a clock-keeping error cost the Blue Devils a shot to tie the game.

At that stage, it didn't much matter.

Finishing 24–10, they had climbed to third in the ACC standings (7–7) and back into the NCAA Tournament for the first time in four years. Most important, Krzyzewski finally beat Carolina and Smith with *his* players, justifying the new contract he had received and finally gaining acceptance from his own fans.

"It was one of the greatest wins in Duke history," Dawkins said of the ACC Tournament triumph. "We beat a team that had Jordan, Perkins, Kenny Smith, Brad Daugherty, and Matt Doherty. That put us over the hump. We knew we could do some special things after that."

Even though Carolina rebounded for the NCAA Tournament by beating Temple in Charlotte, something was wrong. On paper, no team in the country could play with the Tar Heels, but Kenny Smith remained bothered by the cast on his hand, and the chemistry that had made them unbeatable earlier was askew going into a Sweet Sixteen matchup with unranked Indiana in Atlanta.

Every bit as much as his two national championships, Bobby Knight's game against No. 1 North Carolina in 1984 defined him as a true coaching genius. The Hoosiers' late-season run had earned them a No. 4 seed in the East, but they were no match for UNC's stable of stars. All-white Indiana had none, except for promising freshman guard Steve Alford.

Given a week to prepare for an opponent, Knight was the toughest coach in America to beat in one game. He called on unheralded Dan Dakich to roughhouse Jordan on defense, and the frustrated MJ picked up two fouls that sent him to the bench for twelve minutes of the first half as Indiana took a lead. Jordan had a horrible second half, and Dean Smith's stubbornness on defense added to the problem.

With a quick and more athletic team, Carolina kept pressuring Indiana and double-teaming on the perimeter. Knight had four good dribblers and passers who, in the days before the shot clock, moved the ball until an open man got a good look in rhythm. Smith refused to play more straight man-to-man defense, or some zone, and try to win a close, low-scoring game. Indiana shot 65 percent and held on for a 72–68 upset, knocking the favorites out of the NCAA Tournament.

Unranked Virginia, in its first season after Ralph Sampson graduated, played Indiana a more deliberate tempo two days later and eliminated the Hoosiers 50–48 in an improbable win to reach the Final Four. By then, the sorrowful Tar Heels had gone home with a 28–3 record.

The following May, after he was named consensus national player of the year, Jordan reluctantly took Smith's advice and entered the NBA draft a year early. Smith believed he was too good for college basketball and should not risk getting hurt during his senior season and jeopardize the huge rookie contract he had already assured himself.

In the off-season, Duke went head-to-head with Carolina for high school star Danny Ferry, who had grown up a Tar Heel fan.

Ferry attended DeMatha Catholic in Hyattsville, Maryland, whose coach Morgan Wootten was every bit the icon in high school that Dean Smith was on the college level. Plus, Ferry's father, Bob, was general manager of the Washington Bullets when former UNC star Mitch Kupchak helped them win the 1978 NBA championship. As a kid, Danny Ferry hung around Kupchak and other players.

Duke saw him as a milestone recruit because he was expected to play for Smith. With starter Dan Meagher entering his senior year, Krzyzewski had a spot opening up and during a home visit showed Ferry some game tape of Meagher and where he would play as a freshman.

Ferry called Krzyzewski "hungrier" than Smith in his recruitment. The Duke coaches saw more of his games, dropped him notes incessantly, and phoned exactly when they said they would.

"Coach K was more one-on-one," Ferry said. "It was much more of a personal thing. Carolina's recruiting was more corporate. I enjoyed Coach Smith; he was a person I always respected. I *really* enjoyed getting to know Coach K."

Duke was also aided in Ferry's recruitment by DeMatha assistant coach Mike Brey, who grew very close with Krzyzewski's staff and continued to assure them they were in great shape. The Blue Devils entered the 1985 season buoyed by the fact that they were on the verge of leveling the playing field with UNC. They went to Chapel Hill in January of 1985 more determined than ever to break through in Carmichael Auditorium.

Dawkins was having a monster game as Duke broke a 39–39 halftime tie and went up by double digits in the second half. The Carolina crowd sat stunned. Diehard UNC fans believed their team would *never* lose to Duke at home, where it had rallied to win the year before and had come back from eight points behind with seventeen seconds to play in 1974. But the Blue Devils shot an astonishing 45 free throws, making 36, as Carolina kept putting them on the line late in the game. Dawkins finished with 34 points, 8 rebounds and 4 assists. Jay Bilas had 17 points and 11 boards. Alarie added 19 points and 4 assists.

"I got a ticket in the last seat in the last row," recalled Keane, Krzyzewski's secretary, of the 93–77 shocker. "I remember how hot it was and how angry the Carolina fans were. And how new and exciting it was for us."

Ironically, the new Blue Devil regime was anchored by Meagher, the enforcer and badass of the bunch. He had 10 rebounds and drew begrudging praise from Smith, who loved his aggressiveness but thought he was a flopper and a faker on defense.

Carolina wasn't going to relinquish its crown without a fight. In the rematch on Senior Day at Duke, the Tar Heels' Hale made a late three-point play to give them a 78–68 victory and a share of first place in the ACC standings. The win also preserved UNC's streak of finishing first or second in the conference standings for a staggering nineteen straight years.

The 1985 ACC Tournament was the first-ever played in Atlanta, and appropriately it turned out to be Georgia Tech's weekend. The Yellow Jackets bounced Duke in the first round and, with stars Mark Price and John Salley playing all forty minutes, won their first ACC championship two days later over Carolina. After the game, Smith went into the raucous Georgia Tech locker room to congratulate coach Bobby Cremins, the former South Carolina player under Frank McGuire who had become Smith's friend.

The NCAA Tournament expanded to sixty-four teams in 1985, eliminating first-round byes. Duke was seeded third in the Mideast Region, defeated Pepperdine and then led Boston College deep into the second half. The Eagles were coached by Gary Williams, whose relentless style of play was already well-known in the Northeast. In the first of what would be many wild games between Williams's teams and Duke, Boston College won 74–73 and sent the Devils home from the Mideast Region with a 23–8 record.

UNC went South and, in the year Jordan would have been a senior, lost Hale with a separated shoulder in a first-round win over Middle Tennessee. The games were in South Bend, Indiana, and their second-round opponent was Notre Dame and All-American guard David Rivers.

Senior Buzz Peterson replaced Hale and played thirty-six minutes. A near-perfect game was required. The Tar Heels shot 55 percent, out-rebounded the Irish and beat Coach Digger Phelps on his home court to reach the Sweet Sixteen in Birmingham. There, they faced what amounted to another road game against Auburn before seventeen thousand fans at the Civic Center. They led by 10 at the half and hung on to win 62–56.

Carolina was one step from a most improbable Final Four. Leading Villanova by eight points with a few seconds left in the first half, the Tar Heels turned the ball over and gave up a three-point play and the momentum. Villanova got hot in the second half and stayed that way, outscoring UNC by 17 points to win 56–44.

At the Final Four in Lexington, Kentucky, the Wildcats shot 70 percent to shock defending national champion Georgetown for the NCAA title.

That spring, Ferry committed to Duke. When the good-news phone call finally came, assistant coach Chuck Swenson jumped over the desk into Krzyzewski's lap in a giddy office scene.

"He's the first big-name player we beat Carolina for," Krzyzewski said.

With a good chance to play as a freshman, Ferry arrived in the fall of 1985 just happy to be there and in awe of how hard Dawkins and his fellow seniors worked. He figured he'd come off the bench his first season.

The Blue Devils began ranked No. 6 in the nation, based largely on Krzyzewski's two straight 20-win seasons. They opened in the preseason NIT, won two games in Houston, and moved on to Madison Square Garden where they defeated St. John's and Kansas for the title. Ferry started because Bilas was still recuperating from off-season knee surgery.

The '86 Tar Heels, ranked No. 2 in preseason polls, had depth as well, with returning big men Brad Daugherty, Warren Martin, Joe Wolf, and Dave Popson, all at least 6' 10". Smith also had an eye on a high school star from Virginia Beach, a 6' 9", cat-quick forward named J. R. Reid whom he believed would be a better college player than Ferry and, thus, wanted more.

Although David Henderson started most of the season in Meagher's position, as Krzyzewski favored a smaller lineup, Ferry got important early minutes subbing for Bilas and then came off the bench as sixth man when Bilas returned as a starter. That such a highly coveted freshman could be a role player spoke volumes for how well Duke had recruited.

Confident but self-deprecating, the Dukies were picked third in the ACC behind Carolina and Georgia Tech in 1986 and didn't scare many opponents with a lineup of 6' 8" forwards and skinny guards. "We won't win any body-beautiful contests," Krzyzewski said. "We don't strike fear in anyone's hearts. If I was looking at this team, I'd believe I could beat them, too."

Great defense, born from Krzyzewski's insistence to play the pressure, man-to-man for two years, made up for Duke's size and lack of inside scoring. He was changing another paradigm that Smith and Carolina had established, making intensity even more important than execution.

After winning the NIT, the Blue Devils rolled to eleven more victories over unranked teams, stood 16–0 and were ranked third heading to Chapel Hill for the inaugural game at UNC's Student Activities Center on January 18, 1986. The Tar Heels, who had added celebrated freshman shooter Jeff Lebo to their veteran lineup, were 17–0 and had moved up to No. 1 in the polls and stayed there for twelve consecutive weeks.

BLUE BLOOD BITTERNESS

The night before the game, three thousand people, including Smith's mentor McGuire, attended a black-tie gala on the spring-loaded court of the sparkling arena. During dedication ceremonies, UNC officially renamed what had been dubbed the Dean Dome for its already-legendary coach. Smith had objected at first but relented when he decided his name on the building best represented all those who played for him.

The Dean E. Smith Center, plunked into a ravine on eight acres of once-pristine woodlands on the south side of UNC's campus, took nearly four years to build. More than twenty thousand cubic yards of rock were blasted, and twice as much dirt moved. Adjacent residential neighbors groused over the construction inconveniences. Stories about shortcuts in pouring the 18,500 cubic yards of concrete plagued the towering structure, whose Teflon tarp stretched tightly across its massive, crisscrossing steel arches.

Construction delays had postponed completion of the $36 million, eight-sided center with 21,444 baby blue seats. The grand opening was originally sched-uled against UCLA, which Carolina played (and defeated 102–70) in Carmichael Auditorium the previous November 24. UNC's last victory in its old gym came six weeks later when the unbeaten and top-ranked Tar Heels routed N.C. State 90–79.

Because the building had come under such scrutiny, and the first opponent was now Duke, the opening game became the most anticipated event in the history of UNC athletics.

"We didn't select Duke," Smith said.

Hundreds of UNC alumni and fans who had privately funded the project beamed at their personal palace. They were arrogant about the largest college athletic fundraising feat in history and yet unaware of the misjudgments made in financing the building, parking spaces, storage room, and student seating that stereotyped it for years to come. Their money had bought the best seats in the house, and their pride contributed to the wild, capacity crowd that jammed the arena for the historic opener.

Writers from all over the country requested credentials to the nationally tele-vised happening. To pump the pomp, color analyst and former Carolina all-American Billy Cunningham wore a tuxedo.

"That was still as loud as I've heard the place," said Dawkins, who was a Duke senior that day and has since seen eight more games there as an assistant coach. "I'll always remember how electric it was. You could cut the tension with a knife."

From UNC's standpoint, there was more pressure than the NCAA Tourna-ment. No one wanted to *consider* the possibility of a permanent record that showed the Tar Heels had lost the first game in their new home—to Duke!

BLUE BLOOD

Although Mark Alarie had the distinction of scoring the first basket in the Dean Dome (Warren Martin had UNC's first field goal), Carolina built an early lead aided by Krzyzewski getting hit with the first technical foul in the Smith Center. The Tar Heels increased a five-point halftime lead to 64–48 with a run of backdoor baskets against Duke's overplay, getting a career-high 28 points from Hale and 25 from Daugherty, both senior stars.

The Blue Devils scored the last seven points of the game to make the final score 95–92, falling to 16–1.

As the Tar Heels hopped a plane for Milwaukee and a second-straight nationally televised game against Marquette on Sunday (which they won 66–64), most of the stories being written and produced were about the still-unbeaten, No. 1 team in the country and the big win in its new home. Lost in the hoopla was that Duke played well under the circumstances, had four starters in double figures, and shot 52 percent in such hostile surroundings, portending a changing of the guard in the ACC.

The bluebloods remained entwined heading in to the last weeks of the 1986 season. Maryland notched the first visitor's victory in the Dean Dome, when two-time ACC Player of the Year Len Bias scored 35 points. The defeat dropped Carolina to third in the polls and allowed Duke to claim the No. 1 ranking for the first time in Krzyzewski's tenure on February 24.

Late in the Maryland loss, Hale had caught a knee in the chest and suffered a collapsed lung that sidelined him for three games, including the regular-season finale at Cameron. When Hale came out wearing street clothes, his arm in a sling under his sport jacket, the Dukies chanted, "In-Hale, ex-Hale!"

That game on Sunday, March 2, was the first of ten on national television over the next twenty-nine days that permanently etched Duke into the minds of America. Wacky NBC analyst Al McGuire greeted the students wearing the pith hat of an animal trainer, carrying a bullwhip and throwing peanuts into the bleachers. The term "Cameron Crazies" was officially born after NBC featured the pregame hysteria during the broadcast.

Since Carolina moved out of Carmichael Auditorium, Duke and N.C. State were left with the last two hotboxes in the Big Four. The Blue Devils were ascending while Jim Valvano's glory days at State were ending, giving Cameron an edge in atmosphere for most games.

The transformation of college basketball crowds in American can be traced to that 1986 game against UNC. The antics of Duke students hadn't changed;

they distracted opposing free throw shooters with dizzying gestures and organized chants that were planned beforehand and distributed on cheat sheets as they entered the building. Except that this was the first time they had been glorified by the national TV cameras.

Every school sought to emulate the goings-on at Cameron. If Duke did it on national TV, certainly kids could in other arenas, small-college gyms, and high school haunts all over the country. Even brainy Princeton students, who've been dressing up and dissing their Ivy League opponents for longer than Duke, started considering the Crazies their heroes.

There were also basketball reasons the 1986 game was historic.

Behind 27 points from Henderson and 21 from Dawkins, who surpassed Mike Gminski as Duke's all-time leading scorer, the Blue Devils' 82–74 victory relegated UNC to third place in the ACC for the first time in twenty years, snapping perhaps the most remarkable of all of Smith's streaks. It also proved they were the ACC's best team because Carolina played extremely well, shooting 64 percent and pulling down 16 more rebounds.

Unbeaten at home for the first time since 1978, Duke won its first ACC race outright (12–2) in twenty years and completed the long, arduous climb back to the top by surviving three close games in the ACC Tournament—all firsts under Krzyzewski. The Blue Devils had a 32–2 record and won every game they were supposed to win—a sign of their new-found dominance—and earned the top seed in the 1986 NCAA Tournament.

Duke's postseason run began on a scary note. For thirty minutes the Blue Devils trailed tiny Mississippi Valley State, whose coach, Lafayette Stribling, wore an all-white three-piece suit and whose super quick guards baffled Krzyzewski and Duke's defense. The tight Blue Devils looked like they would be first No. 1 seed to lose to a 16 in the history of the Dance.

Krzyzewski has since gone on to compile the best coaching record in the NCAA Tournament, but at that time he was 1–2 with two second-round losses. Would history have been changed by a humiliating defeat to Mississippi Valley State, which forced 23 Duke turnovers while committing just 10 itself?

Dawkins single-handedly saved the terrifying day, scoring 16 points in five minutes of the second half as the Blue Devils pulled it out 85–78. They responded to the near-death experience by winning two more games and sinking Navy and David Robinson 71–50 in the East Regional final at the Meadowlands. As hundreds of Dukies who had found their way into the building chanted, "Abandon Ship! Abandon Ship!" their heroes donned Destination Dallas caps to celebrate yet another Krzyzewski first, a trip to the Final Four.

Arriving at Reunion Arena in Dallas as underdogs, the Blue Devils faced No. 2 Kansas for the second time that season and were not favored to duplicate their preseason NIT win over the veteran Jayhawks. Next to rugged KU forwards Ron Kellogg and Danny Manning, seven-foot center Greg Dreiling and scoring guard Calvin Thompson, Duke looked physically matched.

Alarie held foul-plagued Manning, who had scored 24 points in the first meeting, to a pair of field goals. Duke limited Kansas to two points over the last four minutes, rallying from a four-point deficit to go ahead on Ferry's follow shot and hold on for the 71–67 victory. That Krzyzewski beat KU's Larry Brown for the second time in such a high-profile game solidified his place as America's best young coach. Next up was Louisville, which had won the national championship in 1980 and claimed to be the team of the decade.

"I remember looking around and being a little bit in awe," said Pete Gaudet, Krzyzewski's long-time assistant of coaching in the semifinals. "John Thompson, Dean Smith, Bobby Knight, guys were sitting in the coaches' section watching you. In the back of your mind, it's like, 'Boy this is so special. It may never happen again. You had better enjoy this.' I ended up being a part of seven of those."

Knight was proud of his protégé that weekend, wearing a big Duke button everywhere he went and accepted Krzyzewski's request to address the team before the championship game. His message was clear: Take advantage of this opportunity because it's so hard to get here; concentrate and play hard because no one will remember who finished second.

Balanced scoring had been Duke's hallmark, but in this game only Dawkins hit consistently. Despite shooting almost 60 percent, Louisville still trailed for most of the first thirty-five minutes. Louisville coach Denny Crum was desperate to cool off Dawkins, who had already matched his 24 points against Kansas, and ordered a box-and-one with a different "chaser" each trip down the floor.

The inexperienced Krzyzewski didn't know how to combat Crum's move and couldn't get the ball back into Dawkins's hands or find someone else to score. The rest of the Blue Devils were barely shooting 35 percent.

Louisville's Milt Wagner made the key play when he drove for a score and collided with Bilas. A charging call would have been Wagner's fifth foul, but official Don Rutledge called a block on Bilas and gave Wagner the basket. His three-point play drew the Cardinals within one, and they inched ahead 66–65 on a jumper by Billy Thompson. Drained from working so hard to get open, Dawkins missed a wide-open baseline follow; Louisville rebounded and called timeout with forty-eight seconds left.

Dawkins and Amaker covered Wagner, and Henderson pressured the Cards'

Jeff Hall into firing an airball. In a less-dramatic version of the Hawkeye Whitney-Lorenzo Charles play that sealed N.C. State's national championship in 1983, Louisville freshman Pervis Ellison grabbed the ball in flight and laid it in for a three-point lead.

Dawkins took only two shots in the closing minutes, and Louisville held on to win 72–69. Ellison was the first freshman to win MOP in the Final Four. He scored 25 points against Duke, joining teammate Thompson, and Alarie, Dawkins, and Amaker on the all-tourney team. Krzyzewski blamed himself for the offensive collapse in the final minutes.

Though second best, the Blue Devils arrived home to a tumultuous reception celebrating their return to national prominence, if not their first NCAA title. The Alarie-Bilas-Dawkins-Henderson class put Duke back on the basketball map, setting what in 1986 was an NCAA record of 37 wins and turning their once-unknown coach into one of the hottest names in American sports.

Consensus All-American Dawkins was the lynchpin, Krzyzewski's first National Player of the Year to have his jersey retired. He led the Blue Devils in scoring all four years and set other records for field goals attempted and made.

Despite not winning it all, was the class the most productive in college basketball history? It combined to score more career points than any other recruiting class. Dawkins, with 2,556 points, set the record for an ACC player that still stands; Alarie scored 2,136, Henderson 1,570, Bilas 1,062, Welden Williams 126, and Bill Jackman 87 before he transferred back to Nebraska. The 7,537 total points by one class has never been approached.

The 1986 season bonded the relationship between Krzyzewski and his players. The work, the discipline, the force-fed desire had paid off. Although they might not have won the NCAA title, the Blue Devils won over the media with their wit and personality and their diverse answers. At the Final Four press conference before the championship game, all five starters were asked to pronounce their coach's name. Four said it correctly and then Alarie, perhaps the smartest of the bunch, quipped, "Coach K."

"That's an 80 percent improvement over when they were freshmen," Krzyzewski, seated nearby, said of the tough-love years when he was called anything but Coach by some of his players and Duke fans.

In 1987, the three-point shot from nineteen feet, nine inches became a permanent part of college basketball. It led to contemplation and experimentation from coaches, who had a new percentage to figure out. How many made three-pointers equaled hitting 50 percent of the old two-point field goals? Did three-point shots yield longer caroms and lead to more offensive rebounds? Could a team win over forty minutes by firing it up from behind the arc more times than getting the ball inside?

In Krzyzewski's first six seasons, Duke had steadily improved its field-goal percentage toward the coveted 50 percent barometer that Smith and Carolina had used. Now, what to do? The Blue Devils had lost their cornerstone class, with only point guard Amaker returning as a starter. Dawkins and Alarie were Krzyzewski's first NBA first-round draft choices, Bilas enrolled in Duke law school and Henderson went overseas to play pro basketball.

Carolina added freshman phenom J.R. Reid to its veteran lineup in 1987 and resumed being the team to beat in the ACC. Predictably, the Tar Heels defeated Duke twice and everyone else on the way to their second undefeated regular season (14–0) in four years and their fifth first-place finish of the 1980s.

The expectations Smith had created, however, rendered the regular season next to meaningless if they didn't win either the ACC Tournament or reach the Final Four. Sure enough, they lost a heartbreaker to N.C. State in the ACC title game, after which Smith angrily put his hand over the lens of a TV camera following him off the court. Two weeks later, they were beaten by tenth-ranked Syracuse for the East Region championship. Smith cut short his final post-game press conference in tears, distraught that Kenny Smith, Wolf, Popson, and Hunter joined Daugherty and Hale from the year before as the only classes since 1966 that had not won an ACC Tournament or played in a Final Four.

The mood was solemn all summer in the Carolina basketball office and around the Smith Center. Something had gone terribly awry with college basketball if a team that went 32–4 and undefeated in its own league could finish the season so let down. "We really had a bad year," Bill Guthridge mumbled to himself sarcastically. "We only won 32 games."

Before the 1987–88 season, Chuck Swenson left the Duke staff to become head coach at William & Mary, and Krzyzewski hired Mike Brey, the DeMatha assistant who had been so instrumental in helping the Blue Devils land Ferry. It wasn't as much of a payback for Brey's help as it was an acknowledgement that here was a good high school coach worthy of moving up to the next level, but anyone thinking there was no correlation was foolish.

On January 21, 1988, Duke visited the Tar Heels, who were an overrated No. 2 in the polls. They had lost Kenny Smith and were using Jeff Lebo at point guard while trying to work in freshman King Rice. The Blue Devils' overplaying defense was so effective that Carolina had trouble getting good shots. They led by 5 at halftime and, behind 19 points from Ferry and 22 from Kevin

Strickland, held on for a 70–69 win, their first in the three-year-old Dean Dome.

UNC's Reid hit 11 of his 13 shots to score 27 points, but scored several baskets on offensive rebounds that camouflaged Carolina's scoring problem. Duke's overplaying defense had so disrupted his vaunted passing game that Smith began to think about playing the Dukies differently: using more one-on-one dribble penetration to "break down" their aggressive defense.

The Tar Heels had less trouble with everyone else in the ACC, save a shocking loss to last-place Wake Forest, and won eight straight conference games heading into the rematch at Duke four days after they had clinched first place. In a game when neither defense was much good, the teams combined to make 65 of 114 field goals, 57 percent. The Blue Devils broke it open in the second half, and Krzyzewski swept UNC for the first time, another high point for the forty-one-year-old coach.

Smith often bemoaned the difficulty of beating a good team three times the same season. So as Duke and Carolina advanced to the 1988 ACC Tournament final at the Greensboro Coliseum, it seemed like his turn to win. Coach K, the good solider with the Army background, understood those odds, even if he did not embrace them.

There was something else at stake. In the conference room at a Kansas City hotel on Sunday morning, the NCAA Tournament selection committee decided to let the ACC title determine the No. 2 seeds in the East and West Regions. This was significant because the first two rounds in the East were scheduled for the Smith Center, the last year a team could play on its home court. With the rest of the pairings set, the committee put "ACC 1" on the second line in the East and "ACC 2" on the West line.

Later that day in Greensboro, the Tar Heels broke a halftime tie to lead by five points deep into second half and Smith's adage seemed to be playing out. But at the twelve-and-under TV timeout, Krzyzewski conceded nothing as he knelt in his huddle.

"We have to start playing fucking defense!" he shouted, staring into the eyes of senior leader and defensive specialist Billy King. "We're going to win this game."

The Blue Devils scored on their next possession and then Krzyzewski pointed both index fingers to the ground. They slapped the floor going back on defense, their trademark that they were ready to take things up a notch.

"When they were doing it earlier in the year, they didn't mean it, so I told them to quit," Krzyzewski said later. "They would do it and just play our regular defense. But when you slap the floor like that, it should mean this is a key exchange and you put everything on the line."

Duke locked down the Tar Heels, holding them to 1 of 12 shooting and forcing six turnovers the rest of the way. Quin Snyder contested a fast-break layup by freshman King Rice that would have tied the score in the final seconds, and the Blue Devils won 65–61.

At the buzzer, Krzyzewski thrust both arms in the air, his second ACC Championship secured, and hugged Snyder and other players in an unabashed celebration. He unintentionally ignored Smith, waiting nearby to shake his hand, prompting Krzyzewski later to call himself a "dumb Polack."

The victory meant Krzyzewski had constructed a program beyond one good recruiting class. With a far less-imposing lineup than the Dawkins team, Duke was developing the same mystique Carolina had used to its benefit. Ferry, King, Snyder, Strickland, and a 6' 5" sophomore "center" named Robert Brickey weren't going to scare many opponents. The Blue Devils had finished about where they should have in the ACC race, but March was becoming their month.

The defeat was bitter for UNC and Smith for several reasons, not the least of which was they usually won games under similar circumstances; losing this one symbolized an end to that mastery and some of their own mystique. Also, Smith claimed he had altered his post-season routine and did not treat the tournament as merely a tune-up for NCAA play as they had prior to ACC semifinal losses in 1983, '84, and '86 and losing in the finals of 1985 and '87.

"For the first time in a number of years, we really put an emphasis on winning the [ACC] tournament," Smith said, a comment understandably ridiculed around the league because some inferred that he hadn't really tried to win it since 1982.

Despite winning the ACC again and Smith being named Coach of the Year, the season was already tainted because Carolina could not beat Duke, whose students promptly produced "Triple Crown" T-shirts. UNC also had to relinquish its home for the NCAA Tournament, a bitter pill for the team and fans who had bought up all the tickets to the subregional in the Dean Dome.

The Tar Heels flew out to Salt Lake City while the Blue Devils, awkwardly, bussed over to a Chapel Hill that had been wild with anticipation of the Tar Heels playing their first and only NCAA game there. "They won the tournament and beat us three times," a reticent Smith said.

Duke was booed by some in the half-filled arena who hadn't torn up their tickets, but stoically defeated Boston University and SMU. Meanwhile, three thousand miles from home, Carolina whipped North Texas State and faced high-scoring Loyola-Marymount and Hank Gathers (who died tragically two years later). Smith knew his team could run, too, and also played more defense than Loyola. The Tar Heels made 49 of 62 shots (easily a school-record 79 percent), recorded 36 assists and ran one-dimensional Loyola out of the arena 123–97.

So the Tobacco Road rivals moved on to Sweet Sixteens on opposite coasts.

Duke edged unranked Rhode Island by a point at the New Jersey Meadowlands and drew top-seeded, top-ranked Temple with freshman sensation Mark Macon. Carolina handled No. 10 Michigan in Seattle and faced No. 2 Arizona and All-Americans Steve Kerr and Sean Elliott.

Ironically, they had played each other's Elite Eight opponents during the regular season.

The Blue Devils lost to then top-ranked Arizona in the finals of the Fiesta Bowl Classic on the Wildcats' home court. Krzyzewski was the wildest cat that night, drawing a technical foul over the officiating that eventually sent Arizona to the foul line 42 times.

Temple played at UNC in late February and had blown out the Tar Heels late in the game. Macon scored 19 points after sitting out most of the first half with two fouls, causing Owls' coach John Chaney to spend an entire timeout staring down the officials.

A month later, Chaney and Macon were no match for the two K's—Krzyzewski and the uncompromising King, who had followed Amaker in 1987 as the national defensive player of the year. By using his long arms and bodying up Macon, King held him to 6 of 29 shooting, as Duke erupted in the last few minutes and denied Chaney his best chance to coach in a Final Four. Getting to his second in three years was important for Krzyzewski, who moved into an elite category of coaches with more than one Final Four appearance.

The following day, Carolina played an excellent first half and led Arizona 28–26, but, while overachieving, the 1988 Tar Heels were a mishmash of talented players with no leader or proven point guard. The star-studded Wildcats, who had both, stepped it up after the break. Elliott finished with 24 points and Tom Tolbert 21, while J. R. Reid was held to 10 and no other Tar Heel managed more than 13. The 70–52 loss completed UNC's season at 27–7, the eighteenth consecutive year Smith had won more than 20 games but also the sixth straight he had not won the ACC Tournament or a regional championship.

At the fiftieth Final Four in Kansas City, Duke played Kansas in the semifinals for the second time in three years. The unranked but sentimental favorite Jayhawks were on the NCAA bubble back in February and needed a strong run to get invited as a No. 6 seed in the Mideast. Kansas won 8 of its last 10 regular-season games, but one of the losses was to Duke on February 20 at Allen Fieldhouse.

Still coached by Larry Brown and led by Manning, by then a senior All-American, the Jayhawks scored the first 14 points of the Final Four rematch and led 18–2, then 24–6. The stone-cold Blue Devils were missing badly from both the field and the foul line and trailed by 11 at the half. They kept fighting and staged a second-half rally that cut the deficit to 3 with two minutes left, but Manning scored the last of his game-high 25 points on a tip-in and Kansas ended Duke's season at 28–7.

When Carolina was not participating in the Final Four, Smith usually left after the coaching meetings and semifinals on Saturday. This time, he stayed around to cheer his alma mater and protégé Brown, whom he had helped land the Kansas job in 1983. Smith did not share the hard feelings of those on his staff. Manning was from Greensboro and in 1984 was headed to UNC. Then Brown hired his father, a former pro teammate and friend, as his assistant coach. Ed Manning was out of coaching and driving a truck, so the move looked to have violated an unwritten rule within the Carolina Basketball Family to look out for your own.

Nevertheless, Smith was delighted when Kansas stunned top-ranked Oklahoma, Brown won the national championship and Manning, with 56 points and 28 rebounds in his last two college games, was named MOP of the Final Four. Smith also supported Brown when, a month later, he bolted back to the NBA.

A few days after Brown resigned, Smith walked into the office of his assistant coach, Roy Williams, who was still relatively unknown in the profession. He told Williams not to get excited, or to do anything, but that he might have a chance to get the Kansas job.

"He's finally losing it," Williams thought to himself. "There's no way in hell that I'm going to be the Kansas coach."

A week later, Williams met with KU Athletics Director Bob Frederick in the Delta Crown Room at the Atlanta airport. After Kansas tried to hire a half-dozen sitting head coaches, Smith convinced Frederick to give Williams a chance. "Hell had frozen over," Williams thought on his way to Lawrence, Kansas.

Although Duke and Carolina were now considered colossal college basketball vessels sailing the same waters, they were seen in some circles as big ships passing in the night. Both had won two ACC Tournament titles and reached the Final Four twice in the decade, but Duke's were in 1986 and '88 compared to UNC's in 1981 and '82.

Clearly, some fans perceived Carolina to be in slow decline with an aging coach while Duke boasted hot new stars of the MTV era. Plenty of doubt existed whether Smith and the Tar Heels could retain their preeminence in the ACC, if not the nation. The hurt feelings carried on as Duke protected its 1988–89 preseason No. 1 ranking all the way to late January. The Blue Devils were 13–0 and solidly favored the night the thirteenth-ranked Tar Heels went to Durham with a 14–3 record and Jeff Lebo, their star senior guard, was out with a sprained ankle.

UNC had dropped two of its last three games, including a 23-point pounding at Virginia, while Duke was winning by an average margin of 29 points. Smith thought Carolina's superior size could neutralize the Devils underneath, however, and give his team a chance. He needed a great game from King Rice and to replace Lebo by committee—just the kind of challenges that still juiced the fifty-eight-year-old coach.

Smith rarely attended the pregame meal, leaving that duty to Bill Guthridge, but he hurried through a radio interview and took the two-mile drive to Slug's at the Pines to make sure his players were focused on the nine o'clock tip-off in Cameron Indoor Stadium. Smith was feeding off his own philosophy that a capable team could be most dangerous immediately after suffering its most adversity.

He surprised his players by showing up as the meal was ending and pulled Reid and Scott Williams aside while they were leaving the restaurant.

"We need to get on the boards tonight," he said, looking up at his 6' 9" and 6' 10" postmen. "We have to make up for Jeff's absence by outrebounding them on both ends." His giant juniors nodded their commitment to the coach.

When the Tar Heels took the court about three hours later, Lebo hobbled out with them on crutches. The Blue Devil mascot was waiting with a dozen roses, which was typical of a private school where the students could afford to finance such elaborate pranks. Lebo was not pleased by the gesture and refused the roses.

Ironically, it may have been Lebo's injury that helped Carolina the most on this night. Rice, who replaced Lebo in the starting backcourt, did not have much of an outside shot but was a strong ball handler with good penetration skills. After three losses in 1988 while trying to beat Duke with his passing game, Smith allowed Rice to drive on the Blue Devils and, in the process, found a new way to play them. Krzyzewski played into his adversary's hands by refusing to pull back the pressure and give Rice open shots.

Heeding their coach, the Tar Heels clobbered Duke on the backboards by 17 rebounds, broke open a close game and built an insurmountable lead. During a timeout late in the game, Smith told his players, "The best thing about this win is how quiet this place is right now."

Scott Williams, who had 22 points and 11 rebounds, put his hand to his ear and said to the Duke fans, "I don't hear you now" as the clock wound down on the 91–71 shocker. Rice and senior Steve Bucknall led the backcourt committee, scoring 14 points and dishing out 7 assists in thirty-four brilliant minutes. Freshman Hubert Davis and junior Jeff Denny combined to play an atypical twenty-seven minutes, scoring 12 points to further assuage Lebo's absence.

After the game, in the media room, Smith was talking about Reid, but not the 13 points and 10 rebounds he had contributed to the victory. He had what he thought was a far more important matter on his mind.

Smith had seen a placard in the Duke student section that said, "J. R. Can't Reid." Reluctant to complain after a loss, he took his opportunity on the victory platform to criticize what he considered a racial slur by clever, elitist students. He said that pun wouldn't have been made if Reid were white, and that it was absurd anyway since Reid was an outstanding student from a middle-class home who had been the ACC's only player on the 1988 U.S. Olympic team in Seoul, Korea.

Sportswriters thought Smith was overreacting because a similar "J. R. Can't Reid" sign had popped up at another ACC arena without any recourse from Carolina, but, to Smith, the issue was bigger than one sign. He believed the publicity the networks and national television were giving the Cameron Crazies glorified poor sportsmanship that was being copied all over the country.

Smith loved loud cheering but disdained any crowd behavior meant directly for the opposing team, such as derisive chants and fans waving their arms to distract the free-throw shooter. Duke had taken that to a new level with choreographed group vulgarity that was characterized as a major difference between the respected men coaching each program.

Although Krzyzewski emphasized "cheering for our team and not against the other team," the student antics were tame when compared to a coach caught cursing regularly on television. In retrospect, by not stepping in sooner to control his own crowd, Krzyzewski had become the most influential person in shaping fan behavior in college basketball.

The Reid controversy carried through the regular-season rematch on Senior Day in Chapel Hill. Carolina led midway through the second half before Duke's Quin Snyder drained three late three-pointers to help the Blue Devils even the score. The 88–86 loss added to Smith's orneriness at next week's ACC Tournament in Atlanta.

The Tar Heels arrived with recent nightmares of Atlanta, having lost at Georgia Tech on Dennis Scott's buzzer-beater before dropping the home finale to Duke. The two defeats squandered a chance to win the regular season, left them in second place with the Blue Devils and Virginia and as the tournament's fourth seed after the various tie-breakers.

The UNC players were not only angry from the two defeats, they were also really hot after reading the ACC Tournament preview in the *Daily Tar Heel* that week. Breaking down a possible Duke-Carolina rubber match, sports editor and fellow student David Glenn had checked off "coaching" in the column under the Gothic D logo.

As if the weekend needed another subplot, "JR Can't Reid" hung over the tournament after Smith brought it up again on the ACC conference call the week before.

When Smith got a liberal issue in his craw, he was like a bulldog gnawing leather. He had looked up the SATs of Ferry and freshman Christian Laettner, both white players he had recruited, and found that their combined scores were not as high as those of Reid and Scott Williams, his black duo. Despite violating sensitive issues of privacy, Smith rolled out the comparison.

The media assembled in Atlanta anticipating some off-the-court fireworks between Smith and Krzyzewski. They weren't disappointed.

Told by a local sportswriter and old friend at the tournament practice day that he could not comment on academic information of any players, Smith snapped, "Why not? I didn't give out the specific scores. But I know what they are because I recruited all four."

Carolina had lost any chance at Laettner the year before, and it, too, had something to do with Reid. Laettner's mother had asked about the rivalry with Duke and been told by the UNC coaches that it was basically friendly and overblown by the media. Then, while touring the Granville Towers dorm where the players lived, Laettner and his mother saw "Fuck Duke" written on the door to Reid's room.

Smith still had Laettner's high school records in his files and looked up his SAT scores.

Reid's SATs, by themselves, could not have been higher than Ferry's or Smith would have used that simple comparison (in fact, it was about 200 points lower). To make his point, the old math major from Kansas needed to concoct a formula, and the scores he needed were Williams's 1300 that were several hundred points higher than Laettner's.

Krzyzewski reacted as expected, telling a group of sportswriters at the practice day, "It really pisses me off that he would talk about my players in public." Coaches usually tried to stay above the fray, but at the end of a long, hot season, their nerves were shredded, and they were susceptible to squabbles like anyone else. Especially Smith and Krzyzewski, who were being constantly egged on by their fans, the press, and, sometimes, their own family members.

So the weekend in Atlanta, home of Martin Luther King and a birthplace of the Civil Rights movement, not only had two basketball powers vying for supremacy but two coaching giants tangling over issues of race and privacy.

The Tar Heels called a players-only meeting before the first round of the tournament and responded with their best effort in two weeks by beating Georgia Tech 77–62 in the quarterfinals on Friday. They held another private meeting before the semifinal against last-place Maryland, which was 8–19 and had inexplicably blown out regular-season champion N.C. State by 22 points on opening day.

Maryland coach Bob Wade suffered a mild heart attack after the upset and watched from a hospital bed. Carolina did the blowing out this time, 88–58, to reach the championship game.

Duke, meanwhile, had easy wins over Wake Forest and Virginia. The Blue Devils' in-your-face defense was so difficult to handle that opposing coaches were complaining about a new double standard of officiating, one for Duke and one for the rest of the conference.

During his team's 24-point loss to the Blue Devils, Wake Forest coach Bob Staak stood up in disgust and yelled, "Yeah, Duke plays great fucking defense . . . five guys fouling all the time!"

Duke had more than just defense. On his way to first-team All-American honors, Ferry had set the Duke single-game scoring record with 58 points against Miami and was capping a career in which he played in three Final Fours. Nominated for the Naismith Award as the nation's best collegian, he was the first ACC player to record 2,000 points, 1,000 rebounds, and 500 assists.

Ferry had support from fellow seniors Snyder and John Smith, juniors Brickey, Alaa Abdelnaby, and Phil Henderson. Plus, the 6' 11" Laettner had come on late in February to earn a starting position. None were all-conference players, but they had developed a powerful togetherness behind their leader, Ferry, who was having a superb senior year.

Smith called the next meeting on Sunday morning after the team's pregame meal. He walked into the room and said, "You guys are doing a good job," and walked out. His players needed no prodding; they knew what was at stake: winning UNC's first ACC Tournament since 1982 and beating the Blue Devils for a second time that season.

The atmosphere resembled a heavyweight title fight more than a championship basketball game, so electric was the excitement and anticipation in the old Omni, the site of two of Carolina's most devastating defeats—the 1977 NCAA championship game loss to Marquette and the 1984 Sweet Sixteen shocker to Indiana, Michael Jordan's last game as a Tar Heel. Now came Duke.

"You could *feel* the game," said UNC Sports Information Director Steve Kirschner, then a staffer in his first year watching his first ACC Tournament. "Since then, a lot of people have called it the most intense sporting event they've ever witnessed. It still is for me."

When the teams came out to warm up, so much contentiousness filled the arena that some spectators had trouble breathing normally. Making matters worse, the ACC had unwisely assigned tickets to fans from Duke and UNC in adjacent sections of the arena, separated by a single, narrow aisle.

Before the game, fanatics began yelling insults at each other, and they weren't kidding. Gloating Duke fans felt like they had surpassed Carolina, whose own fans were both proud and hurt, acting as if a new, younger boss was trying to move their father out to pasture.

One other off-court matter involved Snyder and Lebo, opposing point guards and future head coaches, but then social antagonists.

At the time, Snyder was dating Kristy Brown, a UNC coed and the daughter of Larry Brown, the former Tar Heel player and coach. On the nights Brown did not see Snyder, she hung out innocently with Lebo and several of his friends, one of whom was also sweet on her. In the center jump circle, as the starters shook hands before the tip-off, Lebo snickered to Snyder that while they were in Atlanta playing basketball he wondered what was going on back in Chapel Hill.

In general, however, the opposing players were more mature toward each other than their fans. They participated in pickup games on the rival campuses during the off-season, occasionally partied together, and eventually used the same barbershop. The rivalry's roots even extended to the long-time play-by-play announcers, Bob Harris of Duke and Woody Durham of Carolina, who both hailed from Albemarle, North Carolina, and went to high school together in the late 1950s. Harris and Durham were at courtside in Atlanta within a free throw of their respective broadcast locations.

As the 1989 ACC Tournament final unfolded, and the fans kept up a constant din, the head coaches competed as ferociously as their players, quickly sweating through their thousand-dollar suits. The game opened with Lebo hitting three long jumpers to give Carolina a big early lead. Duke responded to close the margin and the intensity and tension were soon off the charts.

UNC center Scott Williams triggered the colorful exchange between Smith and Krzyzewski heard up and down press row. A gangly player who seemed to attract body contact, Williams fell down repeatedly in the paint. After he flopped to the floor following a collision for the third time in the first half, the Duke fans began chanting, "TKO! TKO!"

Krzyzewski thought Williams was playing too rough and told him so when he was in earshot. Smith saw it and yelled down the sideline at Krzyzewski, who retorted with the epithet that he often used, but this was the first time anyone recalled Smith being told off in such a graphic manner.

"Hey, Dean! Fuck you!"

The Tar Heels led 39–35 at halftime and maintained the narrow edge for most of the second half. During one rebounding collision inside, Reid knocked Ferry down and snorted while standing over him, "Take that, Mr. Naismith." When Smith inserted Hubert Davis during a free throw, the freshman was so nervous he ran from the lane to the circle and back to the lane before teammate Kevin Madden dragged him to the right spot behind the shooter.

Carolina maintained control and a small lead, but Duke wouldn't let the Tar Heels get comfortable. With less than two minutes left, the Blue Devils trailed by six points and were getting desperate. Laettner fired the only three-point shot of his freshman year and made it to finish with 15 points and foretelling his career as their all-time leader in three-point percentage.

Still behind 77–74 in the final, frenzied seconds, Duke got one last shot to tie the game. Ferry had the ball seventy-five feet from the basket and lofted a long football pass with amazing accuracy. Standing in front of his bench, Smith followed the flight of the ball, contorting his body as it hit the back of the rim and bounded away.

He grew limp with relief when he heard the horn, saying later, "It was so close an old man could have had a heart attack."

The war had ended, one of the fiercest college basketball games anyone who had seen it could remember. In all, 49 fouls were called, with 59 free throws attempted. Four players fouled out and five others finished the game with four fouls. Most of the combatants excelled, except for Snyder who had an awful afternoon and might have been unnerved by Lebo's crack before the opening tip. He missed 9 of his 10 shots, went 0–7 from three-point range and finished with four points before fouling out.

"I think my comment got into Quin's head," Lebo said later when recounting the story.

Reid had some measure of revenge with 14 points and 9 rebounds and holding Ferry to 6 of 20 shooting and 3 rebounds, winning the tournament MVP trophy in what had been a checkered season.

This was the culmination of a three-year battle that began in high school. Ferry and Reid were the No. 1 recruits in the country a year apart. Reid was two inches shorter but thicker in the arms and chest and was tough to move out of the paint. Plus, he could dribble, spin, and shoot the twelve footer. Ferry was more versatile and, as his career progressed, had a better work ethic, finishing with 2,155 points, 1,003 rebounds and 506 assists.

Duke and Carolina split eight games in which they both played from 1987–89, and each won an ACC championship from the other. Ferry averaged 17 points and just under 7 rebounds against Reid's UNC teams. Reid had 14-plus and 9-plus stats in their head-to-head match-ups. Each made All-ACC in 1987 and again in 1988, when Ferry beat Reid by sixty-five votes for ACC Player of the Year.

However, the 1989 season, when they had their epic battle in Atlanta, separated them. Unanimous All-ACC again, Ferry won his second straight Player of the Year award. Reid, who had been in some off-court trouble and quibbled with Smith over playing time, failed to make any All-ACC team.

They shook hands coldly after their last meeting and led their respective teams into the NCAA Tournament, where another Duke-Carolina controversy was waiting.

By winning their first ACC championship since 1982, Smith thought the fifth-ranked Tar Heels had earned a trip to the NCAA East Regional, scheduled to open in Greensboro the following Thursday. Ironically, their win over Duke had left them ranked too high to be placed in the East, where second-ranked Georgetown was the top seed. In losing, the Blue Devils drew the tougher assignment from the NCAA selection committee.

Kirschner was at the Atlanta airport three hours later, writing down the NCAA pairings on a napkin as he watched them announced in the main terminal. He rode the tram to the Delta concourse with Smith, who squinted as he studied the napkin. Carolina was being sent South, beginning right back in Atlanta the next weekend. If the Tar Heels won two games there, they would advance to Lexington, Kentucky, for the Sweet Sixteen and a likely matchup with Michigan for the third straight year. "That's not right; that makes three years in a row we play them," said Smith, referring to wins over the Wolverines in the second round in 1987 and the third round in '88.

Seeing that Duke was in the East Region, Smith perused the bracket and predicted eleventh seed Minnesota would be the Blue Devils' opponent in the Sweet Sixteen at the Meadowlands, from where they had already reached the Final Four in two of the past three years.

"I'd rather be playing Minnesota," he said, striking the local theme of the 1989 NCAA Tournament.

Back home, Krzyzewski made the first of his snide remarks about Smith. "We don't care where and who we play," he said.

Duke and Carolina won easy openers but got big scares in the second round. The Blue Devils held off seventeenth ranked West Virginia by seven points and the Tar Heels beat UCLA by the same margin, but not before trailing the Bruins for most of the game. They played without Reid, who had been caught with a girl in his hotel room and voted off the trip by Lebo and the other seniors. After watching the win over UCLA back in Chapel Hill, Reid rejoined the team for the Sweet Sixteen in Lexington.

Michigan was different from the last two years. Bill Frieder, the frenetic coach who wore a towel over his shoulder during games, had been fired by

Athletics Director Bo Schembechler in February for having agreed to take the Arizona State coaching job after the season. The Wolverines wanted to prove they could win without Frieder and played hard for elevated assistant coach Steve Fisher. Their star Glen Rice was having a superb senior year, and he burned the Tar Heels for 34 points including the critical fall-away jumper from in front of his bench. The 92–87 loss ended Carolina's season at 29–8 and overshadowed Reid's 26 points in one of the best games of his career.

"I'd still rather be playing Minnesota," Smith said on his way out of Rupp Arena.

Indeed, Duke defeated Minnesota to stand one game away from its second straight Final Four and third in four years. Just as they had against Temple with Macon in 1988, the Blue Devils faced top-seeded Georgetown and its star, center Alonzo Mourning. The Hoyas had edged N.C. State in the regional semifinal, decided at the end on a bogus traveling call against Chris Corchianni by ACC official Rick Hartzell.

While Carolina couldn't muster the emotion to match Michigan, the Duke-Georgetown game further exposed Krzyzewski as the best motivator in college basketball. He had his team, and particularly Laettner, focused to face John Thompson's Hoyas. After Mourning blocked one of his early shots, Laettner stayed with it, picked up the ball, and scored. As with Carolina in 1982, intimidation wasn't going to be a factor in this game.

Duke kept taking it to Georgetown and, buoyed by its traditional following at the Meadowlands, built a 76–51 lead in the second half before the Hoyas made a run and closed to within two. The Blue Devils got the ball to Ferry, who was fouled; his two free throws led to eight straight points and an ultimate 85–77 win that sent them back to the Final Four in Seattle.

The victory was also the breakout game for Laettner, who had been averaging 8 points while hitting a school-record 72 percent of his field goal attempts. He posted a career high of 24 points and 9 rebounds, mostly against Mourning. The veteran players voted not to cut down the nets, a decision Krzyzewski would never let them make again, especially after what happened the next weekend.

Eleventh-ranked Seton Hall from the Big East was a good match for No. 9 Duke in the semifinals at the old King Dome. The Blue Devils led by 18 points in the first half, then the quick Brickey went down with a sprained ankle, turning the tide of the game. Krzyzewski replaced him with 6' 10" Alaa Abdelnaby, who was mismatched against the Pirate's smaller, faster front line led by Australian exchange student Andrew Gaze.

"Alaa got his chance when Brickey got hurt, and he pissed down his [own] leg," assistant coach Pete Gaudet said after Duke faded in the second half and suffered a 35-point turnaround in the 95–78 defeat. Michigan beat Seton Hall in overtime for the title two nights later.

Nevertheless, it ended another strong season in which Duke finished 28–8 and set a school record for field goal percentage (.537). Ferry, who had 34 points and 10 rebounds in a gallant semifinal effort, won the Naismith as national player of the year. The Los Angeles Clippers then selected him second in the NBA draft, Krzyzewski's highest pick to that point.

Reid, whose pro stock had gradually declined since his phenomenal freshman season, decided to enter the draft as a junior when the new Charlotte Hornets told Smith they would make him the fifth pick. Compared to his ballyhooed recruitment and his freshman season in which he made All-ACC and ran away with Rookie of the Year honors, Reid left college as one of the bigger disappointments in UNC history.

Without their main men, Smith and Krzyzewski began preparing for the 1989–90 season and the next decade as the Duke-Carolina rivalry reached a new passage—when what happened *between* them turned secondary. In the past, fans had claimed bragging rights on the home-and-away series and a possible third meeting in the ACC Tournament.

That was now negated if one school played deeper into the NCAA Tournament and, especially, marched on to the Final Four.

Since 1986, Duke and Carolina had split ten games. They had each won three ACC regular-season or tournament championships. Because the Blue Devils had been to three Final Fours, and the Tar Heels to none, no one except those bleeding light blue were saying the programs were even.

RIVALRY RECORD IN THE 1980s
- Carolina won 16; Duke won 9

HOW THEY DID IN THE DECADE
- Carolina 281–63 (.817); Duke 226–101 (.691)
- Coach K vs. Carolina in 1980s: 8–14
- Dean vs. Duke in the 1980s: 16–10

ACC CHAMPIONSHIPS
- Carolina 1981, 1982, 1989; Duke 1980, 1986, 1988

FINAL FOURS
- Carolina 1981, 1982; Duke 1986, 1988, 1989
- NCAA Championships: Carolina 1982; Duke none

BIGGEST WIN
- Duke 77, Carolina 75, March 10, 1984

MOST MEMORABLE GAME
- Carolina 77, Duke 74, March 12, 1989

MOST FAMOUS QUOTE
"So let's get some things straight around here and quit the double standard that sometimes exists in this league."

(Mike Krzyzewski, 1984)

6

BACK-TO-BACK-TO-BACK

In the spring of 1988, Kenny Anderson and Bobby Hurley were the rich man–poor man of high school point guards.

Anderson was the thoroughbred, a lithe lefty who had been a legend since his days on the playgrounds of New York City. He was the first Stephon Marbury and Sebastian Telfair, the boy who played with men and could only avoid college stardom if he didn't do the right thing on the street corner and class room. The college coach who got him might only have him for two years, but those years would make someone's program. That's how good Kenny Anderson was.

Hurley was Seabiscuit from across the sea, or at least the Hudson River. Smaller and slower than Anderson, his pedigree was more impressive than his performance on some nights. He had game, taught to him by a strict coaching father in a hardscrabble neighborhood, but he also had a funny-looking jump shot that he sort of spun off his hands from in front of his forehead. Where Anderson was a can't miss, recruiting analysts debated whether Hurley was good enough to star for a major college.

Anderson was the No. 1 prospect on Dean Smith's list. Smith didn't rule New York recruiting like his predecessor Frank McGuire once had, but Carolina's connections with high school coaches such as Jack Curran of Archbishop Malloy in Queens still made the Tar Heels the favorite for almost any player they wanted. Smith had swooped in at virtually the last minute in 1983 and stolen Kenny Smith away from Virginia. Kenny Smith was related to Kenny Anderson, truly the next great guard out of the City.

Duke recruited Anderson but didn't seem to have much luck with New York City kids. After Johnny Dawkins and Tom Amaker graduated, Mike Krzyzewski's prime target had been Chris Corchianni, another sensational southpaw from Miami, but Coach K was up against Coach V—the Jim Valvano road show. The N.C. State funny man wanted Corchianni, and an Italian kid from Miami was more in

Valvano's comfort zone than the Polish coach from Chicago. Valvano did crazy things in recruiting, including ripping off his dress shirt during a home visit to reveal a T-shirt with the player's picture, or moving the living room furniture around and have all the family members line up in State's offensive set.

Valvano corralled Corchianni, leaving Duke without a true point guard for the 1988 and '89 seasons. That wasn't the end of the world for Krzyzewski, who disdained Smith's system of numbering positions and preferred putting the five best basketball players and athletes on the court and figuring out how to get the ball in the basket. Down to senior Kevin Strickland and junior Quin Snyder in his starting backcourt, Krzyzewski's priority was definitely finding guards for the 1989–90 season and beyond.

Hurley had followed the Tar Heels since attending Smith's summer camp after the seventh grade. His father, Bob Hurley, was the coach at dirt-poor St. Anthony's in Jersey City, which he had turned into a high school powerhouse with basically smoke and mirrors and a lot of elbow grease. Since Jim Spanarkel and Mike O'Koren from rival Hudson Catholic had played for the Blue Devils and Tar Heels, respectively, in the late 1970s, Bob Hurley had followed both teams closely.

Although Smith coveted Anderson, who early on was considered a lock to follow in his cousin Kenny's footsteps, he recruited other point guards. He informed the Hurley family that Anderson was his priority, which had been Smith's long-time policy; generally, he was able to get his second choice to wait to see what No. 1 would do. That's how big playing for Smith and the Tar Heels had become.

Recruiting, however, was changing along with college basketball. High school players received much more publicity, thanks to an increase of all-star games and AAU summer teams and the influx of recruiting services that were now ranking players all the way down to the tenth grade. As Duke had proven, Carolina was no longer the most followed college team. For high school players who didn't much care about yesterday, today's superstar was Michael Jordan of the Bulls, not the erstwhile Tar Heel.

During the summer of 1988, Hurley and his father told Smith they couldn't wait for Anderson's decision. By that time, Duke was already in there solid. Krzyzewski played off Smith's system, forgot Anderson and told Hurley he was Duke's top choice, that they weren't recruiting any other point guards and that he would get to play alongside Billy McCaffery, a shooting guard Duke was also recruiting.

That wasn't going to work at Carolina because Anderson and Hurley were both playmakers who needed to have the basketball. "They had a really good chance at Kenny Anderson, and he was a great player," Hurley said years later. "It looked like he was going to end up there. They suggested us playing together, and tried what they could to keep me interested. But I realized I should move on to other schools."

So Hurley committed to Duke and said he would sign with the Blue Devils before the 1989 season, his senior year at St. Anthony's. Smith continued recruiting Anderson and didn't realize he was losing favor with him. UNC no longer had assistant coach Eddie Fogler, who always had his ear to the ground when it came to recruiting kids in his native New York City. Carolina missed some obvious signs on Anderson.

Georgia Tech coach Bobby Cremins, another New Yorker, had moved in and was chasing Anderson, calling him almost every day and writing him what he eventually estimated as two hundred letters. Plus, Syracuse and coach Jim Boeheim were closing hard. Among coaches, it was common knowledge that Boeheim thought Cremins was going way over the NCAA limit on contacts and visits with Anderson, but coaches rarely blew the whistle on each other.

Anderson, caught up in the hype and with no one from North Carolina to babysit him, told Cremins he didn't think he was going to UNC after all. Rather than joining Dean Smith's stable of stars, he liked the idea of making a new name for himself at Georgia Tech. During the fall signing period of 1988, after Hurley had signed with Duke, Anderson sent his letter of intent to Atlanta instead of Chapel Hill. Cremins welcomed Anderson with the clear understanding that he would stay only until he was a high NBA draft pick.

Smith insisted honesty was still the best policy, but gambling on Anderson left the Tar Heels almost as thin in the backcourt as Duke had been. They had no qualified substitute behind King Rice, leading to Smith's political joke about the beleaguered vice president at the time: "Rice has to remain healthy like [President George H.W.] Bush has to remain healthy, although I don't know who our [Dan] Quayle is."

In retrospect, Hurley was the better choice for Carolina because, regardless of how he turned out, his father's vast connections with high school coaches across the country were going to help whichever program signed his son. Bob Hurley, the long-time UNC fan, turned into a Duke advocate and his son a central figure in the escalating game of one-upsmanship between the two schools that continued into the new decade.

Recruiting had become the second season in college basketball, followed around the ACC as closely as any conference. Duke and Carolina were always "in it" for the top high school players, and it was no coincidence that they usually alternated getting great freshman classes. When one of them loaded up, the other could offer the next year's crop more promise of playing time. As interest grew, other factors were added to the mix.

Krzyzewski and Smith both chafed at how public their private business had become, and how the recruiting services and rankings misled high school players into thinking they were either better than they were or the second and third choices of certain schools when that wasn't the case at all. Prep stars were so coddled and pampered by coaches and various hangers-on that they had a hard time separating fact from fiction. It was easier than ever to get into a youngster's head and distort the truth.

College coaches once had to "sell" a recruit and his family and maybe his high school coach, as well. Now, they had to also deal with AAU summer league coaches, some of whom were already being paid by shoe companies to steer their players toward "Nike or Adidas schools," and the extended families that included relatives and friends inflating their egos with misinformation about their skills and value to the college teams coveting them.

This got worse each year and was much harder on those without the cachet of a Duke or Carolina. The so-called elite programs still commanded the respect of most recruits, their families and the "advisers" who had the players' ears, but even the most famous college coaches had to cooperate with recruiting gurus such as Bob Gibbons and Brick Oettinger who could influence kids by ranking them and evaluating them in Gibbons's *All-Star Sports Report* or Oettinger's column in *The PooP Sheet* sports journal.

For years, both Gibbons and Oettinger were aligned with Carolina, which created skepticism at Duke and other schools.

Gibbons was an insurance salesman in the mountain town of Lenoir, North Carolina, who began following high school players after he got hooked on basketball while a student at UNC. Smith, particularly, paid Gibbons great respect, which in turn gave him credibility with other coaches. It was not uncommon for Gibbons to speak with a dozen head coaches or their assistants every day during the heat of recruiting season. All this made him one of the most influential men in college basketball. Recruiting had become that big.

Oettinger was also a UNC grad and worked for the state Department of Corrections located near Chapel Hill. He went from a local recruiting maven to a national "expert" after aligning with former Carolina player Dennis Wuycik and his controversial *PooP Sheet* publication in the late 1970s. With Wuycik's backing, Oettinger published his own Recruiters' Handbook and got so well known that he had a column in the *Sporting News*.

Gibbons and Oettinger were sensitive about their Tar Heel ties, causing both of them to work hard at befriending and helping other coaches in the ACC. They attended the plethora of summer camps and often knew of ninth and tenth graders before the coaches did. By the time the kids were seniors, there were few secrets in recruiting. How the players did once they were in college, and how long they would stay, was more of a crapshoot.

Now it was the summer of 1989.

Hurley was ready to enroll at Duke, Anderson at Georgia Tech. Having missed on both, UNC had signed two point guards, lightly recruited Scott Cherry and Kenny Harris, who UNC snatched away from Virginia at the last minute. Neither was projected as a future star, or even starter, so Dean Smith and his staff were under pressure to land a great recruiting class that would enter school in the fall of 1990.

In July, rising senior guard Phil Henderson confirmed speculation that he was leaving Duke and transferring to Illinois, his native state university. Henderson had dug himself an academic hole, having been suspended the second semester of his freshman year, and struggled to overcome it despite playing well as a junior when he averaged almost 13 points a game and improved his shooting from 43 percent to 53. Why he would leave with only one season of eligibility remaining, and having to sit out a transfer year, puzzled Blue Devil fans.

But, in late August, Henderson found out that he was ineligible to play for the Illini even after missing the 1989–90 season. An honor student in high school with 1200 on his SATs, he had too many sub-C grades at Duke that Illinois wouldn't accept. Krzyzewski met privately with Henderson several times and after reaching some common ground took him back for his senior year, academic warts and all. With Hurley and McCaffery coming in, Duke needed his experience to stabilize the young backcourt.

UNC recruited hard that summer and, by the fall of 1989, was in solid with four high school seniors it hoped would carry the program back to the Final Four for the first time in eight years and begin to challenge Duke's recent dominance. A fifth was still out there, being sought by both schools.

Grant Hill was the son of former Yale football All-American and NFL all-star Calvin Hill. The 6' 8" Hill grew up in the middle class suburbs of Washington, D.C., where his mother, Janet, worked as a corporate consultant. The Hills kept their only son out of all the high school hoopla of recruiting ratings and all-star games. College coaches, however, knew how good he was and his potential as a collegian.

Like so many others watching college basketball in the 1980s, Hill had been hooked on Michael Jordan and the Tar Heels through his youth. Duke struck his fancy later on when the Blue Devils surfaced, and soon he had narrowed his short list down to the two schools. He scheduled official visits in the fall of his senior year, one weekend at Duke and the next at UNC.

Hill was in Durham in early November of 1989 for the Blue-White scrimmage and annual Legends Game, when former Blue Devils returned to campus. He loved the atmosphere in Cameron Indoor Stadium and got caught up in the excitement of the Crazies. Krzyzewski broke out his favorite line, telling Hill he could come to Duke and "play with the best or go somewhere else and play *against* the best." As the visit ended, he shook Hill's hand and asked for his commitment.

Dean Smith always liked to go into the home *after* a recruit had been to the other school he was considering. Having been invited to dinner at the Hills on the following Wednesday night, Smith arrived believing Grant would finish his scheduled campus visits before making a decision. He ate dinner with the family and, just before adjourning to the living room for the recruiting pitch, was surprised that Hill excused himself from the table and went upstairs to do his homework. Calvin and Janet Hill delivered the news that Grant had committed to Duke the previous weekend.

Saying the commitment was firm, the Hills explained that they thought they owed it to Smith to tell him in person. Smith was not surprised, because he knew Janet Hill, a friend of Hillary Rodham Clinton from their days at Wellesley College, preferred Duke for its more prestigious academic reputation, but he didn't care for how they handled the situation.

"I'm sure Grant will have a great career and we wish him well," Smith said, peeved, "but instead of coming all the way up here to find out he is going to Duke, I could have been home having dinner with *my* family."

Smith countered two weeks later by signing his own celebrated freshmen class for the 1991 season—seven-foot Eric Montross, point guard Derrick Phelps, forwards Clifford Rozier and Pat Sullivan, and swing man Brian Reese, a New York City star whom he stole away from Cremins and Georgia Tech after Hill committed to Duke. The UNC coaches considered it a form of payback for Cremins who signed Anderson the year before.

Recruiting writers called UNC's newest class the best assemblage of high school players by one school, a sign that Smith could still beat the Blue Devils off the court as well as on it. High school ratings, however, remained highly projective and biased.

Gibbons and Oettinger both moved Reese up dramatically in their rankings after he committed to Carolina. Gibbons even put Reese ahead of Hill, ostensibly because Reese had played tougher competition in the Bronx and attended more all-star camps. Coaches who had seen both Reese and Hill knew the truth, that the Blue Devils had much more of a can't-miss player.

The Tar Heels beat Duke and Michigan for Montross. Clicking with his family from the start, Smith theorized they came from "old money" that favored his program's long tradition over Duke's novelty and nouveau-riche hype. Not mesmerized by Cameron, Montross had already played in arenas even bigger than the Dean Dome during his high school career.

Scott Montross played for Michigan on the Cazzie Russell teams of the 1960s and his father-in-law, Jack Townsend, was a two-time All-American for the Wolverines. As one of the most prominent attorneys in Indianapolis, Montross felt pressure for Eric to stay home and play for Bob Knight at Indiana. When that didn't happen, the story leaked out that he once threw Knight out of his office after a legal disagreement.

His son had decided to go away to college and, according to many recruiting analysts, figured to succumb to Krzyzewski's pressure and recent success. Although Montross had a great weekend at Duke, he and his family decided that they would conclude their scheduled campus visits before making a decision. UNC remained his favorite throughout the process. In fact, after leaving Duke, the Montrosses took an impromptu drive through Chapel Hill before flying home to Indianapolis. The word quickly got back to Krzyzewski, who thought the visit had gone well and that the Blue Devils would eventually sign Montross. Now Krzyzewski *knew* otherwise—and, with respect to the rivalry, that the 1990s would be more of the same.

Unlike Carolina, where Smith never started a freshman until he proved his mettle, Duke made Bobby Hurley its starting point guard from the first day of practice for the 1989–90 season. The job was his to lose, and he kept it, despite a rough preseason practice and a first few games of taking bad shots and missing most of them. Krzyzewski was more patient with Hurley than most freshmen, whom he usually broke down and then built up by sending a senior to explain why the coach was so angry. Bad cop, good cop.

UNC fans could care less about Hurley and were still bemoaning the loss of Anderson, especially when the team got off to the worst start in Smith's coaching career. Even in his early losing years, the Tar Heels had never had five losses by the end of December. After a murderous schedule that included three games in Maui, road trips to Alabama and Iowa, and the ACC–Big East Challenge against Georgetown at the Meadowlands, they were 7–4.

The only good that came out of the loss to Georgetown was a suggestion from a fashion-conscious alumnus who lived in New York that it was time for Carolina to update its uniforms and warm-ups. When he got back to Chapel Hill, Smith placed a call to designer and Chapel Hill native Alexander Julian about coming up with a new look for the Tar Heels.

Their fifth loss of the young season was to unranked Colorado State on December 29 in the Mile High Classic, an effortless 78–67 defeat.

Against a much softer schedule, Duke was 8–2 on New Year's Day, 1990. The two losses were narrow, by two points to top-ranked Syracuse in the ACC–Big East Challenge and in overtime at eighth-ranked Michigan. Hurley was still throwing the ball away too much, bricking those awkward jumpers, and suffering some culture shock in the comparatively rural South.

Although he had visited both campuses on separate weekends, Hurley never considered how his recruitment would play into the rivalry until his first Duke-Carolina game on January 17, 1990. The bus ride from Cameron to the tunnel of the Dean Dome took only fifteen minutes. Wow, Hurley thought to himself, these schools are *really* close.

Hooted by the twenty-one thousand fans and taunted by Rice, Hurley spent part of the game on the bench in tears. "Shut the fuck up!" he finally yelled at Rice, who schooled his freshman foe with 13 points and 9 assists compared to Hurley's 2 for 9 shooting and 10 turnovers.

Carolina led by 24 points at the half and was never threatened in the 79–60 win. The Tar Heels went on to win five straight, their longest streak of an otherwise uneven season. Duke rebounded to win six in a row before losing its first game to Virginia since 1983—seven years previously.

In the rematch—on Senior Day in Durham (the afternoon Art Heyman's No. 25 jersey was finally retired)—the Blue Devils shot 39 percent compared to Carolina's 65 and lost again, although Hurley played one of his best freshman games with 16 points and 6 assists. Rice was still better with 20 points and 8 assists in the 87–75 UNC victory that infuriated Krzyzewski because "we didn't play like we've practiced."

In between those losses was Krzyzewski's profanity-laced tirade at ten Duke *Chronicle* staffers for a midseason report card on his players. He had called them to his office, where a secretary directed them to the Duke locker room. There, waiting in closed session, was the entire team and coaching staff. The head coach called the report "full of shit" and went on from there.

One of the reporters secretly tape-recorded the diatribe and excerpted it in the next day's edition. "You're whacked out and you don't appreciate what the fuck is going on and it pisses me off," Krzyzewski was quoted as telling the group that included Seth Davis, the son of former Clinton White House spin doctor Lonnie Davis who went on to write for *Sports Illustrated* and work for CBS as a college basketball analyst, where he's been a Duke apologist ever since.

The episode marked Krzyzewski's first break with local media, which criticized him for the contemptible act. Durham *Morning Herald* columnist Ron Morris called for his firing, saying that any professor treating students that way would have been dismissed. Athletics Director Tom Butters spoke with Krzyzewski, but there was no public apology. In choosing to recognize only its coach's positive qualities, Duke decided to turn a deaf ear and blind eye to his abusive and profane language toward referees, and occasionally his own players, that was heard and seen clearly by courtside observers at Cameron and captured repeatedly on television.

As a team, the 1990 Blue Devils were average for most of the season. They bombed out in the ACC Tournament, losing to Georgia Tech in the semifinals and appearing in complete turmoil leaving the Charlotte Coliseum. After the game, Henderson had stood in front of his locker and told the media that his teammates were a "bunch of fucking babies."

"He's right," Krzyzewski said before boarding the team bus, adding a subtle shot at Dean Smith's penchant for muffling his players. "We don't program our kids and tell them what to say."

Even with the two wins over Duke, the Tar Heels (8–6) still finished behind the Blue Devils (9–5) in the ACC standings. UNC lost more games in 1990 than any Smith-coached team (13) in his thirty-six years, including a first-round ouster from the ACC Tournament by Virginia.

"We're a spot on the shine of Carolina basketball," lamented their senior center, Scott Williams.

Duke, which had been ranked as high as third before fading, was No. 15 going into the NCAA Tournament. UNC had begun as No. 7 and was unranked by the end. Underscoring the mediocrity, the 1990 season marked the only time in ACC history that Duke or Carolina did not have a player on the first All-ACC team. Given all that, neither was expected to go far in the post season. The Blue Devils got the third seed in the East Regional, the Tar Heels the eighth seed in the Midwest.

After beating Southwest Missouri State, giving Smith his twentieth straight twenty-win season, Carolina spread the court in the second-round game in Austin and frustrated top-ranked and high-scoring Oklahoma. The Tar Heels never let the Sooners pull away and trailed by one with only seconds remaining. Rice tied the game on the first of two free throws, and when he missed the second Oklahoma knocked the ball out of bounds in the rebound scramble. After a timeout, Rick Fox got the ball on the right baseline, power driving to the goal. His shot banked in as time expired to give UNC a two-point victory and bounce the favorite from the tournament.

The Tar Heels celebrated like they had won the national championship, and the North Carolina sportswriters in Austin, who thought Oklahoma coach Billy Tubbs had acted like an asshole all weekend, were even cheering and high-fiving as they left the court.

The fun ended the next week in Dallas, where Carolina lost to Arkansas's "Forty Minutes of Hell" in the Sweet Sixteen and finished up 21–13, excellent for most college teams but overwhelmingly average for UNC.

Duke, meanwhile, regrouped enough from its internal acrimony to beat un-ranked Richmond, St. John's, and UCLA in the East Regional on the way to the Elite Eight against top-seed Connecticut, which was still trying to give coach Jim Calhoun his first Final Four team.

Having forced UConn into overtime behind senior Alaa Abdelnaby's career-high 27 points, the Blue Devils trailed 78–77 with 2.6 ticks and had the ball in front of their bench after a timeout in which Krzyzewski had drawn up a last play to win the game.

A UNC fan and high school coach was in the Brendan Byrne Arena at the Meadowlands and saw no Connecticut player guarding Christian Laettner as he readied to inbound the ball. "Cover him! Cover Laettner!" the coach yelled from his seat in the stands. "He's going to get it back."

Krzyzewski saw the same thing and changed the play he had drawn up. He shouted "Special!" to his team, an emergency call designed to get the ball right back to the man who threw it in. Laettner passed the ball in to Brian Davis and, indeed, got it right back. He took two dribbles toward the basket and his hurried fifteen-footer found the net for a 79–78 win. Mobbed by teammates on the floor, the legend of Laettner was born in the first of four memorable NCAA games with UConn. No one would ever leave Laettner unguarded again.

Only two wins from the NCAA title, delirious Duke went to Denver and rallied in the second half behind Henderson's 28 points to beat favored Arkansas. The Blue Devils advanced to the championship game Monday night. Top-ranked and unbeaten UNLV held off ACC Tournament champion Georgia Tech in the other semifinal after a questionable fourth foul on Kenny Anderson helped kill the Jackets' hopes.

The national media in Denver portrayed the Duke-UNLV game as Good vs. Evil. Krzyzewski had become the white knight of college basketball, while the Runnin' Rebels were the black hats after having been dogged by NCAA investigations since their coach Jerry Tarkanian arrived in 1973. With several writers trying to prod him into ripping "Tark the Shark" and his outlaws, Krzyzewski carefully avoided anything other than abject praise for UNLV.

No extra motivation was needed, however, as Vegas turned out to be too tough and experienced for Duke. Hurley went scoreless from the field, running to the locker room several times in the first half with a stomach virus that Krzyzewski coarsely called "diarrhea" in the post-game interview on national television. The Rebels cruised to a 103–73 win and their first national championship in the most one-sided title game in history.

After the surprising, up-and-down 29–9 season, Duke's three outgoing starters, Henderson, Abdelnaby, and Robert Brickey, caused more internal controversy when they failed to graduate on time and Krzyzewski refused to hang the 1990 Final Four banner in Cameron.

Abdelnaby, the native Egyptian who grew up in New Jersey, was a smart and funny guy who wasted most of his career being lazy. He pulled it together as a senior, doubling his scoring and rebounding averages enough to fool Boston into drafting him in the first round. He took the big money, finished up his degree work within a year and bombed out as a pro.

Brickey came from Fayetteville and, like fellow Southerners David Henderson and Billy King, was a borderline student who worked hard to keep up academically. Krzyzewski needed him to graduate to uphold his credibility with the Duke admissions office, and Brickey returned to school to get his degree about a year later.

Nevertheless, Krzyzewski still wouldn't hang the banner because Phil Henderson had not finished his undergraduate work. Not exactly a persona non grata at Duke, Henderson knew he was the sole reason the 1990 banner was not flying at Cameron. Kenny Dennard didn't graduate with his class in 1981 and told Henderson how much "shit" he took from his teammates. Dennard finally got his degree and, like a fraternity brother hazing a pledge, reminded Henderson every chance he got. Henderson took a class here and there, and the banner remained in a closet at the basketball office. (He finally finished almost ten years later, and the banner went up.)

All this was a factor when Dave Gavitt, newly named president of the Boston Celtics, called Tom Butters in the summer of 1990 to say he wanted to hire Krzyzewski. Gavitt told Butters that Larry Bird, the veteran star of the Celtics, had specifically asked Gavitt to pursue Krzyzewski as their new coach.

Butters was worried because Gavitt, the former Providence College coach and the Big East Conference's first commissioner, was among the most respected men in basketball. Also, he was offering Krzyzewski four times what he made at Duke to coach the Celtics and Larry Bird, Kevin McHale, and Robert Parrish in their twilight years, then rebuild the team in his own vision.

"You have the NBA, and then you have the Celtics and Dave Gavitt," Butters said. "Those are two entirely different things. To have the most storied franchise in basketball history and an extraordinary man going after my coach. You don't have that every day."

Krzyzewski met with Gavitt in Boston and returned to contemplate the Celtics' offer. Butters did not counter with "a dime because the difference was ridiculous, and we could be outbid at any moment." He hoped remaining in the college game would save his coach. In the end, it was a question that Gavitt asked that helped Krzyzewski decide.

"Do you think you'll have more influence over thirty-five-year-old million-aires in Boston, or young people in Durham?" Gavitt said.

Krzyzewski was too committed to the Duke program, and leaving when three seniors had embarrassed him, his program, and their school, if not themselves, was not the right thing to do. Plus, no matter how good of an organization the Celtics had, it wouldn't be the same as the family atmosphere he had built at Duke. Gavitt helped him see that with his question and, after Krzyzewski declined, hired Chris Ford to coach the Celtics.

With the local media covering the story daily, UNC's program couldn't help but follow it with interest, and, despite Krzyzewski's decision to stay, Carolina found some comfort from the 1990 season. At least Duke again didn't win it all and, in failing miserably against UNLV, had supplanted Carolina's 78–55 loss to UCLA in 1968 as the widest margin of defeat in an NCAA final. The Tar Heel faithful were also buoyed by their incoming freshman class and the hope that Duke's run of Final Fours was finally over.

The Blue Devils already had set a standard that seemed impossible to match. Despite their glorious past, the Tar Heels had not played on the last weekend of the season since 1982, a reality wearing thin on the players and their fans who were faced with constant reminders of what Duke was doing over and over right under their noses.

Smith's basketball team had to get back to the Final Four to regain some parity and ease the pressure on the "aging coach." That he owned a winning record against Krzyzewski or that James Worthy, Michael Jordan, and J. R. Reid had turned pro early no longer counted in defense of why his Tar Heels had earned only one national championship in the last thirty years.

The 1990–91 season unfolded with escalating intensity and vitriol. Duke opened up as No. 6 in the country, which was too high considering a freshman and two sophomores were in the starting lineup. The Blue Devils lost three games by early January and, after a 17-point drubbing at Virginia—their second straight loss to the Cavaliers after sixteen consecutive victories—dropped all the way to fourteenth in the polls. Carolina started three seniors and maintained a No. 5 ranking by the January 19 visit to Cameron, looking for its third consecutive win in Durham.

The Tar Heels led by four at the break but fell apart in the second half. Antagonists Hurley and Rice both had horrid games, failing to score a single field goal between them. Thomas Hill and Laettner made 14 of their 19 shots to spark Duke's second-half blowout.

They each won nine games over the next six weeks and climbed steadily in the polls heading into their game in Chapel Hill on UNC's Senior Day. They were tied for first in the ACC with 10–3 records, and the winner would not only capture the regular season but gain an unusual first-round bye in the ACC Tournament the following week in Charlotte.

Maryland had been placed on three years probation by the NCAA, stemming from recruiting violations and attempts to cover them up by deposed coach Bob Wade. Among the sanctions was a ban on television appearances during the 1991 season; the ACC voted to exclude the Terrapins from the ACC Tournament, which was totally televised.

Obviously, the team having to play only two games in the ACC Tournament held a huge advantage, so the last game of the 1991 season took on added significance. Not only was it for first place, it was positioning for the conference tournament, which, in turn, determined seeding for the 1991 NCAA Tournament. All Duke-Carolina games were special, but this one seemed even more so when the teams tipped off on March 3 in the Dean Dome.

With five players scoring in double figures, Duke led by 10 at the half and ballooned the lead behind great games from Grant Hill, Laettner, and Hurley, whose second visit to Chapel Hill was far better than the first. He had 18 points, hit 4 of 6 of his three-pointers and dished out 6 assists. The Blue Devils made 53 percent of their shots, while the Tar Heels misfired from three-point range all day. Carolina rallied late in the game and closed to three, but Pete Chilcutt's shot to tie failed. The 83–77 defeat was so bitter that the usually affable Rick Fox stonewalled the media.

Frustrated by their inability to beat Duke in a big game, the Tar Heels went to Charlotte hoping for another shot at the Blue Devils. They got their wish after winning two games and the Blue Devils won one. Duke thought it was fresher and, thus, would beat Carolina for the third time that season.

This time, the Tar Heels broke fast and kept the pressure on. The nasty championship game had players taunting each other and cursing the refs, as fans from both schools yelled and gestured back and forth in the Charlotte Coliseum. It was Duke-Carolina basketball at its best—and worst.

Krzyzewski got hit with an early technical foul from official Lenny Wirtz, who heard cursing coming from the Duke bench and thought it was directed at him (Krzyzewski was, in fact, admonishing one of his players). Duke could do little right and went down by 13 at halftime.

With his team still in control, and seeing Laettner sulking on the Duke bench, Fox said to Hurley loud enough for sportswriters along press row to hear, "When are you gonna put the fag back in the game?" It was a slap at the underground if unfounded rumor about Laettner's sexual preference. Notre Dame fans first yelled the chant at him in 1989, when the Blue Devils crushed the Irish in South Bend, and the tag stuck.

The perception that Laettner was a soft, pretty boy from a prep school in Buffalo, who looked like an actor in *Beverly Hills 90210*, couldn't have been further from the truth. He was from a gritty blue-collar neighborhood, the son of a typesetter who attended prep school on scholarship. Whenever his team played an inner city school, the black kids tried to physically challenge him and were shocked to get it back harder than they gave it. He was closer to a thug than a fag.

Laettner had already drawn Duke's second technical foul for telling official Gerry Donaghy to "fuck off" when he was waiting for play to resume after a TV timeout. He delivered a profanity-laced tirade at the ref that courtside observers heard clearly. Rice, standing by ready to make the inbound pass, kept saying, "Did you hear what he said? Can he say that?" Apparently he could, because Donaghy didn't eject Laettner from the game with a second technical foul.

Angering Krzyzewski even more than the crushing 96–74 loss was his family leaving the coliseum in tears after two hours of heckling from the UNC pep band sitting behind the basket adjacent to the Duke section. Oldest daughter Debbie was in school at Duke but dating a UNC student. She had invited him to the game and caught him cheering for the Tar Heels at the end of the rout. They all filed out in a huff, razzed by Tar Heel fans all the way up the aisle. Krzyzewski saw the incident from the bench and was so incensed that shortly after a family meeting his daughter dumped the boyfriend.

Smith triggered another tête-à-tête as the Carolina press conference was ending and Duke's beginning. He first made a pointed reference to Butters, who was on the NCAA selection committee and whom Smith believed helped Duke get favorable seeding the last two years.

"I asked Mike after the game if he had talked to Tom," Smith said, implying Krzyzewski and his athletics director traded insider information on the pairings.

Krzyzewski was waiting behind the curtain for Smith and his players to finish. Upon entering the interview area, he praised Rice for holding Hurley without a field goal and playing so well on offense.

"Nice game, King," Krzyzewski said, looking at the stat sheet, "12 points and 7 assists . . ."

"The way we keep it, he really had 11 assists," Smith interrupted.

This incensed Krzyzewski, who hated Smith's habit of nit-picking about statistics and other minutiae. To him, there was only one statistic that counted, the final score.

"However the hell you keep it, you had a great game, King," he said before walking out as Smith took the victory podium.

The win not only avenged the two regular-season losses to Duke and captured the ACC Championship, it also gave Carolina the Blue Devils' customary top seed in the East Regional, which they had four of the last five years. That evening, after Duke was assigned to the Midwest Region as the No. 2 seed, Krzyzewski got his team's attention when he said, "We're going to win the national championship."

UNC had snickered at what seemed like Duke's annual cakewalk through unranked opposition in the regional, but had the patsy schedule this time. The Heels beat Northeastern, Villanova, and Eastern Michigan—all unranked—to reach the East championship game against Temple and Mark Macon, now a senior. The Owls were also unranked, not nearly the No. 1 team that Duke had edged four years earlier for a trip to the 1988 Final Four.

This game was just as close as that one after Temple countered Carolina's fast start. With the pressure of the Final Four hanging over their heads, the Tar Heels were clearly holding on until literally the last possession. As Macon's three-pointer to tie missed and the horn sounded, Smith looked relieved when he shook hands with Temple coach John Chaney. He had led his team back to the Final Four for the first time in nine years, snapping a drought no one could have ever imagined when UNC was dominating the ACC in the early 1980s.

At the same time, the Blue Devils rolled through the Midwest, beating Northwest Louisiana, Iowa, and the Big East tandem of UConn and St. John's by an average of 19 points. Laettner and best-buddy teammate Brian Davis, his rumored "boyfriend," rolled around on the floor of the Silver Dome in Pontiac, Michigan, after Duke reached its fourth consecutive Final Four, but the first ever alongside Carolina.

The historic victories occurred within hours of each other on Sunday, March 24. Their fans felt the mixed emotions of the red-hot rivalry—happy they were going but anxious about sharing the stage at the Hoosier Dome in Indianapolis with the archenemy. The possibilities were both tantalizing and taut, given any chance of an NCAA title game between the competing schools and coaching giants.

Still, the prospect seemed remote because of the semifinal pairings.

Duke was to meet top-ranked and unbeaten Nevada-Las Vegas (UNLV) for the second straight year. The defending national champion Rebels appeared even stronger than in 1990, if that was possible. The Blue Devils had to forget that blowout loss and play near-perfect basketball.

The first semifinal pitted UNC against No. 12 Kansas and Smith's protégé, Roy Williams, in only his third year as a head coach but with a lifetime of preparation to play the favored Tar Heels. The folksy, likable Williams, who looked a little like Huckleberry Hound, was a Carolina grad and had served ten years on Dean Smith's staff as a popular but relatively unknown assistant.

Smith was almost giddy to be back. On his last trip in 1982, he had won his first NCAA championship after six previous Final Fours and did not feel the pressure of Krzyzewski to win his first or Tarkanian to repeat. Smith even relaxed a team rule, allowing freshman Montross to stay at home with his family, irritating assistant and by-the-book taskmaster Bill Guthridge. By contrast, Krzyzewski had the single-minded intention to win a title in his fifth Final Four since 1986. Going home empty-handed had become a bore.

At the CBS-sponsored coaches' dinner on Thursday night, Smith played up his second-banana status by jokingly joining the long line of people waiting for Krzyzewski's autograph. The two exchanged awkward smiles.

Smith visited with KU's Williams during Friday's open practices and press conferences. On Saturday morning, Guthridge jogged with Williams and his assistant Jerry Green.

While the coaching approaches might have been different, there was no doubt Duke and Carolina fans felt the pressure of their Saturday games and the possible match-up Monday night. UNC and Duke students were in adjacent lines waiting to pick up their tickets outside the Hoosier Dome.

"Oh for four!" chanted the kids in light blue, referring to Duke's Final Four record under Krzyzewski.

"Long time no see!" retorted the dark blue Dukies.

As the first game tipped off, Carolina fans took some comfort in the fact that if their team lost, Williams's Jayhawks would be in the Monday night game against UNLV. Like everyone else, they figured Duke would fall again to the seemingly invincible Runnin' Rebels.

The Carolina contingent never expected a worst-case scenario, starting with UNC's infamous Final Four shooting woes of the 1990s against Kansas. Fox missed 17 of his 22 field goal attempts, 0–7 from three-point range, in front of friends and family who had watched the Bahamian native and transfer student learn the game and blossom into a star in nearby Warsaw, Indiana.

The Tar Heels got in trouble early, fell behind by nine points at the half and, despite a late rally, never looked like a winner against the Jayhawks. Both teams shot poorly and played raggedly, most likely a product of too much familiarity with each other's offenses and defenses. Then an ugly game turned regrettable.

After Fox fouled out in the last minute, with Carolina trailing by six points, Smith walked a substitute to the scorer's table and baited official Pete Pavia, who had given Smith a technical foul in the first half and whose calls were questioned throughout the game by the UNC bench.

"Pete, how much time do I have? How much time do I have?" Smith shrieked, almost daring Pavia to "T" him up again.

Most officials would have turned away. Pavia was taking medication for cancer that killed him two years later and had no such perspective or patience. He nailed Smith with his second technical foul for leaving the coaching box, which meant automatic ejection and an ignominious exit for one of the sport's most distinguished figures. It had never happened to another head coach in a Final Four, and has not since.

With the Hoosier Dome crowd howling, Smith stopped at the Kansas bench to shake Williams's hand and share a quick embrace. After the 79–73 loss, Guthridge had to be restrained by police and UNC officials from going after Pavia as he left the court ahead of the defeated Tar Heels. The players were more sorrowful for having lost and their revered coach being humiliated on college basketball's biggest stage.

Fox was devastated that his dream of leading North Carolina to another national title failed so miserably. He had discovered college basketball and UNC nine years earlier on Paradise Island, watching Michael Jordan shoot down Georgetown on a big hotel TV screen. The following summer, Fox met the coach of a traveling church team from Indiana and convinced his parents to let him move to America and play basketball. Despite the disappointing end to his college career, Fox would live out the American Dream, playing for the Boston

Celtics and Los Angeles Lakers and marrying former Miss America Vanessa Williams.

All this, of course, was like an early Christmas for the thousands of Duke fans in the building and watching on TV who took devilish delight in what happened. The Dukies there delivered the same irreverent send-off they gave an opposing player who fouled out in Cameron, droning and waving five fingers frantically from side to side and sending Smith into in the tunnel with a loud, "See Ya!"

That alone might have been good enough to make their weekend.

Not their coach, however. Krzyzewski had fought off the naysayers who doubted Duke could beat UNLV after getting crushed the year before. He had challenged his players on the first day of practice for the Final Four, asking if any of them believed they *couldn't* win, then showed them the tape of the 1990 debacle in which his tired team had mailed it in after a long, tumultuous season.

The 1991 Blue Devils were deceptive, young with freshman Grant Hill and sophomores Thomas Hill, Bobby Hurley, and Billy McCaffery in key roles, but hardened from having played fifteen nationally ranked opponents. Krzyzewski said, "We can beat them this time. If it's close at the end, it will be new for them. They haven't been there. We have. Keep it close and the advantage will be ours."

With seniors Larry Johnson, Stacey Augmon, and Greg Anthony, these were basically the same Rebels that dealt Duke its unprecedented NCAA championship game loss and were being conceded a repeat title. These Blue Devils, however, were older, tougher and, by the time they reached Indy, convinced they could shock the world.

Duke led early, 15–6, and eventually surrendered the lead, but, unlike the year before, stayed close. UNLV led by two at the half and by three points with under four minutes to play when Anthony charged into Brian Davis for his fifth foul. The Blue Devils still trailed 76–71 with 2:19 left, and it appeared their gallant effort would fall short. Hurley raced down court with the ball.

CBS broadcaster Billy Packer warned, "They don't need to force a three-pointer here . . ."

After Hurley buried one from the left wing, Packer tried to recover.

". . . unless it comes out of the offense like that one did," he said.

Hurley had brazenly fired, and hit, what turned out to be the biggest shot in Duke history. Had he missed, the game would have been over. Instead, just as Krzyzewski predicted, Tarkanian's team choked away its last possessions beginning with a shot clock violation by one of the highest-scoring teams in the country. UNLV's lead was two points with barely a minute left to play.

Grant Hill hit Davis for a driving layup that resulted in a three-point play;

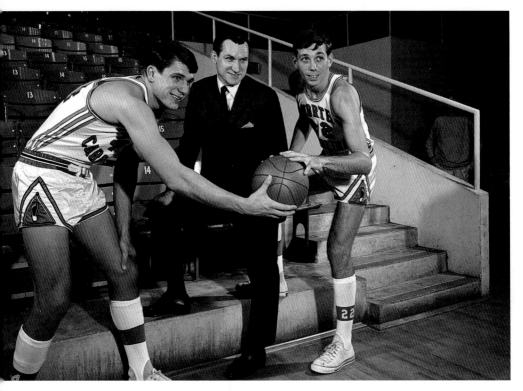

Dean Smith beat Vic Bubas and Duke for his first marquee recruit in 1964 with the help of assistant coach Ken Rosemond. The "L&M Boys" (Bobby Lewis and Larry Miller) began the gradual changing of the guard against dominant Duke. *(Courtesy of the University of North Carolina)*

Duke and Carolina played a total of 14 games between 1979 and 1981—the most in any four-year stretch. In 1979 UNC came back to win the ACC Championship game behind MVP Dudley Bradley and Mike O'Koren. *(Courtesy of Hugh Morton)*

Mike Krzyzewski got a vote of confidence and new contract from Tom Butters and in 1984 put together a team capable of upsetting Sam Perkins (below, shooting), Michael Jordan (23, left), and the top-ranked Tar Heels. *(Courtesy of Robert Crawford)*

Defense was the name of the Duke-Carolina game in the 1980s. Johnny Dawkins tries to score over seven-footer Warren Martin in the opening game at the Dean Smith Center on January 18, 1986. *(Courtesy of Robert Crawford)*

The 1988 ACC Tournament championship game, Duke's third win over Carolina that season, ended in celebration with Coach K. *(Courtesy of Bob Donnan)*

Disconsolate Carolina waited for the runner-up trophy. It was assistant coach Roy Williams's last season before being named head coach at Kansas. *(Courtesy of Bob Donnan)*

The battles between J. R. Reid (34) and Danny Ferry defined Carolina-Duke basketball from 1987 to 1989, culminating in the brutal 1989 ACC championship game in Atlanta won by the Tar Heels, 77–74. *(Courtesy of Bob Donnan)*

Bobby Hurley grew up a UNC fan but picked Duke. *(Courtesy of Bob Donnan)*

Rasheed Wallace ruined Grant Hill's Senior Night in 1994 and made good on his promise that "We ain't ever losing over here." *(Courtesy of Bob Donnan)*

Carolina lost nine players early to the NBA before 1999, when the first Duke players bolted. Elton Brand (42, above left) went happily, but Will Avery (5, above right) left amid controversy. *(Courtesy of Bob Donnan)*

Chris Duhon completes his coast-to-coast drive for a reverse layup to win the 2004 game in Chapel Hill, spoiling Roy Williams's first shot against Duke as UNC's head coach. *(Courtesy of Ned Hinshaw)*

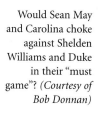

Duke students dress up to welcome UNC coach Roy Williams and remind him that he's not in Kansas anymore. *(Courtesy of Robert Crawford)*

At Cameron in 2005, Williams and Krzyzewski cut up before the game started in which freshman Marvin Williams and DeMarcus Nelson stood out, but Carolina lost when Ray Felton and the Heels couldn't convert for the second straight year. *(Courtesy of Robert Crawford)*

Would Sean May and Carolina choke against Shelden Williams and Duke in their "must game"? *(Courtesy of Bob Donnan)*

Marvin Williams converts Ray Felton's missed free throw for the winning basket. Williams would also have the critical tip-in late in the NCAA championship game a month later and then turn pro after his freshman season. *(Courtesy of Bob Donnan)*

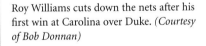

Roy Williams cuts down the nets after his first win at Carolina over Duke. *(Courtesy of Bob Donnan)*

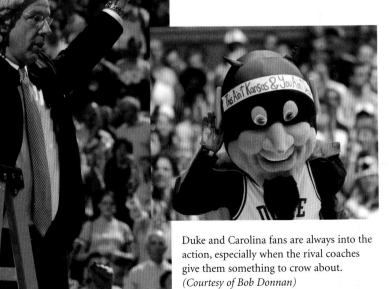

Duke and Carolina fans are always into the action, especially when the rival coaches give them something to crow about. *(Courtesy of Bob Donnan)*

the six straight points pushed Duke ahead 77–76. The Rebels' panic continued with Larry Johnson missing two free throws. Duke was called for a lane violation, giving Johnson a third attempt that he made for a 77–77 tie.

The Hoosier Dome now sounded like a flying saucer getting ready to blast off. Beneath the din, Duke held the ball until fifteen seconds remained and Thomas Hill beat his man and pulled up for a ten-foot bank shot. It missed but Laettner grabbed the rebound under the basket and was fouled before he could go up with the follow. After calmly telling Krzyzewski "I got 'em, coach," Laettner made two free throws for a 79–77 lead.

On UNLV's last possession, Johnson was open on the right wing for the winning three-point attempt. Instead of shooting, he inexplicably passed the ball out to Anderson Hunt for the long-range miss as the clock ran out, and Duke began to celebrate having, indeed, shocked the world.

"I'm not sure we could beat them again but, like last year, we only play once," Krzyzewski said after trying to hold down the pandemonium in his locker room as the Blue Devils delivered a *second* Christmas to their fans.

He wasn't about to let his team overlook Kansas after what it had accomplished—considered such a huge upset that some cynical UNC fans continued to believe that Johnson clutched on his shot because the game was involved in the gambling probe Vegas underwent several years later in which no wrongdoing was uncovered. (Tarkanian left UNLV after the 1992 season and sued the NCAA for tortious interference with his employment contract. In 1998 he received a $2.5 million settlement from the NCAA.)

Kansas fans were happy that the Jayhawks were facing Duke in the championship game, but not their coach. Williams preferred playing Vegas, because they ran and matched up better with his smallish team. Duke led by eight at halftime, spurred by Grant Hill's remarkable alley-oop slam from a Hurley pass that looked like it was going over the basket.

After the emotional win over Vegas, Krzyzewski rested his players in short stints. Laettner played fewer minutes than usual and remained sharp enough to go 12 for 12 from the foul line. Kansas rallied late to cut the deficit to five points in the last minute. Davis's dunk off Grant Hill's lob pass sealed the 72–65 win, which was anticlimactic for all but the Blue Devils and their fans. Laettner earned Final Four MOP and led his teammates in their historic net-cutting ceremony.

Their school had not only won the first national championship since it began playing basketball in 1905, it boasted America's new team with a coach who had his own rags-to-riches success story, and, at long last, made a genius of Tom Butters and the decision he made in 1980 that threatened his life.

Beating Smith trainee Williams made it even sweeter for Duke fans and more painful for Tar Heels, especially those stuck in dreary Indianapolis. Dave Lohse, the long-time sports information assistant at UNC, was so distraught that he did not leave his hotel room all day Sunday and Monday before flying home on Tuesday.

The range of emotion left everyone to ponder just how Duke-Carolina for the national championship would have been handled. The media asked Krzyzewski about it, and he issued his famous opinion that he never wanted the two schools to play in the last game of the season because it would be too devastating for the loser.

"What would happen in this area, people-wise, if one of us beat the other in the championship game?" asked Krzyzewski, whose daughters were taunted in high school by Carolina fans and, worse, by several teachers. "I wouldn't wish that on anybody. It would be so horrible."

The thought did not keep Krzyzewski from his best one-liner of the season at the expense of UNC. On the bus ride from Raleigh-Durham Airport following Duke's national championship, he saw the approaching sign for the turnoff to Chapel Hill.

"Hey," he said to his happy players and the others on board, "you want to cruise down Franklin Street?" The bus broke up in laughter and cheers. Waiting, instead, at Cameron were thousands of their adoring fans ready to toast the new NCAA basketball champions.

Krzyzewski's needle was all part of the entangled rivalry; one school's pleasure was the other's pain. So, it seemed only fitting that when Duke claimed the crown it came with extra heartache for Carolina. As Krzyzewski said, the only meaner scenario would be a title game *between* the Blue Devils and Tar Heels, a possibility that continued to exist as both reloaded for the rest of the decade.

Duke opened the 1991–92 season No. 1 in the polls and sought not only a repeat but to be the first college basketball team since Indiana in 1976 to stay top ranked wire to wire through the Final Four. Starters Bobby Hurley and Thomas Hill at guards and Brian Davis and Grant Hill at forwards ran their motion offense around senior all-everything Christian Laettner, a threat from anywhere on the court. Tony Lang, a sophomore, and freshman center Cherokee Parks came off the bench. These Dukies had rock star quality, two white starters and seven good-looking regulars who were on television so much that they began to split the country between pro-Duke and anti-Duke factions. Early in the season, the Blue Devils played Canisius in Laettner's home town, drawing the largest college basketball crowd in Buffalo's history. The mob was so big outside the backdoor of the arena that several players had to climb out a window to get to the bus. Two months later, after they pulled out a 98–97 win at Clemson, dozen of young girls screamed and clawed at them as they boarded the bus behind Littlejohn Coliseum.

With their uniforms on, though, they were nasty to opponents and occasionally surly to the media and each other. As the leader, Laettner copped an attitude with his underclassmen Hurley, Hill, and Parks that resembled the officer-plebe relationships of Krzyzewski's Army. The result was a tough-love team that made all the big plays and big shots. Laettner, the toughest, always wanted the ball with the game on the line and usually delivered.

Krzyzewski joked about how cocky and self-assured they all were, even the role players. Once, the Blue Devils had a key possession late in the game. Brian Davis, whose career scoring average was less than seven points, claimed in a huddle with several of Duke's greatest players ever that he was the best one to take the shot.

After winning their first 17 games, the Blue Devils' biggest threat turned out to be the February 5 game at the Smith Center. Their last loss was 23 games ago to Carolina in the 1991 ACC Tournament. By the time they steamrolled into Chapel Hill among the most publicized teams ever in the ACC, they were shooting 54 percent and making 44 percent of their three-pointers. They looked damn near unbeatable.

Carolina, which had lost three starters off its Final Four team, was out for blood, literally. Midway through the first half, Montross and Hurley were both bleeding from gashes to their faces after on-court collisions.

"We didn't care that we were bleeding," Hurley said. "In a game like that, everything goes out. You just lace 'em up tight. I played the second half of the game with a broken foot. Pain goes out the window in that game. You just play through it."

UNC out-shot and out-rebounded Duke for most of the night to build an eighteen-point lead in the sweltering Dean Dome. The Blue Devils rallied, cutting the deficit to two, but Carolina's superior free-throw shooting staved them off in the final, frantic seconds. Laettner missed a final shot to tie, one of the few times that happened in his career.

Montross's 12 points, 9 rebounds and 3 blocks were especially vindicating. The Dukies had dissed him before the game by running a full blank page in the *Chronicle* sports section with the caption, "This big, useless white space was put here to remind you of Tar Heel center Eric Montross."

The brutal 75–73 victory left him with a bloodied face and uniform from a head-butt with Laettner, but he still cavorted with hundreds of students on the court. Afterward, as the party on Franklin Street in downtown Chapel Hill swelled to thousands, Montross was telling writers how glad he was that "we got rid of Duke" and said it was not the best team Carolina had played that season. "They're not that good," he insisted.

Hurley broke a bone in his foot late in the game, but Grant Hill moved to point guard and the defending national champions maintained their top ranking by beating No. 22 LSU and Shaquille O'Neal before another wild crowd in Baton Rouge. Laettner outdueled O'Neal for the second straight season; a year earlier, Laettner (and the Cameron Crazies) had humiliated a foul-plagued Shaq in Durham.

This time, O'Neal had a big game, but so did Laettner, who hit late back-to-back three-pointers to push the Blue Devils to a 77–67 victory. They also won at Georgia Tech and N.C. State on the road without Hurley, but lost their next game at Wake Forest. Hurley returned to play at UCLA, where they easily handled the fourth-ranked Bruins.

Carolina, which had been 18–3 and No. 4 in the polls in mid-February, dropped four out of five and was almost out of the rankings. Senior Hubert Davis, Walter's nephew who had gone from lightly recruited to an All-ACC guard, was the team's only consistent player and kept Carolina close by scoring 30, 23, 30, 34, 24, and 27 points in games heading into the regular-season finale at Duke.

The Tar Heels went to Cameron hoping to redeem themselves. They actually loosened up during warm-ups when they saw a Crazy with his face painted like Frankenstein wearing a light blue T-shirt that read "Montross." They all laughed while taking layups.

Laettner and Hurley combined for 10 three-pointers to offset 6 from Hubert Davis (35 points) in a wild shootout that included Duke's Brian Davis yelling at the fired-up Guthridge on the Carolina bench in the closing minutes. The 89–77 win gave the Blue Devils first place in the ACC by three games over Florida State, the newest and ninth member of the league.

They went to the 1992 ACC Tournament in Charlotte with the top seed in the NCAA East Regional locked up and the favorite to defend their NCAA championship. They needed something to fire them up after sleepwalking past eighth-seeded Maryland in their first game.

The Tar Heels had a different problem. Out of confidence and almost out of the polls, they trailed sixth-place Wake Forest at halftime of their tournament opener and were the talk of the media room for their uninspired play. When told before the second half that they were being laughed at and written off by the hacks, Smith shrugged and said, "For a change they may be right." Despite this, Carolina played its best half in a month, beat Wake Forest and advanced to the semifinals against Florida State, hoping to avenge two regular-season losses to the Seminoles.

Duke had an easier time with Georgia Tech in the first game Saturday, and the Blue Devil crowd hung around to watch Carolina play FSU. Just for kicks, with no regard for political correctness, the Krzyzewski family sitting down front brazenly joined in the Tomahawk Chop, creating the tournament buzz of the day and infuriating Carolina fans. Smith claimed neither he nor his team saw it after employing a zone most of the game to beat the Seminoles and advance to championship Sunday and a third game with Duke.

Just as the Krzyzewski family antics fired up Tar Heel fans, Carolina's presence in the title game gave Duke the emotion it needed, especially after the outmatched Heels made a nice run in the first half and led briefly. Duke got engaged behind 25 points by Laettner and 8 for 8 shooting by Grant Hill, easily rolling to a 94–74 win and its first ACC title in four years. The Blue Devils repeated their feat of 1986 as only the fourth team in eighteen years—since David Thompson and N.C. State did it in 1973 and '74—to win the ACC regular season outright and then take home the tourney trophy.

More important to the current Duke players, they turned around their embarrassing 1991 ACC championship loss to the Tar Heels. Unlike that season, however, the teams were headed in opposite directions going into the NCAA Tournament. Duke wanted to repeat as national champs, but Carolina just wanted to win a game or two to stay alive.

The Tar Heels did win twice, ousting Miami (Ohio) and Alabama in Cincinnati to reach the Sweet Sixteen in Lexington, Kentucky, against top-seeded Ohio State in the South Region. They played well early but were awful in the second half. The 80–73 defeat ended their season at 23–10, the second time in three years they reached double digits in the loss column.

Some Carolina fans stayed in Lexington for the weekend as the city shut down to watch the hometown Wildcats take on top-ranked Duke in the East Region championship game in Philadelphia. Among them was Vanderbilt coach Eddie Fogler, a former UNC player and assistant coach under Smith. He had parked his car down the street from Pitino's, a local restaurant owned by the Kentucky coach, and was listening to the final minute of overtime on the radio. When Kentucky's Sean Woods hit the go-ahead basket with two seconds left, Fogler turned off the engine and walked over to join the party that was about to start.

In Philly, Krzyzewski's team was dazed as it huddled up with 2.4 seconds left, but he snapped them back to attention. "We're winning this game!" he shouted.

Krzyzewski wanted to use a play the Blue Devils had tried a month earlier in the final seconds against Wake Forest, a seventy-five-foot pass from Hill to Laettner at the foul line. Hill's pass had hooked badly and Laettner stepped out of bounds, resulting in Duke's only other loss that season than at Carolina. Hill had to throw it straight this time and, if he did, Laettner had time to catch the ball, pivot his body around, square up and launch the winner.

"Can you make the pass?" Krzyzewski asked Hill, who nodded.

"Christian, can you make the shot?" Coach K asked Laettner.

"If Grant can make the pass, I can make the shot," came the cold, confident answer.

Laettner's killer instinct was already out on the table. Earlier in the game, he had walked over fallen Kentucky player Aminu Timberlake and stepped on his chest for good measure. "It's so Laettner," Parks said, looking on from the bench. Laettner got a technical foul as the CBS crew scrambled to show a replay.

Lead announcer Jim Nantz had first thought that Laettner stumbled as he crossed over Timberlake. "No, it was definitely intentional," Nantz said, after reviewing the punk move that was more insulting than injurious.

To everyone but Duke fans, the officials not throwing Laettner out was another example of how they protected Duke's program, and, of course, it left him in the game for the last play.

It didn't hurt that Pitino chose not to have a man face-guard Hill on the baseline, making his low-percentage pass a little easier, and it certainly helped that Laettner was on fire that night. He had already gone 10 for 10 from the free throw line and made all nine of his field-goal attempts.

Since it was after a made basket, Hill could run the baseline, but Pitino's defensive decision gave him a clear shot. After getting the ball from the official, Hill took one step back so he wouldn't go over the baseline before releasing the pass.

Like Roger Staubach hitting his father downfield in the good old days, Hill's pass was right on target. Laettner leaped and caught the ball cleanly as two Kentucky defenders stayed away to avoid fouling. Laettner came down, pivoted to the right and back to the left, squaring his body to the basket. At that point, if not for what was at stake, it became a fairly routine jump shot.

Laettner let fly and he was already backpedaling as his tenth field goal in ten tries went cleanly through the net. He turned and raced the rest of the way right into Hill, who was trailing the play after throwing the pass. The pandemonium that followed became a familiar part of CBS's opening for NCAA telecasts. The shot going in, Laettner running away and toward the camera, and teammate Thomas Hill in tears of disbelief was a staple for years.

The 104–103 epic turned into the signature game of the NCAA Tournament, the greatest ever played on the Road to the Final Four.

Fogler was entering the restaurant when he was nearly trampled by Wildcat fans leaving the bar area in droves. The place emptied out like a bomb had gone off.

"What happened?" he asked someone coming out.

"Duke won. Laettner hit a shot."

. . .

Although Krzyzewski compared the 1992 Blue Devils to any team that had played college basketball, he knew they had to hang another championship banner to back up the boast. He also knew that Laettner was exhausted from the long season of play and pressure. Krzyzewski met with Hurley, who was fresher from having missed a month during the season, and told him he would have to step up his offensive play.

Unlike the year before, when it had to beat an intimidating power like UNLV, Duke got a couple of big breaks with the 1992 Final Four pairings. Indiana, its semifinal opponent, played a familiar style and Krzyzewski was particularly fired up to beat his mentor Knight for the first time. In the other bracket, fourth-seeded Cincinnati faced the sixth-seeded Fab Five of Michigan. Both teams had benefited from five of the eight top seeds not even making it to the Sweet Sixteen. If they played reasonably well, the Blue Devils had it.

Down by 12 points early, Duke closed to within 5 at halftime and began the second half with a 21–3 spurt and held off a late Indiana run to win. Michigan defeated Cincinnati to set up a final game whose story line was the contrast between the Fab Five freshmen and button-down Duke. They had already played once in December at Ann Arbor on national television. Chris Webber had scored 31 points, and even though the Wolverines lost, they became the anti-Duke with their baggy shorts, black shoes, and bravado.

In the national championship rematch, the Blue Devils were woefully flat and trailed by a point at halftime but, after Krzyzewski sucked a last effort from them by smashing a blackboard in the locker room, made it a Big 10 sweep by blowing out the fifteenth-ranked Wolverines 71–51.

As the jumbotrons in the Metro Dome showed Krzyzewski's family celebrating in the final seconds, Duke was already declared the new dynasty in college basketball for becoming the first back-to-back champion since UCLA in 1972 and '73. Laettner had one good half in two games, so the Final Four MOP went to Hurley for his 35 points and 11 assists as the unsung leader who had answered his coach's call for help.

The weekend was not without its heartache for Krzyzewski, who had received an angry letter from Knight before the Final Four, questioning his friendship and loyalty. It hurt Krzyzewski, because he had done nothing to change the relationship and, in fact, believed that Knight resented *his* success.

After Duke held off Indiana, Knight barely shook Krzyzewski's hand and then basically ignored him at the postgame press conference. The snubs first drove Krzyzewski to tears and later to anger. They hardly spoke for almost nine years until Knight delivered his protégé's 2001 induction speech into the Naismith Hall of Fame.

For Tar Heel fans, the 1992 season was pure agony, especially after hearing that the Dukies had chanted, "Mike has two, Dean has one" during their team's second straight raucous reception at Cameron. Carolina had never won consecutive national championships, and it should have confirmed to even those with their heads in the sand that Duke had overtaken UNC. Making matters worse, Krzyzewski's angular jaw, pointed nose, and deep eyes replaced the craggy Smith as college basketball's most famous face.

There he was in the Rose Garden at the White House, kidding with President George H. W. Bush about the future and revealing for the first time publicly his political leanings. Referring to the election that was coming up in six months, Krzyzewski told the incumbent president, "I hope we're both back here next year."

He was suddenly everywhere, rivaling his ubiquitous old adversary, Jim Valvano, after his Cinderella NCAA Championship at N.C. State in 1983. Krzyzewski booked speaking engagements, gave time to various charities and prepared to assist Detroit Pistons coach Chuck Daly on the 1992 Summer Olympic Dream Team.

Laettner, taken by Minnesota as the third pick, was Krzyzewski's fifth first-round draft choice. He was a huge loss, but Hurley, the Hills, Parks, and Lang had enough talent and cachet for the 1993 Blue Devils to be tabbed for a three-peat in some polls.

Sick of Duke's dominance, UNC's returning players openly acknowledged their envy and their determination to make a little noise of their own in the new season. Rising senior George Lynch, particularly, did not hide how tired he had become of hearing about Duke, Duke, Duke.

Lynch was what the Carolina coaches referred to as a "warrior," a sobriquet not awarded lightly. It meant the player had unusual heart, was the hardest worker on the team and, simply, never gave up. Lynch came from Roanoke, Virginia, with a bit of a legend in his past. He had been declared dead at birth with a faint heartbeat before doctors revived him on the last try. As the senior leader of the Tar Heels, Lynch was doggedly determined to unseat Duke and win a championship in his last try.

Lynch exemplified a team that was turning into something special when he capped off a 23-point rally against Florida State in the Smith Center by intercepting a pass and dunking the winner as the Dean Dome erupted. The wild 82–77 victory vindicated an embarrassing home loss to the Seminoles the year before, when FSU's Sam Cassell labeled Tar Heel fans "more like a cheese and wine crowd."

Before Grant Hill's foot injury that would sour their regular season, Duke beat Carolina at Cameron in the Blue Devils' high-water game of the 1993 season. They struggled down the stretch with Hill hurting, losing five of their last ten games. UNC shook off the defeat at Duke and its 26-point pounding by Wake Forest and ACC Player of the Year Rodney Rogers to develop the selfless attitude that Smith always preached.

Their leader and rock, if not rock star, was George Lynch. He inspired teammates to have better than just another good season. The Tar Heels responded with an efficient defense that held opponents to 41 percent shooting and an inside-outside offense of Montross-Lynch and Donald Williams that was in sum better than the individual parts.

In the regular-season finale at Chapel Hill, Lynch's Senior Game, Smith wanted to win so badly that he was not amused by Krzyzewski's ploy during a scorer's table confrontation between coaches and officials. Kidding the refs about how it was just the four of them against everyone else in the packed Dean Dome, Krzyzewski drew Smith's ire.

"Don't you see what he's doing," Smith said to official Lenny Wirtz. "Don't let him do that."

Shaking his head and smiling as he walked back to the Duke bench, Krzyzewski said loudly enough for a dozen people to hear, "Do me a favor, if I ever act like that guy down there, someone take a gun and shoot me."

Carolina won 83–69, finished first in the ACC and No. 1 in the polls and secured top seed in the East Regional. The real goal, however, was to return to the Final Four for the second time in three years, win the NCAA title and, among other things, get its name painted above Duke's on the list of most recent national champions in the main terminal of the Raleigh-Durham Airport, seen daily by thousands of travelers.

With Hill, who missed the last UNC game, slowly recovering through the postseason, Duke was beaten by Georgia Tech in the ACC Tournament and lost to Jason Kidd and Cal in the second round of the NCAA Midwest. Hill and Hurley were great, but Parks broke his leg in the first half and Duke was badly beaten by the Bears underneath.

The 82–77 loss in Krzyzewski's native Chicago ended the Blue Devils' incredible run of five consecutive Final Fours and brought the coach to tears in his post-game press conference. He criticized those who had criticized college sports in any way, saying that the bawling players in his locker room were the only proof he needed of how special the game was.

He said good-bye to Hurley, who benefited from his coach's unwavering faith to become an assist machine and eventually one of the most important players in

BLUE BLOOD

Duke history. Hurley had scored 57 points in his last two NCAA games and passed N.C. State's Chris Corchianni as the career assist leader in college basketball.

The Tar Heels survived their own serious injury to point guard Derrick Phelps, who suffered a severe back bruise against Virginia in the semifinal of the 1993 ACC Tournament. UNC fans had fretted as they watched Phelps wheeled out of the Charlotte Coliseum on a stretcher and into an ambulance that was late arriving because of a snowstorm that day. The Tar Heels had never been to the Final Four without first winning the ACC Tournament, a string that ended after they replaced Phelps by committee and lost the championship game to Georgia Tech the next day.

Phelps returned to play gingerly in wins over East Carolina and Rhode Island. Carolina then survived East Region nail-biters over Arkansas and Cincinnati, with Phelps shutting down Cincy's Nick Van Exel in the second half, and made it back to the Final Four in New Orleans. This time, the Tar Heels weren't merely happy to be there.

The semifinal opponent, as in 1991, was Kansas. Fans dropped the "if we don't win, Roy does" attitude; Carolina got 48 points from Montross and Donald Williams and a double-double from Lynch to defeat the Jayhawks 78–68 and advance to its first national championship game in eleven years. Michigan, with its Fab Five back as sophomores, edged Pitino's Kentucky and earned a second straight shot at the title.

Like Duke a year earlier, UNC showed more tenacity down the stretch against the flakey Wolverines. With Carolina holding a two-point lead, Chris Webber twice called a timeout his team didn't have. The first time, official Jim Stupin gave him a break and looked away, missing Webber's obvious travel in the backcourt. Doubled-teamed in the corner by Phelps and Lynch moments later, Webber got his timeout. The technical resulted in four free throws by Donald Williams that iced the 77–71 victory.

Montross had another great game and Lynch recorded his second double-double of the Final Four, as America's best front court finished the season averaging more than 30 points and 17 rebounds. Dead-eye Williams carved himself into UNC history with his shooting. Spotting up at the arc and waiting for the ball, he nailed five three-pointers for the second consecutive game, finishing with 50 points for the weekend and MOP honors. In four other Final Fours in the 1990s, Carolina's shooting guards were stone cold, making Williams's bulls-eye accuracy at the Superdome even more memorable as years passed.

240

Duke fans back home had to deal with being one-upped by their archenemy, as their own championship run became old news. "Anyone but them," said prominent Duke alum Dan Hill, sighing. Citing Webber's gaffe, they called Carolina lucky again, referring to 1982 when Georgetown's Fred Brown threw the ball away to James Worthy with seconds remaining and the Hoyas down one point. That game was also in the Superdome.

"Okay, call us lucky," Smith said after the Michigan game, "but also call us national champions."

Krzyzewski, a CBS analyst for the Final Four, had to do just that from the television platform situated close enough to hear catcalls from Tar Heel fans during and after UNC's triumph. He had watched Montross, the center he wanted, gain a measure of revenge over Hill and Hurley, two players who had grown up on Carolina basketball, leading Duke to back-to-back titles.

On the celebratory podium, as Smith smiled broadly, the Tar Heels derived extra pleasure from accepting the trophy from Duke's Butters, who had risen to chairman of the NCAA Basketball Committee in 1993. Smith rejoiced as he had always done, only with those close to him. He had a quiet dinner with his family and began preparing to replace Lynch, who would be the twelfth pick in the NBA draft by the Lakers.

Smith's second national championship was won by perhaps his best *team* ever, which had always defined Carolina basketball. Lynch and Montross were considered very good college players but not superstars. Point guard Phelps was a great defender but an awful shooter, and Brian Reese was a talent who became more of a role player as his career progressed. Donald Williams could shoot, alright, but couldn't take defenders off the dribble. Henrik Rodl, Kevin Salvadori and Pat Sullivan were three white reserves whose job it was to give the starters breathers on the bench, period.

Together, the Tar Heels had the right mix, and what Duke was doing down the road made them more concerned with what *they* could accomplish over any individual. It was a special group that validated what Smith had always believed—basketball, above all, was a team game.

Yet, with so many great high school players out there, Smith had already made the decision that to stay competitive he had to recruit the best athletes possible even if they were just as interested in graduating to the NBA as earning a B.A. He had everyone but Lynch returning but was looking for a big man to replace Montross, who had one season remaining. He had his eye on one in Philadelphia, who was perhaps the best player in the country.

The next morning, while Tar Heel fans everywhere slept off their intoxication, Smith and assistant coach Phil Ford boarded a plane to visit 6' 10" high school star Rasheed Wallace, a great athlete with a deft shooting touch. The impact of Smith walking into his inner-city Philly home less than twenty-four hours after he was on their TV set winning the national championship proved immeasurable and helped him close the deal.

Wallace joined a class that already included Jerry Stackhouse and Jeff McInnis, a forward-guard combo that had spent their senior year prepping at Oak Hill Academy in the Virginia mountains. Although Stackhouse hailed from Kinston, North Carolina, and was a distant relative of Michael Jordan, he was not ticketed for the Tar Heels through most of his high school career. An excellent student recruited by several of the ACC schools, Stackhouse was linked mostly to N.C. State and Duke as Krzyzewski's first major recruit from North Carolina.

The worm turned on an unofficial campus visit, where Stackhouse spent most of the time with Ford, who had grown up near him in eastern North Carolina. Stackhouse started to feel more at ease in Chapel Hill, perennially voted among the state universities in America with the most diverse student bodies and "most comfortable" environment for black athletes. N.C. State wanted assistant coach Buzz Peterson, a former Tar Heel player, to tell Stackhouse why he should wear red and not light blue; Peterson couldn't find the right words, choosing not to knock his alma mater. At Duke, where virtually none of the students came from rural North Carolina, Stackhouse was a minority in more ways than one.

Phil Ford had joined Smith's staff in 1988 with no coaching experience and learned the recruiting ropes well enough to both befriend and convince Stackhouse that UNC was the best place for him. Like a few others before him and since, Stackhouse enrolled with the expectations of becoming the "next Jordan" and backboned a freshman class that made loaded Carolina a prohibitive favorite to repeat as national champs and, at the same time, helped destroy the unique team chemistry that had taken the Tar Heels to the 1993 NCAA title.

The cable network ESPN2—known in television lexicon as "the Deuce"—was created with Duke-Carolina basketball in mind. Launched in October of 1993, ESPN2 intended to appeal to a younger audience by focusing on action sports.

However, it needed a hook—and the first Duke-Carolina game each season not only provided one, it sold millions of subscriptions to cable companies across the country in early 1994. For months prior, promos on ESPN told viewers to sign up for the brand new network if they wanted to watch the Blue Devils vs. the Tar Heels on Thursday, February 3, from Chapel Hill.

Raycom/JP Sports won the ACC basketball TV rights in 1982, two years after broadcasting pioneer C. D. Chesley last produced games for an annual rights fee of $1 million. The ACC long believed it was underpaid for its TV rights, but remained loyal to Chesley for having given the ACC television exposure before any other conference—as far back as the 1950s.

Of the Fifty Most Influential People in ACC history, Castleman DeTolley Chesley was voted third behind Everett Case and Dean Smith. Referred to by almost everyone as "Chez," he was also known for the raspy whisper caused by throat cancer and partial removal of his voice box. He learned to speak through a small hole cut in his esophagus and taught patients with the same affliction how to speak and whistle.

Chesley had played freshman football at UNC before transferring to Penn, where he was captain and, true to his promotional flair, a showman in the school's comedy troupe. He later graduated from Penn's Wharton School of Business—but sports remained his first love.

As an assistant athletics director at Penn, Chesley developed Southern contacts with Duke Athletics Director Eddie Cameron and Carolina's Chuck Erickson. He began his TV career producing regional football telecasts for ABC and NBC and for years did Sunday morning replays of Notre Dame games, featuring announcers Lindsey Nelson and Paul Hornung.

Chesley paid the ACC $75,000 to produce three football telecasts in 1956, and the following March he attended the 1957 ACC Tournament in Raleigh, when top-ranked and undefeated UNC defeated Wake Forest on a famous three-point play by All-American Lennie Rosenbluth, who collided with Wake's Wendell Carr on the winning shot. Rosenbluth got the basket and Carr the foul in the classic semifinal game for the ages.

Chesley got the bug. Caught up in the magic of McGuire's Miracle, he set up a five-station network to televise the Tar Heels' Final Four games from Kansas City back to North Carolina. They won both in triple overtime to capture the national championship and the collective heart of a state.

"They were renting TV sets for hospitals," Chesley said. "It was the damnedest thing you every heard of. I knew right there that ACC basketball could be as popular as anything shown on TV in North Carolina."

In 1958, Chesley created the first college conference TV basketball package in the country. He drove his Ford station wagon from Maryland to South Carolina, signing up twenty stations to carry the games, contingent on his finding a sponsor.

Pilot Life Insurance was the first major advertiser on ACC basketball, and "Sail with the Pilot" became a household phrase in the region. Chesley telecast eleven Saturday games and was the ACC's rights holder for the next two decades, first televising the entire ACC Tournament in the late 1960s.

A regional phenomenon, ACC basketball games on Saturday afternoon and Wednesday night changed viewing habits of families and bed times of youngsters from Pennsylvania to South Carolina. High school kids skipped school on the first day of the tournament to watch the afternoon games.

The exposure also helped Duke and Carolina bedrock their programs with some of the best talent in the country. Vic Bubas brought in players from Pennsylvania, Ohio, and West Virginia. One of Dean Smith's early recruits from Washington, D.C., searched through hundreds of letters to find one from UNC after he watched the Tar Heels for the first time on TV.

"No doubt in my mind that TV gave us a leg up on attracting better players," former ACC Commissioner Gene Corrigan said.

On Super Bowl Sunday in 1973, Chesley expanded his telecast between No. 2 N.C. State and No. 3 Maryland, both undefeated, from a sixteen-station network to a patchwork national feed. Long before David Thompson leaped above the fray to tip in the winning basket, the entire country discovered what had been the ACC's secret for years.

Dean Smith, ironically, was still more concerned with radio back then. He was miffed that, during N.C. State's dominant run with Thompson, WBT-AM radio in Charlotte dropped UNC games to carry the Wolfpack. WBT had a massive North-South signal, and for years the New York City fans cultivated by Frank McGuire listened to the Tar Heel broadcasts at night from their apartment buildings. Smith saw that as a recruiting advantage and wanted WBT back. Chapel Hill broadcaster Jim Heavner had connections in Charlotte and acquired UNC's radio rights in 1975 because he convinced the station to air Carolina games again.

Chesley held the ACC TV rights through 1981, when he reluctantly agreed to pay the million dollars for thirty-six exclusive telecasts. He slapped his head in disbelief and frustration, saying he previously "paid each ACC school between $300 and $500 for the right to televise a game."

In the late 1970s, however, other ACC games had been telecast by various competitors, such as Raycom Sports, owned by 1971 UNC graduate Rick Ray, who maxed out his personal credit cards to send N.C. State's games in the Great Alaska Shootout back to North Carolina in 1979.

Raycom filed an antitrust suit against the ACC, and before the case went to court, the ACC opened up its TV rights to a bidding war. Chesley's twenty-four-year relationship with the league ended on a sour note when a Maryland company, MetroSports, paid the ACC $3 million for a package of games during the 1981–82 season.

Chesley, who operated his company from his home in Linville, North Carolina, could not match that bid and lost the business. He died at age sixty-nine in 1983 from the effects of Alzheimer's disease, is buried at the foot of Grandfather Mountain, near Linville, and has been honored posthumously several times by the conference.

Raycom eventually won the contract with a $15 million fee for three years, bringing JP Sports into the partnership that would be renewed several more times as the annual rights fee jumped to $6 million, to $8 million, to $15 million, and to $33 million in the new expanded conference. Whereas the ACC once negotiated certain games separately with the national networks, its TV rights became inclusive and brokered by Raycom to ABC, CBS, ESPN, and Fox. Raycom retained about forty ACC games each year for its own six-state, regional network, underwritten by sponsors and corporate partners. The package included two plums—the entire ACC Tournament and the first Duke-Carolina game. The rest of the country saw both on ESPN or ESPN2.

Asked how the 1994 Duke-Carolina game legitimized ESPN2, John Wildhack, ESPN's senior vice president for programming, said, "It helped create awareness for our network, sending a statement to our viewers, our industry, our advertisers, that we were going to put events of prominence and significance on ESPN2."

Of course, ESPN itself hyped the 1994 game a full week before, sending camera crews and reporters to both campuses to capture the craziness. At UNC, former players and media members were asked to compare this particular game to others that had been played. At Duke, the cameras panned Krzyzewskiville and even caught its namesake leaving Cameron the day before the game.

"What's it like to have Duke and Carolina fans living and working so close to each other?" he was asked.

"It's not too bad," Krzyzewski said, a twinkle in his eye, unable to hold back a really bad joke, "If you're a Duke fan, you just have to clean up a lot."

So the Duke-Carolina rivalry created yet another first with ESPN's new network. Those who did not sign up and missed the match-up of college basketball powerhouses would vow to see it the next year on the Deuce.

Through the five consecutive Final Fours, the back-to-back national championships and assisting with the '92 Olympic team in Barcelona, Krzyzewski learned his life as "just another basketball coach with time to spare" was done. The son of blue-collar Polish immigrants had become one of the more recognizable people in the country.

After the most successful NCAA Tournament run since John Wooden and

UCLA won ten titles in twelve years, Krzyzewski no longer snickered at Smith's cracks about the demands on his time. As with Smith, he had to learn to say no to requests for most interviews, corporate speaking engagements, fund-raisers, and coaches' association meetings.

The change alienated Krzyzewski from the local media, with whom he had been very popular for his candor and early accessibility. Sportswriters from North Carolina found themselves shut out by the coach they had covered since 1980 and, in their minds, treated fairly in his losing years. Krzyzewski stopped holding regular press conferences and eventually cut it to two—before each Carolina game and only then on the urging of school officials.

By comparison, Krzyzewski always seemed to find time for national media such as Dick "Hoops" Weiss of the New York *Daily News,* Skip Myslenki and Gene Wojciechowski from his hometown Chicago plus, of course, Dick Vitale and ESPN. In the 1980s, UNC's Smith had been much the same way but was more willing to meet the press later in his career, which underscored Krzyzewski's break with the local media.

Also unlike Smith, whose control over the UNC athletics department was legendary, Krzyzewski was further frustrated by Duke's reluctance to make the changes he deemed necessary to stay on the cutting edge—and he took it personally. That Krzyzewski felt underappreciated had been building since Duke became only the sixth school in history to win consecutive national championships. All this so annoyed him that his wife grew openly angry about how the administration was treating her husband.

"Mickie was mad at the world," said Donna Keane, Krzyzewski's administrative assistant for twelve years. "She felt that Mike had done so much, and Duke wasn't doing all it could."

Mickie Krzyzewski was involved in every aspect of the program from recruiting to interviewing Keane when she applied for the job, to producing the annual team poster and organizing the post-season banquet, including customized senior videos she choreographed to each player's favorite song. She was the primary editor with approval rights over every word printed in *A Season Is a Lifetime,* a book written on Duke's two national championships.

Mickie had been particularly attentive to Grant Hill, who was unhappy in his early years at Duke. A gentle spirit raised by Yale and Wellesley graduates, Hill chafed under Krzyzewski's military-style discipline and his borderline-abusive language. Several times during his freshman season, Hill called other coaches who had recruited him and talked about transferring.

As his college career extended, Hill developed more respect for his coach's personality and eventually became one of his biggest backers; as a pro, Hill made the first $1 million gift to kick off Krzyzewski's innovative Legacy Fund that endowed Duke basketball.

Cheered on by his ever-present father Calvin, who regularly sat behind the bench in his dark blue ball cap, Grant Hill rebounded from off-season foot surgery to play all five positions as a senior in 1994. He averaged more than thirty-five minutes a game, leading the team in scoring, assists, and steals, and was second to the nearly seven-foot Parks in rebounds and blocked shots.

In carrying a bunch of role players to an unexpectedly fast start, Hill elevated the productivity of other starters Tony Lang, Cherokee Parks, sophomore Chris Collins, and freshman Jeff Capel. The Blue Devils won 15 of their first 16 games and went into their made-for-cable-TV game at Carolina on February 3 as the No. 1 team in the country.

The Tar Heels had opened the season with the unanimous top ranking, odds-on favorite to defend their national championship. They lost only Lynch and had three highly touted freshmen who created a stir from the day they arrived on campus and dominated preseason pickup games. Word quickly got around that Stackhouse, Wallace, and McInnis weren't backing down from the senior starters Reese, Salvadori, and Phelps.

The two returning stars of the 1993 NCAA champs, Eric Montross and Donald Williams, were safe. However, having to contend with the three freshmen every day in practice, Smith fought the public outcry to play the "young guns" after the Tar Heels suffered an early loss to Massachusetts and dropped two more games at Georgia Tech and Virginia, both vastly inferior teams.

Although his seniority system was being sorely tested, Smith wasn't sitting any of the seniors who had led Carolina to the national championship the year before. When Williams missed nine games with a shoulder injury, he moved sophomore Dante Calabria into the lineup ahead of McInnis or Stackhouse, either of whom could have played shooting guard.

It took Duke's visit to Chapel Hill to unify the Tar Heels, who had dropped to No. 4 but moved back to second in the national polls to make this the first-ever Duke-Carolina game when they were ranked No. 1–2.

UNC broke open a tight game in the second half to lead by 15 points before Hill rallied the Blue Devils to within 2. Carolina converted 15 of 18 free throws in the last three minutes to hold on 89–78 and take the top ranking back from Duke. Phelps had 18 points and 6 assists, but McInnis had 8 points and 6 assists in fewer minutes. All eight players who got in scored at least 8 points and the team shot 56 percent in, hands down, its best performance of the season.

Still, the inconsistency played on. Carolina split the six games heading into the rematch at Duke on March 5. The three freshmen continued to think they deserved to start. Smith relented only in Wallace's case, putting him in the lineup because the spectacularly talented forward was playing so well, shooting better than 60 percent and averaging nearly seven rebounds a game.

The Tar Heels again saved their best for the Dukies, shooting the lights out for the second time against the Blue Devils. Wallace's enormous dunk over three of them sealed an 87–77 win and soured Grant Hill's Senior Night at Cameron. Hill had 18 points and Parks 23, but it wasn't enough to beat the hot Heels, who despite the sweep still finished a full game back in the ACC race.

"We're the only ones they hate more than themselves," Duke assistant Mike Brey said pointedly.

Wallace was more emphatic. "As long as me, Touche (McInnis), and Jerry (Stackhouse) are here, we ain't ever losing here (at Duke)."

Carolina won 28 games and the 1994 ACC Tournament but never gelled. The Tar Heels didn't bother with the traditional ritual after their ACC title win over Virginia, which had defeated Duke in the semifinals, claiming they were waiting to cut down bigger nets. They posed for what looked like an unhappy team picture.

In the locker room, the players were sullen and spent from a long season of bitching over who played and for how long. Senior Pat Sullivan, red-shirting because of the log jam in the front court, saw an early out in the NCAA Tournament if they didn't get their "heads out of their asses."

Sullivan proved prophetic. After an uninspired win over Jerry Fallwell's Liberty University, the top-seeded Tar Heels played rugged Boston College in the second round of the East Regional at Landover, Maryland. Smith was livid after BC's Danya Abrams tomahawked Phelps out of the game while chasing a fast break, and despite rallying from an eight-point deficit to tie the game, Carolina couldn't pull it out.

After his streak of thirteen straight years in the Sweet Sixteen was snapped, an angry Smith bitched about Abrams's dirty foul in the postgame press conference, claiming he had warned his team about "No. 23" after watching tape of the eighth-seeded Eagles.

Told that Smith was criticizing his team's rough play, BC coach Jim O'Brien was incredulous that someone with a front line of Montross, Wallace, and Stackhouse could make that charge. "*They* are saying *we're* too physical?" O'Brien asked.

The huffy Heels went home with a 28–7 record. Their selfishness cost them a chance to win a second straight national championship in front of adoring fans after Duke had won back-to-back titles, which would have been the ultimate one up on the Blue Devils.

Charlotte hosted the 1994 Final Four, and the organizing committee was made up of well-heeled UNC alumni who were hoping Smith could put an exclamation point on his career by winning the NCAA Tournament on his and their home turf. The best Carolina could do that year was win the women's national championship. When a few absurd UNC fans dared to crow "back to back," the Tar Heel-haters had a field day full of laughs.

Instead, the Duke team that had looked finished after its lackluster loss to Virginia in the ACC semifinals put on another March rally. As her husband's team advanced, Mickie Krzyzewski remained miffed about Duke's unresponsiveness to her husband's requests and talked about Mike leaving for the NBA, TV broadcast booth, or, most outrageously, a Division III school "so we can get some privacy back in our life."

The Blue Devils won the South Regional in Knoxville by upsetting third-ranked Purdue, with Hill outplaying All-American Glenn "Big Dog" Robinson. Krzyzewski's seventh Final Four in nine years was most remarkable, considering his roster of one star and the rest role players and the professional turmoil swirling around him.

Then, after the team had left for Charlotte, sixteen-year-old Lindy Krzyzewski was robbed in a mall parking lot in Durham. Though their middle daughter only lost her pocketbook and car keys and was otherwise unharmed, it further pushed the family near its emotional edge.

Duke defeated Florida in the national semifinals and then faced Arkansas on Monday night at the Charlotte Coliseum, which was padded-down with security because President (and former Arkansas governor) Bill Clinton wanted to see the game. The crowd was lined up around the coliseum and slowly snaked its way through metal detectors.

Hill had scored 25 points against Florida and was dog-tired during most of the final. He scrapped for 14 rebounds but missed 7 of 11 shots as the Blue Devils lost a 10-point second-half lead to the second-ranked Razorbacks. The game came down to a pair of three-pointers. Arkansas' Scotty Thurman made his over the outstretched arm of Tony Lang as the shot clock wound down, and Collins missed his on the other end. Arkansas won its only NCAA title 76–72. Duke fans applauded their gallant team as it left the court.

Grant Hill wound up among the most decorated players in the nation. He won ACC Player of the Year after accumulating an unprecedented 1,900 points, 700 rebounds, 400 assists, 200 steals, and 100 blocked shots. As a consensus All-American, he had his jersey retired to the rafters at Cameron, joining Christian Laettner and Bobby Hurley for Duke's biggest individual honor. In June, he was the third player taken in the NBA draft by Detroit, giving Duke three straight lottery picks.

Krzyzewski's undermanned 1994 team had finished 28–6 and went further than expected. It was his finest coaching job and he looked more entrenched than ever at Duke, having supplanted Smith as the best coach in college basketball—but looks were deceiving.

"It was the best of times and the worst of times," Donna Keane said. "The best of times because no one thought that (1994) team would go that far. The worst of times because Mike had overextended himself and it was beginning to wear on him."

Besides the national championship, Krzyzewski had lost the free rein he enjoyed at Duke under President Keith Brodie, who had given him anything he wanted. New President Nan Keohane was a different breed, coming from all-women's Wellesley College and demanding accountability from a men's basketball coach who held a degree of power and influence with which she was unfamiliar.

She found out quickly following the 1994 Final Four during her ninth month on the job. Krzyzewski had grown so tired of clashing with Butters that he again flirted with the NBA. The acrimony between Krzyzewski and Butters was acute enough for Keohane to call a meeting in her office so she could play peacekeeper.

Krzyzewski blamed Butters for refusing to make certain upgrades to Cameron Indoor Stadium, such as air-conditioning the fifty-five-year-old building and giving him a private entrance and bathroom in his office so he did not have to walk the public hallways and interact with the staff members and guests he encountered.

In the spring of 1993, after Duke failed to make the Final Four for the first time in six years, Butters had promised Krzyzewski a new exterior door into his office from the side of Cameron facing the woods and a private bathroom in the basketball suite. Those renovations, however, would have to be done the next year because the budget had been allocated.

With the 1994 season over, Krzyzewski wanted construction to begin. Butters was in Florida playing golf—an annual vacation he had written into his contract—when his assistants Joe Alleva and Tom D'Armi told the coach they didn't know of any such plans to renovate. Krzyzewski was furious and decided he was leaving Duke.

Through liaisons Billy Cunningham, the former UNC All-American, and NBA Commissioner David Stern, Krzyzewski was contacted by the Miami Heat (where coach Kevin Loughery had moved into the front office), Portland Trailblazers (Rick Adelman had been fired) and New Jersey Nets (Chuck Daly retired).

Stern was trying to lure superstar college coaches into his league, and within a few weeks Krzyzewski was being wooed by all three franchises.

Then, in May, the Blue Devils abruptly canceled their exhibition tour to Australia because two rising sophomores, Jeff Capel and Greg Newton, had become academically ineligible in the spring and needed to attend both summer school sessions to play the following season. Duke could have gone down under without a full team, but Krzyzewski and his staff voted to cancel the trip, infuriating the Australian promoters who had sold thousands of tickets and had to refund the money.

Duke President Keohane was also mad, believing that the trip was a university commitment and had to be canceled by someone from her office, not the basketball coach. She appointed one of her assistants, Talman Trask, to investigate the situation, further angering Krzyzewski.

"Nan didn't know anything about big-time college athletics," said former newspaper columnist and author Bill Brill, a Duke alumnus and one of Krzyzewski's confidantes. "She gets here and says, 'This guy doesn't have to ask anybody anything? We don't ask any questions? How can this be? Don't we have any control over this guy?'"

Keohane changed her tune while, on vacation, she got the word that Krzyzewski was considering an offer from the Portland Trailblazers. Her office was bombarded by calls and emails, and Keohane got the picture of what it would mean for Duke to lose its famous basketball coach in her first year. She called him and said she was cutting her trip short and asked him not to make any decision until they could meet the next day. By now the speculation was all over Duke and in the media.

This was Krzyzewski's second serious brush with pro basketball after turning down the Celtics four years earlier. So when he called a press conference to say he was declining Portland's offer, Krzyzewski's critics crowed over what they perceived as a grandstand play to hold Duke hostage and make some demands to the school.

Dean Smith even got a chuckle out of it, deadpanning one spring afternoon that he was calling his own news conference to announce, "I'm still the coach at North Carolina."

Keohane's eleventh-hour pledge to help Krzyzewski was essential in his decision to stay. She now understood what basketball meant at her new school and what kind of heat she would catch if a coaching change occurred on her watch. She became Krzyzewski's ally while Butters' influence began to wane. Still, that was far from the end of Coach K's unhappiness.

Subtly suffering through all this turmoil was recruiting, which had turned

Duke into a juggernaut over the previous twelve years. Since failing to sign his top targets his first season, Krzyzewski had recruited with an incredible closing rate. Lately, he was still getting good players but wasn't as hands-on.

He had missed the entire summer-evaluation period in 1992 while coaching at the Olympics. With the official contact periods shortened by the NCAA, Krzyzewski did not have the same amount of time to get to know the prospects as he once had. Having always recruited great players *and* good kids, he admitted being so preoccupied that, when he did speak with recruits and their families, he stopped listening as closely to their answers.

It resulted in taking some prep stars who weren't as single-minded as former Duke recruits, and by 1994 there were players on the roster that Krzyzewski never would have taken before he won his first national championship. Talented but troubled Californian Ricky Price, who was also recruited by Kansas and told by Roy Williams that he would have to play much harder in college, proved to be the poster child of a mismatch for Duke's program.

That summer, Krzyzewski was already stressed out when he thought he pulled a hamstring playing tennis and racquetball. The severe pain was eventually diagnosed as a ruptured disc. His doctors recommended surgery, but he put them off while trying rest, painkillers, and muscle-strengthening exercises. Toughing it out with an athletic and military mentality, he remembered Jim Valvano, the fast-talking New Yorker who was struck down the year before by cancer that had started just above his spine.

Valvano was more of a coaching rival from their days in the Northeast than a close friend. Jimmy V moved to N.C. State from Iona College in 1980, the same year Krzyzewski took the Duke job. Their contrasting personal and professional styles produced some classic ACC matchups, and for years Valvano irritated Krzyzewski by favoring finesse over fundamentals and appearing more interested in himself than his players—to say nothing of beating Duke fourteen of twenty-three times.

At the end, Valvano earned his colleague's compassion.

Forced out at State in 1990 following improprieties in his program, Valvano had turned to TV commentating and expanded his entrepreneurial ventures when he was diagnosed in 1992. Krzyzewski invited him to speak to his team on several occasions. The last time he met with the Blue Devils was in the fall of 1993 just before he checked into the Duke Medical Center. Krzyzewski was among the last to see him alive.

The sudden demise of Coach V had left Coach K to consider his mortality when his own backache began.

. . .

In early October of 1994, Krzyzewski agreed to the surgery and was told to stay out of work for six weeks to recuperate. Had he listened to his doctors, and his wife, he would have rested, recovered, and possibly avoided the catastrophic and controversial season that followed.

But he was back at practice ten days later, looking pale and frail after losing nearly twenty pounds. When he stood, his legs were alarmingly skinny coming out of gym shorts and he spent most of his time in a specially made chair next to the court.

The Blue Devils, without graduated Grant Hill and relying on ballyhooed freshman sharpshooter Trajan Langdon, needed their coach to help develop a young backcourt. Their coach needed to be there, even though the postsurgical back pain was not subsiding.

Mickie Krzyzewski had become the central figure of Duke basketball, far beyond her already omnipotent role as the head coach's wife and godmother to the players. She called Donna Keane, Mike Krzyzewski's administrative assistant, daily to check on her husband's condition and at home changed from feeding his anger to pressuring him to take time off.

"It was unheard of, coming back so fast," said Keane, who now works for an investment company in Charlotte owned by UNC alumni Erskine Bowles and Nelson Schwabe. "I was there when the orthopedist was in the office and said, 'Don't do this; you're ruining everything.' He wouldn't listen.

"He was the most driven individual I'd ever, ever known. He just did it his way and that caused the exhaustion and the back."

The Blue Devils began the 1994–95 season ranked No. 8 in the country and won six of their first seven games, losing only to sixteenth-ranked Connecticut. They beat Michigan at Cameron on December 10, took final exams and made plans to leave for Honolulu and the Rainbow Classic over Christmas. Krzyzewski's doctors wanted him to miss the trip, but he refused and took the ten-hour flight to Hawaii.

His assistants, Pete Gaudet, Tommy Amaker, and Mike Brey, remember him fighting off the pain and discomfort during the week in Honolulu, where Duke lost to Iowa, beat Boston University and Georgia Tech but, more importantly, began to lose Krzyzewski's focus and attention. He was in so much pain that he had to lie on the cabin floor for most of the Delta Airlines commercial flight home.

"It was obviously bothering him," recalled Gaudet, now an assistant women's coach at Ohio State, "but he was such an intense person I don't think anyone thought it was going to hold him back. Nothing held him back.

"He didn't get much sleep anyway. The combination of that, the trip to Hawaii, game after game after game, there comes a point when you don't know how much you can endure. But we never saw him stepping aside.

"You think some people are invincible. The coaches and players all probably thought he was invincible. Coaches aren't allowed to get sick during the season. Coaches lose their voices and have to hurry back from funerals."

The Blue Devils opened their ACC season on January 4, 1995, against unbeaten (8–0) but typically untested Clemson at Cameron.

First-year head coach Rick Barnes had given the Tigers an attitude adjustment and brought in a couple of unknown freshmen. Greg Buckner committed to Barnes when he was the coach at Providence and followed him south. Forward Ike Iturbe was a rugged Spaniard and the catalyst for a famous controversy between Barnes and UNC's Smith at the end of the season.

With Krzyzewski so medicated he couldn't remember much of what happened in the game, Duke fell behind Clemson early and never caught up. Barnes had convinced his no-name players not to be intimidated by the Cameron Crazies. They hit 10 of 15 from three-point range and beat the ninth-ranked Blue Devils 75–70.

Forty-eight hours later, Krzyzewski was in a hospital bed.

Duke practiced in Cameron on Friday afternoon, January 6, and then left for Atlanta and its second game against Georgia Tech in less than two weeks without their head coach. He had been given an ultimatum by his wife: If he didn't leave the team and be hospitalized, she was leaving him.

These were not idle words. Mickie was well known for her strength and resolve, having once sneaked onto the front line with her infant daughter to be with Mike while he was serving in Korea. In this case, she swallowed her pride and enlisted the help of adversary Butters, who told him to take a medical leave to find out what was wrong.

Krzyzewski offered to quit but Butters would have none of it.

"He was in trouble," Butters said. "He didn't know why, I didn't know why. He offered to resign and I said that was crazy . . . let's find out what's wrong, assess the situation and see what to do from there."

Krzyzewski's sudden departure left the program in chaos. As the senior member of the staff, Gaudet became acting coach almost by default, even though several athletics department officials favored Brey if Krzyzewski was going to be out for an extended period. Gaudet was the restricted-earning coach, also taught physical education part-time, and spent hours in the film room putting together scouting reports.

Duke dropped the game at Georgia Tech and lost at Wake Forest, both ranked in the top 25, and then squandered a 23-point lead at home against unranked Virginia before losing in double overtime. Defeats to N.C. State and Florida State gave Duke six straight losses for the first time since 1925.

"What people forget is we were in a little bit of a tailspin before Mike left," said Brey, now the head coach at Notre Dame. "We lost to Clemson at home in his last game, and it wasn't a very good Clemson team.

"Then turn around and go to Tech, and we had just beaten them in Hawaii. They were going to get our ass back. Now you're 0–2 and you're not sure when Mike's coming back, and you've got some young guys in a tough league looking around like it wasn't supposed to be like this."

Krzyzewski went under the confidential care of doctors, tried several new forms of medication and argued with his wife about when he could return. With his background, it was tantamount to abandoning ship. He did not come into the office and was basically placed off-limits by Mickie. Donna Keane made regular trips to the house to drop off tapes and files but rarely saw her boss. For all intents and purposes, Mickie Krzyzewski was running her husband's life. In doing so, she might have also saved it.

With almost daily speculation about Krzyzewski in the news media and around campus, Duke announced that he was out for the season. The news had an unsettling effect; if it were only a bad back why couldn't he appear on TV—lying down, if need be—to tell the world himself? But, while the rumors persisted, at least the constant waiting game had ended.

Gaudet then made the one move that might have doomed him. He basically benched freshman Steve Wojciechowski, a lunch-pail point guard whom Krzyzewski liked because he played good defense and didn't make a lot of mistakes. Without Chris Collins, who never found his game after recovering from a broken foot in December, Gaudet wanted more scoring and assists from his backcourt and gradually cut Wojo's minutes in favor of sophomore Jeff Capel. That created even more tension on the team.

Keane called it a "horrible transition" and said that as the defeats mounted the pressure grew on Gaudet and his staff, transforming an office atmosphere once buoyant and confident into almost constant anxiety. The specter of Krzyzewski hovered over the program. The standard line was he would return after the season, but no one knew for sure.

DEAN VS. DUKE IN 1990s: 12–6

COACH K VS. CAROLINA IN 1990s: 10–12 (MISSED 2 GAMES IN 1995)

NCAA CHAMPIONSHIPS
- Duke 1991, 1992; Carolina 1993

ROUGHEST GAME
- Carolina 75, Duke 73, February 2, 1992

MOST MEMORABLE GAME
- Carolina 102, Duke 100 (2OT), February 2, 1995

BEST QUOTE
"As long as me, Touche (McInnis), and Jerry (Stackhouse) are here, we ain't ever losing here (at Duke)."

(Rasheed Wallace, 1994)

7

ONE RISETH, ANOTHER RETIRES

As college basketball went on during Mike Krzyzewski's mysterious absence, even his closest associates and biggest fans wondered whether he'd be back. The story read like the wealthy and powerful socialite who seemingly had everything—to the surprise of all who considered him untouchable—suddenly stepping out onto the ledge of his penthouse.

From their once-secure perch, the Blue Devils wobbled and wavered, waiting for someone to pull them back inside and tell them they had been sleepwalking through a bad dream. The public looked up in disbelief, wondering what was really happening with an empire so high and mighty it was once called "the perfect program" by *USA Today*.

Duke's unprecedented six-game losing streak in 1995 ended with a win at Notre Dame. The Blue Devils had eighth-ranked Maryland beaten in College Park, only to blow it at the end. Their seventh loss in the last eight starts left them only one game above .500 on the season with No. 2 North Carolina coming to Cameron Indoor Stadium.

Acting coach Pete Gaudet fielded a capable lineup, a roster ten deep with highly recruited players. Besides senior Cherokee Parks, who seemed to thrive without Krzyzewski's tight-fisted discipline, the rest of the group stepped down a notch rather than up as their isolated head coach watched from home and grew more angry with each defeat. The team he left was now officially in decline, its intimidation factor gone and unable to sustain good play over two halves.

To make matters worse, Dean Smith, the once-aging icon, caught a second wind of sorts and took back the mantle as college basketball's best coach. Smith's thin, smallish 1995 Tar Heels got along far better than the overloaded, tempestuous team of a year before that had graduated four seniors. With no true center to go with sophomore forwards Jerry Stackhouse and Rasheed Wallace, Smith started a three-guard lineup of Jeff McInnis, Donald Williams, and Dante Calabria to demonstrate his flexibility.

Over the years, Smith was seen as a rigid coach whose system identified players by their position number; the 5-man was the center, the 4-man the power forward, the 3-man the small forward, the 2-man the "shooting" guard and the "1" the savvy point guard or the quarterback. The Tar Heels tried ad nauseam to get the ball inside and took the outside shot only when higher-percentage options just weren't there. That was their formula for success.

Of course, this too was a mirage. Phil Ford became UNC's all-time leading scorer from the point position and 6' 10" Sam Perkins opened up UNC's offense in 1983 by firing away from the ACC's experimental three-point line, hitting twelve treys for the season. Smith had won the 1982 national championship with Perkins and James Worthy, neither a true center, and played three guards plenty of times in and out of Four Corners.

The last time he fielded a lineup like 1995 was back in the days when he had to "go small" by necessity and couldn't get five quality position players to sign with Carolina. The fans fell hard for this sleeker and slicker version, the freest-shooting and most accurate team of Smith's tenure. The Tar Heels hit 51 percent of their three-point attempts (which set a school record). When they ran off to a 16–1 start, they looked unbeatable by either going inside to their athletic forwards, Stackhouse and Wallace, or bombing away from the perimeter with the three guards.

Despite the teams being bipolar in success, as well as in the ACC standings, Duke and Carolina played a game on February 2, 1995, that reaffirmed the unpredictability of the rivalry. Occurring in Duke's most forgettable season, their double-overtime epic at Cameron has not received its just due, but *because* the Blue Devils were so sorry, the game beats any cliché as an example of what can happen when old foes meet.

Carolina was ranked second and 6–1 in conference games. By that time, Duke was in an 0–7 ACC tailspin (10–9 overall), out of the polls for three weeks and, without Krzyzewski, looking like the worst team in the league. Still, the opposing head coaches *knew* it would be a close game.

When asked about the late, 9:00 P.M. start, Gaudet predicted "we'll still be in overtime" by midnight. He sensed that the sight of Carolina's baby blue uniforms would draw the full attention of his team, a chance to undo the damage of the last month, and win instead of lose in the last few minutes when Krzyzewski's steely focus was sorely needed.

Conversely, Smith worried the most about games he was expected to win. He admittedly wasn't much of a motivator, concentrating on execution and allowing the circumstances to rev his team's emotion. No one had to jack up the Tar Heels when they thought they could lose, but they occasionally came out flat against the "best shot" of a heavy underdog looking to knock them off. Generally, that was never a concern against Duke.

On an atypically warm night, Cameron was such a sweatbox that Smith took off his jacket early and rolled up his shirt sleeves, a rarity for Mr. Manners. The Tar Heels led by 17 points in the first half after Stackhouse's reverse dunk and down court strut that became an ESPN highlight staple for several years with Stackhouse's head bobbing up and down cockily.

The Blue Devils rallied to lead by 12 points in the second. Even with the wild swings, the lead changed hands four more times before Parks tied the game 81–81 with two free throws at the end of regulation.

Duke was behind by a familiar "eight points with seventeen seconds" left in the first overtime, but had it down to three points with only three ticks left. UNC sophomore center Serge Zwikker stood at the free throw line for two shots, either of which would end it. Ricky Price trash-talked loud enough for the other nine players and the three officials to hear, and a shaken Zwikker clanged the first, then the second to keep Duke alive. Jeff Capel crossed midcourt and launched a thirty-five-foot three-pointer that hung in the air forever.

Cameron was actually quiet by the time the ball descended toward the basket. When it swished through the net to tie the game again, the Crazies erupted like something else was at stake than five more minutes of "free basketball." In the crow's nest high above Cameron, ESPN's Dick Vitale jumped out of his chair and banged his bald head against an overhead pipe, opening a wound that took a week to heal.

The clock passed 11:30 P.M. and headed for midnight as Gaudet smiled in the huddle and the second overtime began.

Still deadlocked at 98–98, the game finally turned on a basket by UNC's Donald Williams and a steal and lay-up by McInnis. Price pulled Duke within two on a jumper, but after a Carolina miss the nearly three-hour marathon ended when Steve Wojciechowski's fifteen-footer to force a third OT drew only iron.

The 102–100 loss, the second in double overtime that season, might have seemed like a moral victory to some but it further clouded the future of Gaudet, whose unfortunate team went on to compile Duke's longest ACC losing streak, nine straight, and its worst ACC record, 2–14.

While his program languished in last place, Krzyzewski called seniors Cherokee Parks and Erik Meek to his home, and challenged them to "draw a line in the sand," an old Army term that got into the newspapers and was ridiculed by Carolina fans and those within the UNC program.

Privately, Krzyzewski also told Gaudet to put Wojciechowski back in the lineup for the 1995 ACC Tournament. Wojo had been one of Duke's top seven players early before moving down the bench and representing the first breach of trust between Krzyzewski and the way Gaudet was running his team. Having been relegated to the tournament play-in game against N.C. State, the Blue Devils were likely not to advance past a quarterfinal matchup with top-seeded Wake Forest, but giving the order demonstrated that Krzyzewski was reclaiming control.

Despite having lost the home-and-home series to N.C. State by a combined 22 points, Duke played much better and beat the Wolfpack by 13 in the Thursday night ACC Tournament opener. The Blue Devils faced Wake Forest Friday and led by 18 in the first half. Continuing their pattern of losing leads—further infuriating Krzyzewski, the TV viewer—they succumbed to the Deacons' run behind Randolph Childress and Tim Duncan, losing 87–70.

Duke finished 13–18 for the worst record since Krzyzewski's second year and posted the most losses in the school's storied basketball history.

"I remember getting on the bus in Greensboro after Wake beat us," assistant coach Mike Brey said. "It was like, Jesus, this thing is finally over. We heard that Dick Vitale was saying it would be the only time the NIT invited a losing team. You know what I was saying? 'Please, don't take us. This needs to end *right now*.' "

Krzyzewski soon made his first public appearance in two months, holding a news conference at Cameron prior to an exclusive ESPN *Up Close* interview with Roy Firestone. The recluse look rested and relaxed, revealing none of his hidden fury, and said his back was better and announced his return as coach of the Blue Devils.

Duke was no longer the team to beat in the ACC. Carolina, Maryland, Wake Forest, and Virginia had finished in an unprecedented four-way tie for first place, as if it took all of them to replace the Blue Devils. Wake, with All-American Randolph Childress and future all-pro center Tim Duncan, had beaten UNC for the ACC Tournament championship, but two weeks later the Tar Heels were the last ACC team left standing.

They had survived NCAA first- and second-round games against Murray State and Iowa State, with Wallace hobbling on a sprained ankle, and advanced to the South Regional final by beating Allen Iverson-led Georgetown and Smith's coaching buddy, John Thompson, in Birmingham. There, they faced top-seeded and second-ranked Kentucky for a trip to the Final Four in Seattle.

The favored Wildcats were so sure of winning that their coach, Rick Pitino, reserved a private room in a downtown restaurant for a victory party that night. When Smith found out and told his team before the game, Stackhouse piped up, "Yeah, I'm going to it and celebrate."

Battling relentlessly against the bigger, deeper Wildcats, Carolina withstood a physical first half in which Wallace and Kentucky's Walter McCarty were slapped with technical fouls. Leading 34–31 at the break, the Tar Heels kept going inside to Stackhouse and Wallace, got all four Kentucky big men in foul trouble and finally broke it open in the last few minutes.

Smith had out-dueled Pitino to reach his tenth Final Four with a heart-pounding 74–61 victory that was much closer than 13 points—an old-time upset on which Smith had made his reputation many years before. These were the games he loved most, unknown from the start and a test of not only his coaching but the toughness and resolve of his players. Under such circumstances, he never worried whether they'd be ready to play.

The win was especially sweet for those Carolina fans who still blamed Pitino for not guarding Grant Hill during the 1992 East Regional final, allowing Hill to accurately heave the long pass to Christian Laettner for the shot that kept Duke's back-to-back national championship drive alive.

The Tar Heels moved on to the 1995 Final Four in Seattle, where Duke had bombed out against Seton Hall in the second half of their 1989 semifinal game at the King Dome. Carolina got in trouble much earlier against its opponent on Saturday, sixth-ranked Arkansas.

Stackhouse suffered a deep thigh bruise twelve seconds into the game against the Razorbacks, the defending national champions. Leading by seven points in the final seconds of the first half, the Tar Heels tried to score on a ninety-foot pass from senior Pat Sullivan. The ball slammed against the backboard and ricocheted to half court, where Arkansas 6' 9" back-up center Dwight Stewart grabbed it and flung a desperation three-pointer toward the basket. It went in and UNC's seven-point lead was suddenly four, casting an ominous omen.

Meanwhile, Carolina's Final Four shooting woes from 1991 had returned. All season, Dante Calabria was the beneficiary of defenses worrying about Stackhouse and Wallace and Donald Williams, MVP of the 1993 Final Four. He went to Seattle shooting better than 50 percent from three-point range, which was a UNC record, but mirroring Rick Fox's 5 for 22 against Kansas in Indianapolis in 1991, Calabria missed repeated open looks that could have broken it open in the first half.

Wallace had come out to shoot around before the game wearing a stereo head set and looked just as lackadaisical in the second half trying to stop Arkansas' big Corliss Williamson around the basket. The Razorbacks took control and advanced to their second consecutive championship game, 75–68. Calabria wound up 0–7 from the arc (exactly Fox's numbers in 1991). The 28–6 Tar Heels went home bitterly disappointed because they had already beaten the SEC's best team in Kentucky.

Duke basketball had a vested interest in the 1995 championship game between Arkansas and UCLA, which defeated Oklahoma State in the other semifinal. Not only had the Razorbacks beaten the Blue Devils for the NCAA title the year before, they could duplicate—and somewhat lessen—Duke's feat of 1991 and '92 by winning consecutive crowns themselves.

UCLA's Ed O'Bannon and Toby Bailey combined for 56 points, the Bruins clobbered Arkansas on the boards and someone else besides John Wooden finally won a national championship for the school. (Wooden's last of ten titles had come in 1975 over Kentucky). That someone was coach Jim Harrick, who would be gone within two years for falsifying expense reports and lying about it to school officials.

A few weeks after UNC's 1995 season, Stackhouse and Wallace entered their names in the NBA draft. Stackhouse held his press conference in Chapel Hill, but Wallace opted for his high school gym in Philadelphia. They would be the twenty-third and twenty-fourth of Smith's players to go in the first round, joining Bob McAdoo, James Worthy, Michael Jordan, and J. R. Reid as early departures from Carolina. This marked the first time players left after their sophomore years, rekindling the debate over whether Smith could have won more than two national championships had some of his stars stuck around.

At Duke, the focus was no longer on winning NCAA titles, but whether Krzyzewski could rescue the Blue Devils from their disastrous 1995 season. Rumors persisted about his physical and mental health, but Krzyzewski cared little about what people outside his program believed and, before too long, what a few of them inside thought, too.

At his office, the atmosphere was far from a welcome-back party. Tense was more like it. For weeks, word had filtered down of Krzyzewski's anger over the lost season and Duke's fall from college basketball grace. He had regained his strength while contemplating his life, staying close to his North Durham home and puttering around the garden, his favorite hobby, and in his solitude had determined his next course of action.

"He was a different person when he came back. It was a sad thing," Donna

Keane, Krzyzewski's long-time administrative assistant, said. "The years I worked for him, he was unbelievable to my family. He did so many things for us. It was such a disappointment to see that person fade away and see someone else in his body."

On Krzyzewski's first full day back, he scheduled a morning meeting with his staff. Keane joined Gaudet and Brey, Tom Amaker and Chuck Swenson, who had returned to Duke in 1994 as director of basketball operations, around the conference table. The boss walked in, sat down, and told them all they had all failed to uphold the standards he had established. He called them all replaceable, said only *he* was synonymous with Duke basketball and that they were starting all over again.

As Krzyzewski got up and left, Keane stared blankly at Brey and thought she would faint. Brey was less alarmed, having been in rougher, coaches-only meetings when his boss was equally direct. Within weeks, however, Gaudet took a full-time teaching position at Duke, Brey accepted the Delaware job, and Keane quit altogether. Only Amaker remained on the coaching staff, and Swenson stayed on as director of operations.

Brey had had the most contact with his old boss and revealed that Krzyzewski was more involved than anyone knew, speaking with the coaches almost daily, sometimes late into the night over the objections of his wife. The fall guy was Gaudet, who stayed clear of the basketball office while teaching at Duke, rarely attending games and refusing to talk about what happened.

"I was looking ahead, not behind," Gaudet said. "I had ten great years at Duke. Let's leave it at that." When Duke celebrated its one hundredth anniversary of basketball in 2005, Gaudet did not return for the reunion. His name was left completely out of a book recounting mostly the Blue Devils' glory years.

Gaudet was older than Krzyzewski and a long-time friend who succeeded him as head coach at Army. He helped improve Duke's offense, especially with big men, and scouted opponents when he arrived after the 1983 season. That he was clearly fired for serving involuntarily as "acting head coach" remained a black mark on Krzyzewski's otherwise brilliant career. How could he have made a scapegoat of someone so important to him? Was he that mad over the Wojciechowski benching?

Athletics Director Tom Butters stayed out of any personnel decisions, insisting it was "Mike's program" and he could make any changes he deemed necessary. At the least, Krzyzewski had lost confidence in Gaudet as a leader when he needed to reinstill toughness. At the worst, Gaudet had disobeyed some direct, or implied, orders and was jettisoned like an Army officer would have been discharged in a similar circumstance.

Krzyzewski was also widely criticized for not owning the 4–15 record during his absence but, actually, had no input on the decision.

Soon after it was clear that he would not return for the balance of the 1995 season, Sports Information Director Mike Cragg called the NCAA and was told that Duke could count the wins and losses any way it wanted. Cragg wasn't allowed contact with Krzyzewski at the time and made the decision to credit all the games to Gaudet. When he returned and found out, Krzyzewski did not change it. (Noteworthy, after Utah coach Rick Majerus took a leave of absence during the 2003–04 season, the wins and losses were dumped on the Utes' interim coach, as well.)

"My main regret is not being part of the losing," said Krzyzewski, who, according to Cragg, offered to take the 15 losses on his record but not the four wins. "The fact that we lost was very, very difficult, but that's the way it is, so let's move on."

Years later, Krzyzewski insisted he still considered "Pete a friend, just not with the same frequency of contact." Gaudet went on to coach women's basketball at Vanderbilt and Ohio State and was still regarded as an expert on pivot play, but he was forever linked with 1995.

Duke's 1994–95 season represented the collapse of the nation's most successful college basketball program over the previous ten years. Rivals reveled in the fall of an empire; Carolina fans convinced themselves that Krzyzewski's reign was over and the goodness of Smith had won out again. Born were jokes about coaches with sudden back problems when their teams struggled, wise cracks that popped up any time Krzyzewski lost a couple of games later in his career.

In truth, another college dynasty leveling off was certainly not unusual. It had happened to the greatest of all, UCLA, after Wooden retired; to Kentucky before Pitino resurrected the Wildcats; to Indiana in Bob Knight's crusty final years. Most basketball historians expected Carolina to crack after Smith stepped down.

Duke's decline, however, came while the coach was still in the job, if not *on* the job, and Krzyzewski was getting a second chance. He had flirted with the pros, feuded with his athletics director and fought the effects of a debilitating back injury—but he remained the leader of the Blue Devils.

Obviously, he decided to call upon his past and act as a highly trained military leader trying to save his command. His bad-health hiatus had given him time to reevaluate his life and contemplate whether to leave or stay and reinvent Duke basketball. He chose the latter, at least temporarily.

"When he came back, he had his mind set," said Barry Jacobs, who wrote *Golden Glory: The First 50 Years of the ACC.* "He didn't want to be distracted. It was like, 'We've got to be hungry. We've got to act like we've proven nothing.' Pete Gaudet wasn't around to say, 'Remember who you used to be. Don't lose sight of that.' "

During the summer of 1995, as order was restored and the new season approached, all eyes were still on Duke. But not for the same reasons as usual.

The mid-1990s also marked a transition for Carolina. Stackhouse and Wallace leaving a year earlier than expected forced Smith to rebuild one more time. Fortunately, the Tar Heels had another highly rated recruiting class coming in, namely Vince Carter and Antawn Jamison, to fill the void.

At 6' 5", Carter was a stupendous athlete recruited by virtually everyone in the country (including Krzyzewski, who met with him at his home while lying flat on his aching back). Carter was also the high-stepping, head drum major for his high school marching band in Daytona Beach, but Smith knew he needed to learn the game and not rely on his athletic ability to jump over everyone else on the court. Always trying to lower the expectations for such underdeveloped basketball players, Smith was especially tough on Carter and made him miserable most of his freshman year.

Jamison, a wiry 6' 9" forward, had a better junior year at Providence High in Charlotte. As a senior, his averages had dropped on the court and in the classroom, making his SAT results critical. His initial scores were not high enough, and Smith expected him to spend a year in prep school before enrolling. In his last try during the summer of 1995, Jamison posted his best scores and gained admission under UNC and NCAA guidelines.

That still wasn't enough to boost the spirits in the Carolina basketball office. There existed a feeling that Stackhouse and Wallace had betrayed Smith by turning pro too soon, before he could properly plan for their departure. After Wallace made his NBA announcement in Philadelphia instead of Chapel Hill, attended only by Bill Guthridge, it appeared he did not have Smith's blessing.

Smith had actually endorsed the moves by his two sophomores, whose stock rose dramatically during the Tar Heels' run to the 1995 Final Four.

Stackhouse had made the cover of *Sports Illustrated* as its player of the year, which seemed more like a marketing move for the magazine. The consensus national player of the year in 1995 was lesser-known Maryland star Joe Smith, who was also *ACC* Player of the Year and outpolled Stackhouse in the All-ACC voting. *SI* did not give out the honor annually (doing so next, ironically, for Duke's popular superstar Shane Battier in 2001).

Despite emotional, on-court outbursts, Wallace's athletic ability and shooting touch for a big man could not be denied; a graceful 6' 10", he had long been considered a better pro prospect than Stackhouse by NBA scouts. So when Smith learned they were both lottery picks in the NBA draft—his consistent standard for underclassmen—he told them they *had* to go.

Stackhouse (Philadelphia) and Wallace (Washington) went third and fourth in the 1995 NBA draft, giving UNC eleven first-round draft choices in the foregoing ten years, including Brad Daugherty, Kenny Smith, Joe Wolf, J.R. Reid, Rick Fox, Pete Chilcutt, Hubert Davis, George Lynch, and Eric Montross. Those losses, however, were more a promotional boon for Carolina basketball than a source of pride within the program.

One day in late May of 1995, Smith walked out of his private office to find the secretaries and a couple of returning players talking quietly. He sensed a negative, somber mood and didn't like it. Uncharacteristically, he snapped at them. "We *will* field a basketball team next season," he said, ordering them to change the atmosphere and get back to work.

The big concern was at center, where the only returning big man on the roster was the 7' 2" Serge Zwikker, who had averaged three points and three rebounds in a limited role the year before. A slow, mechanical 270 pounds, Zwikker had never run up and down the court for thirty minutes a game and remained a question heading into the new season. It appeared the Tar Heels would again be only five or six deep, stealing minutes with a sagging man-to-man that protected the basket more than forcing the tempo the way Smith preferred and often made them look like they were loafing on defense.

Speculation also engulfed Duke, as Krzyzewski returned to the bench for the 1995–96 season to much anticipation on campus and around the country. Because he dropped out of sight in such secrecy, rumors persisted that he was coming back from some sort of emotional breakdown. One story had him choking a player in an ugly locker room confrontation; another that he had become addicted to painkillers; and a third that made him and his wife laugh: He was having an affair and she found out.

The forty-eight-year-old Krzyzewski maintained it was a bad back and related exhaustion. His illness resulted in an improved relationship with Butters, who had made his coach sit out the season but assured him the job was still his. Ironically, while Krzyzewski worked to rebuild the Blue Devils, it was Butters who got ill and eventually retired.

"I was so sick, I was not able to do the job at Duke," Krzyzewski said. "My mentality was, 'I'm not the only one who can do this job.' He [Butters] said to take some time, get well, come back and make the decision then. It's your job until you want to come back. I learned that you don't make important decisions when you're sick, tired, or down."

Much of what had changed was his own doing. Not only had Krzyzewski's recruiting fallen off from Duke's back-to-back national championship teams, he had just about cleaned house. He brought back former player Quin Snyder, who had earned a combined law degree and MBA from Duke and dabbled in pro basketball while he was married to the daughter of UNC icon Larry Brown. Tim O'Toole, a former assistant at Syracuse recommended by Orange head coach Jim Boeheim, was also added to the revamped staff.

Two starters had graduated from the 1995 team, bigmen Cherokee Parks and Erik Meek. Krzyzewski didn't mind, because the talented Parks still personified the softness that had infiltrated his program. Although Krzyzewski liked Meek, his father had been a pain in the ass since he and the head coach exchanged heated words over his son's playing time during his sophomore year. Meek's old man, a plumber in the San Diego area, often railed about Krzyzewski whenever he met anyone in California with Duke ties.

As the 1996 season approached, Duke lost a third starter. Sophomore Trajan Langdon developed complications from a sprained knee he suffered playing professional minor league baseball during the summer. The NCAA allowed athletes on scholarship in one sport to turn pro in another, and Langdon had signed with the San Diego Padres organization. Duke decided on surgery and a redshirt season for Langdon, a renowned shooter from Alaska.

Smith, meanwhile, had to start two freshmen for the first time in his coaching tenure. Jamison, who played center facing the basket in high school, surprised him with his quickness in the low post and averaged double figures right away. Carter played too casually for Smith and quickly lost his starting spot to the third freshman in the class, Ademola Okulaja, a tough-nosed club player from Germany.

Carolina got off to a typically fast start. Smith had been at it so long, his teaching method so ingrained, and Bill Guthridge by his side for nearly thirty years, the Tar Heels always seemed to be ahead of the curve early in the season. They won at Maryland on Jamison's buzzer-beater and rallied from 14 down at the half to beat fourth-ranked Wake Forest in Chapel Hill when Okulaja bodied up and shut down the Deacs' Duncan late in the second half. Through 19 games, they were 15–4 and had risen in the polls from an opening-day ranking of No. 20 to No. 8 heading into their biggest game of the season on the last day of January.

Duke had won the Great Alaska Shootout (in the process beating No. 23 Indiana in Krzyzewski's first meeting with his mentor Knight since their split of 1992) that had been scheduled for Anchorage native Langdon. Standing 9–2 on New Year's Day, 1996, the Blue Devils lost five of their next eight games and were a so-so 12–7 when they bussed over to the Dean Dome, where they had not won since 1991.

Ricky Price was now a sophomore enjoying his best college season, given the offensive freedom he coveted and leading the team in scoring. He scored 20 points to help Duke forge a 42–30 lead, but that advantage dwindled as the second half wore on and the nervous Carolina crowd that had been expecting a big win woke up.

In his first of four dominating career games against the Blue Devils, Jamison scored 23 points and grabbed 14 rebounds by the time the Tar Heels pulled within 72–71 in the final, frantic seconds. Duke's Chris Collins got a loose ball first and tried to call timeout, but Calabria tied him up. The possession arrow favored Carolina.

Calabria, the former role player turned primary scorer, then tipped in one of Jamison's few misses to give UNC its first lead with only seconds remaining and the Smith Center going nuts. Duke raced down the court and Price came up short on the other end, leaving the fans delirious over winning a game that looked lost for most of the forty minutes.

Carolina had completed the first half of the ACC schedule at 7–1, far better than anyone expected from a freshman-laden lineup. Smith knew it wouldn't last once opponents started manhandling the wiry Jamison and immobile Zwikker. The second time around the league, foes jammed up Jamison and pushed him out of position. With Calabria and leading scorer McInnis burdened to hit from outside, the Tar Heels dropped three straight ACC games as their offense stalled and their confidence waned.

By late February, they had fallen to 9–6 in the ACC, and nineteenth in the rankings, knocking Smith off pace to pass Adolph Rupp in all-time coaching victories. Smith seemed stuck on 849 career wins, 27 shy of Rupp's 876 total. With his freshmen struggling, Smith's chances the next year did not look much better. Because Smith claimed little interest in breaking Rupp's record, Carolina fans and his former players fretted he would retire before it happened.

The Blue Devils were also struggling as Krzyzewski tried everything to get their old consistency and confidence back.

By Valentine's Day, 1996, Duke hadn't shown him enough signs of recovery. No big man had stepped up to replace Parks and Meek, namely laid-back Canadian center Greg Newton and freshman Taymon Damzalski in the middle. The athletic, 6' 10" Newton had decent numbers, 12 points and 8 rebounds, but was still considered a flake by the coaching staff and his teammates for his eccentricities.

With the Blue Devils 13–10 and 4–7 in the ACC and almost a certainty to miss the NCAA Tournament for a second straight year, Krzyzewski called in Collins, his senior captain, and told him to sit down. Whether a ploy, or truly at wit's end, Krzyzewski said he had taken them as far as he could and what happened from then on was in Collins's hands.

Collins had already become the ad-hoc leader of the team. In January, he helped Duke break a four-game ACC losing streak and notch its first conference win at N.C. State after rallying from a huge second-half deficit. Collins made a miraculous three-pointer as he was falling out of bounds in front of his own bench. His shot hit the back of the rim, bounced high in the air and somehow dropped through for the 71–70 final.

That had been a month previous, and Duke had since lost four more games.

"It's your team now, Chris," Krzyzewski said. "Do whatever you have to do to turn the season around. If you want to take every shot, or not take any shots, it's your decision. I will back you." Krzyzewski's last resort, and perhaps his decision on whether to remain at Duke, rested on Collins's shoulders.

With Collins and Capel sharing the scoring load with Price, and Newton finally asserting himself underneath, the Blue Devils defeated Virginia on Valentine's Day and won five straight, including an upset of sixteenth-ranked UCLA and a 77–75 win at Maryland on Price's last-second shot.

Back in the running for an NCAA Tournament bid the last week of the regular season, Duke was anxious to also beat Carolina for the first time since February of 1993, three years and six rival games ago. Krzyzewskiville, which had some recent vacancies, was beginning to stir again for the Tar Heels' annual visit.

Just as Duke University was once known as Trinity College, the tent village outside Cameron Indoor Stadium did not begin as Krzyzewskiville. To a few brave pioneers, it was known as "Fostertown" for the Blue Devils' last coach, Bill Foster, who was at Duke from 1974–80.

The world's most affluent campground sprung up in 1979, the year after Duke snapped a seven-game, four-year losing streak to the Tar Heels. Desiring the best seats at midcourt for All-American Jim Spanarkel's last home game, several students pitched a tent near the gravel and hardpan lot that has since become a shrine, but Fostertown faded when its honoree moved on and another losing streak to UNC began under Krzyzewski.

Students resumed camping out in earnest in 1986, when they were sure Duke had a regular winner again. That first year, someone wrote KRZYZEWSKIVILLE in magic marker on a piece of cardboard and hung it on a tent. Eventually, an engraved brass and steel sign cemented in the ground christened the sacred camp ground during a university ceremony.

By 1992, the year of Duke's second national championship, Krzyzewskiville had grown to an unofficial record of 205 tents and was also growing out of control. Before Krzyzewski himself got involved and helped Duke take a politically correct stand, one of his own players, Marty Clark, trashed the basketball Woodstock in the local press.

"I think they're crazy," Clark said of the long-term tenants. "I've always thought they were crazy. I don't understand why you would do something like that to yourself for so long—it's cold and it's raining."

As parents bombarded the Allen Building with complaints that their $30,000 annual tuition was going toward breeding bacteria, Duke decided to organize or extinguish Krzyzewskiville. With tents holding as many as ten students, either all of them had to stay there every night or something fair and equitable would be arranged.

The ASDU (Associated Students of Duke University) governing body ruled that only one tent resident had to spend the night to save the places of all the others, but the inability to control and limit who really belonged in each tent turned it into a lawless western plain full of Easterners looking for an angle. For example, Duke athletes were known to give out the code for access to their locker room so their special friends could shower, shave, and shit between tent checks.

Conduct in the commune became mandated by an eight-page, five thousand word *Statute of Undergraduate Admissions Policy for Men's Basketball* that every Cameron Crazy had to embrace. Line monitors with bright vests and loud bullhorns, and the uniformity outside, rivaled the systematic, rhythmic cheering inside that more than one pundit likened to a Hitler Youth rally.

Krzyzewskiville developed all the comforts of a Yuppie excursion up Everest, sans the Sherpas. Duke spent $50,000 to provide wireless Internet access, T-100 telephone lines, and outlets for radios, TVs, and video games. Clean-up crews made sure to minimize the time empty liquor bottles and beer cans littered the campground. They couldn't stop occasional sex in the sooty.

Ridiculed by some schools and emulated by others, Krzyzewskiville remained a controversial phenomenon at Duke that was featured on TV and in national magazines and became the subject of a book by a brainy Duke student who, appropriately, compared the characters and shenanigans to Chaucer's *Canterbury Tales*. "But it's prose, not verse," he clarified.

Basketball was not the only religion in Krzyzewskiville, which had a large Judaic student population. One year, the Freeman Center for Jewish Life brought over an entire Friday night service to the captive, target audience. The result: Jewish tenters attended Shabbat services in a place named for the son of Polish immigrants, praying perhaps for a victory over the Tar Heels.

Local K-Marts and Wal-Marts kept full inventories of tents *after* Christmas. K-ville was the busiest winter account for the Domino's Pizza deliveryman in Durham, hundreds of them purchased by Krzyzewski himself after a particularly long vigil. Nike went there to tape commercials, if not outfit the residents with swoosh-covered clothing to keep them warm and dry.

Rules of engagement were instituted, such as everyone qualifying for the two designated "Krzyzewskiville games"—UNC and one other each season—had to be rowdies in residence a full forty-eight hours before tip-off. Each tenant had to register with a social security card or student ID. The civility allowed most kids and parents to call it a cultural experience of college life rather than sickos sleeping outside in winter.

Patience of the residents ebbed and flowed with Duke's ranking in the polls. In 1996, Krzyzewskiville had dwindled to fifty or sixty dwellings, the lowest since 1993, when those four early ACC losses and a particularly harsh January had students questioning their commitment. Those who stuck it out were hardened by their plight and determined to help the Blue Devils snap the six-game losing streak to UNC.

Once inside for the final game of the 1996 season, the Crazies waved insulting signs and chanted obscenities in what quickly deteriorated into a nasty game. Calabria and Krzyzewski yelled at each other during one on-court flare-up, and both benches did more than the normal pointing at one another.

Amidst the mayhem, Carolina came up with its best effort in a month. Jeff McInnis and Shammond Williams fired away for 51 points and the Tar Heels shot nearly 60 percent to hold a slim lead late in the game. Duke's last hope was to start fouling.

After being hip-checked into the sideline press table by Duke reserve and soccer All-American Jay Heaps, McInnis objected too strenuously to the hard contact and got thrown out of the game. This was the same kind of action-reaction that had triggered the Brown-Heyman fight thirty-five years earlier, a rough foul in the final minute. McInnis was quickly ejected with a technical foul and was nearly uncontrollable, watching the rest of the game from the end of the bench. Several photographers camped on the baseline said that when Smith walked down to calm his player, McInnis shouted, "Fuck you, old man" to the coach.

The Tar Heels hung on for a six-point decision, as they finished 10–6 in the ACC and edged out Duke (8–8) for third place. Even in victory an enraged Smith targeted the "esteemed Duke faculty" for condoning the mob mentality. This wasn't innocent fun, he thought, like the Dukies chanting "Oh, no, not (Pat) Sullivan" at one of his players. He saw the placards about assistant coach Phil Ford's widely rumored marital problems and heard the Dukies calling McInnis "Asshole! Asshole!" throughout the game. If it had been him, Smith said, he would have reacted worse than McInnis.

Krzyzewski waited for the media day before the 1996 ACC Tournament in Greensboro to respond and, surrounded by a group of writers, told Smith to clean up his own house before criticizing anyone else's. As an example, he called Smith a hypocrite for campaigning against beer advertising in college athletics while Coors sponsored UNC's radio network. This was a great example of the programs sniping at each other. Krzyzewski didn't listen to Carolina games on the radio, so someone on his staff was looking for ways to spin his side of the story.

It was 1989 and "J. R. Can't Reid" all over again.

It was also more noise than either of the teams made for the rest of the season.

Both were knocked out in the first round of the ACC Tournament. Duke, which had lost Collins to a sprained ankle late in the UNC game, fell to a Maryland team it had beaten twice in the regular season. Carolina failed to score a field goal in the last nine minutes against a Clemson club it had also whipped twice and lost when Zwikker left Greg Buckner alone on the baseline for the winning dunk.

Collectively, Duke and UNC received their lowest NCAA seeding since the field expanded to sixty-four teams in 1985.

The eighth-seeded, banged up Blue Devils were down to six healthy players, started walk-on Stan Brunson at power forward and got bounced by Eastern Michigan in its first-round game in Indianapolis. At least their 18–13 record was a symbolic reversal from the prior year's 13–18.

Carolina, a sixth seed, lost in the second round to Texas Tech in the dark, dank old Richmond Coliseum. One year removed from his third Final Four of the 1990s, the sixty-five-year-old Smith again heard his longevity questioned by fans who just seemed to want a change. UNC's 21–13 record came with a patch-work squad, and without two would-be juniors (Stackhouse and Wallace) who instead made the NBA All-Rookie team.

The seeding was validated, as neither made it to the Sweet Sixteen for the first time since Black Sunday, 1979.

Kentucky went on to beat Massachusetts and Syracuse at the Meadowlands in the 1996 Final Four, the last to be played in a pure basketball arena and the first since 1987 that did not include either Duke or Carolina, another amazing string snapped. At least one of them had made it for eight straight years (and one would be in the next five Final Fours, making it thirteen of fourteen years).

Carter and Jamison were the future of UNC's program, but Duke needed an-other good recruiting haul to get back on the Tar Heels' talent level. In the fall of 1996, Krzyzewski signed the high school senior class he hoped in two years would return the Blue Devils to the college elite: the celebrated "Killer Bs"—excellent students 6' 8" Shane Battier, 6' 8" Elton Brand, and 6' 10" Chris Burgess—plus guard Will Avery, who was taken amidst snickers from rival coaches after a Cali-fornian named Baron Davis would not make a commitment.

Duke wanted Davis badly, but moved on to Avery after Davis finally opted for UCLA. After the scandal broke that he was driving an SUV bought on the cheap from the son of Jim Harrick, still UCLA's coach at the time, Davis called Krzyzewski and said he wanted to reconsider Duke, but Krzyzewski had make the commitment to Avery and refused.

At first, Duke saw Avery's academic record and balked. He had basically stopped attending school for most of his junior year in rural Georgia. Avery had taken the SATs and reportedly scored a credible 830, which was very low for Duke but not unprecedented (Gene Banks was admitted with about a hundred points lower score in 1977).

By now, Krzyzewski had an excellent relationship with the Duke admission's office. Several questionable prospects—David Henderson and Billy King being two prime examples—had done very well, which helped Krzyzewski push the limits even further. Some of the bigger academic screw-ups—Phil Henderson, Greg Newton—had been very solid high school students, so Coach K's case was strong enough to fight for more academic exceptions.

Some coaches had seen, and most had heard about, Avery's high school tran-script, which wasn't good enough to qualify for many state universities, not to mention prestigious Duke. Supposedly, a deal was struck between Krzyzewski and the admissions office—Avery would have to attend summer school at Oak Hill Academy in Virginia, then spend his senior year there and maintain a B average in several core courses. Avery went, met the standard and was admitted. Krzyzewski had a new class of McDonald's All-Americans, who would enter school in the fall of 1997.

UNC had also recruited Elton Brand and Shane Battier.

Although Smith learned thirty years earlier how to stay ahead of the curve from Vic Bubas, he had fallen behind it again. He made the same mistake with Brand he had with another big man from upstate New York, Christian Laettner in 1988; by the time UNC seriously pursued Brand, Duke had locked him up. Carolina and Kansas were among Battier's final schools, and Duke did a better job with the scholarly son of a mixed-race couple. Smith knew his chances were not good and began his brief visit to the Battier home in Michigan by saying candidly, "Please tell me if Shane is going to Duke, so I can recruit someone else at his position."

A few weeks later, Battier phoned Smith early one morning with the news and thought the Carolina coach blew him off by mumbling something and hanging up. Battier actually woke Smith, who, as was his habit, had watched tape late into the night and slept past eight o'clock.

With the battle rejoined off the court, and Duke's great class on the way, the rivals engaged in some renewed one-upmanship during a 1996–97 season that marked Krzyzewski's rebirth as a coach and the close of Smith's celebrated coaching career.

The Blue Devils had Langdon back and two important additions. Roshown McLeod was Krzyzewski's first transfer from St. John's who had played for Bob Hurley Sr. at St. Anthony's in Jersey City. Hard-nosed freshman Chris Carrawell from St. Louis was the kind of player on which the Duke program was being rebuilt.

Early on, the chemistry was off and their coach still saw too much complacency from his time away and targeted the embattled Newton as his whipping boy. The Duke staff had been together less than two years, and Newton became such a divisive element that the coaches often argued over whether to play, or give up on, the 6' 11" senior center. Krzyzewski preferred using quicker-and-smaller Carrawell, at 6' 6", in the middle of his motion offense and pressure defense.

A good athlete who wore tattoos and pierced various body parts, Newton was yanked out of the starting lineup after a loss at Maryland in late January. Since Gaudet was credited with the two losses to the Terrapins in 1995, the game marked Maryland coach Gary Williams's first win over Krzyzewski, who the next day chewed out his team and threw Newton out of practice for his lack of effort.

At the same time, Smith relied on his patience and experience to tolerate UNC's worst ACC start, three straight losses and nearly a fourth. He applied his own firm, parental touch to his tentative Tar Heels, who were the talk of the ACC and college basketball for their uneven play and poor defense.

After they opened the season with a turnover-plagued loss to nineteenth-ranked Arizona, and then reeled off nine nondescript wins over unranked opposition, Smith was stunned by an 81–57 blowout at Wake Forest. Five days later, he stubbornly refused to call a timeout as the Tar Heels blew a 22-point lead, and the game, at home against Maryland.

Next came a 75–63 loss at Virginia, after which Zwikker shouted in his Dutch accent during a players-only meeting, "When are we going to start playing like a fucking team?"

They rallied from nine points down with 2:09 remaining to beat N.C. State at home but followed up with a loss at Florida State to stand 2–4 in the ACC, drawing rare ridicule on campus. Columnists who continued covering Carolina also wrote them off, claiming that All-ACC forward Jamison was getting little help from the "soft" Carter, the stiff Zwikker, showy Shammond Williams, and turnover-prone freshman point guard Ed Cota.

The Tar Heels faced the distinct possibility of losing to second-ranked Clemson in Chapel Hill for the first time ever, as Smith steadfastly spent extra hours watching tape and talking the players through their shaky confidence.

In his third year at Clemson, Rick Barnes had not only built the traditionally moribund Tigers into a contender, he had become the darling of many ACC fans for standing up to Smith.

During a first-found ACC Tournament game in 1995, Smith had yelled at Clemson forward Iker Iturbe after he aggressively fouled Stackhouse in the lane. Barnes objected to Smith talking to his player, and the young and old coaches went nose-to-nose at the scorer's table. The next season, Smith again yelled at Clemson guard Bill Harder for grabbing Calabria's jersey while playing defense, and Barnes blasted Smith in his postgame press conference. ACC Commissioner Gene Corrigan had to summon both men to his office in Greensboro and order them to knock it off.

"It was a situation that happened," Barnes said a few years later of Smith, whom he had followed while growing up in Hickory, North Carolina, and rooting mostly for N.C. State.

"He was basically taking up for his players. I was doing the same for my players. But I never felt Clemson fans wanted me to go after him. I would hate it if people thought that it was something I planned. I got sick and tired of talking about it. We kept competing, almost like two little kids. I obviously would never expect him to back down. He knew I would compete and not back down."

Playing Clemson was rarely a "statement game" for a program of Carolina's caliber, but because the Tigers were ranked higher and due to the Barnes-Smith feud, this one was. Clemson showed up with uncharacteristic swagger, holding its highest ranking ever and believing Barnes could actually make the school a basketball power.

Smith knew the game would have to be won on defense. He challenged the 6' 5" Carter to cover Clemson's terrific 5' 9" point guard Terrell McIntyre, keep the ball out of Buckner's hands, and cut off the Tigers' head. Using an eight-inch height advantage, Carter never let Clemson get into its offense, and Barnes's club shot 27 percent. The Tar Heels' convincing 61–48 victory reaffirmed Smith as a dangerous, if rare, underdog and underscored his reputation among his adversaries as a wily competitor even at sixty-six years old.

The win came just in time for the first Duke-Carolina game of the 1997 season, always eagerly awaited by both schools and their legions of fans. The Blue Devils were favored for the January 29 clash at Cameron, but the upset of Clemson gave the Tar Heels hope in a game that otherwise had unusually little national significance for the rivalry.

The Duke campus was still wired to break what was now a seven-game losing streak to UNC, and Krzyzewski promised the students a victory when he met with them at his annual private pep talk. Krzyzewski had started the tradition of inviting K-ville residents and other students into Cameron for an off-the-record chat and Q&A the night before the Carolina game, mainly to thank them for their support and fire them up for the next day.

Krzyzewski was more emotional than usual for the 1997 meeting. His mother, Emily, had died the previous summer, and he used her memory as inspiration to get through his grief. They had been extremely close, a working-class mother with the dream of her son attending West Point. He always called her from the locker room after every game.

He clutched his mother's Army pin as a typically taut Duke-Carolina struggle unfolded from the opening tip. Their confidence rekindled, Okulaja's breakaway dunk put the Tar Heels up on the twelfth-ranked Blue Devils by six points early in the second half, quieting Cameron as Duke took a time out and Krzyzewski summoned Newton off the bench.

Making the motivational ploy of the day before look like it had paid off, Newton responded by contributing a dunk and three-point play. Duke rallied to take the lead, but Carolina stayed within range until the last possession.

It came down to a loose ball, like the year before in Chapel Hill. This time, Duke had the possession arrow. During a time out, Smith told his team to switch on as many screens as necessary to stay with Langdon, who had already drained six three-pointers. But the Blue Devils ran the Alaskan Assassin off three picks before he finally popped free moving right at the top of the key. His seventh "three" of the night assured the Blue Devils' 80–73 victory.

A teary-eyed Krzyzewski waved thank you to the students on his way off the court.

"You beat a hell of a basketball team tonight," he told his players, adding a prediction. "I guarantee you they aren't going to lose very often the rest of the season." He showed them his mother's pin and, beginning to cry, said the win would have meant so much to her.

"I think Duke knows it was in a game tonight," Smith said, also feeling much better about his team's chances the second half of the season.

Duke finished the first swing through the ACC race at 5–3, Carolina at 3–5. Both played pretty much lights out in February.

The Blue Devils went to Wake Forest and ended a nine-game losing skid to the second-ranked Deacons as Carrawell replaced Newton at center and, like Okulaja had done the year before in Chapel Hill, held Duncan down during the 73–68 win. They won seven straight before a lackluster loss at UCLA in which the long season first began to show on their stamina and intensity. Duke had enough left to beat Maryland and sew up first place in Jeff Capel's Senior Game, where a lukewarm send-off helped UNC sign his younger brother Jason the next year.

Jeff Capel's career had gone downhill in the eyes of fans since he was the plucky freshman starter who got the ball to Grant Hill in 1994. After that, Capel and all the Duke players found out how much more difficult it was to play without Hill and the double-teaming attention he drew.

Capel's tying three-pointer against Carolina in 1995 symbolized his career; everyone remembered it but, ultimately, it came in a losing cause during a turnover-plagued season. Capel remained a scapegoat in 1996 when, in Langdon's absence, he was the go-to guy on Krzyzewski's worst-shooting Duke team and heard some boos from his own fans while missing 15 of his 23 shots during the disappointing home loss to UNC.

Nevertheless, Capel was enjoying a decent senior season in 1997 on a team with its best personnel in three years.

Carolina won the first seven games of its second swing through the ACC, seriously threatened only in a one-point win at N.C. State, and carried an eight-game winning streak and No. 8 ranking into their Senior Day against seventh-ranked Duke on March 2.

A wild, capacity crowd was in the Dean Dome long before the Sunday afternoon tip-off. Chancellor Michael Hooker, who sat with his wife Carmen on the front row of the student section, was hoisted by the kids and crowd surfed up thirty rows to the concourse level.

Through studying tape and constant teaching in practice, Smith had turned this into an efficient team that got the most out of every possession. The Tar Heels led by 9 at the half, out-rebounded Duke 49–18 and received another monster game of 33 points and 11 rebounds from Jamison. The Blue Devils trailed throughout but hung in and kept it close.

Wojciechowski had the best game for Duke, perhaps the best of his career. He scored 18 points, hit 6 of his 7 three-pointers and had 5 assists and 2 steals. The steals bugged Smith and his staff the most; they believed Wojo had perfected an old soccer trick by bodying up opponents, locking legs and then subtly pushing them to the ground while taking the ball away or forcing a travel call. The Tar Heel bench was all over the officials throughout the game, and Wojo wound up fouling out in the final minutes.

After Carolina won 91–85, Krzyzewski angered the UNC faithful in his press conference by claiming, "We didn't have the edge we would normally have," and suggested his team wasn't emotionally "up" for the game after having clinched first place in the ACC three days earlier. The Blue Devils soon proved it was more than that.

They suffered an embarrassing collapse against eighth-seeded N.C. State in their first game of the 1997 ACC Tournament in Greensboro and, a week later, took quick leave from the NCAA South Region in Charlotte with a second-round loss to Pete Gillen's Providence team after a narrow win over Murray State. That was the weekend that Gillen first cracked his joke about Duke being on television more than reruns of *Leave It To Beaver*.

Jeff Capel closed out his Duke career with 25- and 26-point games in the NCAA Tournament, but again it culminated with a disappointing defeat. He never missed a game in four years, which was part of the problem. He was asked to do too much in the Blue Devils' down period. Although he finished No. 20 on their all-time scoring list, Capel was remembered for as many bricked shots and untimely turnovers, and the experience soured his family on Duke after his name kept popping up in the speculation about coach-player confrontations.

Krzyzewski eventually mended fences by hiring Capel as an administrative assistant and helping him land the head-coaching job at Virginia Commonwealth at age twenty-nine.

Closing with a 24–9 record, Duke's demise was inside, where it had little presence and was out-rebounded as badly as Krzyzewski's early losers.

Dean Smith, in turn, had crafted an incredible comeback for his once-selfish Tar Heels. They had swept through the back half of the conference schedule, then won the ACC Tournament, their veteran coach's thirteenth title, by dethroning Wake Forest and senior Duncan in the semifinals and beating N.C. State in the championship game Sunday. With twenty-four wins on the season, what seemed impossible just a month before was almost a foregone conclusion.

Carolina fans flocked to NCAA first- and second-round games in Winston-Salem to see Smith pass Rupp's 876 career wins. Tickets outside the Lawrence Joel Coliseum, Wake Forest's home court, were selling in the high hundreds. The top-seeded Tar Heels played Fairfield on Thursday night.

Unnerved by the mounting national attention on their coach, they trailed the sixteenth-seeded Stags by seven points at the half after shooting horridly. Behind a double-double by Zwikker, the player Smith entrusted with the center position early in the season, they finally shook off Fairfield, 82–74, as Smith tied Rupp's record.

In the same bracket, Colorado upset Indiana to foil the NCAA's TV-inspired attempt to showcase Smith against Knight, the active coach with the best chance of breaking *his* record, in the second round. After the Hoosiers lost, Knight left the arena on foot and walked in the rain toward the team hotel before being picked up by an assistant coach.

For the potential record-breaker two days later, dozens of Smith's former players found their way into jammed Joel Coliseum, several flying all night from the West Coast to make the noon tip-off. Unlike most years, when CBS televised regional games throughout the first two rounds, the network aired the UNC-Colorado game nationally and announced it would carry the game in its entirety and stay through the post-game interviews.

Again Carolina was behind at halftime and again the Tar Heels rallied to win despite losing Vince Carter to a strained knee in the second half. After the 73–56 victory, as UNC fans chanted "Eight-Seventy-Seven" on their way out of he building, Smith's living legacy staged an emotional celebration with their old coach in the hallway outside the locker rooms, reducing him to gushy hellos, handshakes, and hugs with former players and their wives and kids as he passed through the gauntlet of gratitude for all he had meant to them.

After beating Cal and Louisville in the East Region in Syracuse, giving Smith his eleventh trip to the Final Four, Carolina had won sixteen consecutive games since the defeat at Duke, but the season ended the way it began—with a loss to Arizona. It also ended the way it had the last time the Final Four was in Indianapolis six years earlier, with the Heels shooting 31 percent this time.

Following the 1997 season, more changes occurred for Duke basketball. Amaker left to be Seton Hall's head coach and took O'Toole with him. Krzyzewski then decided he wanted only his former players on the staff. Whether it was because he wasn't a Dukie, O'Toole had a harder time garnering the players' respect. After one loss, he cried openly in the locker room while several Blue Devils laughed at him.

Krzyzewski hired a pair of 1986 graduates from his first Final Four team, David Henderson, whose pro playing days in Europe had ended, and Johnny Dawkins, who had retired from a successful NBA career and was back in Durham working on the Duke radio broadcasts. Copying Smith's long-time blueprint of having ex-players by his side, Krzyzewski wanted well-trained young lieutenants who did all of the grunt work.

As a young man, Krzyzewski's philosophy was to always have an "older coach" on the staff, such as Gaudet and Col. Tom Rogers, both of whom had been with him at Army. Then he realized one day that "I'm now the older coach" and it was okay to surround himself with the people who helped him get there.

"They know me," he said. "Most of the time, I don't even have to ask them to do something because they know exactly what I want."

Meanwhile, the older coach at Carolina was sure the 1997 season was his last. Smith had felt that way after the last two seasons as well, but by the time preseason practice approached he had played enough golf and spent enough time with his family that he was ready to mold another team. He had always said that when the excitement of coaching did not return by October, he would know it was time to go.

In August, Smith told UNC's newly appointed athletics director, Dick Baddour, that he was considering retirement. Baddour was on the job for barely two months after succeeding John Swofford, who had been named commissioner of the ACC. Swofford had left the department with some imminent coaching changes in baseball, golf, and lacrosse, but Baddour never thought basketball would be his first new hire.

Baddour checked with Smith periodically over the next few weeks and, as the beginning of practice approached, had reason to believe he wouldn't have to face, at least for another year, the biggest coaching change in the university's history. Those hopes crashed on Thursday, October 2, 1997. Smith informed Baddour and Chancellor Hooker that he had decided to step down but wanted one more weekend to make sure. Smith was hosting his alumni coaching clinic over the next three days and held private meetings with several of his former assistants, as well as having phone conversations with some of his oldest and closest friends.

Larry Brown was already in Chapel Hill, having brought his Philadelphia 76ers team there for training camp as he had done with the Indiana Pacers for the four previous years. Smith did not confide in Brown right away because he did not want to distract his oldest protégé as he was putting together his first Philly team, but he used Brown as a barometer over the weekend. Periodically wandering in to the Smith Center, where the 76ers practiced during the mornings and evenings, Smith was amazed by the fifty-seven-year-old Brown's enthusiasm for coaching. Smith doubted he still had that kind of fire, and not even his chalk talks with the alumni coaches generated the level of excitement he had always demanded of himself.

When Smith told those closest to him, one by one, they were saddened but not surprised. They had seen him throughout and at the end of recent seasons, and Smith appeared increasingly exhausted by the demands on his time. The ultimate private person, Smith insisted on going through the stacks of mail and correspondence that cluttered the desk in his office. If he could have just prepared practice plans and coached his team, he might have stayed another year or two.

On Wednesday, October 8, 1997, a week before practice began for the new season, UNC sports information director Steve Kirschner started calling out-of-town writers to say a news conference "concerning the men's basketball program" had been called for 2:00 P.M. the next day. At the same time, as media converged on Chapel Hill, the word was leaking out that Smith had told Baddour he was through.

Smith left his office about six o'clock and said, "We're having a press conference and it's about men's basketball, so I guess I have to be there."

Larry Brown was with his old coach for his last official day on the job. So was long-time friend John Thompson, the Georgetown coach who flew down from Washington to attend the historic press conference. They hugged and cried together in private, but Smith did most of the comforting. He had considered retirement from all angles and knew he had made the right decision. Aside from his voice cracking when he said how much he would miss his players, Smith was among the most composed people in the room.

For years, their political leanings aside, UNC alumni and fans had looked to Smith for moral leadership. To them, he was far more than a coach. They regarded his much-publicized principles and ethics as a blueprint by which to live, choosing to dismiss some of the obvious contradictions as human foibles. Smith chain smoked until 1988, always admitting it was a bad habit he longed to change. He never cursed or was accused of cheating in recruiting. He treated his players, from the biggest star to the last man on the bench, like his own children. He won, but with compassion for the loser.

Right down to his nasal voice that many people mimicked, imitation remained the biggest form of flattery.

He wasn't perfect, and that was part of his charm. Some men his age had heard of how Smith agonized over whether to end his first marriage in the mid-1970s. That gave them comfort if things weren't going just right in their own relationships. When he did divorce, and wed a woman fifteen years younger in 1976, it was probably no coincidence that a number of UNC alumni felt it was okay to leave their unhappy marriages as well and start new lives. Despite rising to be a king of the court, Smith never disconnected from the common folk in idealism or practice.

Among Smith's last official duties was to call the two recruits who had already committed for the following season—Jason Capel and Kris Lang—and their families to make sure they knew that nothing, except the head coach, was changing about Carolina Basketball. They said they would still sign with UNC in November, although both were obviously hoping to play for Smith at least part of their careers. Capel barely considered Duke because he had witnessed how tough his older brother, Jeff, had it playing for Krzyzewski and in front of the critical Cameron fans. Lang, who had been raised by a single mother in Gastonia, North Carolina, was looking to Smith as a father figure as well as a coach.

At the press conference, Smith confirmed he was stepping down and handing a returning top-10 team led by juniors Jamison and Carter to Guthridge— "letting Bill take over" as Smith told the media throng, more than a hundred UNC athletics department personnel, coaches, and athletes, and a few dozen fans who sneaked into the emotional scene in the cavernous Bowles Hall. Students congregating outside held WE LOVE YOU, COACH placards against the windows.

Well-wishes and congratulations poured in from friend and foe, alike. Krzyzewski was one of the first people sought out by the media for a comment about the end of this historic chapter.

"I'm going to miss him; I loved competing against him," Krzyzewski said.

"He was the best to compete against, and he brought out the best in you. Even when I was a young coach, he always treated me with respect. He never big-timed you. That's an example I've always tried to use."

Dean Smith's retirement after thirty-six seasons may have shocked the rest of college basketball, but it brought some unexpected relief at the University of Kansas, where Roy Williams was in his tenth season after ten years on Smith's staff at Carolina, the first eight working seven days a week as UNC's restricted-earnings assistant coach.

He had gotten the job in 1988 with the prospect of Kansas going on NCAA probation for recruiting violations under the regime of former coach Larry Brown. Williams's honeymoon season, while the Jayhawks served a one-year sanction, got off to a fast start, and the team and rookie coach survived eight straight losses in February to finish 19–12. Williams then began a string of twenty-plus-win seasons and NCAA Tournament invitations to become a KU fixture.

During the decade of the 1990s, Smith's old friends and fellow alumni at Kansas showered him with compliments about how good, how healthy, how *young* he looked. They wanted him to work forever, because if he did there was no chance they would lose their coach and Smith's protégé.

Since he had begun achieving success on his own, Williams figured he would someday face the question of whether to leave Kansas and return to UNC. This was a foregone conclusion among Carolina's inside family of former players and coaches; namely Smith, Guthridge, Brown, Eddie Fogler, and Williams, plus their financial advisor, Bill Miller. Because Smith always insisted he would retire *before* the start of the next season rather than in the spring, there would be a transitional step.

That group had convened after the 1995 season at the Florida condominium of Bill Miller, the Charlotte-based investment broker who died of cancer in 2002. They played golf and talked some about the future of Carolina basketball. As with everyone else in the group, Williams believed that, whenever Smith decided to step down, Guthridge should first get the job for as long as he wanted it.

The transition was as seamless as a legend leaving could be. Besides keeping the entire program running with precision, Guthridge was a savvy talent scout and one of the best big-man teachers in the country. He had earned the chance through his three decades of loyalty and richly deserved the head-coaching chair and all of its perks.

Smith stayed on as a consultant to Baddour. He eventually swapped offices in the basketball suite with Guthridge and gradually weaned himself away from the daily operation, but he still retained the ultimate say on who would follow Guthridge.

Or so he thought.

Smith has since confirmed that his plan was for Williams to take over whenever Guthridge, in turn, decided to retire. There was no set time frame; it could be one year or five.

"All Coach Smith told me," Williams said, "was to be ready, he (Guthridge) doesn't know how long he's going to do it."

Williams was prepared to go when Kansas ruled the newly expanded Big 12 Conference but kept getting bounced out early from the NCAA Tournament. Despite building the highest winning percentage among active coaches, with a streak of ten consecutive twenty-win seasons and earning high NCAA seeds almost ever year, Williams had not taken a team back to the Final Four, and advanced as far as the Elite Eight only once, since 1993.

In 1997, for example, Kansas had lost only two games (34–2), won both the Big 12 regular season and tournament and remained No. 1 in the polls for a school-record fifteen consecutive weeks. The lineup was loaded with big men Raef LaFrentz and Scott Pollard, All-American forward Paul Pierce and guards Jerod Haase and Jacques Vaughn, but the Jayhawks lost to late-blooming Arizona in the Sweet Sixteen round in Birmingham, and Williams went home devastated.

Amazingly, with such success, things had gotten a bit stale in Lawrence, and both the school and coach seemed ripe for change. Truth be told, Williams felt betrayed by the seedy side of recruiting, which had become more cutthroat than ever with the infusion of shoe companies and AAU leagues into the mix. For the first time in his ten years at Kansas, he had also run afoul of a few sportswriters who questioned his squeaky clean image.

One, *Basketball Times* columnist Dan Wetzel, criticized Williams's role in the sordid recruitment of Kansas City prep star Jaron Rush, befriended since early childhood by a wealthy insurance man, KU graduate, and Jayhawk booster Tom Grant. A rangy 6' 7" slasher, Rush had lived the good life off Grant, who paid for his private schooling, put braces on his teeth, gave him $300 a week spending money, and leased a new GEO Tracker that he allowed Rush to drive as his permanent car. Rush was also the star of Grant's Nike-sponsored AAU Children's Mercy Hospital 76ers, coached by one-time crack cocaine dealer and Nike pitchman Myron Piggie, exposed in Wetzel's 2000 bestselling exposé *Sole Influence*.

Kansas withdrew its scholarship offer to Jaron Rush after he criticized Williams's frequent substitution methods on a statewide radio show. Williams was furious, but the situation smelled bad for long before that.

The 76ers represented all that was wrong with summer basketball, according to many college coaches, as Piggie filled the roster with local prep stars that included Rush's younger brother, Kareem, and recruited out-of-town talents such as high school All-Americans Korleone Young and Corey Maggette. Nike's national sales manager, former college coach George Raveling, supplied the 76ers with shoes and uniforms and, according to Piggie, gave them $50,000 for travel expenses.

As the 1997–98 season opened, Williams did not know how long he would remain at Kansas but was fairly sure it wouldn't be forever. He had sent his son Scott to Carolina, where he played jayvee basketball for two seasons and had made the varsity as a junior. His daughter Kimberly was a freshman and had just made the UNC dance team. Williams made one in-season visit to Chapel Hill during a recruiting trip each year to catch both of their squads in action.

He still had family and close friends in the mountains of North Carolina, where he grew up, taking his golf posse there for a week every summer. He and his wife, Wanda, bought their first beach home at Wild Dunes outside of Charleston, where he spent as much of the summer as his schedule allowed. Among his guests there were as many people with Carolina connections as Kansas.

Of course, there were certain heavy hitters in Kansas who hoped to keep Williams as long as he coached. They were making plans to give him a $5 million annuity that would mature after his twentieth season. Others wanted to put it in writing that if he stayed, Williams would either have his name added to Allen Fieldhouse or a brand new arena in Lawrence.

Even on the clearest Kansas day, Williams's future remained foggy.

JFK was president and the Beatles were a bar band in Liverpool the last time UNC had a different head basketball coach. That year, 1961, Carolina and Duke had staged their famous fight that cost UNC coach Frank McGuire his job and resulted in his thirty-year-old assistant taking over.

Thirty-six years later, Dean Smith left, dominating the Duke series (59–35) after beating Krzyzewski 24 times out of 38 games in 17 seasons of head-to-head combat. His combined record against the other Duke coaches he had engaged— Vic Bubas, Bucky Waters, Neil McGeachy, Bill Foster, and Pete Gaudet—was 35–21. Bubas beat Smith the first seven times their teams played, but after that, the Carolina coach defeated Duke almost 2–1.

Only after Smith departed did the Blue Devils take command of the rivalry. Despite having lost eight of their last nine games to Carolina, Krzyzewski had put them back on firmer footing than in the previous three years and Duke was poised to dominate. Beyond victories, Krzyzewski was building a power base at Duke that would surpass Smith's at Carolina. His influence reached clear across campus and into the prestigious alumni ranks, where he knew how to get what he wanted.

Cameron Indoor Stadium finally received the long-awaited updates Butters had been promising beyond cosmetic changes of brass railings and mahogany trim to the upper level that had been made in the late 1980s. The real work began with a new concourse (named for Bubas) added to the west side and the new dressing rooms underneath that replaced the cramped quarters with old-timey wire lockers. Ground was also broken for a new basketball administration building as part of Duke's $75 million athletic facilities renovation.

Krzyzewski's new office was originally planned for two stories, but he lobbied for something much bigger outside the brick courtyard adjacent to Cameron and Krzyzewskiville. When Butters suffered a heart attack in the fall of 1997 and stayed out of work for nine weeks, Krzyzewski pressured Duke President Nan Keohane to make it six stories and include floors for weight training, a players' lounge, and women's basketball. He agreed to help her raise the extra money for what would become K's castle where he overlooked the Duke campus.

That became the precursor to the Legacy Fund, a spin-off of the Iron Dukes athletic booster club and dedicated solely to men's basketball. With Krzyzewski making a half-dozen personal visits a year to ask for minimum gifts of $1 million, the goal of the Legacy Fund was to endow all men's basketball scholarships and raise a principle balance of more than $50 million that could also be spent on capital improvements. It eventually paid four full-time employees, including one of Krzyzewski's daughters as director of external affairs, basically the head coach's PR woman.

Whether coincidence or natural evolution, Krzyzewski's ascension to Smith-like status happened as his long-time rival had ended his era. Once referred to as "Mike" by those he worked with him in his early years at Duke, his colleagues, alumni, and fans reverently called him "Coach K"—no longer the cheesy nickname that it had seemed in 1980. "Coach Smith" had the same respect; even fifty- and sixty-year-old former players didn't dare call him Dean.

Such coaches held the rest of their universities hostage because of their popularity and power, mainly the money their programs made to support other sports. While not the most important thing at Duke and Carolina, basketball was the most visible. Winning seasons had a documented effect on applicant pools, fund-raising, and the sale of licensed products—all benefiting the university rather than just the athletics department.

Of course, the basketball programs themselves generated millions through TV rights, tournament payoffs, and ticket sales, far in excess of their seven-figure budgets. Smith was not hesitant to remind his "bosses" at UNC that he brought in more than twice what he spent, so chartering NBA planes for road games and staying at five-star hotels was his prerogative. Duke traveled in the same lap of luxury.

Smith and Krzyzewski, Midwesterners from modest means, wound up wealthy beyond their wildest dreams. Above their university salaries, radio and TV deals paid them hundreds of thousands of dollars for an hour at the microphone or a half hour in front of the camera each week. Krzyzewski, in fact, gave up his radio show after getting sick in 1995, turning it (and presumably the money) over to his assistant coaches. Income from their sold-out summer camps was split between the head coach and those assistants who ran them.

Nike wanted the Blue Devils and Tar Heels to wear their shoes on national television and made massive deals with both coaches. Besides saving Duke and UNC money by providing shoes and apparel, Nike paid Smith and Krzyzewski millions in consulting fees, which they considered tantamount to bonuses awarded CEOs at profitable corporations. Smith got mild pushback on some of his endeavors, mostly because he worked at a regulated state university. Krzyzewski pretty much did what he wanted, as long as everyone agreed it was good for Duke, too. Every year, it seemed, his name graced a new program on campus, a charity he supported or a product he endorsed.

Smith retired comfortably, his five children grown and out from under his responsibility. Krzyzewski wanted and needed more every year, as his daughters married and his grandchildren began arriving. With an annual income almost forty times his original Duke salary of $48,000, Krzyzewski exceeded Smith's standard for aristocracy and envy. A joke among Duke athletics department employees was the "coach's handshake"—palms open, pinkies touching, in a receiving manner.

K might have stood for "king," but Krzyzewski was now also the dean of college basketball.

Guthridge, whom Smith put in the job to reap some of those financial rewards, inherited a battled-tested team in 1998. The Tar Heels opened ranked fourth, won their first 17 games and climbed to No. 1 by mid-January.

Infused with young talent to join veterans McLeod, Wojciechowski, Langdon, and Carrawell, Duke's roster was reminiscent of those Krzyzewski had while winning the national championships. He had again signed tough, as well as talented, kids to bring the Blue Devils back to where he wanted them.

Duke began as No. 3. Despite losing freshman Brand, their leading rebounder, with a broken foot after 12 games, the Blue Devils won 20 of their first 21 games and took over the top ranking after Carolina lost its first game at Maryland on January 14, 1998.

No. 1 Duke and No. 2 Carolina played on Thursday, February 5, marking only their second meeting (the other was in 1994) as the two top-ranked teams. The nationally televised game, in a packed Smith Center, was close early in each half before the alley-ooping, hot-dogging Heels exploded for big runs triggered by Jamison's scoring in the low post.

In Lawrence, Kansas, watching at O'Henry's because it was the only place in town that had ESPN2, teetotaler Roy Williams kept his back to the bar crowd and marveled at Jamison's play, thinking he was even quicker around the basket than the James Worthy he had known at UNC.

Carolina's first big lead disappeared when Makhtar Ndiaye's personal foul and ensuing technical sparked a Duke rally. Then the Tar Heels broke it open for good late in the second half. After getting blown out *twice* in the same game, a contrite Krzyzewski conceded, "They're the real deal."

Afterward, ESPN revealed that it had put a clock on Jamison every time the quick-twitch forward touched the ball and calculated that his 35 points against Duke came in a cumulative fifty-two seconds of possession.

A week before the rematch, the Cameron Crazies had a surprise visitor to Krzyzewskiville, UNC's Shammond Williams. In the first half of a game at Virginia on February 11, Williams had left the bench in tears after a smart exchange with Guthridge. Williams, who belonged to a black fraternity headquartered in Durham, heard the Dukies were planning to taunt him and wave Kleenex and made a preemptive strike at the tent village on Friday night to spend time socializing with student adversaries.

The next afternoon, Carolina suffered a fourteen-point loss to unranked N.C. State at home; on Sunday, the Blue Devils welcomed Brand back to the lineup by crushing UCLA 120–84 and reclaiming the No. 1 ranking. They won easily at Georgia Tech and went home to prepare for the regular-season finale, Senior Day for McLeod and Wojciechowski, against the Tar Heels who had dropped to No. 3 in the polls.

An unprecedented media crush for both the UCLA and UNC games left Duke denying access to some reporters, who were told they had to watch the games on television in Card Gym. Due to 70-degree weather, Cameron was both bursting *and* sweltering when Carolina arrived on Saturday afternoon, February 28, 1998.

The veteran visitors opened as hot as the air, hit almost everything they threw up, and led by 12 at the break. Krzyzewski came out for the second half wearing a golf shirt under his suit jacket, ostensibly because he had sweated through his dress shirt; actually, he had torn it off raging at his players, calling them "fucking pussies" for their soft play under the basket. Cameron continued to bake and Carolina continued to lead, once by 17 points, before Duke climbed back into the game.

Fueled by Brand's 16 points while abusing the Tar Heel big men trying to halt his bullish moves in the paint, the rally required nearly every remaining tick of the second-half clock. The Blue Devils finally took the lead on the last of McLeod's 23 points, and UNC missed potentially tying free throws by Cota and freshman Brendan Haywood as time expired.

Wojciechowski, who had 11 assists, ran directly into the arms of Krzyzewski after his five hundredth win as a head coach. As they bear-hugged, tears streamed down both of their faces. A few feet and seconds removed from the heartfelt scene, Duke fans erupted in a wild celebration that for most of the game they never figured on having.

One student jumped into the mass where the Tar Heel players were trying to get off the court. Startled by the body flying at him, UNC's Okulaja greeted the Crazy with a quick right hand punch that split his nose open and bloodied his face. Okulaja kept moving through the throng as ushers rushed the student to the first aid station. A bitter dispute between the two programs and schools was expected.

Police officers visited both locker rooms to take statements from witnesses. Okulaja claimed he was defending himself, and after several conversations between school administrators Duke Sports Information Director Mike Cragg talked the student out of pressing charges or suing. Fearful the publicity might result in stricter postgame rules that would be impossible to enforce, Duke managed to keep the incident quiet.

The 77–75 victory secured a second consecutive ACC first-place finish for the 15–1 Blue Devils, who remained ranked No. 1 after nine straight wins. The enigmatic Tar Heels finished two games behind and dropped another notch to fourth heading into the ACC Tournament in Greensboro.

Their consistency waning at times, Guthridge appeared powerless to keep them at an even keel. He still called it "Dean's team" and coached like it was on autopilot, leaving the leadership to his "six starters" Carter, Cota, Jamison, Ndiaye, Okulaja, and Williams, whom he rotated alphabetically as the first sub off the bench. This seemed strange because Ndiaye was clearly the sixth best of those players and, as a transfer, did not rate the same say as upperclassmen who were recruited as freshmen. But Ndiaye was one of two seniors and popular with his teammates, so Guthridge chose the rotation over a potential morale problem.

Clearly, Carolina's talent pool was the best in the country and, despite Duke's higher ranking and regular-season title, the Tar Heels were tabbed the ACC Tournament favorite. It was widely held that All-American juniors Jamison and Carter were heading for the NBA and bent on winning both the conference and national championships.

Enormous interest, and rampant speculation, followed the rivals as they advanced to the championship game on Sunday, March 8, at the Greensboro Coliseum. Jamison had strained his groin in the overtime win against Maryland in the semifinal, and UNC trainer Marc Davis doubted he could play against the Blue Devils.

Guthridge considered holding Jamison out, but his team needed a second win over Duke for the NCAA selection committee to keep it in the East Regional, which was scheduled back in Greensboro after first- and second-round games in Hartford. When Jamison took the court for warm-ups, he told Davis and Guthridge that his groin felt fine. Hurting or not, the player Guthridge often called a warrior wasn't missing this game.

The Tar Heels broke out early, led 40–36 at the half and repelled Duke's second-half comeback by scoring the last 15 points of the game. The 83–68 victory touched off a wild celebration for Carolina's second consecutive ACC championship. The once-doubtful Jamison had played all forty minutes, scoring 22 points and clearing 18 rebounds to win the tournament MVP.

In the Heels' hysteria, the cocky Carter and Shammond Williams began drumming with the UNC pep band, and several players danced on press row. Remaining in the coliseum and watching from their first-row seats were members of Krzyzewski's family. Ndiaye mounted a table directly in front of them and pounded his heart, making dramatic stabbing gestures that the Duke contingent believed were directed at them.

Krzyzewski did not see the incident but, after hearing about it from his wife and daughters, used his NCAA Tournament press conference the following day to criticize Carolina for allowing its players to posture in such a way. He specifically questioned Ndiaye's graphic celebration that certain athletes used to depict "killing" an opponent.

Newspapers printed letters to the editor, mostly critical of Krzyzewski, which merely confirmed to him the "Carolina bias" that he long believed existed in the local and statewide media. He had not bothered to contact Guthridge or Carolina before going public with his criticism.

In a press conference that sounded a lot like one of Smith's, Krzyzewski also whined about Duke being sent "out of our natural region"—clearly mimicking his old adversary's habit and further inflaming the relationship with UNC. No one reminded Krzyzewski of his sarcastic plea made five years earlier that, "If I ever acted like [Smith], someone take a gun and shoot me."

No comment came from Chapel Hill except a private snicker from Linda Woods, the long-time basketball office secretary. "They still lost the game," she said.

Raw from the wounds of insult, the rival camps watched each other closely as their teams entered the NCAA Tournament as No. 1 seeds in different regions, the Tar Heels in the East and Blue Devils in the South.

The more fanatical fans had a game to worry about each day, either theirs or the enemy's. In the macro, the goal was to reach the Final Four and win the national championship. In the micro, the pressure was on UNC to win one day and for Duke to hold serve the next.

Carolina opened the tournament with a 36-point blowout of Navy on Thursday, March 12, at the Hartford Civic Center; Duke routed Radford by the exact margin on Friday in Lexington, Kentucky. The Tar Heels survived overtime against fired-up UNC-Charlotte on Saturday; the Blue Devils barely beat Oklahoma State on Sunday to also advance to the Sweet Sixteen.

UNC returned to Greensboro and wore down a young Michigan State team that would win the national championship two years later. Twenty-four hours after the Tar Heels' victory came Duke's regional semifinal in St. Petersburg, where the Blue Devils dispatched Syracuse by 17.

Now it was a UNC-Duke weekend, two of the Elite Eight vying for spots at the Final Four in San Antonio.

Carolina held off Connecticut's second-half rally, dealing coach Jim Calhoun and the Huskies their third regional final loss in nine years. Carter sealed the 75–64 decision with a breakaway in which he turned in midair and laid the ball in as the Tar Heels reached their second straight Final Four and fifth in the 1990s.

In the South championship game the next day, Duke began losing a 17-point lead over Kentucky midway through the second half. Krzyzewski stubbornly stuck with Wojciechowski, who was beaten repeatedly by the Wildcats' Wayne Turner, instead of using quicker, inexperienced Avery.

Going into the game, Krzyzewski knew he would be at a disadvantage in the backcourt. He had hoped that Ricky Price, now a senior who had returned after a first-semester suspension, could become his stopper with his long arms and quickness—the kind of perimeter defender he needed against Turner. Price had refused to accept that role and, when he did get in that season, seemed more determined to try to make spectacular offensive plays.

Kentucky completed its remarkable rally with a barrage of three-pointers to pull out the 86–84 victory for the final spot in San Antonio with Stanford, Utah and Carolina. Actress and UK graduate Ashley Judd celebrated in the Wildcats' locker room with the players. Duke was distraught, having blown a chance to win another national title.

Even though they were no longer on a collision course, the archrivals still stuck it to each other that weekend.

Hundreds of UNC students had poured from the bars on Franklin Street on Saturday evening after their win for the Final Four. While many also cheered Duke's defeat the next day, Krzyzewski made pointed remarks in his postgame press conference of how "classy" Kentucky had been in victory. The zinger referenced the way the Tar Heels had whooped it up two weeks earlier at the ACC Tournament.

Oddsmakers favored Kentucky and Carolina to advance to the national championship game at the Alamo Dome on Monday night. The Wildcats needed overtime but finally subdued Stanford in the first Saturday semifinal. The Tar Heels waited around nervously for an extra twenty minutes before they could come out to warm up.

If there was ever a time for Guthridge to come off his alphabetical starting lineup, this was it—the biggest game of the year and the statistics right in his hand.

Shammond Williams was the odd man out who had shot poorly coming off the bench all season—almost 10 percentage points lower than as a starter. Plus, Williams was already wary of the depth-perception difference in domes compared to basketball arenas. At Indianapolis the year before, he had gone 1–13 against Arizona and missed 7 of his 8 three-pointers; he could have used the confidence boost of starting his last Final Four. But Guthridge stayed with the routine.

The Tar Heels fell behind Utah by double digits three minutes into the game. Williams went in and, immediately trying to shoot his team back in the game, found the Alamo Dome as unforgiving as the RCA Dome had been the year before. He again fired bricks from beyond the arc, missing 10 of 12, most of them not even close. Inside, Jamison couldn't find the basket either and Carolina's comeback fell short. After the 65–59 loss, Jamison kissed the NCAA logo on the floor, a sure sign he was turning pro.

The poor performance was not only a bitter pill, but it turned ugly when, after the game, Ndiaye accused Utah's Britton Johnsen of calling him a "nigger" during one tussle under the basket. UNC's season ended on unsavory and controversial notes, as the embarrassed Tar Heels suffered negative national publicity as they headed home with a 34–4 record.

Butters, who had retired as Duke's athletics director in late February of 1998, attended the Final Four as a former member of the NCAA Basketball Committee. He was removed enough from his old job to admit he was pulling hard for the Tar Heels in San Antonio. Encountering some UNC alumni on the trip back, he seemed generally disappointed their school had fallen short.

"You had the best team," Butters said. "I know because I watched you kick our ass twice—no, two-and-a-half times—this season. So I had no doubt you were going to win the whole thing."

Having learned on the way home that Ndiaye made up the charge against Utah's Johnsen, Guthridge had him issue a public apology. He also seriously contemplated quitting, angry that one of his players would tell a lie borne from the frustration of losing. A transfer from Michigan by way of Wake Forest, Ndiaye apparently did not understand how an act so callous would humiliate Carolina's tradition-rich program.

The UNC campus fell into a low mood, as students waited for spring to arrive in full bloom. Guthridge was in Los Angeles in late April when Jamison won the Wooden Award, UNC's first national player of the year since Michael Jordan in 1984. Roy Williams was also there. He told Guthridge that, if he decided to retire, it was a good time to leave Kansas because he could coach his son, Scott, a rising senior reserve at Carolina. Williams believed his Kansas players would accept that reason.

The Jayhawks had endured another disappointing finish in 1998. They won 35 games and again swept through the Big 12 regular season and tournament. But they went out to hot-shooting Rhode Island in the second round in Oklahoma City. Bashed for his fourth straight NCAA Tournament wipeout as a No. 1 or No. 2 seed, and feeling the pull of his alma mater and family, Williams was ready to leave Lawrence that spring if Guthridge quit.

Had Carolina won the national championship, it likely would have been one and done for Guthridge, but he couldn't walk away on such a season-ending sour note and decided to return for a second year.

As expected, Jamison and Carter entered the NBA draft and were lottery picks, fourth and fifth to Toronto and Golden State (which then swapped them). Some highly recruited players remained, but no superior talent of the last five years. In October, Guthridge got a commitment from a potential superstar, Joseph Forte, whom he could have used right away.

UNC appeared to be hanging on with leftovers. The Heels won their first eight games, including the preseason NIT, to reach No. 3 in the rankings. As the season stretched into the new year, the opposition got wiser and made their weaknesses more apparent. Except for Okulaja, who emerged as a senior to make All-ACC, nobody stepped up to help a good team become great. That platitude went to Duke after an early hiccup.

Over Thanksgiving, the Blue Devils lost to fifteenth-ranked Cincinnati in the final of the Great Alaska Shootout, which Krzyzewski returned to for the second time in four years so Langdon got another chance to play in front of his family, friends, and fans after being injured during the 1995 tournament. Langdon's college career added to his legend in Alaska where, for example, he had been the guest speaker as a *junior* at a rival high school. *Sports Illustrated* listed him as the No. 1 athlete ever out of the forty-ninth state; the only other contemporary celebrity of note from Alaska was his eighth-grade lab partner, a young singer who went on to be known as Jewell.

From the loss in Alaska, the Blue Devils morphed into greatness. They defeated No. 9 Michigan State (the first of four in a row over coach Tom Izzo's team), third-ranked Kentucky, fourth-ranked Maryland and won at No. 8 St. John's before going home to play Carolina, which was hanging on at No. 10 despite three losses in the last eight games.

Some Duke students, probably figuring their team would win big, were up to no good. The morning of the game, UNC officials discovered that Michael Jordan's oversized No. 23 retired jersey had been pilfered from the steel girders of the Dean Dome. Not surprising since UNC pranksters had swiped Grant Hill's ACC Athlete of the Year trophy from a glassed case the year before. They notified their Duke counterparts, who canvassed Cameron and the surrounding area and found nothing.

Duke gave up, believing that if the jersey materialized it might magically appear in the crowd that night where two thousand students couldn't be arrested en masse. Such skullduggery was common the week of the Duke-Carolina games every year, when at least something got slapped with the opposite shade of blue paint.

Mike Sobb, Duke's sports marketing director, was standing outside Cameron that afternoon and noticed a wire running from one of the trees on the west side of the building. The maintenance staff found the wire ran through an open window at the top of the gym and was connected to rolled-up garment stuffed in the rafters. They cut the wire and Jordan's jersey unfurled from the sky—with the No. 23 doctored with tape to a *33*, which was Hill's number at Duke. Only a few people saw what would have been among the greatest pranks in the rivalry's history.

The Tar Heels played conservatively in Cameron, attempting only five three-pointers, and hoped their superior size could pound out an upset. With Cota, now a junior, on his way to a career-high 20 points and 7 assists, they trailed by only 4 at halftime and were killing Duke on the boards. But a 12–1 run secured a fifteenth consecutive win for the Blue Devils, who put all five starters in double figures to demonstrate their versatility if not their vigor.

Krzyzewski harped on rebounding before the rematch in Chapel Hill. Carolina was within two at the half after Cota threw in a prayer at the buzzer. Behind Brand's 13 rebounds and 11 from freshman Corey Maggette, Duke dominated the boards and won its twenty-fourth straight game, but more impressively became the first team to run the table (16–0) in the nine-team ACC.

Clearly, Duke basketball was back on top of the ACC and the rivalry and needed only a return to the Final Four to reclaim the full measure of its national prominence. Unlike the early 1990s, however, Krzyzewski's program looked more like a small corporation than the pride of the school's athletics department. Smith had always pooh-poohed that sovereignty, but Krzyzewski operated like it was the only way to assure its success in the future.

He wanted absolute and total control. He decided that Assistant Athletics Director Chris Kennedy, the academic guru of Duke athletics who was once responsible for every athlete's eligibility, should no longer be in charge of the basketball Blue Devils. Krzyzewski hired his own academic counselor who also had other duties but all within the program.

While adhering to NCAA rules about the limits on (four) assistant coaches, Duke's bench began growing with guys in dark suits who had titles. Retired Army Colonel Tom Rogers, whom Krzyzewski had known since Army, was still around for home games as a special assistant. The new academic counselor was also the recruiting coordinator, and eventually those positions were split into separate jobs. In later years, adults held titles of assistant player development director, head team manager (there were as many as twelve student managers) and assistant intern. When those who sat at the end of the bench stood along the home baseline at Cameron for the National Anthem, they stretched beyond the basket.

Most of them had specific in-game duties and some carried clipboards, charting every kind of statistic imaginable, stuff that Krzyzewski once privately chided Smith about. At time outs, they came bounding off the bench with towels and water bottles and stat sheets. Ushers at Cameron began calling them the "flying monkeys" for their high-energy routine while Krzyzewski talked to the team.

Carolina looked much the same with Guthridge in Smith's seat. There were assistant coaches with their own clipboards and several managers to tend to the players and wipe off the coaches' chairs so they wouldn't soil their expensive suits. The long-time trainer, Marc Davis, sat at the end of the bench with any out-of-uniform players, and the student managers either sat with him or behind the team. Once considered the model for college basketball programs, the operation somehow looked less regal than what was happening down on the Duke end where Krzyzewski appeared more like an intimidating, sideline CEO than a basketball coach.

The Tar Heels' 22–8 record in 1999 also paled next to their top-ranked rival's 29–1. They had beaten just one ranked opponent—No. 14 Clemson to extend the Tigers' 0-for-Chapel Hill streak—since November and entered the ACC Tournament hoping for the best. They got it by avenging two regular-season losses to fifteenth-ranked Maryland when Okulaja threw a court-length football pass to sophomore Brian Bersticker for the winning dunk.

Unfortunately, they drew Duke for a third time in the ACC championship game and got the worst whipping of all. The Blue Devils' 23-point victory confirmed their brilliance of 19 consecutive wins over conference opponents and the frustration coming out of the Carolina camp.

Cota, who never seemed to get any better, gave up 29 points to Duke's sophomore Avery and, incredulously, still insisted his team was as good as the Blue Devils. "He's not so hard to guard," Cota said of Avery, as sportswriters tried to keep their faces straight. On the other side of the locker room, Okulaja was saying, "Nobody can beat Carolina but Carolina."

The absurd statements became a point of ridicule for the Dukies, who chased another NCAA title as the No. 1 seed in the East. The third-seeded Tar Heels went west and faced fourteen-seed Weber State in Seattle.

The 1999 season seriously damaged the contemporary Duke-Carolina rivalry, because the Blue Devils were the best team in the country and UNC looked like the program in decline.

Giving up 36 points to Harold "the Show" Arceneaux—matching the most relinquished by the Tar Heels in the NCAA Tournament since Purdue's Rick Mount thirty years earlier—Carolina got bounced by the Broncos. The loss resonated across the nation and at home; Duke students began buying Weber State T-shirts on the Internet and saved them to taunt the Tar Heels when they came to Cameron the next season.

Long before that, the media was having a renewed field day with the pettiness of the rivalry. Back in 1992, the night after Duke had won its second NCAA title in Minneapolis, UNC grad and columnist Mark Whicker and several fellow sportswriters parodied a few stanzas of the country and western song, "Here's A Quarter, Call Someone Who Cares," entitled "Dean's Lament."

> *I won it all in Old Montreal*
> *When Duke couldn't beat Delaware*
> *Now K has Hurley and I go home early,*
> *Here's a quarter, call someone who cares.*

On the night Weber State stunned Carolina, about a dozen North Carolina writers were in Charlotte covering Duke's early NCAA games. They got together in the hospitality room of the media hotel, chugged a few beers and added some new verses, one referring to Krzyzewski having an official on his side, as Smith supposedly had for years.

> *K's still in the Final Eight,*
> *While we lose to Weber State*
> *You get calls like those, when you've got Larry Rose,*
> *Here's a quarter, call someone who cares.*

Riding a thirty-one-game winning streak that included four double-digit wins in the 1999 East Regional, Duke was the solid favorite to win its third national championship, but when the Blue Devils arrived in St. Petersburg, their coach was not on his game. Krzyzewski was popping more and more painkillers to soothe a damaged hip scheduled for replacement surgery after the season.

Leading Michigan State by 12 at the half of the national semifinals, Krzyzewski sent Quin Snyder to do the mandatory exit interview with CBS, a practice he had started with his assistants to give them national TV exposure. While other head coaches wondered how Krzyzewski could skip what was supposedly a requirement of the new TV contract, Duke fans fretted that he was in too much pain to face the camera, one on one.

Michigan State used a zone in the second half after Brand sat down with four fouls and cut Duke's lead to three points. Consecutive three-pointers by Avery and Langdon (his only trey of the game) gave the Blue Devils breathing room and they hung on for a 68–62 win. Brand had 18 points and 15 rebounds despite missing a good deal of the second half.

Connecticut, in its first Final Four, whipped Ohio State to set up its fourth-ever NCAA Tournament meeting with Duke and the third since 1990. Whether overconfident or in too much pain, Krzyzewski canceled full practice the day before the game and held only a team meeting and walk-through, puzzling his staff, his own players, and the fans who found out.

Third-ranked UConn was formidable in its own right with Richard Freeman, "Rip" Hamilton, and Khalid El-Amin. The Huskies had held the No. 1 ranking for two months, longer than Duke, but had portrayed themselves as underdogs against a team that had been perfect since the November 28 loss to Cincinnati, thirty-two games ago.

"We're going to shock the world," El-Amin said in a taped interview upon entering Tropicana Field. Announcers from Digger to Dickie V. and Nantz to Packer admired El-Amin's pluck but still picked the Blue Devils.

Jake Voskuhl, UConn's great white hope of a center, took only one shot and scored two points but forced the game into the hands of the guards by limiting Brand's touches. Trailing 75–74 with the ball and a chance to win on the last basket, Duke disdained a timeout and hoped to score before the Huskies set their defense. Langdon drove up court, tried to reverse his dribble and fell down as the ball—and the national championship—slipped away.

The outcome stunned the Blue Devils and their fans.

Critics roasted Krzyzewski for the last play, but it was sound strategy. Langdon, in his last college game, already had 25 points on 7 of 15 shooting. Avery had missed 9 of his 12 shots and was shaky with the ball all night. At the end of the first half, Langdon had gone one-on-one against UConn defensive ace Ricky Moore and converted a four-point play. Krzyzewski clearly designated him to make something happen on the final play and accepted responsibility for it after the game.

"They did a good job funneling me toward the sideline," Langdon said. "I got tripped a little bit. I tried to get a shot off but I was stripped."

"It was clean; everything about the game was clean," Krzyzewski added.

Duke's pain was again Carolina's party. In Chapel Hill, students dropped furniture from the balconies of high-rise dorms on South Campus, and diagrams of the botched last play hit e-mail list servers almost immediately. It began a stretch of misplaced pleasure for UNC's fan base that filled the void of their own significant wins with enjoyment over Duke losing big games and a string of players bolting for the NBA.

ONE RISETH, ANOTHER RETIRES

The Dukies had an easy comeback, pointing to Carolina's early ouster from the NCAA Tournament, the loss that wouldn't go away and kept the critics on Guthridge about how long he would stay. Once again, an embarrassing end to the season left him in conflict. Close friends and associates *knew* he was in it for the short run, more because Smith had asked him than because he wanted to be a head coach.

Still, Guthridge was assured he could keep the job as long as he wanted it and go out on his own terms. Three losses to Duke and getting whipped by Weber State weren't exactly his own terms.

RIVALRY RECORD IN THE 1990s
- Carolina won 14; Duke won 10

HOW THEY DID IN THE DECADE
- Duke 271–78 (.777); Carolina 270–78 (.776) [*Note:* Carolina beat Duke seven straight, 1993–96; Duke beat Carolina five straight, 1999–2000]
- Coach K vs. Dean Smith: 14–24 (missed 2 games in 1995)
- Guthridge vs. Duke: 2–4

DEAN VS. DUKE
- All-Time: 59–35
- Dean's record at Duke/Cameron Indoor Stadium: 18–18

ACC CHAMPIONSHIPS
- Duke 1992, 1999; Carolina 1991, 1994, 1997, 1998

FINAL FOURS
- Duke 1990, 1991, 1992, 1994, 1999; Carolina 1991, 1993, 1995, 1997, 1998

BEST QUOTES
"Only Carolina can beat Carolina."
> (Ademola Okulaja, 1999)

"Only Duke can beat Duke."
> (Nate James, 2000)

8

THE FALL OF AN EMPIRE

During the 1999 season, even as Kansas overcame the departure of stars Paul Pierce and Raef Lafrentz to the NBA, Roy Williams was still thinking about North Carolina. Despite the Jayhawks losing nearly 55 points per game of scoring from the year before, Williams brought them along masterfully to tie for second place in the Big 12 and dismantle Oklahoma State in the championship game to win a third straight conference tournament.

At the NCAA Midwest Regional in New Orleans, they defeated Evansville and then lost an overtime heartbreaker to defending national champion Kentucky. The 23–10 season was among Williams's best coaching accomplishments, but all the talk that weekend was about his *next* job at North Carolina. A regular topic of conversation for more than five years, the speculation increased because a new biography on Dean Smith said Williams would bolt from Kansas whenever Bill Guthridge decided to leave the Tar Heel bench. Williams angrily denied that report but knew Guthridge came close to quitting after the 1998 season and was seriously considering it again.

By now, it was like a double whammy for Williams. He had no idea how long Guthridge would coach, and he faced even more questions about his own longevity at Kansas every time he visited with high school stars and their families.

He had landed a mother lode recruiting class, beating Duke for forwards Nick Collison and Drew Gooden, and adding athletic guard Kirk Hinrich. They were all good young players and better kids who allowed Williams to enjoy the process more than he had in years. None of them, however, wanted to commit unless he committed to them for four years. Frustrated with the Carolina situation and comfortable again with the idea of remaining at Kansas, Williams gave them all his word.

Privately, Williams beat himself up for spending so much time worrying about KU *and* Carolina. He felt like he was responsible for two teams and hated the fact that he couldn't control his own anxiety as much as he disliked the distraction itself. When Guthridge decided to stay for another season, after contemplating retirement, Williams told Dean Smith that he was focusing on Kansas, period. If UNC ever came open, he would think about it again.

Williams did go to Chapel Hill that spring, but not for good. In May, he attended graduation ceremonies for his son, Scott, whom he once hoped to coach as a walk-on guard for the Tar Heels. They took a family picture, Roy and his wife Wanda, his daughter, Kimberly, a sophomore at UNC, and Scott in his light blue cap and gown. They all smiled happily, and Williams went back to Lawrence with a new resolve—that he would finish his career at Kansas.

Meanwhile, Duke set another record in June of 1999 when four players, three of them underclassmen and three of them starters, were selected in the first round of the same NBA draft. The Blue Devils also lost a back-up center projected to be a starter, which in other years would have been manageable. The departures came with both consent and controversy and seemingly depleted the Blue Devils to also-ran status in the ACC.

The starters (sophomores Elton Brand and Will Avery and senior Trajan Langdon) and a sixth man (freshman Corey Maggette who scored as many points per minute as any starter) had left a team that *couldn't* lose the national championship, but did. Plus, since-forgotten sophomore Chris Burgess transferred to Utah, his home state university, closer to his disgruntled family.

Ken Burgess had bugged Mike Krzyzewski about his son's playing time and called the Duke coach "petty and dishonest" over what he said was a broken promise that the Killer Bs (Chris Burgess, Elton Brand and Shane Battier) would play together on the front line. Burgess actually started 17 games as a sophomore, but his minutes faded as Battier emerged.

"I won't say Coach promised me certain miracles," Burgess said, "but he did guarantee Elton, Shane, and I would play together."

His father was less diplomatic about Krzyzewski.

"If you aren't on his good side, he doesn't fix that," Ken Burgess said. "If you are, you can do no wrong. Like Shane Battier—he can't do anything wrong. He (Krzyzewski) has no sons, and he picks one of the boys to be his son, and he can do no wrong. Even the players called Shane 'Shane Krzyzewski.'"

Battier was one of three returning players who visited Krzyzewski at his home while he recuperated from his first hip replacement surgery amidst widespread rumors of the mass exodus. Together with Chris Carrawell and Nate James, they wanted to know if Krzyzewski had confidence in those who were coming back. When the coach demonstrated that he did, unwaveringly, Carrawell said, "If you have faith in us, that's all we care about."

Brand's exit was expected, given his foot injury as a freshman and his status as reigning national player of the year, and strongly supported by Krzyzewski. Brand had little else to prove on the college level, and his family in working-class upstate New York could use the money. Accordingly, he was picked first overall by the Chicago Bulls and signed a guaranteed $13 million contract.

Langdon went on the eleventh pick to Cleveland, getting the boost of coming from a great program that many Carolina players had enjoyed over the years. Duke provided the kind of publicity someone like Langdon from the outpost of Alaska might have never received otherwise. A deadly shooter, for sure, Langdon's speed, ball handling, and defense were considered pro liabilities, but he had won so much, and played for Krzyzewski, so the Cavaliers gambled with their first-round selection.

Duke's next two draftees gave Krzyzewski as much heartburn as the first two had given him pride.

Maggette virtually disappeared after the season, unduly influenced by an overblown column in his hometown *Chicago Sun-Times* written during the 1999 NCAA Tournament by Sam Smith (who authored *The Jordan Rules*) that said he would go first in the draft to the Bulls. Maggette was already the subject of an NCAA probe into his summers of AAU ball before he enrolled at Duke. He was naively led to believe that if he came out, the Bulls would make him one of their three lottery picks that year.

Plus, his family was hurt that Krzyzewski gave him less than eighteen minutes a game and benched him late against UConn in the 1999 national championship game. Most importantly, the mess in Kansas City the summer of 1997 between his junior and senior years in high school had put his college eligibility in jeopardy.

Prosecutors in Missouri were trying to nail admitted cocaine dealer Myron Piggie on a new scam. In 1987 they couldn't prove that Piggie dealt enough drugs for a ten-year prison term, but then Piggie was funneling Nike money to members of his Children's Mercy Hospital 76ers AAU team. Paying amateurs was not technically illegal, so they charged Piggie with conspiring with his players to defraud several NCAA schools by keeping their payments secret.

Duke had gotten in on Maggette late in the fall of 1997 after losing recruits Danny Miller to Maryland and Dane Fife to Indiana. Krzyzewski recruited Maggette through his prep coach and wound up beating Stanford for his commitment. He did receive a vague warning that players on the 76ers were paid and there might be some dirty laundry with Maggette, but the official probe in

Kansas City did not come out until after Maggette had turned pro. The real fault of coaches like Krzyzewski (Dean Smith, and Roy Williams, etc.) was their continued association with Nike, a company that exploited child labor in Southeast Asia and remained an influence with AAU basketball by underwriting teams like the 76ers.

Nearly one hundred credits shy of graduation, Maggette applied to enter the draft the week before the deadline and went No. 13 to Seattle, from where he was immediately traded to Orlando. He eventually admitted accepting AAU money, but Duke got off because it was ruled to have had no knowledge of what happened during the summer of 1997. Otherwise, the Blue Devils' 37 wins in 1999 in which Maggette played, including their second-place in the NCAA Tournament, could have been forfeited.

Krzyzewski badly wanted Avery back for one more year, his junior season, to help groom incoming freshman Jason Williams and give Duke *some* depth in the backcourt. Without him, the Blue Devils would have only one true guard among their top nine players. So when Avery promised him he would return, Duke still looked like the team to beat in 2000.

But Avery did not keep his word. He entered the draft and went to Minnesota on the fourteenth pick, right after Maggette. That led to controversy and a story in *ESPN The Magazine* that infuriated Dukies everywhere.

The basis of the ESPN article was a meeting between Krzyzewski and Avery's mother, who traveled to Durham from her home in Augusta, Georgia, where she lived just above the poverty line and worked at a power plant until she got laid off. That Avery might turn pro miffed Krzyzewski because he had made a personal commitment to helping him and thought he owed Duke another year.

"Your son is going to fuck my program," Krzyzewski told Terry Simonton, Avery's mother, according to the magazine story.

"Coach K got bad-mouth, rude, personal. He forgot who he was talking to," Simonton was quoted.

Krzyzewski did not deny he used such language. "I talked to William like I always talked to William," he said in the article. "I told him what I felt was the truth. If you don't want to hear that, you're not going to like what I say. But that's what I owe William."

Simonton countered, "Coach K is selfish. He talks about a so-called close Duke family. But he just wants to protect his program. He lied to us about where William would go in the draft. Late in the first round? Maybe even second round? Come on. Even I could pick up the papers and read he was going earlier than that."

The article had another twist that further angered Duke. Published in August of 1999 and entitled "The Blue Flew," it was written by 1965 UNC grad Curry Kirkpatrick, inflaming the controversy. The story chronicled all of the Duke departures, including assistant coach Quin Snyder leaving to take the Missouri job, but the Avery coverage obviously hurt the most.

Kirkpatrick was a long-time Duke nemesis, just as 1977 Duke graduate and best-selling author John Feinstein was considered a Carolina antagonist by their fans and athletic officials. Feinstein infuriated Tar Heels after the 1991 ACC Tournament when he penned a controversial column in the defunct *National* sports daily depicting Smith as "A Winner And A Whiner." He also publicly predicted, correctly, in 1995 that Rasheed Wallace would turn pro after his sophomore season, and said Wallace had stopped going to class. Smith denied that part of it vehemently—at first reacting, "You have to remember, John is a Duke graduate"—and while Wallace did enter the draft he could have returned to UNC for his junior year.

Kirkpatrick said he told his editors at *ESPN The Magazine* not to assign him the Duke story because he "knew no matter what I wrote or how it came out, it would seem to the Duke people overwhelmingly negative, prejudiced, and one-sided." During Kirkpatrick's days as senior college basketball writer at *Sports Illustrated,* he claimed to be identified "as an NC guy" by those associated with Duke whenever and wherever he covered the Blue Devils. Feinstein has said the same about Tar Heel loyalists.

Kirkpatrick had interviewed Krzyzewski for the story at a high school all-star camp in Indianapolis in June of 1999, sitting with him on folding chairs at the far end of the court in clear view of other coaches in attendance. They spent a half-hour together, during which Kirkpatrick said he took careful notes because he expected a strong response from Duke after Simonton's remarks were published.

After the story came out, Mike Cragg, Duke's sports information director at the time, wrote a harsh letter to John Papanek, editor of *ESPN The Magazine,* claiming Krzyzewski did not use curse words with Simonton and that the article was slanted because of its author. Cragg also said Kirkpatrick was no longer welcomed at Duke athletic events.

Over the next few months, others recanted the story. Simonton said that Krzyzewski never cursed in front of her, and Avery allowed that while his coach used profanity he did not hear any with his mother. Avery also said he believed Krzyzewski had his best interest in mind when he asked him to stay one more year and polish his skills. That, of course, was borne out by Avery leaving the NBA before his three-year guaranteed contract was up.

In December of 1999, Kirkpatrick requested a media credential for Duke's home game against DePaul. Cragg, who was also most miffed by the repeated use of the derogatory term "Dookies" in the article, said there were no more press seats available. Kirkpatrick got into the game on a ticket from DePaul Athletics Director Bill Bradshaw and eventually had his press privileges restored at Duke.

Nevertheless, the hard feelings hardly went away. The next time he covered a Duke-Carolina game in Cameron Indoor Stadium, Kirkpatrick wound up on the wrong side of *both* schools.

As the turn of the century approached, and college basketball continued to grow and change, the biggest question at Duke was: Could the Blue Devils manage to rebound from the early NBA losses—as Smith and Carolina had for three decades?

Robert McAdoo, the junior-college transfer and lynchpin of UNC's 1972 Final Four team, was the first player to leave early. Smith replaced him with another eventual first-round draft choice, Bobby Jones. Next went James Worthy and Michael Jordan, national players of the year, followed by J. R. Reid in 1989. UNC still had the highest winning percentage of any college program in the decade. In the 1990s, Rasheed Wallace, Jerry Stackhouse, Vince Carter, and Antawn Jamison left a total of six college seasons on the table, but that didn't stop the Tar Heels from reaching five more Final Fours. Guard Jeff McInnis also gave up his senior year against the advice of Smith, who wanted him to stay for the 1997 season and replaced him with freshman Ed Cota (the Tar Heels made two straight Final Fours anyway).

Now that the same migration had begun with Krzyzewski's program, could the Blue Devils do as well?

After having his hip replaced, Krzyzewski held a midsummer press conference and addressed the issue. He said the early departures had a domino effect, allowing underclassmen to get recognized before their time. "If Jamison and Carter don't leave UNC early, Elton Brand's picture is not on all the preseason magazines," he said. "Kids are widely publicized before they've had a chance to do very much."

Fortunately, Duke had taken advantage of Smith's retirement and signed two of the best recruits in the country. Jason Williams and Mike Dunleavy narrowed their choices to the two rivals and both made decisions based on who was coaching at one school and who wasn't coaching at the other.

Carolina cooled on Jason Williams because he wanted to play point guard (Guthridge considered him more of a small shooting guard), and the Heels had the celebrated Ronald Curry on their roster. Krzyzewski said he had a spot for

Williams and would give him the ball, just as he had Bobby Hurley, Jeff Capel, Chris Collins, and Steve Wojciechowski as underclassmen.

Dunleavy might have gone to Carolina had Smith still been active. Mike Dunleavy Sr., the long-time NBA coach, played for Frank McGuire at South Carolina and against UNC. He sat with Smith in the Dean Dome during their official visit and said he could see his son as a Tar Heel. Mike Jr. and his mother, however, both favored playing for Krzyzewski, who must have known something because he passed on higher-rated Californian Casey Jacobson (Stanford) to wait on Dunleavy.

Along with Alaskan Carlos Boozer, who was signed late after Brand announced he was leaving, Williams and Dunleavy positioned the young Blue Devils to maintain their domination over the ACC in 2000, despite playing a one-guard lineup all season. Krzyzewski was healthy again, teaching and more engaged in practice than he had been in three years. Duke's stars were Carrawell and Battier and the emerging Jason Williams at point guard.

The Blue Devils opened the 2000 season with two straight defeats for the first time in forty-one years, but they beat themselves both times with horrendous shooting at the Coaches vs. Cancer Classic in New York. They hit less than 30 percent in an overtime loss to thirteenth-ranked Stanford and weren't much better in losing to top-ranked UConn the next night.

Just like the year before, they went on a tear, winning 16 straight games before going to Chapel Hill on February 3 for an expected mismatch. Carolina had lost four straight games for the first time in eight years and, despite a veteran lineup and hotshot freshman Joseph Forte, couldn't seem to get it together. The Tar Heels had opened the season ranked fifth but had already lost three games at home and dropped out of the polls by the time Duke got to town.

The Heels' fan base was howling for Guthridge's scalp, saying enough was enough for the veteran coach who supposedly never wanted the job anyway. When they were down by 17 points at the half, the students who had lynched Dean Smith in effigy thirty-five years earlier were now angry middle-aged men watching somewhere. But basketball was still two halves.

Duke was up 19 with fourteen minutes left when Cota led a dramatic Carolina rally. Racing the second-half clock the Heels suddenly played to their preseason hype, chopped away at the lead and tied the score at 73–73 on Forte's three-pointer with five seconds left to force overtime. But three inside feeds and layups by Boozer gave the Blue Devils a record sixteenth consecutive ACC road win and dealt the Heels a fourth loss at home.

Unranked for the remainder of the season, Carolina lost to Duke for a fifth straight time on Carrawell's Senior Day, when the Weber State-clad Crazies went especially nuts over Battier hitting six three-pointers and hanging 30 on the Tar Heels. It was a record-breaking afternoon for the program.

Duke finished 15–1 and first in the ACC for the fourth straight season, completing a three-year run of going 46–2 in conference games that included new marks for consecutive victories at home (31) and as well as away (24 and counting). Krzyzewski won several national coach of the year awards for sustaining his success in light of the early NBA losses.

Struggling UNC, which concluded the regular season 18–12, avoided what surely would have been a sixth straight defeat to Duke by sleep-walking through its 2000 ACC Tournament opener against Wake Forest and letting the Deacons take the hit in the semifinals. After the half-hearted loss to Wake, Guthridge appeared despondent at the press conference and the UNC fat cats *were* furious at the tailgate dinner between sessions. Boosters besieged Rams Club officials demanding that something change.

"It's up to Dean, it's up to Dean," one club officer repeated, holding up two palms.

Two days later, Duke took home a second consecutive ACC title by swamping Maryland in the championship game to secure the top seed in the NCAA East Regional, where it was favored to roll on to another Final Four. Reflecting the Blue Devils' surprise success, unheralded Carrawell won ACC Player of the Year. Krzyzewski, who had been named coach of the *decade* (1990s) by his peers, also won ACC Coach of the Year for the fifth time.

Having lost four of its last six games, Carolina limped to a No. 8 seed in the South on the basis of an 18–13 record and third-place in the ACC (9–7) and was expected to be an early out. If the Tar Heels got by Missouri (coached by former Dukie Quin Snyder) in the first round, they would certainly be sent packing by top-seeded Stanford.

March can be so maddening, however, and Carolina pulled off a crazy comeback that no one saw coming.

Humiliated by their play going in, the resuscitated Tar Heels handled Missouri and took advantage of the No. 1 seed most vulnerable to their size and quickness. Finally playing to their preseason promise, they clobbered Stanford inside and won on freshman Forte's late three-pointer with the shot clock expiring.

At the South Regional in Austin, Texas, they rallied to beat fourth-seeded Tennessee at about the same time top-ranked but tired Duke was losing to eleventh-ranked Florida in the Syracuse Sweet Sixteen; just like that, they had a chance to trump the Blue Devils by making it all the way to Indianapolis. Two days later, Forte's 28 points were too much for Bill Self's last Tulsa team, and un-ranked UNC became the worst-rated team to ever make the Final Four.

Carolina's Ratings Percentage Index (RPI) of 41 was the highest of any Final Four team since the NCAA began using the standard. Wisconsin had an RPI of 32, Florida 18 and Michigan State, the only top seed making it, was 13, to fill out the weakest Final Four in history. Duke had a higher RPI than all of them, but its lack of depth proved fatal after relying on a versatile six-man team all season. The Blue Devils had faded in the second half against Florida; instead of a second consecutive Final Four, they had to settle for going home with a 29–5 record.

For a change, Carolina had lasted longer in the tournament, which was as important to many Tar Heels as making their second Final Four under Guthridge and UNC's sixth in the last ten years. Their second-half rally against Florida fell short, but how the Tar Heels completed their 22–14 season was more than enough to make their fans happy.

They could also throw Krzyzewski's new standard back in his face, that the team with the longer NCAA run had the better season regardless of what hap-pened in the head-to-head games. Duke had beaten Carolina twice but flamed out in the East Regional. Carolina had somehow rallied to not only upset Stan-ford but make another Final Four when least expected to do it. Who had the bet-ter year in 2000? It was arguable.

It also played right into the speculation that Guthridge could now step down and allow Roy Williams to come home at last. The UNC faithful thought it had seen the foreshadowing two weeks earlier in an NCAA second-round game in Winston-Salem, where eighth-seeded Kansas took on No. 1 Duke.

During the second half, Krzyzewski and Williams were nose to nose at the scorer's table, arguing with official Lenny Wirtz about Krzyzewski's complaint that Williams was out of the coach's box.

"Mike, I'm yelling at my players, not the officials,'" Williams shouted.

"You're still out of the coach's box," Krzyzewski countered.

"Bullshit!" Williams told him, inches from his face.

It was something neither coach considered a big deal after Duke won 69–64. Nevertheless, the confrontation stayed on the minds of Carolina fans through their team's return from Indianapolis. They clamored to know how long Guthridge would stay, most believing the timing was better than ever for his re-tirement with honor and a transition to the Williams era.

Having fallen back in love with Kansas, Roy Williams found himself wishing that Guthridge would coach forever at Carolina. The Rush-Grant-Piggie controversy had passed, and Williams couldn't see leaving his prized class of rising sophomores that had renewed his faith in the recruiting process.

"If it weren't for them, I would have left college coaching; that's how disillusioned I had become with recruiting." Williams said.

Collison and Gooden had started as freshmen and Hinrich played in every game, starting the last 13. Kansas did not place first in the Big 12 or win the conference tournament for the first time in six years but, ironically, the 1999–2000 Jayhawks gave Williams one of his most satisfying seasons. He loved his young team and was merely defending it when he clashed with Krzyzewski, no message intended.

Although Kansas had dropped 10 games for the second straight season and suffered its worst Big 12 finish since 1989, his first year in Lawrence, Williams was losing no significant seniors and looked forward to coaching Collison, Gooden, and Hinrich as upperclassmen. Then Smith called in May of 2000 to tell him the sixty-three-year-old Guthridge was definitely retiring but wanted to wait until after UNC's summer camp ended in late June to announce it.

Williams said he wouldn't know what to tell his players, and Smith advised him to say it was best for his family and that KU would hire an excellent coach. Over the next few weeks, as Smith confided to several close friends that "Bill is stepping down, and Roy's coming," Williams could not get comfortable with the idea of taking the job he had wanted for most of his professional life. The harder he tried, the closer he felt to Kansas.

As late as three days before Guthridge announced his retirement, Williams tried to talk him out of it while Smith continued scripting words and phrases for his protégé to use with his Kansas players.

Williams and Guthridge spoke on Thursday, June 29, about how hard it would be to tell their respective teams. "There's one difference, though," Williams said. "You're retiring. I'm trading my players in for another group."

UNC abruptly called a press conference for Friday. More than to announce Guthridge's retirement, it was a celebration of his remarkable interim period. He won more games than any other head coach in his first two seasons (58), tied Everett Case for wins after three years (80) and joined two distinguished coaches who were working when Guthridge played at Kansas State. Like Guthridge, Ohio State's Fred Taylor reached two Final Fours in his first three years. In distinction, they trailed only Cincinnati's Ed Jucker, whose first two Bearcat teams won NCAA titles and his third lost the national championship game in overtime.

Guthridge's day also touched off an agonizing week that unfolded across the states of North Carolina and Kansas. Dean Smith sat on the dais and was almost glib about his role in selecting the next Tar Heel coach. He interrupted Athletics

Director Dick Baddour once, saying, "We know a little something about basket-ball," and clearly implied the decision, like the one to elevate Guthridge, would be his.

News swept through the press conference that Roy Williams would issue a statement that night, followed by the obvious speculation that he was resigning at KU to become Carolina's new coach. Compelled to say something, Williams appeared at his own press conference in Lawrence with Athletics Director Bob Frederick, wearing a black shirt and looking somber.

He said he faced the most difficult decision of his life, leaving no doubt that he had been offered the UNC position, and asked for a few days to consider whether he would return to his alma mater. That surprised Smith and those in the loop at Carolina, who were counting on Williams to be in Chapel Hill over the weekend and then introduced as the new coach on Monday.

Smith spoke to him that night and again suggested what he should tell his players. Although Williams wanted a few more days of contemplation, Smith re-mained confident and assured assistant coaches Dave Hanners and Phil Ford at lunch on Monday that "Roy's coming; of course he's coming."

Williams spent the weekend prior to July 4 at his beach house outside Charleston. He had dinner one night at his favorite restaurant, Hank's, when the head bartender brought a sparkling light blue drink over to his table.

"I know it's a tough decision, coach, but this is what I think you should do," the bartender told him.

He visited Chapel Hill on Tuesday, July 4. The Carolina campus had emptied out for the holiday, and no one except insiders knew he was there. When he men-tioned how much he loved North Carolina barbecue, UNC Sports Information Director Steve Kirschner and a colleague drove more than an hour to get a pound of pulled pork for him to take back to the beach. Meanwhile, Williams met with Smith and Baddour, played nine holes of golf with UNC pro Johnny Cake and walked the deserted campus.

"I was hoping for some kind of sign that this was the right move at the right time," Williams recalled. "But it never came. I went back to the beach still unsure of what I was going to do."

Carolina offered Williams a seven-year contract. Bill Miller, his financial ad-viser, continued working on the details of the deal. His goal was to craft the best contract a college basketball coach had ever signed, but more money and perks were the last things Williams cared about. He was already wealthier than he had ever dreamed.

Williams flew back to Kansas City after the holiday to find bed sheets hang-ing from overpasses between the airport and Lawrence begging him, DON'T GO!

Hundreds of people held vigil outside his office at Allen Fieldhouse and his secretary had hundreds more supportive e-mails waiting for him inside. Someone had chalked PLEASE STAY on the sidewalk.

Although he had told his best golfing buddies the week before that he was probably playing his last round with them as the Kansas coach, Williams couldn't pull the trigger. On Thursday morning, July 6, he went to see KU Chancellor Robert Hemenway and said he would make his decision that afternoon but needed to spend a few more hours by himself on campus.

Hemenway led Williams through the side door of his office so he could avoid dozens of reporters and cameramen waiting out front in the 100-degree heat. At about 2:00 P.M., Williams called Frederick and said he was staying. Then he phoned Baddour at home and told him he wouldn't be coming after all. At the same time, Baddour's cell phone rang; it was Smith who learned the bad news for himself.

Baddour was back in his office when the *Charlotte Observer* Web site broke the story in midafternoon that Williams would remain at Kansas.

"What do we say to the media?" Baddour asked Kirschner.

"We have to say something; they're all hanging around outside," Kirschner said. He then led the athletics director to meet with the throng of reporters and cameramen who had been camped in the Smith Center parking lot for almost a week.

Baddour said the expected under the circumstances; he was disappointed with Williams' decision and the university would move ahead to hire the next best coach available. The glaring omission was Smith, nowhere to be found and leaving Baddour to answer the question everyone asked, "What happened?"

The timing, once so good for the move, was all off. Had Guthridge retired after either the 1998 or 1999 seasons, Williams would have made the transition back to Carolina almost as smoothly as fans at both schools had come to expect it since he began winning big at Kansas.

During each of his last several seasons in Lawrence, Kansas people knew that Williams returned to UNC to see his son Scott's team play and watch his daughter Kimberly on the women's dance team. That he also remained friendly with influential Tar Heel alumni, including then Chancellor Michael Hooker, only fueled speculation that Williams would answer when summoned.

No one in the loop could be blamed for assuming Williams was coming. After all, during that spring trip to Florida with Dean and his other disciples, the plan had been hatched for Williams to follow the Smith regime and continue the Carolina family tradition. It turned out to be too risky because Guthridge did not know how long he would coach.

In retrospect, promoting the lifetime assistant was far more to honor his service to the program than insure its future. Rival coaches had been waiting for Smith to retire, and such a long transition gave them more reason to say UNC's salad days were history. Smith may have anticipated a slippage in recruiting, but he figured Williams would fix it on the back end.

Williams has insisted he never promised anyone he'd take over at Carolina, that it always depended on when the job opened and the ongoing circumstances at Kansas. "I don't think they were listening," he said later.

Nevertheless, he got strong feedback from old friends and associates in North Carolina, criticizing him more for prolonging his decision a week and then allowing KU to hold a pep rally of sorts in the football stadium, where twenty thousand Jayhawks fans watched his press conference on the big screen.

"I'm staying," he said simply to a huge roar. Then he uttered the phrase he lived to regret, that this was the last such press conference they would hold unless he was "dying or retiring."

At the time, Williams didn't realize just how bad that looked to the people of his home state. "By then, I just wanted it to be over," he said.

It was just beginning for Carolina, which had no Plan B because of Smith's assurances that Williams would take the job. Many critics, Tar Heel fans among them, blamed what happened next on the two-year decline of UNC basketball. This soap opera could not have been created; it involved a new chancellor who hadn't moved to Chapel Hill yet, an embarrassed athletics director, and a Hall of Fame coach who felt insulted in his own home.

Nebraska Chancellor James Moeser had been named to the same position at UNC in April of 2000. He was finishing up his tenure in Lincoln and literally packing boxes when he learned of Guthridge's retirement. Like everyone else, he assumed Williams was leaving Kansas to return to Carolina. That pleased Moeser, who had been on the KU faculty for twenty years from 1966 to 1986 and had followed the Jayhawks' success under Williams.

When Williams turned UNC down, Moeser spoke with Baddour, who had met the new chancellor briefly and established a long-distance relationship with him. Baddour had not enjoyed the same confidence level with the impetuous Hooker, who had died suddenly in 1998 from acute lymphoma. Moeser asked Baddour what they were going to do now.

"Coach Smith says Larry Brown will come," Baddour told Moeser.

The fifty-nine-year-old Brown, a former Carolina player and assistant to

Smith who was on his seventh NBA stop with the 76ers, had held two college coaching jobs, UCLA and Kansas, in his Hall of Fame career. The second, coincidentally, further spun UNC's dilemma out of control.

Brown had preceded Williams at Kansas and led the Jayhawks to the 1988 national championship. Still, his reputation troubled Chancellor Moeser, who knew Brown ran a loose ship and left Kansas on NCAA probation when he jumped back to the NBA.

That placed Dick Baddour in a vice grip between his new boss and Smith, the man who had orchestrated his ascension to athletics director in 1997. Despite Smith's insistence that "Larry's coming . . . just tell him when to be here for the press conference," Baddour decided to go to Brown's Malibu beach home and interview him for the job. He flew to California with UNC faculty athletic chairman Jack Evans, his good friend and confidante.

Baddour, Evans, and Brown met for about two hours. Brown's third wife, Shelley, whom he had met and married while coaching the Los Angeles Clippers in 1991, was in the house for part of the time but did not participate in the discussion. Evans has maintained that "Dick conducted a very professional interview." Brown considered it less than that.

"The first hour he (Baddour) spent telling me how Roy Williams was so perfect," Brown said. "The second hour he spent telling me that I was too old, that I couldn't accept less money, and why I shouldn't take the job."

Brown agreed that Williams was a great coach and how he had wanted him to be next at Carolina. "But I'm not chopped liver," he said, "and it's up to me to decide whether I'm worried about the money or not. Not you."

The meeting ended awkwardly and Brown, now realizing he was not a unanimous choice at his alma mater, called Baddour the next day and said he didn't think the athletics director wanted to hire him. Baddour confirmed that Carolina was going in another direction, and that afternoon Brown announced he had withdrawn his name from the UNC coaching search.

Brown felt betrayed by his school and immediately changed plans for his team to hold its preseason training camp in Chapel Hill, where it had for eight years. Mum at first, he eventually gave interviews to ESPN The Magazine and the Philadelphia newspapers about his dealings with his alma mater.

Those who knew and supported Brown were furious, and some stayed mad for three years. Sure, Brown left two schools (Kansas and UCLA) on probation, but they saw that as errors of omission rather than overt acts and were sure, under Smith's thumb, that Brown would not make those mistakes again. Mainly, they wanted someone popularly considered to be the best active basketball coach in the world for the next five years while a long-term successor was groomed.

THE FALL OF AN EMPIRE

They respected Moeser's concerns but believed he should have allowed the hire and set stringent demands to make sure Brown obeyed the rules.

The money wasn't an issue for Brown, who grew up a poor kid and had earned far more than he could ever spend. He loved UNC, had always dreamed of being the head coach there, and told Smith that whenever he needed him, just call.

"I honestly think he would walk to Chapel Hill and coach Carolina for nothing," said Ashley McGeachy, the NBA beat writer in Philadelphia and daughter of the former Duke coach Neil McGeachy.

Smith had also called South Carolina coach Eddie Fogler and Middle Tennessee's Randy Wiel, two other former players and protégés, but by then Baddour had tracked down Notre Dame coach Matt Doherty at a Wal-Mart in South Bend and asked him to interview. Doherty flew into Raleigh the next day, met for six hours with Baddour, talked strategy with Smith and emerged as the leading, and, by then, the only viable, candidate.

A groundswell of support had elevated Doherty's stock far higher than was deserved for a one-year head coach being considered to take over the most storied college team over the past thirty years. However, prominent alumni and boosters, who knew little of what it took to coach major college basketball and often were allowed inappropriate influence, had convinced themselves that Doherty was the answer.

He was tall, handsome, and had gotten some recent national TV time while leading the Irish through an NIT run in his first season after serving on Williams's staff at Kansas for seven years. He was green for sure but had the pedigree of having played on Smith's 1982 national champions and working alongside Williams, who was now pushing him for the job. Besides the winning season, Doherty had recruited well at Notre Dame, signing incoming freshman guard Chris Thomas and Oklahoma transfer Ryan Humphries.

Aloof as a player and having gone into coaching after an unhappy stint as a stockbroker on Wall Street, Doherty was not the pick of many former UNC players, who wondered whether the volatile personality of a native New Yorker could follow smoothly the noncussing, more mild-mannered Midwestern methods of Smith and Guthridge. With both Guthridge and Baddour listening in, Smith called one former player whose opinion he respected and said that Carolina was about to hire Doherty. "Big mistake, big mistake," the player warned.

Nevertheless, Carolina went with the high-profile Doherty. Introduced on July 11, 2000, he revealed he was bringing his entire coaching staff from Notre Dame—four assistants, none with any ties to UNC—a move that undermined his tenure from Day One because they were considered stepchildren to the fabled Carolina Family.

Smith was not on the dais this time and watched from the back of the same hall in which he and Guthridge had both held their retirement events. Publicly supportive, Smith nevertheless said it also felt "like a funeral" because his longtime assistants Ford and Hanners, along with young aide Pat Sullivan, were losing their jobs and employment at UNC.

"They are all so capable and I'm very sad for them," Smith said, biting his lip.

Guthridge had been biting his tongue for a week, angry that Williams had turned down the job and foiled the plan. It brought criticism from parties who could not understand why Guthridge waited until midsummer to step down and how it looked like he didn't care what happened to his staff.

That had been another issue for Williams in considering the move. Had he come, he would have brought his assistants with him just as Doherty had done. Perhaps there would have been room for one UNC coach to stay, but not all three.

Doherty had joined the Kansas staff before the 1993 season, which ended with the Jayhawks losing to Carolina in the Final Four. He had gone back into basketball as a broadcaster and then as an assistant at Davidson, working for his old Long Island high school coach, Bob McKillop, after his five years on Wall Street.

A hard-working recruiter, Doherty stayed on the phone endlessly and dogged prospects even though Williams personally handled the top Kansas targets each year.

After his seventh season at KU, almost overnight, Doherty got the Notre Dame job. Williams and Smith cornered Irish Athletics Director Kevin White at the 1999 Final Four in St. Petersburg, telling them that Doherty—an up-and-coming coach and an Irish Catholic to boot—was his man. White was struggling to shake Notre Dame out of the basketball lethargy that existed since Digger Phelps' departure. He interviewed Doherty and then hired him the next week.

Fourteen months later, after a 22–13 record and a loss to Wake Forest in the 2000 NIT title game, Doherty was the new Carolina coach. He was given a six-year contract, including many of the benefits that had been planned for Williams. He and his new staff hit Chapel Hill running hard, impressing the prominent alumni who had backed his hire with his aggressiveness, but getting mixed reviews from others.

At the first meeting with those players who were on campus in July (the others listened in on a conference call), Doherty told them they didn't work hard enough and didn't know how to win. Since the Tar Heels had played in the 2000 Final Four, and had eight regulars returning, they were bewildered and offended by what Doherty obviously intended as a motivational message.

It was the first of many remarks the blunt new coach made to people that were not taken exactly as intended. The word immediately got back to Guthridge and Smith, who expressed concern to friends. Smith decided he would "stop by" a few of Doherty's early practices to see how things were going.

At Duke, the Blue Devils watched with interest. They, too, had been expecting to face Williams, the same coach who had taken them to the wire the previous March in the NCAA Tournament. Many of their fans actually regarded Doherty as more of a long-term threat because of his youth and exuberance.

On the other hand, it no longer mattered as much who was coaching Carolina. Duke was so established that the rivalry had become secondary to its own national aspirations each year. The Blue Devils had ended 2000 ranked No. 1 and dropped only one notch in the Associated Press preseason poll, returning four starters and adding highly touted freshman guard Chris Duhon.

Gone was the over-achieving Carrawell, who had been drafted forty-first by San Antonio, snapping Duke's string of five consecutive first-rounder picks. Carrawell sniped at Krzyzewski for not working the NBA circuit as hard for him as he had for higher draft choices Roshown McLeod, Brand, and Langdon the last two years.

"The whole system let me down," Carrawell said. "Whether it was the NBA scouts, my agent, the NBA, or Coach K not lobbying for me enough—never in history had an ACC Player of the Year gone so low."

Neither was there another Final Four banner to hang. A more enduring ceremony, however, was held during a second-round preseason NIT home game against Villanova, which not coincidentally was Krzyzewski's five hundredth win at Duke. The school dedicated the Cameron floor to him with the words Coach K Court—one of the appliqués placed directly in front of the visiting bench for a maximum intimidation factor. Still trailing Dean Smith's 879 wins, Krzyzewski owned more than twice the victories of any other current ACC coach at his school heading into the 2000–01 season.

Justifying its ranking by winning the preseason NIT, Duke edged Temple in the first of two games against the Owls within nine days. The Devils moved up to No. 1 after beating Illinois in the ACC-Big 10 Challenge, the first of four wins over top 10-ranked opponents in December and January. In streaking to a 19–1 start, their only loss was a blown lead to third-ranked Stanford and one-time recruit Jacobson in the Pete Newell Challenge in Oakland, California, during Christmas week.

Back in North Carolina, the team with the excitable young coach opened slowly but soon began making some noise of its own, validating a preseason placement of No. 6 in the national polls.

Doherty had delighted the Dean Dome crowd by drawing a technical foul minutes into his first game for stomping the floor with his size-eleven loafers. After three seasons of Guthridge rarely getting up, Doherty's arm-waving dance down the sideline was a welcome contrast. Carolina lost to Michigan State and Kentucky to fall out of the top 10, then Doherty inserted Ronald Curry, the erstwhile high school legend, into the lineup at point guard.

Curry, national prep player of the year in both football and basketball from Hampton, Virginia, had originally committed to Virginia in the fall of 1997. He never signed his national football letter of intent, and instead enrolled at UNC because he said he preferred playing Carolina basketball over Virginia. Curry's relationship with Nike, which sponsored his Boo Williams AAU team, might have also been an influence—UNC was a Nike school; Virginia was not.

After starting quarterback Oscar Davenport went down on the first series of the 1998 football season, Curry took over and eventually won MVP honors in the Las Vegas Bowl. Not joining Guthridge's 1999 squad full-time until January, he played sparingly as a freshman and averaged less than 3 points in 26 games. He then missed the entire next season recovering from a torn Achilles tendon he suffered on the football field at Georgia Tech.

Curry suited up for Doherty's first team as a question mark. He went in against Miami in the sixth game, sparked a comeback victory and was a starter from then on. The Tar Heels began a winning streak that drove them steadily up the rankings and shielded any internal problems with the demanding Doherty, the anti-Smith and Guthridge. Toward the end of the exhilarating, ten-week run came the single game that sent fans over the edge with excitement and expectation.

In Doherty's first visit to Duke, the Tar Heels carried a five-game losing streak against the Blue Devils but kept the Cameron crowd anxious most of the night. Near the end of the game, with his team hanging on to a small lead, Doherty told a private joke in the huddle that got out and later made national news.

Worried that Duke would pull off another miracle finish as it had against UConn and Kentucky and others in years past, and trying to keep his team loose, Doherty said while killing the end of a two-minute TV timeout, "Duke still has the ugliest cheerleaders in the ACC."

Doherty compared the tension-breaker to the many sly and sarcastic barbs he had heard Smith make, confidentially, over the years during tight situations. He had tried the same at Notre Dame, cracking on the band or music or telling a stupid joke to make someone laugh and break the tension. At Duke, Doherty chose the cheerleaders to let his players know he had been in their shoes during his own playing career.

Duke indeed did tie the game on a near-miraculous three-pointer by Dunleavy, but with the game apparently headed for overtime, Shane Battier—one of the smartest players in ACC history—committed one of the dumbest fouls in ACC history, bumping Brendan Haywood thirty feet from the basket. Haywood, who had missed two free throws when he could have tied the score in the final seconds of the 1998 game, redeemed himself by sinking both shots for the 85–83 lead.

After Duhon's desperation heave fell short, several UNC fans sitting behind the visitors' bench ran onto the floor for a victory dance on the Duke logo. An hour later, a ring of still-stewing students remained, hands clasped to protect the gothic "D" insignia until Krzyzewski came out in a warm-up suit.

Speaking quietly, he assured them that it was only one game and, despite how badly they felt that night, it wasn't the end of the world. "We'll be all right," said Krzyzewski. "I promise you. Go home."

Ecstatic UNC students scrawled "Doherty is God" on campus sidewalks and spawned a generation of kids wearing T-shirts promoting DOHERTY'S DISCIPLES. The upset at Duke turned Doherty's request for a million-dollar-plus expansion of the locker room and practice gym into a slam dunk with the executive committee of the UNC boosters the next morning.

Doherty began by saying, "This is a good time to have a meeting and ask for this." The fat cats gleefully agreed, approving the project. "Give him what he wants," said Rams Club majordomo Maurice Koury.

Overheard by the brother of a Tar Heel player, Doherty's joke about the Duke cheerleaders wound up in an ESPN.com column by Curry Kirkpatrick, angering both schools. In turn, the column sparked a debate between two commentators on the cable sports network. The episode typified Doherty's star-crossed career, marked by as much bad luck as bad behavior. He apologized publicly, but while embarrassing, the episode did little to dull the euphoria over Carolina toppling Duke on the court and in the polls as the Tar Heels went on to complete their 18-game winning streak and reach No. 1.

No one was happier for Doherty than Roy Williams, who attended the UNC-Florida State game later in the season to watch his daughter on the dance team. Sitting behind the scorer's table, he smiled when the Carolina students mockingly cheered him by chanting, "Thanks for staying!"

"I would have bet Matt coached (at UNC) for twenty years," Williams said two years later, "and by that time I would be retired and on the golf course somewhere."

Things were decidedly different as the rematch with Duke in Chapel Hill approached on March 4. The Tar Heels had lost their first ACC game at Clemson on February 18, when there was a halftime blow-up between players and coaches. Since then, they had lost again at Virginia by 20 points and Forte's game was falling off amidst rumors of a rift with Doherty.

Duke, meanwhile, had lost thrice by a combined five points and still trailed UNC in the ACC race. After blowing out Georgia Tech, the night Battier became the first Duke player to have his jersey retired since Grant Hill in 1994, and after winning at Wake Forest by two, the Blue Devils got the ironic break that was to make them even better.

Late in an 11-point loss to Maryland at Cameron, sophomore center Carlos Boozer landed awkwardly, broke a bone in his foot and was lost for a month. To most observers, it was the death knell for Duke's season.

Following an all-nighter with his staff to decide how to replace Boozer, Krzyzewski told his worried players at practice the next day that if they did what he said, they would win the national championship. Challenged to make up for the absence of Boozer, who was averaging 15 points and 7 rebounds, they began their 2001 postseason drive with a small lineup and racehorse style that utilized their quickness and three-point shooting.

When Boozer went out, Krzyzewski could move little-used sophomore Casey Sanders into the lineup or "go small" by inserting sixth-man Chris Duhon as a starter. Sanders was considered a liability even by Duke fans who thought he was soft and lazy. At the beginning of his sophomore season, Sanders had been chided by senior Battier.

"I heard Coach K call you *Casey* Sanders today, is that your name?" Battier said. "I thought it was *Pussy* Sanders, because that's what Coach K called you all last year. Nice to meet you, *Casey* Sanders."

Surprisingly, Krzyzewski started both Sanders (using football player Reggie Love as a backup center) and Duhon as a third guard. That relegated fifth-year senior Nate James to a sixth-man role, but—in what could be seen as contrast to the bickering and selfishness under Doherty—James accepted the demotion and the son of a Marine officer became a spark off the bench.

The switch augured Krzyzewski's commitment to up-tempo, aggressive basketball for the rest of the season. Doherty said he hated Boozer getting hurt because it cast Duke in a rare underdog role and actually made the Blue Devils harder to defend.

"Now, they didn't have to pass the ball inside and they had no pressure," Doherty said. "It was an interesting dynamic going into the game, and in the second half we didn't handle it very well."

Including the coach. Instead of slowing the tempo and leveraging his superior size, Doherty chose to run with the far fleeter Blue Devils, who broke open a close game at halftime and ran away from the Tar Heels.

Playing a new brand of "Battier ball," the Blue Devils shot a school-record 38 times from three-point range and made 14 of them, including 7 from Jason Williams. Their strategy on both ends of the court was best explained by Battier, the three-time national defensive player of the year, who said, "Coach told me to run around and make plays."

Among them was blocking a breakaway layup by Forte at a key juncture of the game. While one play did not spell victory or defeat, the running, free-shooting style transformed a Duke team that had not looked like a Final Four lock with the bigger, slower Boozer in the lineup.

Krzyzewski relished the challenge of playing small-ball but was far from surprised when they won so easily at a stunned Smith Center. "We're beyond under-dog; we're Duke," he said. "You've still got to beat Duke."

The 95–81 victory left the Blue Devils tied for first place in the ACC with UNC at 13–3, but gave them all the momentum heading into the post-season tournaments.

They met again one week later in the ACC championship game at the Georgia Dome, as the tournament moved to a football stadium for the first time. Doherty dubbed it his "longest hour in coaching."

Carolina almost didn't get Duke in the finals. The Blue Devils survived a dramatic overtime game against Maryland on James's tip-in. It was their third meeting of the season, and rubber match, temporarily elevating their rivalry past Duke-Carolina in the public's perception—just as UNC-South Carolina in the 1960s, UNC-N.C. State in the 1970s, UNC-Virginia in the 1980s, and UNC-Wake Forest in the 1990s had done for brief periods.

In the championship game Sunday afternoon, Duke bolted to a 20-point lead at halftime. Wearing a gleaming white shirt, Doherty stood stoically in front of his bench before thirty-five thousand people as a national television audience watched the Blue Devils humiliate him and his team and then literally laugh at them as the sloppy second half wound down. He said it seemed "like years" since that first win at Cameron.

"We're behind 25, there are twelve minutes to go and the clock is not moving," Doherty recalled of the second most lopsided ACC championship game ever. "There are forty thousand people, and national TV watching you get blown out. You feel like your guts are being ripped open and millions of people are looking at you."

Neither team shot 30 percent in the second half and by the buzzer only Blue Devil fans remained in the cavernous dome. While Duke cut down the ACC nets for the third straight year, tying a record set by UNC from 1967 to 1969, Doherty snapped at the first question from Chapel Hill broadcaster Jim Heavner in the postgame press conference.

Pointing out the Tar Heels had split their last eight games and were playing poorly, Heavner asked Doherty, "Where do you go from here?"

"I don't understand your question, Jim," Doherty said. "We just played in the ACC Tournament final and tied for first in the regular season. What do you mean where do we go from here? We're going to the NCAA Tournament."

Carolina, 25–6, got the No. 2 seed in the South Region and went to New Orleans for the first- and second-round game, the site of its last two national championships, surrounded by questions. This was not the same program, however, that had twice celebrated on the Superdome floor. The Tar Heels did not appear to be a happy team, beaten down by the losses and the already-growing rumors about their relationship with Doherty.

Still nationally sixth-ranked, they fought off fifteenth-seeded Princeton, then coached by John Thompson Jr., before losing to seven-seed Penn State in the second round during which TV commentator Billy Packer repeatedly ripped them for careless play, particularly their twenty-two turnovers.

Doherty's misplaced emotion characterized him as a coach who cared more about himself than his players. Fighting back tears in his first losing NCAA press conference, he concluded by sniffling and blurting out, "I gave it my best shot."

Top-seeded Duke, meanwhile, left the rivalry behind by rolling through the East, including a win over Snyder's Missouri Tigers in Greensboro and a sweep of West Coast rivals UCLA and Southern Cal, with Boozer returning as a substitute in Duke's new lineup. Battier and Jason Williams tore up the regional, combining for 106 points in two games as the Blue Devils advanced to the Final Four in Minneapolis, Krzyzewski's ninth and the school's thirteenth.

There, they faced Maryland for a fourth time that season and the third in barely a month. Duke missed its first eight three-pointers and fell behind the fired-up Terps by 22 points with less than seven minutes to go in the first half when an incensed Krzyzewski called time out.

"What the hell are you afraid of, losing by 40?" he snorted at them. "What difference does it make? A loss is a loss. I'm not calling any more plays. Just go play basketball."

With the crowd howling over several disputed calls, Maryland center Lonny Baxter fell into foul trouble and the Blue Devils cut the deficit to 11 by halftime.

Maryland coach Gary Williams, by then sick of Krzyzewski and Duke, got defensive when asked by CBS interviewer Bonnie Bernstein what he would say at the half.

"We're up on Duke by 11 points. I'm telling them to keep doing what they're doing," he said, clearly annoyed.

That did not happen as Boozer, Battier, and Williams (who teamed for 67 points) led a second-half rout and, after Baxter's controversial fifth foul (when he grabbed Boozer's shorts to gain an advantage) sent the sweaty Maryland coach through the domed roof, Duke won going away to advance to the championship game against Arizona.

Publicity about Baxter's fifth foul, including Packer's rant on national TV, essentially turned the final into a road game for Duke. The Metro Dome crowd booed loudest after Jason Williams straddled Arizona's Jason Gardner on a no-harm-no-foul no call. But behind Dunleavy's three clutch three-pointers the Blue Devils prevailed 82–72 and won their third national championship in eleven years; Arizona settled for second and sending five players to the NBA the following June.

Duke completed an incredible run that set a precedent for winning all six NCAA Tournament games by at least 10 points. Battier's class also broke a record for victories in a four-year period (133). He and Williams were both consensus All-Americans and each won a national player of the year award, the first time ever for teammates in the same season.

Krzyzewski, in turn, earned icon status in his profession, joining John Wooden (ten), Adolph Rupp (four) and Bobby Knight (three) as coaches who had won more than two national championships. The long-retired Smith, of course, was among the latter group, which still delighted Duke fans almost as much as their own coach's accomplishment.

As they had in 1991 and '92, the Blue Devils went to the White House and met the *other* President Bush. Krzyzewski made an encore appearance on the *Late Show with David Letterman* and was again all over the national media, reestablishing himself as the best and best-known coach in college basketball.

While the archrival basked in the glory of the NCAA title, Doherty tried to keep his team together. Haywood was graduating and three more of UNC's top six players contemplated leaving. Forte, co-ACC Player of the Year with Battier, was considering the NBA draft. Unhappiness with Doherty would play into his decision to stay or go.

Smith did his due diligence, told Forte he was a mid-to-late first-round pick and advised him to return for his junior season. Forte didn't practice very hard and took the most shots, thus becoming a whipping boy for the late-season skid.

His mother, Wanda Hightower, also had taken a job with Octagon, the Washington, D.C., agency for pro athletes that was recruiting her son as a client, which could affect Forte's eligibility moving forward. Hightower was in all kinds of trouble, including a string of car rentals that she did not return properly. One report alleged that UNC's Smith intervened to offer free legal help from a lawyer friend in Washington while her son was still at Carolina. If true, that would have been an NCAA violation.

Doherty and UNC were upset that the same level of local media exploitation did not follow a column in the *Boston Globe* about Carlos Boozer's out-of-work father moving from Alaska after his son enrolled and landing a steady job with GlaxoSmithKline in the Durham division of the pharmaceutical giant whose president, Bob Ingram, was a close friend of Krzyzewski. Or a story in the New Orleans *Times-Picayune* about Chris Duhon's mother, Vivian Harper, whose house in Slidell, Louisiana, disappeared from six months of public foreclosure proceedings before she, too, moved to Durham during Duhon's freshman year. Harper went to work for, and received a raise after four months from, NCN Capital Management Company, a billion-dollar firm owned by Maceo Sloan, among whose prized possessions was an autographed ball from the 1991 Duke NCAA champs. Neither, by NCAA bylaws, was illegal as long as Boozer's father and Harper were qualified to hold their jobs.

It was not a totally uncommon practice. Rasheed Wallace's mother, Jackie, had moved from Philadelphia to Durham during his career and got a UNC-related position through her connections with the basketball program.

Despite urging from both Smith and Doherty to stay in school, Joseph Forte entered the draft just before the May 10 deadline and, a month later, was taken by the Boston Celtics with the twenty-first pick, one selection after Brendan Haywood by the Washington Wizards and their newest owner, Michael Jordan. Earlier, Memphis had nabbed Shane Battier with the sixth pick.

The same month, two-sport stars Ronald Curry and Julius Peppers told Doherty they were concentrating on the 2002 NFL draft and not to count on them for any part of the next season. That left Carolina with only two returning starters, seniors Jason Capel and Kris Lang, and four reserves with any experience, Brian Bersticker, Adam Boone, Will Johnson and Brian Morrison.

Over Memorial Day weekend, a few hundred Duke and Carolina fans got into it at an AAU tournament game in the Smith Center, where four Blue Devil recruits took on the Tar Heels' future point guard. A team of Dukies-to-be J. J. Redick, Shavlik Randolph, and Michael Thompson went up by 18 points over a team led by Raymond Felton. The second-half shootout between Redick and Felton had about two thousand spectators going wild, as Felton's team finally pulled out the game.

THE FALL OF AN EMPIRE

That spring, Krzyzewski was voted into the Basketball Hall of Fame, joining Temple's John Chaney and Bobby Knight as the only still-active coaches to be admitted; he joined Smith (1982) as the only active coaches to make it in their first season of eligibility. In September, the Krzyzewski family began an academic scholarship endowment at Duke with a $100,000 gift, and he was named "America's Best Coach" in any sport, on any level by CNN and *Time* magazine.

In October, he had some measure of reconciliation with Knight, who gave his induction speech into the Naismith Hall of Fame. In November, Duke rewarded him with a lifetime contract, also making him a special assistant to the president.

On November 19, 2001, the Blue Devils opened another season ranked No. 1 while the depleted Tar Heels were left out of some polls and picked to finish somewhere in the middle of the ACC race.

At UNC, Doherty had gone from a fiery young coach to a hothead that had run off office personnel, offended co-workers, and alienated players while his team encountered hard times on and off the court. Three long-time Smith-Guthridge office staffers secretaries Angela Lee, Ruth Kirkendall, and Linda Woods, wound up working elsewhere and were understandably hurt. Former players didn't come back, as they once had, amidst rumors of a family fractured.

From first sky-rocketing in the polls and then flaming out in the NCAA Tournament, Doherty's future turned cloudy as Carolina embarked on what was expected to be a difficult season with the loss of two seniors starters (Cota and Haywood), plus Forte and the football duo of Curry and Peppers.

Doherty claimed that, when he took the job, he looked ahead and saw a down second season, but it started out worse than anyone could have imagined. There were home losses to lightweights Hampton, Davidson, and an ordinary Indiana team. The Tar Heels rebounded over Georgia Tech in their ACC opener—ironically to take first place in the conference—but two more losses to Kentucky and Charleston sent them into the new year with a 5–5 record and premature talk of not making it back to the NCAA Tournament.

That, of course, was blasphemous for UNC basketball, which owned the record for consecutive tickets to the Big Dance—twenty-seven years. Doherty was also dangling two more of Dean Smith's revered records over the fire, successive twenty-win seasons (31) and, perhaps the most astonishing, top-three finishes in the ACC (37). Fortunately, Doherty was winning the "other" season that could help him: recruiting.

In November, he had signed three players among the best in the high school class of 2002. As unlucky as Doherty was with Forte, Curry, and Peppers, he had some divine guidance in landing this trio.

Point guard Raymond Felton was Carolina's to lose, no matter who was coaching. Growing up in rural Latta, South Carolina, where most people paid attention to football at Clemson and the University of South Carolina, Felton played basketball every day and learned to dribble in the dark. He was an admitted UNC fan from an early age.

Since his sophomore year in high school, he was ticketed to be a Tar Heel. Eddie Fogler, the one-time Smith assistant who was then the head coach at South Carolina, recruited Felton hard but always said, "He's going to Chapel Hill." Doherty merely had to keep from screwing it up. On Felton's official visit for "Midnight with Matt and the Tar Heels" in October of 2001, Doherty had a customized Carolina jersey waiting for him with his name and a No. 1 embroidered on the back. The six-foot ball handling wizard was the first to sign.

Rashad McCants grew up a Vince Carter and North Carolina fan in Asheville, where he was both a star and a loner. He fell off the recruiting radar somewhat when he moved to the boonies of New Hampshire to play his junior year at New Hampton Prep, but popped back on everyone's screen after winning MVP at the Boo Williams AAU tournament that summer in Virginia.

Roy Williams recruited him for Kansas and asked him, "Is it 90–10 that you are going to North Carolina?" McCants said it was "more like 70–30," but Williams knew he, and everyone else, had very little chance of getting him.

Once McCants signed, he said he wanted to wear No. 32 because it was the reverse of Michael Jordan's retired number. He claimed he wanted to follow Jordan's path, win a national championship and then turn pro early.

Sean May would have never gone south had Bobby Knight still coached at Indiana. He was raised in Bloomington, the son of celebrated former Hoosiers' All-American Scott May, who had gotten rich buying apartment buildings. *Everyone* knew Sean May from a very early age, the 6' 8" size and the skills, the great hands and soft shooting touch, but everyone also figured he was a lock to play for Knight—until, of course, Knight got fired before the 2000–01 season started.

May knew Mike Davis, who took over for Knight, and might have gone to Indiana anyway, but Knight told Scott May he did not want his son to be a Hoosier after his ousting. Knight took the job at Texas Tech in 2001 and asked May to play for him. During a visit, he put the hard sell on father and son, but if May wasn't going to Indiana, he wasn't going to Lubbock, Texas, either.

Scott May had played for Dean Smith on the 1976 Olympic team. Since then, he kept a close friendship with Smith and Phil Ford, his running mate with the Gold Medalists in Montreal. May also knew that, while their styles differed, Smith and Knight were good friends and shared many of the same standards and beliefs about basketball and life. So it was natural that Sean May would consider Carolina as a compromise choice.

Doherty recruited him with vigor, but he had little to do with the final decision. He just couldn't screw that one up, either. The Mays spent as much time on their recruiting visits with Smith, Guthridge, and Ford, who by then was working as a fund-raiser for the athletics department, as they did with Doherty and his staff. While all the speculation centered around whether May would play for Knight at Texas Tech, Doherty and his staff knew the secret: He wasn't going anywhere but Chapel Hill and was the third to sign.

When Scott May voiced concern about his son playing for the green and already controversial Doherty, Smith assured him, "Don't worry, I'll look after him."

Doherty added three more to his second recruiting class, two centers (Byron Sanders and Damion Grant) he signed only after losing high school big men to Duke, Notre Dame, Texas, and Villanova, and a UNC football recruit who was going to walk-on but decided to play just basketball. Already having committed the maximum five scholarships in any given year, Doherty told David Noel that if he would pay his own way as a freshman he would get a scholarship as a sophomore. Noel agreed and gave up his football free ride.

This was the future freshman class that saved what was left of Doherty's sanity and hope of the fans as the 2002 Tar Heels lost 11 of their first 12 games after the new year and their season went down the tubes.

Regularly blown out, they suffered 10 defeats by 18-plus points and lowered the elite bar that had measured Smith's program for three decades. It got so bad at one point that prominent alumni and trustees, who were still trying to justify hiring Doherty, seemed content with a 15-point home loss to Maryland because "we looked better, didn't we?"

During the dismal decline, the Tar Heels even evoked some sympathy from Duke. On January 31, Krzyzewski admonished his once-beaten and No. 1-ranked defending national champions during a timeout huddle as the Blue Devils were sending Carolina to its worst loss ever in the Smith Center.

"Hey, there's been some great basketball played in this building," he said to a suddenly attentive squad, "and there will be again. So no celebrating after the game ends. Shake their hands and walk off the court. Nobody act like an asshole, okay?"

In the stands were assholes of both colors. Frustrated Tar Heel fans alternately yelled at Krzyzewski and the officials, as if somehow the refs were responsible for their 30-point deficit. Some of the several hundred Dukies who always got into the Dean Dome rubbed it in so smugly that an Internet columnist and UNC grad had already decided to open his next piece with the question, "God, were we THIS arrogant?"

On the court, Krzyzewski ordered a ball-control offense that burned the clock and held the final margin under 30 points when it easily could have been 40 or 50. Doherty appreciated that bit of sportsmanship and told Krzyzewski as much when they shook hands at the scorer's table after the game.

Duke did the same thing in winning the rematch by 25 points in Durham, and when they played five days later in the ACC Tournament, Doherty tried a shot-clock version, of a slowdown Smith had used in 1966. Duke was never in serious jeopardy, but at least Carolina kept the score closer in the 60–48 loss.

The Tar Heels nosedived to an unprecedented 8–20, their first losing record since 1962 and painfully ending Dean Smith's sacred streaks. After reaching six Final Fours in a ten-year period, they had missed *making* the NCAA Tournament altogether for the first time since 1974.

In trying to explain away the season, Doherty didn't want to criticize Guthridge for leaving him with a team of a senior center, two football players whose hardwood futures were questionable, and one highly recruited star who probably wouldn't stay all four years.

After 8–20, however, Doherty needed to defend himself.

Of course, Carolina fans spread the blame around, and some of it landed back on Roy Williams for turning down the Tar Heels. Had he come in 2000, he would have recruited a better initial freshman class than Doherty, who took three players (Jackie Manuel, Melvin Scott, and Jawad Williams) he had gotten to know while recruiting at Notre Dame. Coach Williams would have closed on several players the old staff was chasing and convinced a Kansas recruit or two to follow him to Chapel Hill.

Carolina's collapse left Duke to dominate the ACC and the rivalry. The Blue Devils were now the only constant, an automatic entry in the NCAA Tournament and national news, win or lose. They did not win the ACC regular season for the first time in six years, losing their top ranking and the crown to Maryland on February 17 in College Park, but they won an unprecedented fourth consecutive ACC Tournament championship by handling Wake Forest in the semifinals and blowing out N.C. State in the championship game.

Their 31–4 season came to a shocking end when they lost a 16-point lead to Indiana in the Mideast Regional semifinal. After seemingly losing the game, Jason Williams nearly pulled it out by drilling a three-pointer and getting fouled in the final seconds. He missed his free throw to tie, and Carlos Boozer came down with the offensive rebound. Boozer had pushed off to get it and then got grabbed by Indiana's Jared Jeffries as he went back up with the winning shot, missing it badly.

Officials have rarely blown the whistle in last-second scrums under the basket, but Bruce Benedict carried that too far in this game. The former Atlanta Braves catcher gagged on both Boozer's push-off and Jeffries' hold, causing a confrontation with seventh-year Duke senior Matt Christensen near the end of Duke's bench. Christensen (who first played for Duke in 1995–96 before going on a two-year Mormon mission) chased Benedict off the court and was restrained by Krzyzewski—shades of Guthridge's temper tantrum toward Pete Pavia for having thrown Smith out of the 1991 Final Four in Indianapolis.

Duke's 74–73 loss was a huge story, nearly as big as Maryland winning its first NCAA title the next weekend in Atlanta. Without having to contend with Duke this year, the Terrapins beat Kansas by nine in the national semifinals and then pounded Indiana in the second half of the championship game.

Krzyzewski and his program couldn't make a move, on of off the court, without some kind of scrutiny from somebody. Not trying to effect such an outcome, and having no idea how they did it, the Blue Devils had polarized the college basketball world like the Yankees, Celtics, and Cowboys dynasties of old. You either loved 'em or hated 'em. There was precious little middle ground.

There was plenty of coverage when Duke lost three more players early to the NBA—making it six in three years to surpass Carolina's five from 1995–98. Krzyzewski had planned for the departure of Jason Williams and Boozer, but Dunleavy's decision to go blindsided him. He believed Dunleavy would be the favorite for both ACC and national player of the year honors as a senior.

Through his father's NBA connections, Dunleavy was assured he'd be a high first-round pick and guaranteed a $15 million contract. He also feared that, without Williams's penetration and Boozer's inside presence, the outside looks that helped him make 38 percent of his three-pointers and average 17.3 points would not be as good. Dunleavy was drafted third by Golden State behind top pick Yao Ming (Houston) and No. 2 Williams by the Bulls.

Krzyzewski knew Williams and Boozer, who was drafted in the second round by Cleveland, were graduating after their junior years. They had attended every summer session on the way to the 112 credits required for a Duke degree which, compared to the 124 needed at most other universities, aided those players who wanted to earn diplomas ahead of their classes. Along with the new NCAA rule that allowed recruits to go on scholarship the summer *before* their freshman year, it also helped Krzyzewski hatch a plan he hoped would keep his program ahead of the NBA curve.

In order to offset the lure of the NBA for high school stars, Krzyzewski said he would fast-track the career of any player whose primary goal was to reach the NBA. "If you're good enough to get into Duke, you're good enough to graduate in three years," he told the most qualified recruits. Because NBA rookies had restricted contracts, minimizing the money they made for three or four years, Krzyzewski wanted to help them hasten the pace. He even had his assistants check to see if the most academically gifted recruits might be eligible to graduate from *high school* in three years, beating the clock from both ends.

Krzyzewski also found a loophole that allowed his 2002–03 team to begin practice two weeks early in order to go to England in October for four exhibition games against European opponents. It was no coincidence that the parents of Duke's chief recruiting target, Loul Deng, lived in London and could see the Blue Devils up close and personal. When other coaches learned of the trip, they complained so loudly that the rule was changed to prohibit preseason trips abroad after school was in session.

Not surprisingly, the 6' 8" Deng chose Duke during the fall signing period. What was once said of Carolina—the overused and exaggerated claim that "they don't recruit, they select"—was now said of Duke and Krzyzewski. While neither program got every player it wanted, the Blue Devils had continued upping the ante and, due to the transition at the school down the road, had sprinted ahead of the Tar Heels in perception as well as hard facts.

Surviving the NBA purge as well as UNC ever had, Duke now enveloped the rivalry and was the new measuring stick in the ACC, if not the nation. Krzyzewski had better postseason success than Carolina, reaching the national championship game seven times. Besides three NCAA titles, Duke also had more tournament wins and Final Four trips than any school since UCLA's run ended in 1975.

This all grated on those favoring the lighter shade of blue. The touted incoming freshman class boosted their spirits for the 2002–03 season. Behind Felton, McCants, and May, the Tar Heels showed early signs of recovery by upsetting Kansas on the way to the preseason NIT championship and a 5–0 start, climbing back into the national rankings before May went down with a broken foot in December.

They were still 11–5 after stunning sixth-ranked UConn at home but then lost four straight heading to Durham on February 5. Doherty hoped the hostile atmosphere would spur them to challenge a Duke team that had lost three of its last five games, dropped to No. 9 in the rankings and driven its angry coach to a drastic move.

The day after losing at Florida State for the second straight season, the Blue Devils arrived at practice to find their new locker room stripped bare. The spoils of victory and reminders of Duke's glory years, such as pictures of past championship teams, were gone. Their once-personalized lockers had only pieces of tape with their names on them. Replacing the cushy, padded chair in front of each locker was a metal folding chair, just like in the Army.

Krzyzewski's message was loud and clear: They had earned nothing and had to play a helluva lot harder and better to live up to the Duke tradition. It was not a good time for Carolina to be coming to Cameron. The Blue Devils had been humiliated by their coach and were hurt. They were ready to fight, at least on the court, and nothing fired them up more than the sight of powder blue.

In the first half, Dahntay Jones, a transfer from Rutgers without the historical perspective of other Blue Devils, pushed Doherty when his momentum carried him along the Carolina sideline. Doherty hurried down to Krzyzewski, told him what had happened and the incident died innocently. Jones, however, would be a central figure in a far bigger brouhaha in the rematch at Chapel Hill five weeks later.

Seconds before halftime, with Carolina's young team leading 43–38, a skinny streaker painted in dark blue and wearing only tennis shoes and a scarf ran out from behind the bleachers with his arms flailing and his private parts flapping. The students cheered at first and then got quiet. This wasn't listed on their cheat sheets of organized pranks, was it?

The streaker bolted from baseline to baseline and was headed out the main exit of Cameron, where a friend was waiting with his car running, but the naked nerd decided to take a victory lap. He got nailed by a flying tackle from one of the Durham policemen who slammed him to the floor, smearing blue paint everywhere, handcuffed him and dragged him away.

(The streaker, student Robert Findly, was taken to jail, where he was charged with indecent exposure and disorderly conduct and posted a $1,000 bail for his court date on March 25. He was later ordered to perform community service and pay court costs.)

Up in Section 7, Row G, 1963 Duke graduate Herb Neubauer—aka the Crazy Towel Guy—loved the extracurrics. Neubauer got his title in 1985 after he kept bringing a towel to home games because he sweated too much and began waving it during Duke scoring rallies. The "Cra-zee Towel Guy" cheer became a regular first-half ritual. One of his towels, signed by him and Krzyzewski, later brought $25,000 at a charity auction.

The game was delayed briefly while body paint was cleaned off the court. On the Duke bench, freshman Lee Melchionni shrugged, "He even painted his ding-a-ling blue." The wide-eyed UNC players, among them freshmen Felton and Mc-Cants, were amused and curious. At Carolina home games, students painted their faces and got rowdy, but they had never seen anything quite like this.

These were also different Tar Heels than those that had lost five straight to the Blue Devils. With no May, and McCants scoring only two points, they hung around behind 25 points from Felton and 19 each from Jawad Williams and David Noel. But without May, Carolina couldn't get enough scoring, lost the board battle, and eventually the game.

Duke's Jones led his teammates to the 83–74 victory with 23 points and 13 rebounds, and the next day their locker room returned to normal. The shrewd Krzyzewski had made his point, and the renewed Blue Devils won six of their next seven games, losing only in double OT at Wake Forest.

They continued breaking in their own freshman class of guards J. J. Redick and Sean Dockery, forwards Shavlik Randolph and Lee Melchionni, and big men Shelden Williams and Michael Thompson. With upperclassmen Chris Duhon, Dahntay Jones, Daniel Ewing, Nick Horvath, and Casey Sanders, Krzyzewski at least had one of his deepest teams ever.

After a second-half meltdown at St. John's, they were still 21–5 and ranked tenth going into the regular-season finale at Carolina on Sunday, March 9, 2003. Even though the last game had been closer, Duke had taken the last six games from UNC by an average margin of 20 points, but Doherty believed his young team was ready to spring an upset.

The rivalry remained alive in the media, where memorable Duke-Carolina games were aired all week on the ESPN Classic network. Although Duke had a much better record and was headed back to the NCAA Tournament, the Tar Heels' young talent promised a close game. In one sense, it was the good old days again. Fans on both sides felt they could win.

They got another ESPN Classic, but for different reasons.

"Mike, he's a dirty player. He threw an elbow at my guy," Doherty said to official Mike Wood, accusing Dahntay Jones of a flagrant foul on Raymond Felton midway through the second half with the score tied at 64–64.

"That's not what happened, Coach," Wood said to Doherty, who by then was standing over his fallen player in front of the Duke bench.

Assistant coach Chris Collins, a Carolina nemesis as a Blue Devil player seven years earlier, stepped three feet onto the court and yelled to get Wood's attention.

"Hey, Mike," Collins shouted, "did he come out here to check on his guy or bitch and whine about the play?"

Doherty started at Collins. "Shut the fuck up, motherfucker!" he screamed.

Collins, a half-foot shorter than Doherty, held his ground and shot back as the Carolina coach reached him, "No, you shut the fuck up, motherfucker!"

Doherty stuck out his chest and bumped Collins, who raised both palms to receive what turned out to be a minor blow. As opposing players and coaches jostled each other, a black-uniformed figure jumped into the fray.

Andre Buckner, a benchwarmer for Duke and the brother of the former

Clemson star who had crushed Carolina with a last-second dunk back in 1996, stepped between the two coaches and shoved Doherty. Wood and fellow officials John Clougherty and Ray Natili were now in the scrum, pulling and pushing bodies with different color uniforms away from each other.

"This is wrong," Wood told Doherty and Krzyzewski after bringing them to the scorer's table. "This is embarrassing to a great league, two great universities, and two great basketball programs. It has to end now."

The coaches nodded and shook hands. A great game now lessened, the Tar Heels shot 56 percent and went on to upset the tenth-ranked Blue Devils behind McCants's 26 points, 5 rebounds, and 3 steals. Their last 82–79 lead stood up after Jones's long three-pointer failed to beat the final horn.

Krzyzewski, who was so upset with his defense that he tried a rare zone, came off the bench waving his arms and saying to Wood, "It was too late, Mike." Later he said, "It was like an alarm clock went off. The game's over, they won. Let's quit fooling around."

The altercation upstaged Carolina's first win over Duke since 2001. The ACC reprimanded Doherty and Collins but did not suspend Buckner the mandatory one game for leaving the bench area or shoving an opposing coach. Buckner later told *Devils' Den,* an unofficial Duke Web site, that "pushing Coach Doherty" was one of his biggest thrills at Duke along with winning the national championship.

ACC Commissioner John Swofford, UNC's former athletics director for seventeen years, as far back as when Doherty played there, delivered the reprimands by telephone. Swofford asked Doherty if he realized how close he had come to starting a fistfight and, consequently, losing his job.

"John, I'm an athlete," Doherty responded, attempting to justify his competitive spirit to Swofford, himself a former college football player.

"You were an athlete twenty years ago," Swofford said sharply, "now, you're the head basketball coach at the University of North Carolina."

Doherty and Collins were also rebuked by their own schools, and according to Doherty the incident was mentioned again by the UNC administration when reviewing his job status a week after the season.

"If I had to do it over again, I wouldn't have stepped toward Chris Collins," Doherty said. "Maybe I would have gone to Coach K and said, 'What is he [Collins] doing?' It was like two kids at the playground. Your testosterone is going. But I do remember, as I fronted him, I'm thinking 'this is ridiculous . . . twenty thousand people and a national television audience (are watching).' We're two competitive people in a very heated game. I'm not going to punch him, but I'm going to defend my player. That's part of the heat of that rivalry."

By the time the basketball bluebloods played again six days later in the ACC Tournament, Duke had turned a slow burn into desire for revenge. UNC felt slighted.

Carolina claimed that Buckner should have been suspended for Duke's next game, and that only favoritism from the conference office prevented it. Moreover, an assistant coach coming on the court to challenge an opposing head coach deserved the stronger of two reprimands.

All was not forgotten for Duke either. Assistant coach Johnny Dawkins refused a pregame handshake with Doherty, waving him off as the surprised UNC staff walked by before the start of their semifinal.

This was Krzyzewski's game, just as it would have been Smith's years ago. He fed off the loss in Chapel Hill, challenged his players' pride and their school's tradition and sent them out to extract revenge and satisfaction. The results were in by halftime when Duke led by 19 points.

Following the Blue Devils' 75–63 victory, Doherty grabbed Dawkins, against whom he had played in high school and college, and made him shake hands as they left the court. Dawkins did so reluctantly.

"I felt in the game before, the things that happened at the eight-minute mark were preventable," Dawkins said. "As coaches we have to maintain a certain level of control. I thought a line may have been crossed during that game."

After beating Carolina for the twelfth time in five years, Duke rallied from 15 points behind N.C. State midway through the second half on the incredible long-range shooting of Redick. He hit four three-pointers and outscored State by himself 23–22 to lead the amazing comeback and secure the Blue Devils' fifth consecutive ACC Championship. The young Blue Devils, who had finished two games behind regular-season champion Wake Forest, returned to the NCAA Tournament for the eighth straight year and were seeded third in the West behind Arizona and Kansas.

UNC accepted an NIT bid and, after beating DePaul and Wyoming, fell one game short of 20 wins (19–16) by losing to Georgetown. Instead of going back to New York to try to become the first ever to win both the pre- and post-NITs in the same season, they sat home as UNC officials decided Doherty's fate. Athletics Director Baddour held private meetings with most of the players; only Raymond Felton and David Noel supported Doherty's return.

Things were also percolating in Kansas after an unsettling year.

Prominent boosters noting the decline of other sports at KU, had forced Bob

Frederick, the man who gambled and hired Roy Williams as an unknown assistant in 1988, into retirement. KU replaced him with outspoken former Fresno State athletics director Al Bohl, who wanted to oust football coach, and Williams's good friend, Terry Allen. Williams gave his support to Allen, and Bohl responded to the media, "Roy Williams is our basketball coach. I make the decisions about football."

Bohl fired Allen at midseason and eventually hired rotund Oklahoma offensive coordinator Mark Mangino. Suddenly, what Williams considered the perfect job became tense and uncomfortable. Bohl tried to take away some of his recruiting seats behind the bench and put boosters on the Kansas team plane without clearing it with Williams. He waited by the bench to glad-hand Williams before tip-off of home games, then accused the most popular figure in the athletics department, and arguably the most beloved person in the state, of not being a team player. Williams was hurt, angry, and, what had once seemed incomprehensible, unhappy at Kansas.

Now the class he loved most—Collison, Hinrich, and Gooden (who had turned pro after his junior year)—was concluding its college career. Williams was still getting commitments from great high-school players, but they weren't in Lawrence yet to form the same bond. Word began leaking out that it was no longer a foregone conclusion Williams would end his coaching career at KU.

One of his old friends from Carolina told a UNC Trustee that if Doherty did not make it, Williams might now be interested in coming back. That got out, sparking speculation further. There had been other indicators, as well.

In the two-plus years since turning down the job, Williams had run into various Tar Heel alumni and fans in airports, at the beach in South Carolina and other places, often stopping to tell people he hardly knew what a difficult decision it had been in 2000 and how he hoped they understood.

Mike Cooke, who played for Smith in the early 1960s, introduced himself to Williams at the 2001 Peach Jam AAU tournament in Augusta, Georgia. "He spent a half hour with me, explaining why he hadn't taken the job," Cooke said. "He told me, 'I just want the older guys to know that I love North Carolina. I just couldn't leave my kids.'"

Williams had also run into Baddour more recently and told him how miserable it was with Bohl in charge. "If you were my athletics director, I would be a lot happier," Williams said. The statement was meant as a compliment, but it gave Baddour reason to believe the outcome might be different if UNC went after Williams a second time.

Rumors almost ruined one of the most glorious weekends in Kansas basketball history at the West Regional in Anaheim. Williams defeated Duke for the first time in his head-coaching career, ending the Blue Devils' 2003 season at 26–7. His Jayhawks then edged Arizona, settling an NCAA Tournament score from 1997 when they lost to the Wildcats after being ranked No. 1 in the country for fifteen consecutive weeks, to reach a second straight Final Four. The buzz kept Kansas folks from fully enjoying it.

Dick "Hoops" Weiss of the New York *Daily News* reported Doherty was on the way out, and that Carolina would make another run at Williams. As the Jayhawks headed home to prepare for their trip to New Orleans, their fans seemed almost as interested in who would be their coach next season as how *this* season ended.

On Monday, March 31, Doherty was told he could not return because of irreparable relationships with his players. He was given the choice to be fired or resign, as his attorneys negotiated a settlement to the three years left on his contract. UNC called a news conference for 8:00 P.M. on Tuesday night. Doherty chose to take the high road, but everyone knew the truth.

"The resignation is also not just a result of the meetings we had with current players," Baddour said in a statement. "It would be extremely unfair to those players and would be an unqualified mistake to say the resignation was a result of only their concerns and questions."

Williams's aura hung heavy over the hour-long press conference, attended unfortunately by several UNC players who were photographed in baggy jeans and caps, underscoring their bad rap as malcontents who got the coach fired. Baddour and Moeser acknowledged Williams would be one of the people considered for the job but denied he had been contacted or, according to the wildest rumors, that he had already agreed to come.

Williams spent a murderous week, preparing his team for the Final Four while dodging details about his future. Kansas administrators and fans grew more worried that he refused to simply say he was their coach forever but did not press the issue while the season was still playing out.

It all hit the fan a few minutes after the Jayhawks' 81–78 loss to Syracuse in the title game at the Superdome, when Williams was asked about his plans by CBS reporter Bonnie Bernstein in the post-game interview. Her first attempt drew a terse, but politically correct answer from Williams that he didn't want to address the subject, that he was only concerned with his kids at Kansas. When she pressed him, Williams blew up.

"I couldn't give a shit about North Carolina right now," he snapped. "I care about those thirteen players in the locker room."

Sean May, who had returned from his broken foot to play an ineffectual ten minutes in the last Duke game, was home in Bloomington, watching the final game with his father. "I told my dad, 'Coach Williams is gone. We might as well find somebody else.'"

Smith went to New Orleans for the championship game, sat with some fellow Kansas alumni in the stands, and visited with Williams following the disappointing loss. He maintained they did not discuss the Carolina job until a phone call Tuesday night after both men had returned home and in person for the first time when he flew out to Lawrence later that week.

For the second time in less than three years, Roy Williams had to make the decision of a lifetime. Williams couldn't turn down his old coach again. Or could he?

UNC had two private planes on call to pick Williams up in Lawrence once he said yes. The Kansas population fretted that he had not reaffirmed he was staying when, in retrospect, that he didn't, meant he was leaving. In North Carolina, skeptics still sore about his decision of 2000, grew impatient with having to wait another week. "He knows whether he's coming or not," they said. "Why doesn't he just say it."

Kansas abruptly fired Athletics Director Bohl, hoping his eradication would convince Williams to remain and have more of a hand at selecting Bohl's successor. Nevertheless, the bitter feelings of the last two years were still lodged in his throat, and this time he had let the North Carolina question go too far.

In his last conversation with Smith on April 14, 2003, Williams asked his mentor three things.

"Do you think everyone there will be pleased with me coming back?"

"Would I be their choice"

"Are you sure you want me to take this job?"

When Smith answered "Yes" to all three, Williams told him that he would talk with his Kansas team that afternoon, and to have the plane waiting when the meeting was over. After telling his players and encountering several angry reactions, the ESPN cameras caught the teary-eyed, T-shirt clad Williams leaving Allen Fieldhouse and boarding the jet.

"If I had known how hard that was going to be, I never would have done it," he said, shaken to his bones.

In Chapel Hill, a press conference was announced for that evening. As the jet landed at Raleigh-Durham airport, the healing began. In the welcoming party was Bill Guthridge, who had not spoken with Williams since he turned down the job in 2000. Guthridge believed Williams went back on his word and hurt North Carolina basketball. He was willing to let bygones go because Roy's return was now the best thing for the future of the program.

Alexander Julian, the designer and native of Chapel Hill who created the Tar Heels' argyle-laced uniforms in 1992, had two Carolina blue ties delivered to the basketball office. When Williams walked into the press conference, he was still wearing his red Kansas tie and appeared exactly what he was: a man torn between two universities, one of which he could not reject again for very personal reasons.

He spent most of the time talking about what his fifteen years at Kansas there meant to him. His sadness was genuine, but it still rankled some Carolina people that he seemed so reticent. With such a deep-rooted connection existing between the two schools, and being back, it made him think of Kansas even more.

"The family business needed me," he said, "and I couldn't turn Coach Smith down for a second time."

His new players were assembled in the corner of the room, neatly dressed in jackets, ties, and turtlenecks, a marked contrast from those who had shown up at Doherty's dismissal in gangsta garb. He raised an open hand, closed his fist and promised if they played together and did what he said, they would be successful.

Williams put on one of the Julian ties the next day and met students at an informal gathering at the Old Well campus landmark, handing out Krispy Kreme doughnuts. Then he was gone for six weeks to help with the U.S.A. Olympic team coached by Larry Brown, while his wife tried to sell their two homes in Lawrence and find one in Chapel Hill.

When he returned in June for the Carolina summer camp, the ACC was embroiled in a controversy over expansion to twelve members so there could be two six-team divisions in football and a championship game. The move was money-driven, but those opposed wondered whether splitting the increased revenue twelve ways would leave the original schools with as much as they currently made.

The ACC presidents argued whether they wanted Syracuse, Virginia Tech, or Boston College to join Miami as the new members. Politics in Virginia, where Virginia Tech grads put pressure on the Governor, were creating problems, as was the decision of Duke and North Carolina to oppose adding *any* schools.

They said they doubted the ACC's financial projections, but basketball was at the core of their reasoning. The programs that had dominated the league for thirty years did not want to further share TV exposure or ACC Tournament tickets, or mess with the tradition that had taken them to the top of the best conference in the country.

Krzyzewski was the most outspoken critic of expansion, going against the stated position of his school and suggesting the ACC take Miami only and lobby the NCAA to allow a ten-team league to hold a football playoff. "First try to change the rule," he said. "Rules can be changed easier than expanding a conference."

Williams was caught in the crosshairs of the controversy when he returned and was asked about living through the Big 12's expansion from the old Big 8. He said he didn't like it at first because some traditional rivalries were lost but it seemed to have worked out. Informed that he was not consistent with UNC's official position, he replied when asked again, "I'm supposed to say I'm against it, so I'm against it."

The ACC settled on taking in two new schools, Miami and Virginia Tech, beginning in 2004–05 with an eye toward a twelfth member. Boston College eventually agreed to join the conference, effective the following year. The basketball coaches went back to their own business.

For the second time in ten years, Krzyzewski had to rush to the bedside of a former player who was nearly killed. Jason Williams, his All-American point guard who had just finished his rookie season with the Chicago Bulls, lost control of his Harley Davidson motorcycle and wound up in the ICU of a Chicago hospital. Like Bobby Hurley, whose horrific automobile collision in 1993 cut short his pro career, Williams faced a long rehabilitation to repair a devastated knee and serious internal injuries. Krzyzewski told Williams to rehab at the Duke Medical Center as soon as his doctors would allow it.

This was also part of coaching, the occasional tragedies that close-knit programs had to endure. By the time he retired, Dean Smith had already attended the funeral of several former players and managers. In 1988, he faced what he called "the toughest thing I've ever had to do"—telling his sophomore center Scott Williams that his father had shot his mother to death and then killed himself in a domestic dispute. Roy Williams once recruited a star high school player who the summer before he enrolled at Kansas lost his foot in a train accident. Williams honored the kid's scholarship and made him a team manager.

As summer turned into fall, and Duke and Carolina both opened practice for the 2003–04 season with their own versions of Midnight Madness, other stories about the high-profile basketball coaches broke.

Krzyzewski was named "executive-in-residence" at the Fuqua School of Business, lending his name and time to the newly created Fuqua/Coach K Center of Leadership and Ethics that was raising $10 million for two endowed professorships and to teach courses and conduct research on ethical leadership in business. One of the early commitments of $1.5 million came from the Maxcor Financial Group, whose Chairman of the Board and CEO Gilbert Scharf graduated from Duke in 1971.

A joint effort between the business school, athletics department, and Kenan Institute for Ethics at Duke, which was already holding an annual leadership conference, the Fuqua/Coach K Center was officially rolled out at a press conference on Monday, October 20, led by Duke President Nan Keohane, who introduced the coach as Professor Krzyzewski. The new role gave him the one remaining status symbol he coveted at Duke: academic standing. "Now I'll have to get rid of all of my professor jokes," Krzyzewski quipped.

Also chuckling were many UNC fans, college basketball followers, and even some people with Duke ties who remembered him ambushing a dozen student reporters, running off a long-time assistant and secretary after a losing season and allowing Duke to expunge the 4 wins and 15 losses his team compiled when he was sidelined with a bad back in 1995 from his career record.

More recently, Krzyzewski's ethics were questioned by signing Corey Maggette, who stayed one season before turning pro and later admitted accepting money illegally from an AAU sponsor in high school.

The public's perception of ethical behavior generally included keeping profanity out of the King's English. Krzyzewski's liberal use of four-letter words on the bench, and in student gatherings, had been glossed over by the Duke administration for most of his quarter-century in Durham. While the West Point graduate and former Army captain boasted a strong record of ethical behavior and high moral standards otherwise, Krzyzewski's foul mouth went well beyond typical coach-speak and apparently was considered such a part of his persona that he could not and would not change.

"Growing up on the streets of Chicago," explained Matthew Laurance, a Duke radio announcer and good friend of the coach, "it was who he was and how they communicated in that environment. If he changed that suddenly, after all these years, he might not be as effective getting his points across."

Claiming it had no communication at all with Duke, the Kenan family of Chapel Hill, philanthropists who donated $10 million to start the Kenan Institute for Ethics, had to read about its supposed involvement in the Fuqua/Coach K Center in the newspaper.

"They aren't putting a dime into this particular program, but their name is being used to legitimize it," said a close friend of the family. "Don't you think someone from Duke or Fuqua should have called them?"

A week later, Coach K was back in the news when he and his wife, Mickie, donated $1 million to the Duke Basketball Legacy Fund in the name of Bill Krzyzewski, a retired Chicago fireman and the coach's older brother. Their gift was the twenty-fourth of a million-plus dollars toward endowing thirteen basketball scholarships and four coaching positions, plus capital improvements such as a separate training facility for the team that Krzyzewski was pushing. Started in 2000, the Legacy Fund already had an endowment of more than $25 million.

Williams, meanwhile, finally made it official by signing his own multi-million-dollar contract exactly six months after he took the job. Carolina agreed to pay him twice what Matt Doherty made, using some legislative wrangling and local arm-twisting to guarantee the richest compensation package UNC had ever given anyone in any position.

The UNC Board of Trustees needed approval from the Board of Governors, which ran the state's sixteen-campus system, for an exemption to a twelve-year-old policy intended to avoid excessive buyouts, stemming from the combined $1.4 million severance pay given to former UNC football coach Dick Crum when he resigned and to deposed N.C. State basketball coach Jim Valvano between 1988 and 1990.

Williams was guaranteed a total of $4.6 million ($575,000 a year) if he were fired "without cause" at any time over the duration of the eight-year deal. Without cause meant, essentially, fired for not winning enough games. Doherty had accepted a $337,000 buyout when the remainder of his contract called for $510,000, and it was speculated that issues of player-coach relationships caused him to forgo the difference.

Williams's total annual income began at $1.6 million, escalating from there due to a private annuity that jumped each year from $357,000 to $481,000 to $780,000 to $879,000 to just under $1.4 million in 2008, when it was scheduled to end and Williams's Carolina head-coaching income would exceed $2.6 million. He justified his embarrassment of riches by calculating that his "average salary my first twelve years in coaching was $31,000 . . . so it evens out."

Carolina raised the extra money for the annuity from forty boosters and high-powered Chapel Hill investors, who each agreed to pay $100,000 over four years, because Williams's one stipulation when hired was that he not "go backward" from his deal at Kansas. He had had similar guarantees as long as he stayed there.

Besides the private payment, Williams received $260,000 in annual base salary, which was more than UNC's chancellor and athletics director made, plus $327,000 for his four months of weekly radio and television shows, plus the $500,000 personal payment Nike transferred from Kansas to UNC, plus incentives that were worth another $100,000 each season. Then there was the Carolina Basketball School, which grossed a half-million dollars in two weeks that went mostly to Williams's staff that ran the summer camp.

The contract immediately drew criticism from certain faculty circles, including former UNC system president Bill Friday. In retirement, Friday had served on the Knight Commission, which among other things crusaded for curbing the so-called college athletics arms race, "Especially," he said, "when funded in part by excessive corporate sources."

"Recently we were told the university had failed to retain bright and talented faculty members because no funds were available," Friday said. "Here, over $3.8 million was raised quickly in these salary negotiations to meet the competition."

One bonus that particularly rankled Friday, and Williams eventually said he did not want, was a month's salary (about $21,000) if the graduation rate of his players equaled that of the student body. Williams said he would take a bonus for something else, but that graduating players was part of his job.

Krzyzewski earned an estimated $2 million annually. Duke, as a private school, did not have to—and refused to—publicize any of its faculty and staff compensation. Unquestionably, however, the Blue Devils' head basketball coach was its highest-paid employee. Even at the Duke Medical Center, where it was *truly* a matter of life and death, the top administrators made less money than Coach K.

The coaches' enormous incomes underscored remarkable success stories.

One was raised a Carolina country boy and nicknamed "Mountain Man" by his coaching colleagues, worked his way through UNC by keeping stats and refereeing intramural games while studying to be a coach and teacher. He had an alcoholic father and a mother who ironed to earn extra money, some of it so her son didn't have to work and could play ball with his friends after school. Williams, whose mother was deceased, returned to UNC from Kansas, in part, so he could be closer to his remaining family in Asheville.

The other grew up a blue-collar kid from Chicago's Polish inner city, making his family proud by earning an appointment to the U.S. Military Academy that they insisted he accept. His parents were both high school dropouts; his father operated an elevator and owned a tavern, his mother cleaned the Chicago Athletic Club. Krzyzewski was all about family and especially cherished his late mother, Emily, helping to build a local community center in her name near Duke and supporting numerous other local charities.

Their incredible financial windfalls also mirrored miraculous coaching careers.

Williams' first college job was as a twenty-eight-year-old part-time assistant at UNC, making $2,700 a year and selling Carolina Basketball Calendars to help feed his family. He was considered a good coach by those who knew him but spent most of his time at Carolina as the third, nonrecruiting assistant. After Kansas took a chance on him after the 1988 season, he won more games faster than any other head coach in the history of the college game.

Krzyzewski began at Duke making less than $50,000 and wearing off-the-rack suits. Criticized by his own players and fans, he had a losing record after three season and was nearly fired during the fourth. Twenty-one years and three national championships later, he was inducted into the Naismith Hall of Fame, his profession's highest honor.

Both coaches raised their families in modest neighborhoods in college towns and only well into their forties did they start enjoying the material fruits of their labor. Williams bought a big beach house near Charleston, and the Krzyzewskis finally built their five-thousand-square-foot dream home in Duke Forest.

Begrudgingly, both became comfortable with their fame and fortune. Williams's idea of clout was to play any golf course he wanted, anywhere in the world. He hopped on a booster's private jet for Pine Valley or Augusta or Pebble Beach, where old friend and UNC graduate Cody Plott was the CFO.

"When I first went to Kansas, I was making more money than I thought they could print," Williams liked to say in his "ah, shucks" hyperbole.

Being generous to his family, which included three daughters and two grand-children (with two more on the way) and close friends gave Krzyzewski the most pleasure. He hung out with Las Vegas billionaire Steve Wynn and also became a wine connoisseur, featured for his private collection in *Wine Spectator* magazine.

"I never planned on being a celebrity," Krzyzewski said. "And when I became one, I had no idea how to handle it."

With two superstar coaches again caretakers to the rivalry, another era of Duke-Carolina basketball commenced. Although each school relished beating the other's brains in, they really preferred the games to be even and hotly contested. That's the way it had been for most of the last fifty years, how this annual, ongoing battle turned into a cultural phenomenon.

Duke-Carolina, the hyphenated rivalry, has proven stronger than any single brand, any coach or player. As college basketball evolved, and the road map grew more uncertain each season, it continued to define the game.

Almost as if connected by an eight-mile umbilical cord, they were never out of each other's sight or mind. The Duke dynasty fell and recovered in the 1990s; the Carolina kingdom collapsed and rebuilt itself ten years later. Stable again, they promised five, eight, or ten more seasons of the bluest-blood battle rejoined, a tradition preserved until it would again be left for others to carry on.

RIVALRY RECORD IN THE 2000s

- Duke has won 12; Carolina has won 3

NCAA CHAMPIONSHIPS

- Duke 2001, Carolina 2005

HOW THEY DID IN THE DECADE

- Duke 179–32 (.848); Carolina 128–72 (.640)
- Doherty vs. Duke: 2–7

ACC CHAMPIONSHIPS

- Duke 2000, 2001, 2002, 2003, 2005; Carolina none

FINAL FOURS

- Duke 2001, 2004; Carolina 2000, 2005

RIVALRY FACT

- Duke won the 2001 national championship with the highest average margin of victory in NCAA Tournament history.

MOST INFAMOUS QUOTE

"Duke still has the ugliest cheerleaders in the ACC."

(Matt Doherty)

POSTSCRIPT
TWENTY-FIRST CENTURY
DUKE-CAROLINA

The scene reeked of irony.

On the court of the Dean Smith Center, three University of North Carolina basketball players and their coach held a bittersweet press conference on precisely the same spot of a much unhappier gathering in the recent past.

Sean May, Raymond Felton, and Marvin Williams, with teammate Rashad McCants watching in the wings, ended a record-breaking eighteen days for the Tar Heels and continued a mind-bending two years for their coach, Roy Williams.

The Tar Heels had won the 2005 NCAA championship on April 4 in St. Louis, setting a record for the quickest turnaround from a losing season. In 2002, before all five of them had arrived in Chapel Hill, Carolina shockingly lost 20 of 28 games. With May, Felton, and McCants the next year, the record improved to 19–16 but not enough to save their unpopular coach's job.

On April Fool's Day, 2003, in the same gym on the same end of the court, Matt Doherty was fired in a press conference that marked a low for the legendary basketball program. Several of the players sat off to the side, wearing caps and rough clothing that made many perceive them as punks who had pulled off a mutiny.

Exactly two years and twenty-two days later, three UNC players were on the podium neatly dressed and looking more like young gentlemen than jerks with an ax to grind. Their new coach sat alongside in a summer sport coat over a knit, collarless shirt. He, too, acted upbeat, but the last two of his soon-to-be fifty-five years showed on his wrinkled face. Newly tanned from several rounds of golf between recruiting trips, his puffy eyes told a different story.

The players were announcing the end of their college careers, declaring for the upcoming NBA draft. McCants, wearing a Philadelphia 76ers jersey and standing close enough to be a secondary part of the scene, had done the same the week before.

Roy Williams had finished individual meetings with all four youngsters. He knew McCants was going since the middle of the season and, after two years of high maintenanced management, encouraged the gifted but grumpy junior to enter the draft. He also had no qualms about Felton, the explosive and fearless point guard who was among the best in the country and could most easily adapt to playing the same position in the NBA.

The other two weren't as clear cut.

May had maintained all season that he was coming back for his senior year and, consequently, did not discuss the NBA with Williams until after he had 26 points and 24 rebounds in the home-season-ending win against Duke. At that point, with an impressive string of double-doubles, his pro stock was rising with his reputation. He completed the transition from a "soft" center playing out of position to a mobile, maturing big man with suction cups for hands and savvy beyond his barely two years of college basketball, culminating with 48 points, 17 rebounds and the Most Outstanding Player award in the Final Four.

Their meeting was the toughest because May had changed his mind and wanted to hold firm when Williams went over the pros and cons of turning pro. He had become a dominating back-to-the-basket postman, but Williams thought May needed to develop a face-up game to be as successful on the next level. The veteran coach suggested the best place to do that might be a senior year at UNC. May said he had made up his mind, his stock would never be higher and he was gone. Williams grew teary-eyed and capitulated.

The last domino to fall was freshman Marvin Williams, the raw-but-spectacular specimen. He had text-messaged May, "I'm not playing in the middle next year without you!" Projected as the highest draft pick of the four, he *had* to go, too. Despite never starting a college game, Williams's athletic ability and quickness for someone 6' 9" made him a can't-miss "futures" player in the NBA. Why return and risk an injury or face the possibility of playing for a depleted, losing team?

No school had ever lost four underclassmen to the NBA draft in the same year. In 1999, Duke University lost two sophomores and a freshman early. Arizona, after losing to Duke in the 2001 national championship game, also had four underclassmen put their names in the draft before one, Jason Gardner, pulled out and returned for his junior year. Now Carolina had set a new record, its second precedent in those eighteen days.

Sitting about one hundred feet away in the visitors' runway was the arena's namesake, Dean Smith, the retired coach of the Tar Heels. Smith watched the proceedings silently, occasionally smiling and one time shaking his head. It took Smith seventeen years to lose his first four underclassmen to the NBA—from Robert McAdoo in 1972 to J. R. Reid in 1989 (with a couple of guys names Worthy and Jordan in between). It took approximately seventeen *minutes* for May, Felton, and Marvin Williams to make their statements and for Roy Williams to mention McCants, as well.

For Coach Williams, these were the best of times following the worst of times. He inherited a talented group but not the one he would have hand-picked had he been recruiting for Carolina at the time. He struggled to adjust to his new job and team, looking longingly like the Kansas coach with regrets for most of his first year. By early in his second, Williams had his stepchildren thinking and playing his way.

That turned out to be his personal irony. Williams won it all with someone else's guys. Doherty had recruited seven of the Tar Heels' top eight players. Now, including three seniors who were graduating, Williams was losing seven of them. He had four good recruits coming in but still faced the biggest rebuilding job of his coaching life.

In Durham that morning, two men from the Duke athletics department were having breakfast when a gray-haired woman who recognized them approached their table. She had read the newspaper report of the mass exodus at Carolina and was smiling. She said several kids in her son's sixth-grade class were Tar Heel fans and had been bragging uncontrollably for the past two weeks, but they were probably sad today.

"If they need me to," she said, "I'll be happy to go over to Chapel Hill today and help those boys pack up for the NBA."

Duke was not losing any of its star players to the pros, which made the day even harder for UNC fans who looked ahead with trepidation. The Blue Devils hadn't escaped the lure of the NBA, having themselves sent seven underclassmen out in the last six years, but would return most of their team for the 2006 season. Only senior starter Daniel Ewing was graduating and their Hall of Fame coach Mike Krzyzewski had managed to prevent all but one unexpected defection.

Junior J. J. Redick, the daring and deadly marksman who was the ACC's leading scorer and best player, never wavered from his early decision to complete his college career. Classmate Shelden Williams, a dominating defender and improved low-post player who was Krzyzewski's first to average double-figure rebounding, thought about declaring for the draft, not hiring an agent and attending the NBA tryout camp in Chicago. Since he could not be assured of being a high first-round or lottery pick, he stayed in school for his senior year to "accomplish some of the same things Carolina did last year" and become Duke's all-time leader in blocked shots.

Oft-injured junior Shavlik Randolph, the former prep protégé of his grandfather and N.C. State legend Ronnie Shavlik, who started 36 games in three seasons at Duke, gave up his senior year of eligibility amidst rumors of family financial troubles. His father, Kenny Randolph (a UNC graduate), owed federal and state taxes since two of the companies he and his family had inherited from Ronnie Shavlik filed for bankruptcy in 2002. Shavlik Randolph, who had a 6-point college career scoring average, applied for the 2005 NBA draft with little chance of being selected. He worked out for several pro teams and, after failing to get drafted, hoped to sign a free-agent contract to play either home or abroad.

Despite his inconsistent career, the talented Blue Devils still could have used Randolph's experience in 2005–06.

Duke had signed another stellar recruiting class of high school stars, led by lanky forward Josh McRoberts and two-sport quarterback Greg Paulus. They were two of the best players in the 2005 McDonald's All-American Game, promising Krzyzewski his deepest roster of quality players since 1999. Who knew how long they would all stay, given the capricious state of college basketball, but it would be at least one year—and that was enough for now.

Although Carolina had finished the last season ranked No. 1 and brought back the NCAA championship, the school's fourth, many of their faithful couldn't fully enjoy the accomplishment because of their anxiety over next year. Fretful Tar Heels were trying desperately to retain the gleam from their march to the arch, but attention quickly shifted to how thin the departure of Felton, May, McCants, and Marvin Williams, who were all drafted in the first round, had left their program.

The Blue Devils, meanwhile, were loading up and sure to begin the new season *ranked* No. 1—a favorite to cut down the 2006 nets in Indianapolis, where they had done it for the first of three times in 1991. The Dukies were acting arrogantly, licking their chops like next year was already theirs.

The sport had grown quirky and speculative. There was often more fascination with the players who weren't in school than those already there. Preoccupation with who Duke had coming in and who Roy Williams was recruiting for the *following* year made it harder to live in the moment.

If Duke-Carolina basketball has taught us anything, it's that a rivalry can't be judged on record alone. Perhaps Søren Kierkegaard, one of Dean's Smith's best reading buddies, said it best, "Life must be lived forward but can only be understood backward."

Carolina was the last team to hang a national championship banner, which has become the benchmark of the rivalry as well as college basketball. Still, Duke remained on firmer footing, and it went beyond the premature loss of players, which would have devastated most programs besides these two. As UNC has proven for nearly twenty-five years and Duke for the last five, they will both survive such attrition.

Indeed, what's happened in the past can preview the future.

There exists no better metaphor than where the current head coaches work, Mike Krzyzewski in an austere six-story tower next to a courtyard that bears a derivative of his name, and Roy Williams in an eight-sided monument to the Smith years.

To reach Krzyzewski, you have to take an elevator up five levels, check in with the receptionist and then be escorted to the private sixth floor, where an American flag drapes down from the window-covered wall of the head coach's office. The building has every imaginable wrinkle of technology showcasing Duke teams and titles over the past twenty years, and the journey must be mind-boggling for eighteen-year-old recruits.

At Carolina, visitors enter from side, ground-floor doors of the Smith Center with unremarkable signage. The basketball office is a one-story suite that used an outdated standard when it was built in the 1980s. Compared to cramped Carmichael Auditorium, it *was* blue heaven, but it grew obsolete quickly and had little room to expand with the mushrooming interest that followed Smith's first national championship in 1982.

For the last eight years, Duke has embarked on a carefully conceived plan to "use its biggest asset"—Krzyzewski's program—to not only maximize men's basketball but to enhance other areas of the university. It has become the twenty-first century model for how to operate a major college athletics program in a corporate environment. Krzyzewski's high-powered agent David Falk uses many of the marketing and business philosophies with which, ironically, he made former Tar Heel Michael Jordan an icon.

In the last eight years, Carolina has changed head coaches three times and struggled to keep a firm foundation underneath its program. Players have left, others did not come, and now Williams faces a major rebuilding job following his own first national championship. He remains much more of a pure basketball coach compared to Krzyzewski the CEO, and while his rival completes corporate obligations as his assistants hunt for players, Williams, himself, logs most of the recruiting miles.

Carolina would have a brand new team in 2006, built around freshman Tyler Hansbrough, a big, white center like so many others Williams had at Kansas. After the Final Four, one of the first high school players Williams visited was junior Wayne Ellington, a Merion, Pennsylvania, teammate of major Duke target Gerald Henderson.

In a spring-time recruiting battle worthy of this rivalry, Duke got a commitment from Henderson and two other top-25 high school players from the class of 2006. Carolina countered with verbals from two top-10 players, including Ellington. They battled head-to-head through the summer for the top power forward in the country, Brandan Wright, a 6' 9" Tennessean. None of them could sign scholarships until the following November.

As the new season approached, Carolina found itself somehow looking *up* from the mountaintop. Both prestigious programs have to negotiate the newest landscape of college basketball, which wasn't leveling off with any certainty, but Duke had the stability of one coach over the last twenty-five years, just as UNC had Smith for thirty-six. The bond to past players and their families, the loyalty to their alma mater among its assistant coaches, the connections in communities near and far all favored the school that has been there, done that longer.

Krzyzewski is 58, Williams 55. They figure to stalk the sideline at least five more seasons.

The Duke coach has already broken Dean Smith's record for NCAA Tournament wins (66). Several more milestones are within his reach: a fourth national championship to match Adolph Rupp and a fifth to put him in a class second only to John Wooden; 4 more ACC Tournament championships and 7 more regular-season titles will catch Smith's record of 13 and 17, respectively. With 721 career wins, he would have to coach at least six seasons to pass Smith's 879 and longer if his mentor, Bob Knight, breaks Smith's mark in the next two years.

Williams can't compete for most of the above records because, at thirty-eight, he became a head coach thirteen years later than Knight, ten years later than Krzyzewski and eight years later than Smith. Williams, however, owns, and can maintain, the highest winning percentage among active head coaches (.802). He can also win multiple ACC and NCAA championships. The irony of having won the national title with mostly players he inherited from Doherty was not lost on him; it has given him added incentive to restock the Carolina roster and prove that he can win with *his* players. Beyond the locker room, he will have to strengthen the bond and loyalty among former players, coaches, alumni, and fans that only years at the same school can guarantee.

It will be surprising if either coach quits, or moves on, before reaching retirement age. Krzyzewski has had his serious flirtations with the NBA and reaffirmed his place as Duke's coach and, later, as a professor, fund-raiser, and continued force in college basketball. Williams only wants to coach—at Carolina for as long as he has the passion and health and after that as a little league coach for his yet-unborn grandchildren.

When Krzyzewski does retire, he will most likely copy Dean Smith and put his trusted chief assistant, Johnny Dawkins, in the head coach's chair. If Dawkins doesn't want it, Krzyzewski will orchestrate finding the best person for the long-term success of Duke basketball, Blue Devil ties or not.

Although Williams has his own coaching tree from fifteen years at Kansas, it is unlikely that UNC will venture away from Smith's family. Best-positioned to be the next Carolina coach is thirty-eight-year-old Jeff Lebo, a proven winner whose latest success has come at Auburn and remains close enough to be remembered.

Until then, what will the rivalry look like?

Back to Kierkegaard.

When Krzyzewski arrived at Duke, he used Smith as a yardstick—for some aspects he wanted to emulate and for others he thought he could do differently.

He loved Carolina's unselfishness but gave his players more freedom within the team concept. He favored the Darwinian "best guy plays" theory over Smith's seniority system. He decided that effort was even more important than execution. He wanted the regular-season series to be secondary to what happened in March.

It gave him something to shoot for and made him a better coach faster. The way the Blue Devils played defense, conversely, had Smith put on his thinking cap in his senior years, and the one team Duke could not beat consistently was Carolina.

Now Williams cannot avoid looking eight miles down the road to the program that has passed the Tar Heels in national popularity and become America's team to love or loathe, but always to notice. From TV ratings to newspaper polls to Internet page views, Duke remains No. 1 and UNC a narrow No. 2. There is no close third.

Krzyzewski has earned the arrogance that shows when he defends himself over the American Express controversy. "C'mon, it's not like we haven't recruited great players here before I started doing the commercials," he says.

Roy Williams was once the biggest coach in the state of Kansas. Now he is not even the biggest in his new area code. Can he do what he does best, and learn something from Duke, well enough to pull Carolina even, and perhaps ahead, in this two-horse race, unquestionably the greatest rivalry in college sports?

All who watch and care will live it forward and someday try to understand it looking back.

APPENDIX

MISCELLANEOUS RECORDS
All-ACC Players
- Carolina 116, Duke 114

ACC Players of the Year
- Duke 12, Carolina 11

1,000-Point Career Scorers
- Carolina 57, Duke 54

Final No. 1 Rankings (AP/UPI or Coaches)
- Duke 12, Carolina 9

Weeks Ranked No. 1
- Duke 96, Carolina 86

Consensus All-American Players
- Carolina 18, Duke 16

NCAA TOURNAMENT STATISTICS
Tournament Appearances
- Carolina 37, Duke 29

Consecutive Tournaments
- Carolina 27 (1975–2001); Duke 11 (1984–94)

Current Consecutive Tournaments
- Duke 10, Carolina 2

Total Tournament Games
- Carolina 124, Duke 109

Consecutive Tournament Wins
- Duke 13 (1991–93); Carolina 7 (twice: 1982–83; 1993–94)

APPENDIX

Tournament Records
- Duke 83–26 (.761), Carolina 88–36 (.710)

Sweet 16 Appearances
- Carolina 26, Duke 22

Most Consecutive Sweet 16s
- Carolina 13 (1981–93), Duke 8 (1998–2005)

Final Fours
- Carolina 16, Duke 14

Final Four Games
- Carolina 27, Duke 25

Consecutive Final Fours
- Duke 5 (1988–1992), Carolina 3 (1967–69)

Final Four Victories
- Duke 14, Carolina 13

Final Four Winning Percentage
- Duke .560 (14–11), Carolina .481 (13–14)

NCAA Championships
- Carolina 4, Duke 3

Consecutive NCAA Championships
- Duke 2, Carolina 1

MISCELLANEOUS FACTS
- Between 1991 and 2001, Duke or Carolina finished first in the ACC every year except 1996.
- Duke and/or Carolina played in 13 consecutive ACC Tournament championship games between 1957 and 1969. Duke has played in the last eight consecutive ACC Tournament championship games.
- Duke and/or Carolina have advanced to 42 of the 52 ACC Tournament championship games played, but they met for the title in only 10 of those years.
- Since 1980, Duke has the best winning percentage (.776) of any other team in the country; Carolina is second (.761).
- Either Duke or Carolina has played in 20 of the last 29 Final Fours; only once, in 1991, have both made it. They have never played in the NCAA Tournament.
- Duke's 10 Final Fours since 1980 is the most of any school in the country; Carolina's 9 is second.
- Carolina has played in more NCAA Sweet 16s (18) since 1980, Duke is second with 16; either school has made it in 25 of those 26 years, both in 10 of those years.

INDEX

INDEX

INDEX

INDEX

INDEX

INDEX

INDEX